CliffsNotes®

AP® English Language and Composition

5TH EDITION

by
Barbara V. Swovelin

Houghton Mifflin Harcourt
Boston • New York

About the Author

Barbara V. Swovelin taught AP and Honors classes at Torrey Pines High School in Del Mar, California, for 34 years before retiring in 2014. She is an experienced AP English Exam Reader and a College Board Consultant, working both nationally and internationally. Additionally, she prepares new AP English teachers at College Board Institutes and Workshops. She has also taught graduate-level test preparation classes at California universities since 1986, specializing in the GRE, GMAT, and LSAT exams. Swovelin is also a co-author of *CliffsNotes AP English Literature and Composition*.

Acknowledgments

I am forever indebted to Dr. Jerry Bobrow, in memoriam, for believing in me and to Dr. Allen Casson, in memoriam, for his meticulous technical assistance in the first two editions of this book.

Dedication

This book is dedicated to my husband, Jerry, who helped and encouraged me in every step of the process. I also dedicate it to the thousands of students I had over the years, who taught and inspired me more than I can express.

Editorial

Executive Editor: Greg Tubach

Senior Editor: Christina Stambaugh

Production Editor: Jennifer Freilach

Copy Editor: Lynn Northrup

Technical Editor: Jane R. Burstein

Proofreader: Susan Moritz

CliffsNotes® AP® English Language and Composition, 5th Edition

Copyright © 2019 by Houghton Mifflin Harcourt Publishing Company

All rights reserved.

Library of Congress Control Number: 2018952973
ISBN: 978-1-328-46583-2 (pbk)

Printed in the United States of America
DOO 10 9 8 7 6 5 4 3 2 1

For information about permission to reproduce selections from this book, write to trade.permissions@hmhco.com or to Permissions, Houghton Mifflin Harcourt Publishing Company, 3 Park Avenue, 19th Floor, New York, New York 10016.

www.hmhco.com

Table of Contents

Text Permissions

The following excerpts have been reprinted with permission.

Gather Together in My Name by Maya Angelou. Copyright © 1974 by Maya Angelou. Used with permission of Random House, Inc.

"Do Public Subsidies Leverage Private Philanthropy for the Arts? Empirical Evidence on Symphony Orchestras" by Arthur C. Brooks, *Nonprofit and Voluntary Sector Quarterly* 28:32–45. Copyright © 1999 by *Nonprofit and Voluntary Sector Quarterly*. Reprinted with permission of SAGE Publications LTD and conveyed through Copyright Clearance Center, Inc.

"Athletes Salaries Too High? Sports Fans, Blame Yourselves" by Gene Callahan. Copyright © 2007 by *The Foundation for Economic Education*. Reprinted with permission.

"At What Cost Does Innovation Come?" by Ali Carr-Chellman. Reprinted with permission of the author.

"Catastrophe on Camera: Why Media Coverage of Natural Disasters Is Flawed" by Patrick Cockburn. Copyright © 2011 by *The Independent*. Reprinted with permission.

"The Culture War: When Government Is a Critic" by David Cole. Reprinted with permission of the author.

The Writing Life by Annie Dillard. Copyright © 1989 by Annie Dillard. Reprinted with permission of HarperCollins Publishers.

A Considerable Town by M. F. K. Fisher. Copyright © 1964, 1977, 1978 by M. F. K. Fisher. Used with permission of Alfred A. Knopf, an imprint of the Knopf Doubleday Publishing Group, a division of Penguin Random House LLC. All rights reserved. Any third-party use of this material, outside of this publication, is prohibited. Interested parties must apply directly to Penguin Random House LLC for permission.

Cities on a Hill by Frances FitzGerald. Copyright © 1986 by Frances FitzGerald. Reprinted with permission of Scribner, a division of Simon & Schuster, Inc. All rights reserved.

"Alerting America: Effective Risk Communication" by Ruxandra Floroiu. Copyright © 2002 by *The National Academies Press*. Reprinted with permission.

"Polling Isn't Perfect" by John Fund. Originally published in *The Wall Street Journal* 14 Nov. 2002. Copyright © 2006 by Dow Jones & Co., Inc. Reprinted with permission of *The Wall Street Journal*. All rights reserved worldwide. License number 4191530975654.

Taking Flight: Inventing the Aerial Age, From Antiquity Through the First World War by Richard P. Hallion. Copyright © 2003 by Richard P. Hallion. Used with permission of Oxford University Press, USA.

"Who Makes More Money: Athletes, Actors, National Leaders, or CEOs?" by Audrey Henderson. Copyright © 2017 by *Supermoney*. Used with permission.

"Bargain or Bust" by Cameron Hollway, as it appeared in the 8/3/2005 *St. Louis Post-Dispatch*. Reprinted with permission of the *St. Louis Post-Dispatch,* copyright © 2005.

"Who Should Pay for the Arts in America?" by Andy Horwitz. Copyright © 2016 by *The Atlantic Monthly*. Reprinted with permission of The Atlantic Monthly Group, Inc. and conveyed through Copyright Clearance Center, Inc.

"ISDR Joins Asia-Pacific Broadcasting Union to Boost Information, Education on Disasters." Copyright © 2005 by UNESCAP News Services.

Michelangelo and the Pope's Ceiling by Ross King. Copyright © 2003 by Ross King. Used with permission of Bloomsbury Publishing.

Art Credits

Study Guide Checklist

- ❏ Become familiar with the exam format (p. 1).
- ❏ Carefully read chapters 1 and 2.
- ❏ Take the Diagnostic Mini-Test in Chapter 3, strictly observing the time allotments for each section.
- ❏ Check your answers, analyze your results, and read the sample essays and analyses, beginning on p. 63.
- ❏ Familiarize yourself with the AP exam terminology by carefully reading Appendix A.
- ❏ Review the past essay topics in Appendix B.
- ❏ To further prepare for the AP exam, familiarize yourself with the items in the suggested reading list in Appendix C.
- ❏ Take Practice Exam 1 in Chapter 4, strictly observing the time allotments for each section.
- ❏ Check your answers and analyze your results, beginning on p. 106.
- ❏ For Practice Exam 1, study *all* of the answers and explanations, including the student essays and analyses beginning on p. 112.
- ❏ Take Practice Exam 2 in Chapter 5, strictly observing the time allotments for each section.
- ❏ Check your answers and analyze your results, beginning on p. 161.
- ❏ For Practice Exam 2, study *all* of the answers and explanations, including the student essays and analyses beginning on p. 167.
- ❏ Take Practice Exam 3 in Chapter 6, strictly observing the time allotments for each section.
- ❏ Check your answers and analyze your results, beginning on p. 216.
- ❏ For Practice Exam 3, study *all* of the answers and explanations, including the student essays and analyses beginning on p. 222.
- ❏ Take Practice Exam 4 in Chapter 7, strictly observing the time allotments for each section.
- ❏ Check your answers and analyze your results, beginning on p. 268.
- ❏ For Practice Exam 4, study *all* of the answers and explanations, including the student essays and analyses beginning on p. 274.

Introduction

About the Exam

The AP English Language and Composition Exam is used by colleges to assess your ability to perform college-level work. Actual college credit (either for one semester or for an entire year) may be offered by colleges and universities. The exam lasts 3 hours and 15 minutes and consists of two major sections: multiple choice and free response.

The first section of the exam consists of approximately 55 multiple-choice questions that address four or five reading passages. All the questions in this section have equal value, and no penalty is deducted for an incorrect answer. You have 1 hour to answer the multiple-choice questions.

The multiple-choice questions are designed to test your ability to analyze prose passages. These passages are drawn from a variety of sources, rhetorical modes, historical or literary periods, and disciplines. You will be asked questions about the passages' style, content, and rhetoric. Expect four or five reading passages with between 10 and 15 questions per passage. The multiple-choice questions are carefully written and screened by the AP Test Development Committee and the Educational Testing Service (ETS). The committee is ethnically and geographically balanced, and its members represent public and private high schools, as well as colleges and universities. The committee is responsible for choosing the passages for both the multiple-choice section and the free-response section. All of the multiple-choice questions are pretested in college classes before they are used on AP examinations.

In the free-response section, you are given three essay topics, and you must write an essay on each of the three topics in 2 hours and 15 minutes. The suggested time allotment for each essay is 40 minutes, with an extra 15 minutes for reading the essay prompts. Each of the essays is of equal value in your final score.

The free-response questions test your writing ability in a variety of modes and for a variety of purposes. These timed essays measure your expository and analytical writing skills, which are essential to success on many college exams. In general, the three essays will give you an opportunity to demonstrate that you can do the following:

1. Synthesize ideas from multiple short passages into an argument of your own.
2. Analyze how an author's rhetorical strategies create meaning, based on one given reading passage.
3. Analyze an author's key point(s) in a given passage and create an argument that discusses the validity of the author's message.

The essay responses are read and scored during a 7-day period in early June. In 2000, more than 300 AP Readers representing the United States, Canada, and other countries read more than 115,000 AP English Language exams; by 2005, more than 700 AP Readers scored essays from 240,000 test-takers; by 2011, approximately 1,000 AP Readers scored essays from more than 360,000 test-takers; in 2017, over 500,000 students took the AP English Language and Composition Exam. More than half of the AP Readers are college or university instructors; fewer than half are high school teachers. Each Reader is assigned to score only one essay question during the reading session; therefore, each student's work is read by at least three different Readers. Some essays are read and chosen as samples to be examined by all the Readers, while others are checked by the table leaders and question leaders after an individual Reader has scored the essay. You can trust that the essay scoring is as professional and accurate as possible. All AP Readers are thoroughly trained and retrained throughout the week of scoring.

Before the actual scoring session in June, a committee reads a large number of randomly selected essays and creates a scoring guide on a scale of 0 to 9 for each of the three essay questions. Therefore, the scoring guide is based on the students' *actual performance* in writing the essays, not on how the test-makers *anticipate* they should perform.

Overall, the entire exam is designed to show your awareness of how an author creates meaning through use of language, genre conventions, and rhetorical choices, and how well you can do the same in your own writing. A qualifying score demonstrates your ability to perform college-level work.

How the Exam Is Scored

In the multiple-choice section, you earn 1 point for each correct answer. No penalty is deducted for wrong answers. Unanswered questions do not count for or against your score. The multiple-choice section accounts for 45 percent of the total exam score.

The three essays are each scored holistically, which means that the AP Reader will read the entire essay and give it an overall score based on its quality. The scores range from 0 to 9. (A score of 0 is given for a blank paper or one that does not attempt to answer the question.) The essay scores are then calculated to equal 55 percent of the total exam score. You can read more detailed information on how the essays are scored in Chapter 2, "The Free-Response Section."

The score for the multiple-choice section is added to the score for the free-response section to produce a composite (or total) score. This composite score is translated into a 5-point scale:

5 Extremely well qualified
4 Well qualified
3 Qualified
2 Possibly qualified
1 No recommendation

Scores are reported in July to you, your secondary school, and any college you designate.

Frequently Asked Questions

Q: Who administers the exam?
A: The Advanced Placement exams are sponsored by the College Board. The exam is administered through the Educational Testing Service.

Q: What materials may I bring to the exam?
A: Bring an identification card, as well as plenty of pens for the free-response questions and pencils for the multiple-choice questions. You may not bring a dictionary, a thesaurus, or any other reference book.

Q: May I cancel my score following the exam?
A: Yes. You always have this option. Check the current AP Bulletin for procedures and deadlines, which is available at www.collegeboard.com/ap or from your school counselor.

Q: Is there a penalty for a wrong answer to the multiple-choice questions?
A: No. As of 2011, no AP exams will deduct any points for wrong answers.

Q: How can I prepare?
A: Practice! Become comfortable with the exam and its format. Take several practice exams to work on your timing. Learn new or unfamiliar terms that you might be expected to know for the exam. Practice your essay planning and timed writing. Practice paraphrasing what you read so that this skill becomes second nature before the exam.

Q: How do I register for an AP exam?
A: See your school counseling office for registration information. Most schools register candidates in March for the upcoming May AP exams.

Q: Is paper provided for the essays?

A: Yes. In fact, you'll write all of your essays in a special book that conceals your identity from the Readers who score it. You are permitted to write in the exam booklet itself, but nothing written inside the exam booklet will affect your score.

Q: Why are there two AP English exams?

A: Because not all colleges offer the same curriculum for freshman English. The two exams—AP English Language and Composition and AP English Literature and Composition—permit each college to designate the exam that best reflects its curriculum.

Q: What's the difference between the two AP English exams?

A: The two exams are similar; both test your ability to analyze the written word and to prove that you can communicate intelligent ideas on a given subject. However, the AP English Language and Composition Exam asks questions about nonfiction; it never presents poetry or fiction. The language exam also places more emphasis on rhetorical analysis and the study of *how* language works. In contrast, the AP English Literature and Composition Exam places greater emphasis on literary analysis; it includes poetry, fiction, and drama. You will be asked to analyze several poems on the literature exam.

Q: Which exam should I take?

A: The best way to decide which exam to take is to ask the college you plan to attend. A college may offer either one or two semesters of credit, depending on its freshman English curriculum. Generally, a school that has a literary component combined with expository writing skills in its freshman English course gives up to a full year's course credit for the literature exam. A school that has a full year of freshman writing in various rhetorical modes may give up to a full year's credit for the language exam. In addition, it helps to consider your own strengths and weaknesses and your likes and dislikes. If you enjoy reading prose and writing well-argued, analytical essays, then the language exam is for you. If you have a strong literary background, especially in American and British literature and poetry analysis, then the literature exam will be a better fit.

Q: Is one exam easier than the other?

A: They are equally rigorous.

Q: What is an average score?

A: At a typical exam administration, approximately two-thirds of all test-takers receive a score of 3 or higher. To earn an average score of 3, you must answer approximately 50 to 60 percent of the questions correctly on the multiple-choice section and also write three adequate free-response essays that score in the 5 or above range.

Q: Can I take both the literature exam and the language exam in the same school year?

A: Yes, they are administered on different days.

Q: How can I find out how much college credit I'll get if I pass the exam?

A: Contact the college and ask the admissions office for a clear, written response. Do not be surprised to find that this is a somewhat confusing issue, compounded by the fact that two English exams exist. Additionally, some colleges and universities consider an overall score of 3 as passing, while other colleges require a 4 or even a 5. Some colleges require that all freshmen take their freshman English class, usually a composition course. In addition, some schools or programs within a college have different requirements.

Q: Do colleges get separate scores for my multiple-choice and free-response sections? May I get the two separate scores?

A: No to both questions. Only your overall score, based on a scale of 1 to 5, will be released to you or to any college.

Q: **What if my school does not offer an AP course or I did not enroll in the course? May I take the exam anyway?**

A: Sure! Although an AP course is theoretically designed to prepare students for the exam, much of that "preparation" consists of reading quality literature—both fiction and nonfiction—and practicing analysis, critical thinking, and close reading, in addition to taking practice AP exams and understanding the format of the exam. You can do this on your own, especially if you have disciplined study habits. However, I do strongly recommend that you read this test-preparation book carefully, and, if you can, also explore the College Board website at www.collegeboard.com/ap.

Q: **When will I receive my AP exam scores?**

A: You will receive your scores at about the same time as the colleges do, in early July.

Q: **How can I obtain previous exams to use for practice?**

A: You may order previously released exams directly from the College Board; the AP section of College Board information can be found at the College Board's online store at www.collegeboard.com/ap.

Q: **How often are previous exams released to the public?**

A: Multiple-choice exams are released every 5 years; essay topics are released every year.

Q: **Can I still pass the exam even if I don't finish all the multiple-choice questions in time?**

A: Yes! Many students don't finish all the questions and still receive a passing score. Naturally, if you don't finish, you need to do very well on the questions you do complete and write three strong essays. However, since you will not be penalized for any wrong answers, you'll want to fill in something for every question if you see yourself running out of time.

Q: **Should I answer the multiple-choice passages in the order they appear on the exam?**

A: Most students choose to answer the multiple-choice passages in the order they appear on the exam, as it is a very systematic and logical approach. However, keep a steady pace and do not let one passage eat up too much of your time, subsequently causing you to rush on the last passage(s). Overall, remember that your score is determined by the total number of questions you answer correctly.

Q: **Does the scoring give extra weight to one of the essays?**

A: No, all three essays are counted equally. Because the free-response portion of the exam is 55 percent of your total score, each essay equals 18.3 percent of your essay score.

Q: **Should I plan my essay in advance?**

A: In general, yes, planning your essay in advance is a good strategy. An outline is never required and will never be seen by the AP Readers anyway, but clear and logical organization is, indeed, an important criterion on which your essay is scored. You need to at least organize what points you intend to make and the order in which you plan to present them. Your exam booklet has ample blank space for planning.

Q: **How many paragraphs should I write for each essay?**

A: Write as many paragraphs as you need to fully develop and present your ideas. Although the introduction-body-conclusion format is most frequently used, the number of body paragraphs presented varies from student to student and topic to topic. An introductory paragraph that contains a thesis is understandably an appropriate beginning, but don't worry if you don't get to the conclusion. Read more about essay organization and development in Chapter 2.

Q: **How many pages should each essay be?**

A: No set length is required; however, most high-scoring essays are *at least* two pages long. Naturally, some essays are shorter and some are longer. Instead of worrying about length, concentrate on addressing all of the tasks of the topic and thoroughly developing your ideas. Be aware that very short essays, such as those that are only about half a page in length, are considered "unacceptably brief" and score very low; they simply do not demonstrate enough development of ideas to receive a passing score. In Chapter 2, you can read sample student essays and get a feel for length.

Q: How much should I worry about grammar and spelling?

A: Good news! You don't have to worry too much about your spelling. If you can spell reasonably well, no AP Reader will dock your score for occasional spelling errors. When you read any of the scoring guides for essays, you will notice that the word "spelling" is never mentioned. The Readers are remarkably tolerant; they want to reward you for what you do well. Grammar and punctuation can be another issue, though. The Readers are always willing to overlook what they call "minor errors" or "honest mistakes" that are made under time pressures. They understand that what you have produced is a first draft that is likely to have a few flaws. However, if your errors are persistent and serious, the Reader will have to lower your score. In fact, the scoring guide states that no essay that is particularly poorly written—one with errors so severe that they continually distract the Reader's attention from the student's ideas—may receive a score higher than 2.

Q: Should I write my essays in cursive or should I print?

A: You need to write as legibly as you can, so use whatever is easiest to read. The Readers want to be able to reward you for your essay; to do so, they have to be able to read the words. Please don't forget to use a nice black- or blue-ink pen; avoid ones that bleed through paper, because you'll want to write on the back of the page.

Q: Do the essays need a title?

A: Not at all. It will never affect your score. I can guarantee that AP Readers are bored by dull titles anyway. Why not just get started on the essay itself?

Q: May I be creative in my essay writing?

A: The number-one rule is that you must address the essay question; if you can do so in a creative fashion, you may be rewarded, as long as it works well. However, writing something as far-fetched as a poem or short story would be unacceptable. Again, when you read some sample scoring guides, you'll notice that creativity is never mentioned as a specific criterion for scoring. The basic tenets are that your essay must be focused on the topic, organized, and well developed. Accomplish all of that in a creative style with a strong voice and the AP Reader may be pleasantly surprised.

Q: How much of the passage in the prompt should I quote?

A: No set, formulaic answer exists. Yes, you do need to refer to the passage appropriately in order to support your ideas, and many of those examples should take the form of quotations. However, a string of irrelevant quotations, glued together with a few of your own words, will not help your score at all. Read the sample essays in this book to get a feel for what's appropriate.

Q: Can I pass the test if I don't finish an essay?

A: Of course! Understandably, a radically unfinished essay will receive a very low score, so try to pace yourself accordingly, devoting approximately 40 minutes to each essay. Doing so should allow you time to finish each one. Also, practice your pacing many times before the test. I also advise practicing the planning period over and over. If, within approximately 10 to 12 minutes, you can organize what you're going to say and the order in which you're going to present it, you should have enough time to actually write the sentences. Finally, if you find yourself in a time crunch on test day, remember that body paragraphs are much more important than concluding paragraphs—especially conclusions that merely summarize. You should devote your time to getting your ideas down on paper. The AP Readers' constant motto is: "Reward the writers for what they do well."

Q: How can I approximate my score from my practice tests into an AP-scaled score of 1 through 5?

A: Approximating your score is a bit more complicated than simply counting the number of right and wrong answers, but follow these directions. Additionally, you will find a sample scoring worksheet in this book after each full-length sample exam.

The total number of points on the exam is 150. Because the free-response and multiple-choice parts are weighted 55 percent and 45 percent, respectively, there are 82.5 points for the essays and 67.5 points for the multiple-choice questions. Because the three essays are graded on a 9-point scale, each point on your essay raw score will be multiplied by 3.0556. Three 9s would total 27, and 27×3.0556 would total 82.5. If there are 55 multiple-choice questions, each point in the raw score would be multiplied by 1.2272 to equal 67.5.

The total number of points required for a final score of 3, 4, or 5 varies each year, but a very reasonable assumption is that you need to accumulate approximately 114 to 150 points for a score of 5, 98 to 113 for a score of 4, and 81 to 97 for a score of 3.

Some Successful Testing Strategies

1. Increase your awareness of the structure of the exam. Know how many questions you'll be asked, how much time you'll have, what basic skills you'll need, and so forth. Of course, these preliminaries are all covered in this book.

2. Understand the thought process behind the exam. If you understand what the test-makers have in mind when they write questions and answers, you'll avoid fighting the exam, and eliminating wrong answer choices in the multiple-choice section will go faster.

3. Read the exam directions carefully! Become familiar with the wording of the directions in advance so that you'll be as comfortable as possible on test day.

4. Mark your answer sheet carefully. If you skip a question, mark it in your exam booklet, and then carefully enter the next answer on your answer sheet.

5. Practice your pacing and timing skills. For multiple-choice questions, complete the easiest ones first; in the free-response section, follow your preplanned strategy.

6. Overall, be prepared! Become familiar with the exam. Remember that increased comfort builds confidence and relieves anxiety. The essential skills can all be improved by practicing frequently.

Chapter 1

The Multiple-Choice Section

The multiple-choice section is 1 hour long and consists of about 52–55 questions. You should expect four or five reading passages that represent a variety of rhetorical modes such as narration, argumentation, persuasion, and description. (To provide you with practice in as many passages as possible, this book will use five passages in most of the practice exams.) The passages may vary in length from about 300 to about 800 words. Each passage is followed by 10 to 15 questions based on its content. These questions are not ordered by level of difficulty. The total number of questions is approximately the same on every exam.

Remember that you're not expected to be familiar with the passage or its specific content. Consider this section akin to a scavenger hunt; the passage will give you everything you need, it's just up to you to find it and think about it accurately. Any technical information crucial to comprehending the passage, as well as unusual or foreign phrases, will be defined for you.

You will be more comfortable with both the free-response and multiple-choice sections if you are adept at reading works from many genres and time periods. For example, the exam can cover excerpts from autobiographies, biographies, historical writing, essays and literary criticisms, journalism, political writing, nature writing, and scientific writing. The exam passages can be up to about 400 years old, so you'll need to practice comprehending and appreciating the styles of older pieces as well as contemporary ones. A student who practices only with modern-day authors will not be as relaxed or efficient during the exam as one who has been exposed to John Milton, Cotton Mather, or Dr. Samuel Johnson.

At least one multiple-choice passage will contain documentation of some sort, such as footnotes. Expect some questions about this documentation, such as what information is provided in a footnote or what inferences you can draw from the source in it; some questions may ask you to compare information from different footnotes. You will *not* be asked about proper citation form or punctuation. The reading passage that has documentation will, of course, ask questions about the passage's content; only a few questions will concentrate on the documentation.

Abilities Tested

The multiple-choice section tests your ability to analyze the linguistic and rhetorical choices of an author. You are expected to show an awareness of the stylistic effects created by specific word choices and syntactic decisions. These questions also test your ability to examine prose passages critically; to understand the author's meaning and purpose; to comprehend structural organization; to recognize rhetorical modes; and to analyze syntax, figurative language, style, and tone. The level of difficulty reflects college-level study.

Basic Skills Necessary

In general, you need to be able to glean the gist of a given passage, have skills in literary and rhetorical analysis, and demonstrate an adequate background in grammar. Although the questions don't specifically ask for definitions of terms (such as *subordinate clause* or *syntax*), you should be familiar with terms that may show up in the question stems or in the answer choices. See "Terms for the Multiple-Choice and Free-Response Sections" in Appendix A for a review of the terms you're likely to encounter on the exam. In addition, you need to be proficient in careful reading so you can analyze and interpret the passages. You can gain this proficiency by using active, visual reading.

Analysis of the Directions

The directions you see on the AP English Language and Composition Exam will look like this:

> **Directions:** This section contains selections from prose works and questions on their content, style, and form. Read each selection carefully. Choose the best answer of the five choices.

The following tips will help ensure your success on the exam.

- Use self-discipline to manage your time effectively during the exam. You can develop this skill through practice. You should divide your time for each passage accordingly. Do not let yourself fall further and further behind as the exam progresses.

- Answer all the questions to the best of your ability before going on to the next passage. This strategy prevents you from having to return to any passage at the end of the exam just to answer a few skipped questions. If you put yourself in the position of returning to a passage, you'll have to reread it and that process is too time-consuming.

- Read each passage carefully and critically. First, paraphrase the author's ideas as you read; then, concentrate on the author's effective word choices. Avoid getting bogged down in diction, whether it's a word you don't know or the structure of a sentence that's confusing. Simply keep trying to get the main point, and then let the questions guide what you need to know.

- Read all the answer choices. Remember that the directions ask for the *best* answer, which means there can be more than one reasonable choice for each question. However, never forget that the wrong answer is wrong for a reason. The correct response will never have a single inaccurate word in it. Eliminate wrong answer choices as you go. You can become more proficient at eliminating wrong answer choices by practicing spotting the wrong word or phrase in the incorrect responses.

Test-Taking Strategies

You can do well on the AP English Language and Composition Exam by using some proven test-taking strategies.

Skim the Questions

First, skim the questions to find out what you should concentrate on. Skimming the questions before reading the passage helps you focus on what the test-makers found important. Skimming involves a very fast reading speed—approximately 1,000 words per minute—so be aware that during this skimming, you are really just glancing at the questions. Ignore any "generic" questions, such as ones that ask you the author's main purpose or main point; instead, try to find approximately three to five specific ideas that you can look for while you read the passage. Do not try to memorize the questions; you're just glancing at them to help you focus while you read.

This technique works well, but you must practice it frequently enough before the exam for it to become second nature. You should look for the specific content of each question. For example, don't merely note that a question asks you to draw an inference. You must also focus on the specific content included in the inference. Prior practice is essential for you to become comfortable with the strategy of skimming the questions before reading the passage.

Read Each Passage Actively and Visually

Active reading means you should underline and mark key words and ideas (just the most important ones) as you read. Don't sit passively and merely let your eyes move across the page. Scientific studies support the idea that active readers gain higher immediate retention than do passive readers, and immediate retention is all you need in this case. You won't be concerned at all with long-term memory on the day of the exam.

Visual reading means you should picture any action of the passage in your mind; create a movie, if you will. Visual reading is a valuable tool for eliminating distractions while reading. It gives your brain a task to perform and helps keep your mind on the content of the passage. Most people are visual learners; they remember more after they have "seen" something, even if it's in their imagination.

Both of these strategies enhance your immediate retention and concentration—just what you need for this exam. Practice these skills daily and watch them become more effective with continued use.

Paraphrase While You Read

This technique also helps your immediate retention and understanding of the author's ideas. By definition, paraphrasing, like summarizing, means restating the author's ideas in your own words. This is an essential skill for comprehension, and, like visual reading, it gives your brain something to do that is on task while you read. Every question that asks about a passage's main ideas or an author's point can be answered correctly if you paraphrase accurately.

For any given passage, paraphrase each paragraph as a unit, and then paraphrase the author's overall point that covers all of the paragraphs. Initially, practice by writing down your concise statement of an author's point immediately after reading a paragraph or a whole passage. Later, you can develop this skill to the point that it's internalized, and you can paraphrase very quickly. You'll find that, eventually, you can paraphrase effectively while you're reading.

Read the Questions Carefully

Read the question carefully after you've read the passage. Don't assume from your earlier skimming that you know each question well. You must understand exactly what you're being asked. Students frequently choose the wrong answer because they have misread the question, either by reading too quickly or by not being sure what's actually being asked.

Read the Answer Choices Carefully

Eliminate a wrong answer choice as you read it by crossing out that letter in the exam booklet. Never waste time rereading the wrong answers. Make sure the answer choice you select is accurate according to the passage and that it answers the question.

Understanding how to eliminate incorrect answer choices saves time and increases accuracy. Of course, the test-makers are trying to mislead you. If you understand the tricks they frequently throw at you, you'll work faster to eliminate wrong answer choices and you'll be less likely to be deceived by them. When trying to eliminate wrong answers, remember to think like a test-maker, not a test-taker. Remember to cross out each wrong answer choice in the exam booklet; don't waste time rereading them. Wrong answer choices can be:

- **Contradictory to the passage:** If you read the passage carefully and paraphrase it accurately, you won't be tricked into the time-consuming process of rereading it to decide if the answer choice is consistent with the passage.

- **Irrelevant to the question:** These incorrect answer choices may sound good, but they simply do not answer the specific question. Be sure to read the question carefully, know what it asks, and match the answer accordingly.

- **Never addressed in the passage:** Again, poor readers are tricked into rereading to look for ideas that weren't there in the first place. Readers who are accurate at paraphrasing can quickly eliminate an answer choice that has no evidence in the passage.

- **Unreasonable:** If the answer choice makes you shake your head and ask, "Where did they get that idea?", it's unreasonable. You can learn to quickly spot unreasonable answer choices.

- **Too general or too specific for the question:** Understand the degree of specificity that you need for a correct answer and then eliminate incorrect answer choices accordingly. For example, if the question asks about the overall point of a passage, you need a general answer, one that encompasses the content of the entire passage. On the other hand, if you're asked about the author's use of a certain quotation, the correct answer is likely to be quite specific.

Finally, never forget that a wrong answer choice is wrong for a specific reason and will *always* contain an inaccurate word or phrase. Practice crossing out the exact word or phrase that is wrong, and you'll find you can perform faster and with greater confidence. The correct answer will not have a single word that is inaccurate.

Leave the Most Difficult Questions for Later

Leave the most difficult questions until the end of each passage. From the practice exams, you can learn to recognize which questions are harder for you and which ones you can do accurately and quickly. Then use this knowledge as part of your personal strategy to get the most correct answers you possibly can. Remember to treat each passage as a unit and answer all the questions for that passage within your time limit before going on to the next passage. Because you will not be penalized for a wrong answer, be sure to choose an answer for each question.

One way to increase your score is to always analyze the questions you get wrong on the practice exams. Try to identify the specific reason why you selected each incorrect answer choice. Did you misread the question? Did you misread the answer choice? Did you work too quickly? Try to detect any trends; for example, a certain question type may always be the hardest for you. Then you can study, analyze, and understand why the correct answer is better than your choice. This analysis will help you to stop repeating the same mistakes.

Remember: Practice! With extensive practice, you'll increase your familiarity with the question types. Thus, you'll begin to think like the test-makers, not the test-takers, and your score will improve.

Question Categories

In general, the exam questions tend to fall into just a few categories. By becoming familiar with these, you can more quickly understand what you're being asked. Also, you'll be more comfortable with the exam format and able to work faster. As with all testing strategies, it is essential to practice recognizing the question types *before* the exam.

A brief analysis of these question types follows.

Note: Be aware that these question types do not constitute a complete list. You will encounter questions that don't seem to fit into a category. However, by understanding what question types appear most frequently, you will increase your familiarity with the exam and improve your understanding of how to find the correct answers. Don't be thrown off balance by questions that don't seem to fall into set categories.

Questions about Rhetoric

Many of the questions on the exam are about rhetoric and test your ability to understand *how* language works in each passage. These questions ask you to analyze the *syntax* (sentence structure and word order), *diction* (word choice), point of view, and figurative language and its effects. Your mere recognition of these elements is not enough; you must be able to understand precisely how and why the devices of rhetoric produce particular effects.

Here are some of the ways this question type may be worded on the exam.

- The shift in point of view has the effect of . . .
- The syntax of lines _____ serves to . . .
- Which of the following choices best describes what _____ symbolizes?
- The second sentence is unified by metaphorical references to . . .
- As lines _____ are constructed, "_____" is parallel to which of the following?
- The antecedent for "_____" is . . .
- The third sentence remains coherent because of the use of . . .
- The phrase "_____" has the effect of . . .
- The style of the passage can best be characterized as . . .

- The sentence "_____" is chiefly remarkable for which of the following stylistic features?
- In line _____, the word "_____" functions as a metaphor for . . .
- Compared to the rest of the passage, the diction of lines _____ is best characterized as . . .
- In lines _____, the author develops her rhetorical purpose by . . .

Questions about the Author's Meaning and Purpose

These question types also appear quite frequently on the exam. They measure your ability to interpret the author's theme, meaning, or purpose. As with the questions about rhetoric, these questions are closely tied to specific word choices. However, now you must determine *why* the author chooses the wording, not what effect it produces. These questions demonstrate your understanding of the author's thematic reason for choosing certain phrases. They might refer to the passage as a whole or to a specific portion of the passage, such as only one paragraph or one sentence.

Here are some of the ways this question type may be worded on the exam.

- Which of the following best identifies the meaning of "_____"?
- Which of the following best describes the author's purpose in the last sentence?
- The main purpose of _____ is to make clear . . .
- The author emphasizes _____ in order to . . .
- The sympathy referred to in line _____ is called _____ because it . . .
- What is the function of _____?
- By "_____," the author most likely means . . .
- In context, which of the following meanings are contained in _____?
- In the commentary in the second footnote, the author's primary purpose is most likely . . .
- The author italicizes the word "_____" in order to . . .
- The author places quotation marks around the phrase "_____" in order to . . .

Questions about the Main Idea

These questions also appear quite frequently. They test your understanding of the author's ideas, attitude, and tone. To prepare for these questions, paraphrase everything you read. First, make yourself practice this skill in writing—literally write down an author's point in a sentence or two. After such practice, you'll be able to do it internally while you read, and you'll have greater comprehension.

Here are some of the ways this question type may be worded on the exam.

- The theme of the second paragraph is . . .
- The speaker's attitude is best described as one of . . .
- The speaker interests the audience by stressing the idea that . . .
- It can be inferred from the description of _____ that which of the following qualities are valued by the author?
- In context, the sentence "_____" is best interpreted as which of the following?
- The atmosphere is one of . . .
- Which of the following would the author be LEAST likely to encourage?
- Which of the following is true about the various assertions made in the passage?
- All of the following ideas may be found in the passage EXCEPT . . .
- Footnote #1 supports which of the author's ideas?
- The information in footnote #1 and footnote #2 differs in that . . .

Questions about Implications and Inferences

These questions require that you read between the lines and consider ideas that are not expressed explicitly. To answer these questions, think about what is NOT stated directly, but rather what is logically *implied* in the passage. Remember that the correct answer has to be the very BEST answer choice; therefore, whenever you are asked to read between the lines, select the answer choice that is most obvious, most plausible, and most likely to be true. Test-takers sometimes think that the correct answer should be more obscure than it really is—beware of talking yourself out of the correct answer!

Here are some of the ways this question type may be worded on the exam.

- The passage implies that . . .
- The phrase "_____" suggests that . . .
- It can be inferred from _____ that . . .
- In context, the phrase "_____" is meant to indicate that . . .
- From footnote #4, one can infer that . . .
- The image of _____ suggests that . . .

Questions about Organization and Structure

Appearing less frequently than the first four question types detailed here, these questions test your ability to perceive how the passage is organized. For example, you need to know if the passage follows a compare/contrast structure or if it gives a definition followed by examples. Other passages may be organized around descriptive statements that then lead to a generalization. These methods are just a few of the ones an author may use to organize ideas. You also need to understand how the structure of the passage works. For example, you must know how one paragraph relates to another paragraph or how a single sentence works within a paragraph. You will know to pay attention to the passage's organization if you skim the questions before reading and spot one of these question types.

Here are some of the ways this question type may be worded on the exam.

- The quotation "_____" signals a shift from . . .
- The speaker's mention of _____ is appropriate to the development of her argument by . . .
- The type of argument employed by the author is most similar to which of the following?
- The speaker describes _____ in an order best described as moving from _____ to . . .
- The relationship between _____ and _____ is explained primarily by the use of which of the following?
- The author's discussion depends on which of the following structures?
- Which of the following best describes the function of the third paragraph in relation to the first two paragraphs?
- The organization of the passage can best be described as . . .
- When the passage transitions from paragraph one to paragraph two, it also moves from . . .
- The last paragraph signals a shift from _____ to . . .

Questions about Rhetorical Modes

You should expect only a few questions of this type on the exam. These questions ask you to identify and recognize the various rhetorical modes the author uses. You must know the difference between narration, description, argumentation, and exposition. Understanding *why* a particular mode is effective for the author's ideas is also helpful.

Here are some of the ways this question type may be worded on the exam.

- The pattern of exposition exemplified in the passage can best be described as . . .
- The author's use of description is appropriate because . . .
- Which of the following best describes the author's method?
- Because the author uses expository format, he is able to . . .
- The speaker's rhetorical strategy is to . . .
- The author develops the passage primarily through which of the following?

Practice

This section contains two passages that are typical of the ones chosen for the multiple-choice section of the exam, followed by sample questions. The answers and their explanations follow.

Questions

Directions: This section consists of selections from prose works and questions on their content, style, and form. Read each selection carefully. Choose the best answer of the five choices.

Questions 1–15 refer to the following passage from a 20th-century British book of biographies.

Everyone knows the popular conception of Florence Nightingale. The saintly, self-sacrificing woman, the delicate maiden of high degree who threw aside the pleasures of a life of ease to
(5) succour the afflicted, the Lady with the Lamp, gliding through the horrors of the hospital at Scutari, and consecrating with the radiance of her goodness the dying soldier's couch—the vision is familiar to all. But the truth was
(10) different. The Miss Nightingale of fact was not as facile fancy painted her. She worked in another fashion, and toward another end; she moved under the stress of an impetus which finds no place in the popular imagination. A Demon
(15) possessed her. Now demons, whatever else they may be, are full of interest. And so it happens that in the real Miss Nightingale there was more that was interesting than in the legendary one; there was also less that was agreeable.
(20) What was the secret voice in her ear, if it was not a call? Why had she felt from her earliest years, those mysterious promptings towards . . . she hardly knew what but certainly towards something very different from anything around
(25) her? Why, as a child in the nursery, when her sister had shown a healthy pleasure in tearing her dolls to pieces, had she shown an almost morbid one in sewing them up again? Why was she driven now to minister to the poor in their cottages, to
(30) watch by sick-beds, to put her dog's wounded paw into elaborate splints as if it was a human being? Why was her head filled with the queer imaginations of the country house at Embley turned, by some enchantment, into a hospital,
(35) with herself as matron moving among the beds? Why was even her vision of heaven itself filled with suffering patients to whom she was being useful? So she dreamed and wondered, and taking out her diary, she poured into it the
(40) agitations of her soul.

A weaker spirit would have been overwhelmed by the load of such distress—would have yielded or snapped. But this extraordinary young woman held firm, and fought her way to victory. With an
(45) amazing persistency, during the eight years that followed her rebuff over Salisbury Hospital, she struggled and worked and planned. While superficially she was carrying on the life of a brilliant girl in high society, while internally she
(50) was a prey to the tortures of regret and remorse, she yet possessed the energy to collect the knowledge and to undergo the experience which alone could enable her to do what she had determined she would do in the end. In secret she
(55) devoured the reports of medical commissions, the pamphlets of sanitary authorities, the histories of hospitals and homes. She spent the intervals of the London season in ragged schools and workhouses. When she went abroad with her
(60) family, she used her spare time so well that there was hardly a great hospital in Europe with which she was not acquainted, hardly a great city whose slums she had not passed through.

(65) Three more years passed, and then at last the pressure of time told; her family seemed to realise that she was old enough and strong enough to have her way; and she became superintendent of a charitable nursing home in Harley Street. She had gained her independence,
(70) though it was in a meagre sphere enough; and her mother was still not quite resigned: surely Florence might at least spend the summer in the country. At times, indeed, among her intimates, Mrs. Nightingale almost wept. "We are ducks,"
(75) she said with tears in her eyes, "who have hatched a wild swan." But the poor lady was wrong; it was not a swan that they had hatched; it was an eagle.

1. Which of the following best describes the structure of the first paragraph?

    A. It is divided into two parts, beginning with general statements, and moving to specific commentary.

    B. It is divided into two contrasting parts, with the division coming in line 9.

    C. It alternates a short sentence followed by a long sentence throughout.

    D. It moves from the presentation of Florence Nightingale's strengths (lines 1–9) to the presentation of her weaknesses (lines 9–19).

    E. It presents Florence Nightingale first in figurative language (lines 1–9) and then in literal language (lines 9–19).

2. Which of the following best defines the word "succour" in line 5?

    A. oversee

    B. treat with medicines

    C. relieve

    D. rally

    E. convert

3. In the first paragraph, all of the following words and phrases are used to present the popular conception of Florence Nightingale EXCEPT

    A. "saintly" (line 2)

    B. "self-sacrificing" (line 2)

    C. "the Lady with the Lamp" (line 5)

    D. "interesting" (line 18)

    E. "legendary" (line 18)

4. The first paragraph of the passage employs all of the following contrasts EXCEPT

    A. "the vision" and "the truth" (lines 8–9)

    B. "fact" and "fancy" (lines 10–11)

    C. "another fashion" and "no place in the popular imagination" (lines 11–14)

    D. "the real" and "the legendary" (lines 17–18)

    E. "more that was interesting" and "less that was agreeable" (lines 17–19)

5. In the first paragraph, all of the following words have specific religious meanings EXCEPT

    A. "saintly" (line 2)

    B. "maiden" (line 3)

    C. "consecrating" (line 7)

    D. "Demon" (line 14)

    E. "possessed" (line 15)

6. In which of the following sentences from the first paragraph is the use of parallel structure most important?

    A. the first ("Everyone knows . . .", lines 1–2)

    B. the third ("But the . . .", lines 9–10)

    C. the fourth ("The Miss . . .", lines 10–11)

    D. the seventh ("Now demons . . .", lines 15–16)

    E. the eighth ("And so . . .", lines 16–19)

7. All of the following words and phrases serve a similar purpose EXCEPT

    A. "popular conception" (line 1)

    B. "vision" (line 9)

    C. "as facile fancy painted" (line 11)

    D. "demons" (line 15)

    E. "the legendary one" (line 18)

8. In which sentence in the first paragraph does the author use archaic diction and clichés?

    A. the first ("Everyone knows . . .", lines 1–2)

    B. the second ("The saintly . . .", lines 2–9)

    C. the third ("But the . . .", lines 9–10)

    D. the sixth ("A Demon . . .", lines 14–15)

    E. the eighth ("And so . . .", lines 16–19)

9. Which of the following phrases in the first paragraph employs BOTH hyperbole and metaphor?

A. "the Lady with the Lamp" (line 5)

B. "the horrors of the hospital at Scutari" (lines 6–7)

C. "consecrating with the radiance of her goodness" (lines 7–8)

D. "as facile fancy painted her" (line 11)

E. "no place in the popular imagination" (lines 13–14)

10. The words "call" (line 21) and "mysterious" (line 22) in the second paragraph are related to the diction of the first paragraph because their meanings are associated with

A. medicine

B. religion

C. social position

D. psychology

E. feminism

11. In the second paragraph, the sentence that is most likely to surprise the conventional expectations of a reader is the

A. first ("What was . . .", lines 20–21)

B. second ("Why had she . . .", lines 21–25)

C. third ("Why, as a . . .", lines 25–28)

D. fourth ("Why was she . . .", lines 28–32)

E. fifth ("Why was her . . .", lines 32–35)

12. The significant difference between the syntax of the second paragraph and that of the rest of the passage is its use of

A. both loose and periodic sentences

B. parallel structure

C. sentence fragments

D. interrogative sentences

E. connotative diction

13. The third paragraph implies a contrast between all of the following EXCEPT

A. "weaker spirit . . . extraordinary young woman" (lines 41–43)

B. "superficially . . . internally" (lines 48–49)

C. "reports of medical commissions . . . histories of hospitals" (lines 55–57)

D. "the London season in ragged schools and workhouses" (lines 58–59)

E. "abroad with her family . . . slums" (lines 59–63)

14. Which of the following best describes the structure of the passage as a whole?

A. The entire passage is developed chronologically.

B. The first paragraph gives an overview, and the second, third, and fourth paragraphs develop chronologically.

C. The first paragraph uses only the point of view of the author, the second and third paragraphs only that of Florence Nightingale, and the fourth paragraph only that of her mother.

D. The first and second paragraphs generalize about Florence Nightingale, while the third and fourth paragraphs use specific detail.

E. The first three paragraphs use a first-person narrator, while the fourth paragraph employs direct and indirect discourse.

15. Which of the following is the climactic contrast of the passage?

A. "Three more years . . . the pressure of time" (lines 64–65)

B. "independence . . . meagre sphere" (lines 69–70)

C. "Harley Street . . . the country" (lines 69–73)

D. "'ducks . . . wild swan'" (lines 74–76)

E. "swan . . . eagle" (lines 77–78)

Questions 16–25 refer to the following passage from an American 19th-century autobiography.

Very soon after I went to live with Mr. and Mrs. Auld, she very kindly commenced to teach me the ABCs. After I had learned this, she assisted me in learning to spell words of three or four
(5) letters. Just at this point of my progress, Mr. Auld found out what was going on, and at once forbade Mrs. Auld to instruct me further, telling her, among other things, that it was unlawful, as well as unsafe, to teach a slave to read. It would forever
(10) unfit him to be a slave. He would at once become unmanageable, and of no value to his master. As to himself, it could do him no good, but a great deal of harm. It would make him discontented and unhappy. These words sank deep into my
(15) heart, stirred up sentiments within that lay slumbering, and called into existence an entirely new train of thought. It was a new and special revelation, explaining dark and mysterious things, with which my youthful understanding had
(20) struggled, but struggled in vain. I now understood

what had been to me a most perplexing difficulty—to wit, the white man's power to enslave the black man. It was a grand achievement, and I prized it highly. From that moment, I understood the (25) pathway from slavery to freedom. It was just what I wanted, and I got it at a time when I least expected it. Whilst I was saddened by the thought of losing the aid of my kind mistress, I was gladdened by the invaluable instruction which, by (30) the merest accident, I had gained from my master. Though conscious of the difficulty of learning without a teacher, I set out with high hope, and a fixed purpose, at whatever cost of trouble, to learn how to read.

(35)   The very decided manner with which he spoke, and strove to impress his wife with the evil consequences of giving me instruction, served to convince me that he was deeply sensible of the truths he was uttering. It gave me the best (40) assurance that I might rely with the utmost confidence on the results which, he said, would flow from teaching me how to read. What he most dreaded, that I most desired. What he most loved, that I most hated. That which to him was (45) a great evil, to be carefully shunned, was to me a great good, to be diligently sought; and the argument which he so warmly urged, against my learning to read, only served to inspire me with a desire and determination to learn. In learning to (50) read, I owe almost as much to the bitter opposition of my master, as to the kindly aid of my mistress. I acknowledge the benefit of both.

16. From the report of Mr. Auld's words in lines 8–14, we can infer that he believed that the illiterate slave was

   A. valuable legal property
   B. incapable of learning to read
   C. eventually unmanageable
   D. discontent with his position in life
   E. likely to revolt over his master

17. Of the following, which phrase is figurative rather than literal?

   A. "learning to spell words of three or four letters" (lines 4–5)
   B. "He would at once become unmanageable" (lines 10–11)
   C. "the pathway from slavery to freedom" (lines 24–25)
   D. "whatever cost of trouble" (line 33)
   E. "sensible of the truths he was uttering" (lines 38–39)

18. The antecedent of both uses of the pronoun "it" in lines 23 and 25 is

   A. "revelation" (line 18)
   B. "things" (line 18)
   C. "understanding" (line 19)
   D. "difficulty" (line 21)
   E. "power" (line 22)

19. In line 35, the word "decided" can be best defined as

   A. judgmental
   B. definite
   C. inclusive
   D. stentorian
   E. patriarchal

20. In lines 43–44 ("What he most loved, that I most hated"), the author uses all of the following EXCEPT

   A. two sentences in parallel structure
   B. a parallel structure in the first sentence
   C. a parallel structure in the second sentence
   D. opening subordinate clauses
   E. circumlocution to create juxtaposition

21. In lines 44–46 ("That which to him . . . to be diligently sought"), all of the following are balanced against one another EXCEPT

   A. "that which . . . was to me"
   B. "him . . . me"
   C. "great . . . great"
   D. "evil . . . good"
   E. "carefully . . . diligently"

22. In line 52, if the word "benefit," which can mean "a kindly act" or "anything contributing to improvement," is used to denote the first of these meanings, the final line of the passage is an example of

   A. paradox
   B. overstatement
   C. metaphor
   D. irony
   E. personification

23. The passage could best be used to effectively support a general argument about

    A. the kinder treatment of slaves by women than by men
    B. the importance of motivation to learning
    C. the physical cruelty in the treatment of slaves
    D. the dangers of education
    E. the corruption that results from power

24. All of the following describe the style of the passage EXCEPT

    A. the use of carefully balanced sentences
    B. the occasional use of short, loose sentences
    C. the use of the first-person pronoun
    D. the use of original metaphors and similes
    E. the use of indirect discourse

25. The passage illustrates the truth of the paradox that

    A. learning may be power
    B. slavery may be freedom
    C. a foe may be an ally
    D. poverty may be wealth
    E. a falsehood may be truth

Answer Key

1. B	**6.** E	**11.** C	**16.** A	**21.** A
2. C	**7.** D	**12.** D	**17.** C	**22.** D
3. D	**8.** B	**13.** C	**18.** A	**23.** B
4. C	**9.** C	**14.** B	**19.** B	**24.** D
5. B	**10.** B	**15.** E	**20.** E	**25.** C

Answer Explanations

1. B. The first paragraph has two distinct parts. The first nine lines present the "popular" idealized notion of Florence Nightingale. The division is clearly marked by the sentence "But the truth was different." The rest of the paragraph begins the presentation of what the author claims is the "real Miss Nightingale." Though the paragraph uses both long and short sentences, the alternation is not consistent. Both the third and fourth sentences are short, and the fifth is long only because it uses semicolons in place of periods. The contrast is not between Nightingale's strength and weakness, but between a romantic conception of her and a realistic account.

2. C. To succour (the American spelling is *succor*) is to relieve, to ameliorate at a time of distress.

3. D. All but "interesting" are used to present the popular idea of Florence Nightingale. The author argues the *real* woman was "more . . . interesting" though less saintly than the woman of the legend.

4. C. Four of these pairs are part of the legendary versus real contrast in the paragraph. "Another fashion" and "no place in the popular imagination," however, are both part of a sentence describing the "real" woman and are not contrasts.

5. B. Though "maiden" might be used in a religious context, of itself it is simply the word for a virgin or an unmarried girl or woman. The four other words have specific religious denotations. As it appears here, "possessed" is used (metaphorically) to mean controlled by a spirit.

6. E. None of the first four options uses parallel structure. The eighth sentence, however, plays "in the real" against "in the legendary" and "there was more that was interesting" against "there was also less that was agreeable."

7. D. Four of these words or phrases refer to the popular concept of the sainted Florence Nightingale. "Demons" does not.

8. B. The second sentence employs both archaisms like "maiden of high degree" or "couch" and clichés like "saintly, self-sacrificing," "delicate maiden of high degree," and "to succour the afflicted," as the author mocks the sentimental idea of Florence Nightingale. The other sentences avoid these excesses.

9. C. The "horrors of the hospital" is not hyperbolic or figurative, and "facile fancy" is not hyperbole, though it is metaphoric. The overstatement is the claim that the "radiance" (a metaphor) of Nightingale's goodness "consecrated" the dying soldiers' deathbeds. She may have made the dying more comfortable, but she did not make them sacred.

10. B. Though "call" and "mysterious" can be used without any religious reference, both have specific religious meanings. The word "call" can mean a religious vocation regarded as divinely inspired, and "mysterious" has several different religious meanings; for example, pertaining to that which only faith can explain.

11. C. Most modern readers are unlikely to expect the sister's pleasure in "tearing her dolls to pieces" to be described as "healthy," while Florence Nightingale's repairing the victims is "morbid."

12. D. Unlike the rest of the passage, the second paragraph depends almost entirely on the use of questions. Six of its seven sentences are interrogative. All of the paragraphs employ connotative diction.

13. **C.** The contrast of choices A and B is clear. In D and E, "the London season" and "abroad with her family" suggest situations associated with the high social position of Florence's well-to-do family, but Florence's concern on these occasions is the world of poverty, of "workhouses" and "slums." The "reports" and "histories" noted in choice C are alike, not contrasted; they are both the subjects of Florence Nightingale's studies.

14. **B.** The first paragraph establishes the basic contrast of the passage, that of the conventional view of Florence Nightingale with the realistic view that this passage will present. The second, third, and fourth paragraphs move chronologically from Florence Nightingale's youth, to her preparation, to her first success.

15. **E.** This final metaphor is the climax of the passage. The author has emphasized the contrast by the parallel construction of the sentence ("it was not a swan . . . it was an eagle"). The sentence is a final instance of the more genteel notion of Florence Nightingale ("a swan") and the author's vision of her strength and power ("an eagle").

16. **A.** We can infer the value of the illiterate slave from the slave owner's fear that the literate slave will have "no value." Because Mr. Auld takes pains to withhold education from his slave, he cannot believe that slaves are incapable of learning to read. All other answer choices present what Mr. Auld believes about literate slaves, not illiterate ones.

17. **C.** When Douglass comprehends that learning to read was a "pathway from slavery to freedom," he employs figurative, imaginative language; he is not referring to a literal path or trail. All other answer choices are literal.

18. **A.** It is tempting to see the whole clause "I now understood . . . the most perplexing difficulty" as the antecedent of *it;* if the pronouns refer to a single word, it must be "revelation" (line 18) rather than "understanding" (line 19) because this "understanding" is "in vain." The antecedent must be an "achievement" of the speaker.

19. **B.** As it is used here, *decided* is an adjective meaning "definite" or "unhesitatingly."

20. **E.** The author does not use circumlocution, which refers to long-winded, overly complex language. There are three parallels in the two sentences. Both short sentences balance the "What he . . ." clause with the "that I . . ." clause, and the two sentences use the same parallel structure. Both sentences begin with a subordinate clause.

21. **A.** The phrase "that which" is not repeated or balanced. It is the subject of both parts of this compound sentence, while the phrase "was to me" serves as the predicate.

22. **D.** If "benefit" is used with its associations of kindness, it is ironic in this context because Mr. Auld's real purpose was to maintain his power over his slave. That Mr. Auld's attempt to prevent his slave from learning to read motivates him to do so is also an example of dramatic irony.

23. **B.** The passage is essentially about Frederick Douglass learning to read, and he gives much of the credit for this achievement to his motivation, his "fixed purpose, at whatever cost of trouble." The other topics are perhaps true, but none is really an issue in this passage.

24. **D.** There are no similes and only a few commonplace metaphors in the passage. Lines 27–30 are carefully balanced. The last sentence of the passage is a good example of a short, simple sentence. Lines 7–14 use indirect discourse, and the whole passage employs a first-person speaker.

25. **C.** The paradox central to the passage is Mr. Auld's double role of oppressor and benefactor.

Chapter 2

The Free-Response Section

The free-response section of the AP English Language and Composition Exam, also called the essay section, requires you to write three essays. You will be given 2 hours and 15 minutes to complete the essays. The extra 15 minutes are allotted for reading the prompts and passages in the exam booklet and preparing your responses; you may begin writing in the answer booklet as soon as you are ready. Of course, you may jot any notes you want in the exam booklet as you read. The suggested time for writing each essay is 40 minutes. You must complete all three essays within the 2 hours and 15 minutes time limit. Each of the three essays is equally weighted at one-third of the total essay score, and the total for the free-response section accounts for 55 percent of the entire AP exam score.

Abilities Tested

This section tests your ability to:

- Synthesize material from multiple sources to compose an informed and well-reasoned position on an issue.
- Construct a coherent and convincing argument.
- Demonstrate an understanding of *how* language works in developing ideas and arguments.
- Communicate intelligent ideas in essay form.

You should read the prose passages very carefully and then quickly articulate your ideas. Each essay should be written in approximately 40 minutes.

Basic Skills Necessary

The basic skill you need for the free-response section is the ability to articulate and prove a thesis through concrete examples. You must be able to write on any assigned subject. Your paragraphs should be well developed, your overall essay organization should make sense, and your writing should demonstrate college-level thinking and style. The basic writing format of presenting an introduction, body, and conclusion is helpful, but to achieve a high score, you *must* demonstrate *depth of thought*. Overall, you must show that you can read the prompt and any subsequent passages carefully, plan an intelligent thesis, organize and present valid and sufficient evidence while connecting your evidence to the thesis, and demonstrate college-level skill with your use of language.

Analysis of the Directions

Each essay prompt has its own wording and, therefore, its own directions.

Test-Taking Strategies

Remember the following as you practice writing your essays.

- Use the exam booklet to plan your essay. A poorly planned or an unplanned essay frequently reveals problems in organization and development.
- Consider using the standard format with an introduction, body, and conclusion, but do not force a formulaic and overly predictable five-paragraph essay.
- Clearly divide ideas into separate paragraphs; clearly indent the paragraphs.

- Stay on topic; avoid irrelevant comments or ideas.
- Use sophisticated diction and sentences with syntactic variety.
- Be organized and logical in your presentation.
- Be sure to address all the tasks the essay question requires.
- Develop your body paragraphs thoroughly with evidence, examples, and your analysis.
- Write as legibly as possible; the Reader must be able to read your essay.

The following sections offer more specific strategies having to do with pacing, planning, and writing your essays.

Pacing the Essay

With an average time of only 40 minutes per essay, you should divide your time as follows:

- **Spend about 10 minutes rereading the topic and the passage(s) carefully and planning your essay.** This organizational time is crucial to producing a high-scoring essay. In the first 10 minutes of your writing time, you need to follow the steps below. Do it efficiently, and you'll know what you want to write and the order in which you'll present your ideas. Although you are given 15 minutes at the beginning of the essay portion to read the topics, do not assume you don't need to skim the content again.

1. Reread the prompt carefully and underline the specific task(s).
2. Reread the passage(s) carefully, noting what ideas, evidence, and rhetorical devices are relevant to the specific essay prompt.
3. Conceive your thesis statement, which will be placed in your introductory paragraph.
4. Organize your body paragraphs, deciding what evidence from the passage(s) you'll include (using at least three sources in the synthesis essay) or what appropriate examples you'll use from your knowledge of the world. Know what relevant remarks you'll make about the evidence. Understand your body paragraph divisions—when you'll begin a new paragraph and what idea unifies each paragraph.

The importance of this planning phase cannot be overemphasized. When your essay has been well planned, your writing flows faster, your essay stays on topic and is well organized, and the paragraphs are well developed. You must practice this essential planning step several times before you take the actual AP exam.

- **Take about 25 minutes to write the essay.** If you've planned well, your writing should be fluent and continuous. Avoid stopping to reread what you've written. Twenty-five minutes is sufficient time to produce all the writing needed for a good score. In general, most high-scoring essays are at least two full pages of writing, usually more.
- **Save about 5 minutes to proofread your essay.** Reserving a few minutes to proofread allows you time to catch the "honest mistakes" that can be corrected easily, such as a misspelled word or a punctuation error. In addition, this time lets you set the essay to rest, knowing that what you've written is the best draft you can produce under the circumstances. Then you can go on to the next essay prompt and give it your full attention.

Planning the Essay

Your planning and organizing should be done in the exam booklet, which provides space for that purpose. Begin by reading the essay question carefully. Underline the key words and phrases of the prompt so that you *thoroughly* understand what your tasks are. Then read any accompanying passage(s) analytically, always keeping the essay question in mind. As you read, underline important ideas and phrases that relate to the topic. Your goals while reading are to:

- Understand and critique the author's point.
- Relate the passage to the free-response question.
- Begin gathering evidence to support the points of your essay.
- Look for nuances of diction and syntax (for essay topics on rhetorical strategies).

After you've read both the question and the passage carefully, you're ready to plan and organize your essay. Again, use the space provided in the exam booklet. Organize your thoughts using whatever method you're most comfortable with—outlining, clustering, listing, and so forth. Planning at this stage is crucial to producing a well-written essay and should provide the following:

- Your thesis statement
- A list of what you plan on addressing in each body paragraph (your topic sentence idea)
- A list of supporting evidence
- The order of presentation for that supporting evidence
- Notes on analysis or commentary to be added regarding the evidence (analysis that connects your evidence both to your thesis and to the essay question)

Be careful to manage your time during the planning stage. If you overplan, you may run out of time to commit all your ideas to paper. If you fail to plan sufficiently, you're likely to produce an unorganized essay or one that's not as thoroughly developed as it should be. Remember that you do not have time to write out full sentences for everything that is in the preceding list, with the possible exception of the thesis. Simply jot down phrases and ideas quickly. Your goal here is only to plan the essay; if you do that well, your writing will go much faster. You'll then need only to put it all down on paper in complete sentences, and you'll have produced a well-written essay.

Writing the Essay

A convenient format for essay writing uses the standard structure of introduction, body, and conclusion. The body should be made up of several paragraphs, but the introduction and conclusion need only one paragraph each.

The Introduction

In your introduction, make sure you include a strong, analytical thesis statement, a sentence that explains your main idea and defines the scope of your essay. Also, be sure the introduction lets the Reader know that you're on topic; use key phrases from the question if necessary. The introductory paragraph should be brief—only a few sentences are necessary to state your thesis. However, do try to establish the importance of the topic, especially the central issue of the argument and synthesis essays.

Avoid merely repeating the topic in your thesis. Instead, let the thesis present what it is that you will specifically analyze. Imagine, for example, that one of the topics asks you to "analyze the ways in which the author re-creates his experience, perhaps considering such devices as diction, imagery, pacing, and contrast." A bland, repetitive thesis might read, "The author uses diction, imagery, and contrast to re-create his experience." A more effective thesis might state, "The author's terrifying experience is vividly reconstructed through fast-paced diction, darkly menacing imagery, and stark contrasts in pacing." Although this second thesis still uses the structure of the topic, it at least identifies the thrust of the student's ideas and an awareness of the content of the passage.

The Body Paragraphs

The body paragraphs are the heart of the essay. Each paragraph should be guided by a topic sentence idea that is a relevant part of the introductory thesis statement, although the topic doesn't need to be stated in the first sentence.

In the synthesis essay, be sure to cite at least three of the sources as you develop your paragraphs. For the rhetorical strategies essay, always supply a *great deal* of relevant evidence from the passage to support your ideas; feel free to quote the passage liberally as you analyze. In your argument essay, provide appropriate and sufficient evidence from the passage and your knowledge of the world. Prove that you are capable of intelligent civil discourse, a discussion of important ideas.

Always be sure to connect your ideas to the thesis. Explain exactly how the evidence you present leads to your thesis. Avoid obvious commentary. A medium- to low-scoring paper merely reports what's in the passage. A high-scoring paper makes relevant, insightful, analytical points about the passage. Remember to stay on topic.

AP Exam Readers give high scores to essays that thoroughly develop intelligent ideas. Students who notice more details and concepts in the prompt and present their relevant ideas in articulate, thoughtful prose receive higher scores than those who see only a few ideas to comment on and present them with simplicity. Therefore, strive to make your body paragraphs strong. Generously use examples from the passages, both implicitly and explicitly. In other words, sometimes weave direct quotations and phrases from the prompt into your own sentences and sometimes refer to the author's ideas in your own words. Thoroughly explore and explain the relationship between the text examples you present and your ideas; do not assume the Reader can also read your mind.

Additionally, understanding the writer's rhetorical appeal will help you analyze the persuasive tools the writer uses to sway an audience's response. Three appeals that are commonly referred to are:

- An appeal to **logos** uses logical reasoning, combining a clear idea (or multiple ideas) with well-thought-out and appropriate examples and details. These examples are logically presented and rationally lead to the writer's conclusion.

- An appeal to **ethos** establishes credibility in the writer. Since, by definition, "ethos" means the common attitudes, beliefs, and characteristics of a group or time period, this appeal sets up believability in the writer. He or she becomes someone who is trusted and concerned with the readers' best interests.

- An appeal to **pathos** plays on the reader's emotions and interests. A sympathetic audience is more likely to accept a writer's assertions, so this appeal draws on that understanding and uses it to the writer's advantage.

The Conclusion

Your conclusion, like your introduction, shouldn't be longwinded or elaborate. Do attempt, however, to provide more than a mere summary; try to make a point beyond the obvious, which will indicate your essay's superiority. In other words, try to address the essay's greater importance in your conclusion. As one AP Reader remarked, "I ask my students to get *global and noble*."

Of course, you should also keep in mind that a conclusion is not absolutely necessary to receive a high score, and many students incorporate their concluding ideas in the last body paragraph. Never forget that your body paragraphs are more important than the conclusion, so don't slight them merely to tack on a conclusion.

Remember to save a few minutes to proofread and to correct misspelled words, revise punctuation errors, and replace an occasional word or phrase with a more dynamic one. Do not make major editing changes while proofreading. Trust your original planning of organization and ideas, and only correct any obvious errors that you spot.

Some Suggestions about Style

On the actual exam, you won't have enough time during your proofreading to make major adjustments to your style. However, as you practice, you can experiment with some stylistic devices that you can easily incorporate into your writing. Remember that top-scoring essays are stylistically mature and that your goal is to produce college-level writing. By answering the following questions and then practicing these suggestions, you'll improve your writing.

- How long are your sentences? You should try for some variety in sentence length. Remember that the occasional concise, simple sentence can pack a punch and grab a Reader's attention when it's placed among a series of longer sentences. If an essay's sentences are all of the same length, none will stand out.

- What words do you use to begin your sentences? Again, variety is desirable. Try to avoid "there is" or "there are" (or any other dull wording). Also avoid beginning every sentence with the subject. For variety, try such grammatical constructions as a participial phrase, an adverbial clause, and so on.

- Does every word you use help your essay? Some bland, vague words to avoid include "a lot," "a little," "things," "much," and "very." Additionally, phrases like "I think," "I believe," "I feel," "in my opinion," "so as you can see," and "in conclusion" are unnecessary.

- How many linking verbs do you use? A linking verb (usually a form of the verb "to be") has no action, is vastly overused, and produces unimaginative prose. Replace as many of these as possible with action verbs.

- What sentence patterns do you use? Again, you should aim for variety; avoid using the same pattern over and over. Also, try inverting the normal order. For example, try putting a direct object before the subject for emphasis. Poets frequently do this, as illustrated by Edward Taylor's line "A curious knot God made in paradise," which would normally be written as "God made a curious knot in paradise."

- Are all your compound sentences joined in the same way? The usual method is to use a comma and a coordinating conjunction (such as "and," "but," or "yet"). Try experimenting with the semicolon and the dash to add emphasis and variety (but be sure you're using these more sophisticated punctuation devices correctly).

- How many prepositional phrases do you see? Eliminate as many as possible, especially possessive prepositional phrases. For example, change "the words of Homer" to "Homer's words."

- Do you use any parallel construction? Develop your ability to produce parallelisms and your writing will appear more polished and memorable. Parallel construction also adds a delightful, sophisticated rhythm to your sentences. You can find examples of parallelism in "Terms for the Multiple-Choice and Free-Response Sections" in Appendix A, as well as in many of the high-scoring sample essays in this book.

- Do you use any figures of speech? If you practice incorporating the occasional use of alliteration, repetition, imagery, and other figures of speech, your writing will be more vivid and engaging.

- What does your essay sound like? Have a friend read your essay aloud to you and listen to how it sounds.

Finally, a word about vocabulary. Of course, the use of sophisticated language is one of your goals, but do not use words you're unfamiliar with. In your practice, look up new words in a dictionary before you use them, especially if you find them in a thesaurus. Of course, you are not permitted to use a dictionary or a thesaurus during the actual exam. Variety in word choice is as essential as variety in sentences, but don't try to overload an essay with fancy, multisyllabic words. Use succinct words that specifically fit your purpose.

Essay Scoring

Each of the three essays equals one-third of the total essay score, and the entire free-response section accounts for 55 percent of the total exam score.

Each essay is read by experienced, well-trained high school AP teachers or college professors. The essay is given a holistic score from 1 to 9. The Reader will assign a score based on the essay's merits as a whole, on what the essay does well; the Readers don't look for or count errors. (A score of 0 is recorded for a student who writes completely off the topic or merely repeats the prompt. A student who doesn't even attempt an essay and leaves a blank page will receive the equivalent of a 0 score, but it is noted as a dash [—] on the Reader's scoring sheet.) Although each essay prompt has its own scoring guide (or rubric) based on that prompt's specific information, a generic scoring guide for synthesis, rhetorical strategies, and argument essays follows here. Notice that, on the whole, essay-scoring guides encompass four essential points AP Readers look for in an essay. It should be:

- On topic
- Well organized
- Thoroughly developed
- Correct in mechanics and sophisticated in style

High Score (8–9)

High-scoring essays thoroughly address all the tasks of the essay prompt in well-organized responses. The writing demonstrates stylistic sophistication and control over the elements of effective writing, although it is not necessarily faultless. Overall, high-scoring essays present thoroughly developed, intelligent ideas; sound and logical organization; strong evidence; and articulate diction.

- *Synthesis essays* demonstrate the ability to effectively develop a convincing position on an issue, incorporating at least three of the sources with appropriate explanation.

- *Rhetorical strategies essays* demonstrate significant understanding of the passage, its intent, and how the rhetorical strategies that the author uses enhance meaning.
- *Argument essays* demonstrate the ability to construct a compelling argument, observe the author's underlying assumptions, and discuss many sides of the issues with appropriate evidence.

Medium-High Score (6–7)

Medium-scoring essays complete the tasks of the essay topic well—they show some insight but usually with less precision, development, and clarity than high-scoring essays. There may be lapses in correct diction or sophisticated language, but the essay is generally well written.

- *Synthesis essays* demonstrate the ability to adequately develop a position on an issue, incorporating at least three of the sources with sufficient explanation.
- *Rhetorical strategies essays* demonstrate sufficient examination of the author's point and how the rhetorical strategies that he or she uses create the central idea.
- *Argument essays* demonstrate the ability to construct an adequate argument, understand the author's point, and discuss its implications with suitable evidence.

Medium Score (5)

Essays that earn a medium score complete the essay task, but with no special insights. The analysis lacks depth and merely states the obvious. Frequently, the ideas are predictable and the paragraph development is weak. Although the writing conveys the student's ideas, these are presented simplistically, and the writing often contains lapses in diction or syntax.

- *Synthesis essays* demonstrate the ability to develop a position on the issue, using at least three sources to some degree. Oversimplification of the issue(s) might minimize the essay's effectiveness.
- *Rhetorical strategies essays* demonstrate uneven or insufficient understanding of how rhetorical strategies create an author's point. Often, the student merely lists what he or she observes in the passage instead of analyzing the effect(s) of rhetorical strategies.
- *Argument essays* demonstrate the ability to present an argument, but they frequently provide limited and inadequate discussion, explanation, or evidence for the student's ideas.

Medium-Low Score (3–4)

These essays are weaker than the 5 score because the student overlooks or perhaps misreads important ideas in the passage. The student may summarize the passage's ideas instead of analyzing them. Although the student's ideas are generally understandable, the control of language is often immature.

- *Synthesis essays* demonstrate little ability to develop a position on the issue. They may reference at least two or more of the sources, but the references may be too brief to be convincing. Sometimes the student's use of the sources dominates the essay, weakening the connections between the sources and the student's position.
- *Rhetorical strategies essays* demonstrate little discussion of how rhetorical strategies create meaning or present incorrect identification and/or analysis of the author's strategies.
- *Argument essays* demonstrate little ability to construct an argument. They may not clearly identify the author's point, and/or may not offer adequate evidence for the student's position.

Low Score (1–2)

These essays demonstrate minimal understanding of the topic or the passage. Perhaps unfinished, these essays offer no analysis of the passage and little or no evidence for the student's ideas. Incorrect assertions may be made about the passage. Stylistically, these essays may show consistent grammatical problems, and sentence structure is frequently simple and unimaginative.

- *Synthesis essays* demonstrate little ability to develop any position on the issue. Instead of citing specific references to the sources, these essays may simply allude to the sources, misread them, or substitute a simpler task.

- *Rhetorical strategies essays* demonstrate little ability to identify or analyze rhetorical strategies and how they create effects. Sometimes students misread the prompt and replace it with easier tasks, such as paraphrasing the passage or listing some strategies the author uses.

- *Argument essays* demonstrate little ability to understand the author's point and then construct an argument that analyzes it. Minimal or nonexistent evidence hurts the essay's effectiveness. Some students may substitute an easier task by presenting tangential or irrelevant ideas, evidence, or explanation.

Types of Essay Topics

Although the wording varies, the exam essentially presents three types of essays: the synthesis essay, the rhetorical strategies essay, and the argument essay. Become familiar with each type so that you can efficiently and quickly plan your essays on the day of the exam and stay on topic.

- **The synthesis essay:** This essay type presents six or seven sources on the same subject. One of these documents will likely be a visual one (such as a chart, photograph, or political cartoon). You need to read all the documents carefully and then, using at least three of them, synthesize the various authors' points while intelligently discussing their validity. Therefore, this essay is similar to the argument essay, only it asks you to incorporate more viewpoints from more sources to support your position on the issue. In that regard, it is like a "mini research" essay. Incorporate explicit and implicit evidence from the sources, plus your own ideas based on your knowledge of the world and its history. Your purpose is to present an intelligent and thoughtful discussion on a subject, acknowledging various viewpoints from the authors, while bringing in your awareness of the world. This is the first essay prompt in the exam booklet.

- **The rhetorical strategies essay:** This essay presents a passage and asks you to analyze the rhetorical and literary strategies the author uses to create effect or meaning. Accurately identify the devices the author uses and evaluate *how* these devices create meaning. Be sure you understand the effect and author's meaning before you begin writing. Uncertainty results in muddled ideas. Refer to the passage liberally, incorporating quotations into your own ideas. Usually, this is the second essay prompt in the exam booklet.

- **The argument essay:** This essay presents one passage; read it carefully and formulate an essay discussing the extent with which you agree or disagree with the author's points. Like the synthesis essay, you will be well served if you intelligently address multiple sides of the issue and persuasively explore evidence from the passage, while incorporating examples from your understanding of the world based on your readings, observations, and experiences. Usually, this is the third essay prompt in the exam booklet.

The Synthesis Essay

Think of the synthesis essay as a variation of the argument essay in that you will be asked to take a stance on an issue and then support it with sound logic and concrete examples. It differs in that you will be given multiple sources to peruse (six or seven instead of one), and you must incorporate at least three of these sources into your essay to earn a good score. The synthesis essay is like a mini research paper, wherein you demonstrate your ability to weave different ideas from the various sources into your discussion of the issue.

In crafting an intelligent response to the issue, keep in mind that the AP Readers (high school English teachers and college professors) are impressed by a student who can conduct civil discourse, demonstrating a good understanding of all sides while presenting a stance. Avoid both oversimplification and jumping to conclusions. Remember the adage "Judgment stops discussion."

It's okay to let the Reader watch your ideas develop throughout the essay, instead of stating the conclusion up front and then spending the whole essay trying to justify it. Read the topic carefully and keep in mind that you may not have to take only one side in the issue. Frequently, a very good essay demonstrates a thorough understanding of multiple sides of an issue and presents a qualifying argument that appreciates these many sides.

The directions for this prompt will typically be organized into three paragraphs, although, of course, you should be prepared for some variation. The first paragraph will introduce the issue(s) of the prompt and establish their importance. It will define or clarify any terms you may need. The second paragraph will narrow down the directions. You will be directed to read the sources (and their introductory material), then synthesize details from at least three of them into an essay that discusses the issue(s) and examines their validity. The final paragraph will present generic guidelines that are reprinted each year (perhaps with small variations in wording). You will be reminded that your argument, your stance on the issue, is central; you must use the sources to support your argument. In other words, do not merely summarize the sources. You will also be reminded that you should cite the sources appropriately, whether you do it parenthetically or within your sentences. You can use the author's name (when given), the name or title of the source (when given), or simply refer to it as Source A, Source B, and so forth.

Here are some specific strategies for writing the synthesis essay.

- While reading the sources, think about the following.
  - Pay attention to the introductory material for each source (typically enclosed in a box above the source itself). Try to draw inferences about who wrote it, what type of source it is, when it was written (and any related historical context), and what intended audience it may have had. Think about whether this information implies objectivity or bias in the author and/or the source.
  - To make sure you understand the gist and the content of each source, read actively, underlining key points and jotting brief notes in the margin as necessary.
  - Understand the author's attitude about the issue; is it positive, negative, or neutral? Perhaps put a + or – on the page.
  - You know in advance that the different sources will provide a variety of outlooks or attitudes on the issue. Think about this as you read, looking for evidence you can use to support your stance.
  - Every synthesis topic will include at least one visual document, such as a chart, graph, photo, advertisement, or cartoon. Carefully interpret the point in this source and its relationship to the written sources.
  - Think about your stance on the issue as you judge the validity of each source, looking for examples that will strengthen your argument and counterexamples you can refute or minimize.
- When writing the essay itself, do the following.
  - Don't use only the sources that support your argument. Show that you understand the opposing sides and that you can intelligently dismiss them.
  - Use as many examples as you can from the sources, remembering that you must cite at least three different sources. Citing more sources can help your score if they are accompanied by intelligent discourse, but do not feel obligated to try to incorporate all the sources.
  - Discussing more than one source in any given paragraph helps demonstrate a greater awareness of how to synthesize materials; do not forget that's the name of the essay! In other words, avoid discussing only one source in each of your paragraphs.
  - Show fairness in your essay. Use undistorted language and avoid hyperbole. Also avoid using absolute words that can be inaccurate, such as "never," "only," "all," "must," "will," or "everyone." Instead, use more general terms that are much more likely to be accurate, such as "some," "often," "frequently," "might," "occasionally," or "likely."
  - Incorporate the sources into your essay with sophistication, variety, and style. You can use direct quotations (blending them into your own sentences for greatest effect), or you can paraphrase, summarize, and so forth.
  - Cite the source properly. You may refer to the source parenthetically at the end of your sentence, using either the author's name or the source letter designation, or you can refer to the author and/or the title directly in your sentence. *Always cite the source for every idea or quotation you incorporate.*
  - Embellish and expand your argument with concrete examples from your own reading, observation, and experience. Show that you can relate the issues in these sources to your knowledge of the world.

- Demonstrate your logical reasoning skills. Avoid logical fallacies such as circular reasoning, non sequitur arguments, or begging the question.
- Be sincere. Show that you find the topic interesting and worthy of intelligent discussion.
- Know your audience. All AP Readers are high school English teachers or college professors.

Example

Online education has been increasingly incorporated into K–12 school districts and college programs in the past decade. In contrast to the many benefits of online education, such as its flexible learning schedule, many people argue that online education is tearing down the stability that has been traditionally found in the school academic structure.

Considering the pros and cons of online education, read the following six sources (including any introductory information) carefully. Then, synthesizing at least three of the sources, write a coherent, well-written essay in which you defend, challenge, or qualify the idea that the effects of online education are beneficial to students and the school system.

Always remember that your argument should be central; the sources should be used to support this argument. Therefore, avoid merely summarizing sources. Clearly cite which sources you use, both directly and indirectly. Refer to the sources by their title, their source letter (Source A, Source B, etc.), or by their description in parentheses, which is usually the author's name.

Source A (Smith, D. Frank)

Source B (Department of Education)

Source C (Miron)

Source D (Smith, Nicole)

Source E (Carr-Chellman)

Source F (DePaoli, et al.)

Source A

Smith, D. Frank. "7 Telling Statistics About the State of K–12 Online Learning." *EdTech magazine.* 26 Nov. 2014. Web. 1 Sept. 2017.

The following article, written by a social media journalist, explores the availability of online learning opportunities and mentions some of the reasons for a lack of online educational opportunities in some states.

A new report on the state of K–12 online education shows growth in the world of connected instruction, but some states are still putting up barriers to bringing classrooms online.

"Keeping Pace with K–12 Digital Learning," the 11th edition of Evergreen Education Group's annual study, is a 176-page, detailed analysis on how schools across the country have been incorporating online instruction. The report reaches two conclusions: Students have more online learning options than ever before, but wide gaps remain in how these options are distributed among schools. The report also raises concerns about the lack of studies tracking digital learning activities.

"Online schools and courses are meeting needs for students in those cases where students do not have access to adequate physical school and course options. However, meaningful information and evidence are lacking for most digital learning activity," the report states. "Plenty of examples show that digital content and tools can assist in boosting outcomes, but the broad base of digital learning usage and effectiveness is unstudied."

Different grade levels incorporate online learning techniques in different ways. The online options at the elementary school level are often "deliberately designed to exclude online collaboration with other people," the report states.

High school students are afforded a wider variety of online course options and tools. The level of supervision is also different at the high school level.

"High schools are more likely than middle or elementary schools to have online courses in which the teacher is online, or the teacher of record is in the same building, but does not share a regular class period with students," according to the report.

Just as school policies on implementing online learning vary, so do state policies. Some 30 states and Washington, D.C., have fully online schools open to students statewide, while 20 states prohibit open enrollment in online schools. Various restrictions are not necessarily a result of outdated policies; some are the unintended consequence of strict standards meant to safeguard student data.

"New laws are being considered in many states—and too often are passing—that have the laudable goal of protecting student privacy, but are written in ways that will slow the spread of data usage in ways that will help schools and students," the report says.

Facts About the State of K–12 Online Learning
- **316,320** students attended online schools in the 2013–2014 school year
- **30** states offer fully online statewide schools
- **20** states prohibit open enrollment in online schools
- **26** states offer state virtual schooling
- **16%** of the U.S. K–12 student population is enrolled in online schools, charter schools, or private schools
- **20** states have enacted a combined total of 28 laws related to data privacy in 2014
- **11** states offer online course choice programs

Source B

"Reimagining the Role of Technology in Education: 2017 National Education Technology Plan Update."
Department of Education, Office of Technology. N.D. Web. 2 Sept. 2017.

The following success story about an Iowa school district was published in chapter 3, "Leadership: Creating a Culture and Conditions for Innovation and Change," in the 2017 National Education Technology Plan Update.

John Carver, Superintendent of Howard-Winn Community School District, faced less than optimal conditions when he initiated a digital learning transformation project modeled on Future Ready Schools. The district was experiencing declining enrollment and was failing to meet the standards of No Child Left Behind in reading comprehension, and almost half of the district's students qualified for free or reduced-priced lunch. Many districts face similar challenges; what set Howard-Winn apart was the district's decision to view failure as an opportunity to learn and improve.

Despite a lack of funding and community reluctance to change, Carver successfully gained support by working closely with teachers, the school board, and the district's School Improvement Advisory Committee to set an ambitious goal: By the year 2020, children in Howard-Winn will be the best prepared, most recruited kids on the planet.[1]

Creating a new brand, *2020 Howard-Winn*, helped Carver communicate the district vision of technology embedded in all parts of instruction, social and online systems of support for district professionals, and active community buy-in and participation. Behind these three pillars are leadership attributes essential to change: the courage to identify challenges and create a sense of urgency; openness to invest time, build trust, and cultivate relationships with stakeholders; and constant availability, visibility, and ownership as the drivers and face of change.

Although the implementation is still in its early stages, the district has acquired 1,300 laptops and implemented a 1:1 program. Teachers are challenged to be digital explorers and are asked to seek professional development opportunities proactively by using technology and to teach their students to be good digital citizens.

Since implementing these measures, student attendance at Howard-Winn schools has improved 90 percent, and a tech-enabled partnership with Northeast Iowa Community College has saved students between $9,000 and $10,000 in tuition fees by allowing district students to access college coursework while still in high school. The district also has seen a 17 percent increase in students meeting and exceeding summative assessment benchmarks. With more than $250,000 in support from stakeholders, the district also has been able to implement sustainable and cost-saving measures such as solar-powered Wi-Fi routers and propane-powered buses. The district has also created and publicized #2020HowardWinn—which reflects their commitment to be a transformed 21st century educational system by the year 2020.

As the district continues to implement its vision of digital learning, Carver says he and other leaders have been driven by the following question: "Do we love our kids enough to stop doing the things that do not work anymore?"

---

[1] John Carver. (2015). 2020 Howard-Winn Admin Update. Retrieved from http://2020hwinnadminupdates.blogspot.com/2015/10/jcc-october-16-2015.html?_sm_au_=iVVZSvStrsDP4TqR

Source C

Miron, Gary and Charisse Gulosino. "Full-Time Virtual Schools: Enrollment, Student Characteristics, and Performance." *National Education Policy Center*. 2015. Web. 11 Sept. 2017.

The following Executive Summary was published by the National Education Policy Center in its study titled "Virtual Schools in the U.S. 2015: Politics, Performance, Policy, and Research Evidence."

This section provides a detailed overview and inventory of full-time virtual schools. Such schools deliver all curriculum and instruction via the Internet and electronic communication, usually asynchronously with students at home and teachers at a remote location. Although increasing numbers of parents and students are choosing this option, we know little about virtual schooling in general, and very little about full-time virtual schools in particular. Nevertheless, the evidence suggests that strong growth in enrollment has continued. Large virtual schools operated by for-profit education management organizations (EMOs) continued to dominate this sector. While more districts are opening their own virtual schools, district-run schools have typically been small, with limited enrollment. This report provides a census of full-time virtual schools. It also includes student demographics, state-specific school performance ratings, and a comparison of virtual school ratings and national norms.

Current scope of full-time virtual schools:

- Our 2012–13 inventory identified 400 full-time virtual schools that enrolled close to 261,000 students.
- Although only 40.2% of the full-time virtual schools were operated by private education management organizations (EMOs), they accounted for 70.7% of all enrollments.
- Virtual schools operated by for-profit EMOs enrolled an average 1,166 students. In contrast, those operated by non-profit EMOs enrolled an average 350 students, and public virtual schools operating independently enrolled an average 322 students.
- Among the schools in the inventory, 52% are charter schools; together they accounted for 84% of enrollment. School districts have been increasingly creating their own virtual schools, but these tended to enroll far fewer students.
- Relative to national public school enrollment, virtual schools had substantially fewer minority students, fewer low-income students, fewer students with disabilities, and fewer students classified as English language learners.
- While the average student-teacher ratio was 16 students per teacher in the nation's public schools, virtual schools reported more than twice as many students per teacher. Virtual schools operated by for-profit EMOs reported the highest student-teacher ratio: 40 students per teacher.

School performance data:

- Most states have implemented school performance ratings or scores. These have typically been based on a variety of measures combined to produce an overall evaluation of school performance.
- In 2013–14, 28% of virtual schools received no state accountability/performance rating. Of the 285 schools that were rated, only 41% were deemed academically acceptable.
- Independent virtual schools were more likely to receive an acceptable rating than virtual schools operated by private EMOs: 48% compared with 27.6%.
- During the 2013–14 school year, charter virtual schools lagged behind their district-operated virtual schools in terms of acceptable school performance ratings by seven percentage points: 37.6% compared with 44.9%.
- As schools transitioned from the adequate yearly progress (AYP) measure to multiple performance measures under ESEA flexibility waivers, differences in performance outcomes of independent virtual schools and those run by private EMOs continued. In addition, full-time virtual schools continued to lag significantly behind traditional brick-and-mortar schools.

- Only 154 virtual schools reported a score related to on-time graduation in 2013–14. Based on data available in states' annual federal reports, the on-time graduation rate (or four-year graduation rate) for full-time virtual schools was nearly half the national average: 43.0% and 78.6%, respectively.

Recommendations:

- Policymakers slow or stop growth in the number of virtual schools and the size of their enrollment until the reasons for their relatively poor performance have been identified and addressed.
- Policymakers specify and enforce sanctions for virtual schools if they fail to improve performance.
- Policymakers require virtual schools to devote more resources to instruction, particularly by reducing the ratio of students to teachers. Given that all measures of school performance indicate insufficient or ineffective instruction and learning, these virtual schools should be required to devote more resources toward instruction. Other factors, such as the curriculum and the nature of student-teacher interactions, should also be studied to see if they are negatively affecting student learning.
- Policymakers and other stake holders support more research for better understanding of the characteristics of full-time virtual schools. More research is also needed to identify which policy options—especially those impacting funding and accountability mechanisms—are most likely to promote successful virtual schools.
- State education agencies and the federal National Center for Education Statistics clearly identify full-time virtual schools in their datasets, distinguishing them from other instructional models. This will facilitate further research on this subgroup of schools.
- State agencies ensure that virtual schools fully report data related to the population of students they serve and the teachers they employ.
- State and federal policymakers promote efforts to design new outcome measures appropriate to the unique characteristics of full-time virtual schools. The waivers from ESEA present an opportunity for those states with a growing virtual school sector to improve upon their accountability systems for reporting data on school performance measures.

Source D

Smith, Nicole. "An Argument Against Online Classes: In Defense of the Traditional Classroom." *Article Myriad*. 2010. Web. 29 Mar. 2011.

The following excerpt is from an online article about problems with online education.

Eliminating the traditional K–12 classroom in exchange for impersonal online classes would be the biggest possible mistake for students and teachers alike . . . . Aside from academics, one of the most important aspects of college life is the social interaction that comes with daily meetings of other students. Considering that a large part of a student's life revolves around this personal contact, removing this valuable part of students' lives would be a loss that not only the students themselves would feel, but the faculty as well. Online classrooms lack the ability to be personalized and will have a negative impact on both the social and educational lives of their students.

Also of importance, students will lose the motivation necessary to actually complete the work necessary since there are no teachers "there" physically to ensure the student's success. "Motivating students can challenge instructors who have moved from traditional to online classrooms. Online student motivation can vary owing to difficulty with content, challenges with access to technology or technology itself, isolation, poor communication with instructors, English as a second language, and lack of connection between content and students' needs" (Beffa-Negrini, 2002). The points made here are certainly worth considering since they are far-reaching and don't just include teachers or students, but learners of different types. Aside from the lost social interaction mentioned above, this problem of motivation on both the parts of students and teachers alike would likely be an issue.

Works Cited

Beffa-Negrini. (November/December 2002). *Journal of Nutrition Education and Behavior.* Strategies to Motivate Students in Online Learning Environments. Vol. 34, Issue 6, p334, 7p, 2 charts.

Source E

Carr-Chellman, Ali. "At What Cost Does Innovation Come?" *Education Week.* 8 Feb. 2012. Web. 12 Sept. 2017.

The following commentary responds to a web-series discussion about the degree to which online learning is beneficial for students.

I have been teaching in an online environment for many years. But it wasn't without great trepidation that I approached the enterprise of online learning in higher education. The research here is pretty clear: meta analyses of empirical research studies have shown that really there is "no significant difference" between online and face-to-face in traditional measures of achievement in most contexts. This is good news, it means that online learning is "working."

While this may be true, there is a great deal of research on the other side suggesting that it will bring on the downfall of the university or school system. David Noble is among my favorite critics of online learning in terms of ways that this enterprise may serve to hasten some very nasty potential results, particularly for the "life of the mind" that has been the hallmark of university life . . ..

I believe that the research will show likewise—that K–12 online learning, when we carefully compare similar groups of children in terms of their achievement scores on standardized tests, will be very similar. We'll find again that there is little or "no significant difference" between the online mode and the face-to-face mode of delivery. But the question, particularly for our public schools, goes far beyond whether it "works." Is it good for us as a society, as a community?

Online learning in K–12 settings is a significant boon for Olympic-level skaters, severe asthmatics, and some ADHD children who really cannot exist within the confines of a traditional school setting for a variety of reasons. And for certain specific applications I can definitely understand the usefulness of this approach and medium.

However, I've been exploring a number of concerns within cyber charters and am quite concerned by several important issues. Did you know some of the following?

- Cyber charter schools have no limitations on the amount of money they can spend to advertise and/or lobby politicians (and these expenditures allow them to remain non-profit).
- Cyber charter populations tend to be bimodal rather than similar to the larger general schooling population with a large number of high achievement and special needs learners.
- Traditional public schools must pay cyber charters for every child who leaves their school for a cyber charter and in PA alone, this amount now approaches $1 billion (with a B) leaving underfunded traditional K–12 schools.
- There is no real regulation on the ability of parents to include religious education in the regular school day, or to link religious lessons throughout the curriculum of a cyber charter if they wish to. That is, the separation of church and state in these schools cannot realistically be policed.
- Cyber charter schools use a great deal of their money on expensive curricular materials, which are generally published by the same company that owns the "non-profit" cyber charter school.
- There is very little ability of cyber charter schools to monitor cheating.
- Exercising choice for individual achievement in the form of cyber charter schooling will likely leave our most vulnerable children behind in underfunded schools. Research on school choice indicates that parents with more education and better resources are the most likely to exercise choice in any form.
- The CEO of the largest provider of cyber charter curriculum, sold specifically to their own non-profit schools, made more than $28 million last year.

These facts make me very concerned. Is capitalism really the way we want a publicly funded school system to function? I do believe that schools where significant losses of students have led to innovations of their own represent an exciting possibility for the future of school change. But I worry at what cost that innovation comes. If the trade-off is capitalist schooling models that create huge profits, religious education in public schools, unfettered lobbying and enormous advertising budgets within the realm of public schools, I fear we are no longer seeing any service of the public good from public schools, and instead are only concerned about our highest aspirations as individuals and not our greatest successes as a society.

Source F

DePaoli, J., Balfanz, R., and Bridgeland, J. "2016: Building a Grad Nation: Progress and Challenge in Raising High School Graduation Rates." *GradNation*. 12 May 2015. Web. 4 Dec. 2017.

The following chart compares graduation rates at different types of high schools.

Low-Graduation-Rate High Schools, High-Graduation-Rate High Schools, and Average Adjusted Cohort Graduation Rates (ACGR), by School Type, 2014

School Type	Percent of High Schools 67% and Below	Percent of High Schools 85% and Above	Average ACGR
Regular	7%	64%	85%
Alternative	57%	8%	52%
Charter	30%	44%	70%
Virtual	87%	4%	40%

Note: The high schools in the above table have a total enrollment of 100 students or more. "Regular" includes only district-run public schools that are non-charter and non-virtual. "Alternative" includes only district-operated alternative high schools. "Charter" includes only regular (non-alternative), non-virtual charter schools. "Virtual" includes only regular (non-alternative) virtual schools.

Sources: U.S. Department of Education, National Center for Education Statistics. (1998–2015). Public Elementary/Secondary School Universe Surveys. U.S. Department of Education through provisional data file of SY2013–14 School Level Four-Year Regulatory Adjusted Cohort Graduation Rates.

Before we look at the scoring guide and sample student essays, let's first examine how one can approach this (and any other) synthesis essay using our previously listed suggestions. First, clarify the issue and your position on it. Next, understand what each source says and which ideas you can use from the sources to support your stance. Remember that your essay must reference at least three sources. Consider creating a quick chart that will help your organization. The following sample chart is much more detailed (and time-consuming) than you should need. Try practicing with something like this, using abbreviations and phrases that you can easily understand.

The topic: Defend, challenge, or qualify the idea that online education (OE) is beneficial to students and schools.

My stance:

Source	Brief Summary	Does It Support or Refute the Idea?	What Might I Use?
A (Frank Smith)	30 states offer fully online school 20 prohibit open enrollment 26 offer state virtual schooling 16% of K–12 enrolled in online, charter, or private	Neutral/Both pros and cons	1-more OE options 2-wide gaps in how options are distributed 3-concerns about lack of studies tracking student activities
B (Dept. of Education)	Success story of one district in Iowa Superintendent worked closely w/ teachers, school board, and dist. committee Get 1,300 laptops, 1:1 program, teachers seek pro dev.	Defends/Supports	Attendance up 90% HS students can access college coursework at local CC +17% students meeting and exceeding summative assessments
C (Miron)	Studies full-time virtual schools only (students at home; teachers at remote location) VS = bad performance ratings Much more research and policy adjustments needed	Challenges/Refutes	VS enrollment growing; most enrollment at for-profit organizations (EMO) 52% are charter schools Far fewer minorities, disabled, and English Language Learners VS have more than twice student-per-teacher ratio EMOs only 27.6% acceptable rating! VS grad rate = half national avg!
D (Nicole Smith/online article)	Eliminating traditional classroom for OE = biggest mistake; no social interaction; impersonal; possible loss of motivation	Refutes	Social interaction is important, but is anyone really proposing completely eliminating traditional classrooms? Not a strong argument; list of things that can lower motivation is good

continued

Source	Brief Summary	Does It Support or Refute the Idea?	What Might I Use?
E (Carr-Chellman)	Likes OE, but has several worries	Defends but with qualifications	OE great for certain students, but . . . No regulations regarding separation of church and state Charter schools pay big $ for materials that are published by the co. that owns the charter Little ability to monitor cheating More students in cyber charters = leaves most vulnerable students in underfunded public schools
F (DePaoli/chart)		Refutes	Regular HS avg 85% grad rate Virtual schools avg 40%! All other schools lower than regular schools

After creating your chart, you can then decide which sources you will use and the order in which you'll present your ideas. As you organize, don't forget to group ideas into coherent and logical paragraphs.

Scoring

Scoring Guide

Score	Description	Criteria
9	Successful	Essays that earn a score of 9 meet the criteria for essays that receive a score of 8; in addition, they are especially sophisticated in their explanation and argument. They may also present particularly remarkable control of language.
8	Successful	Essays that receive a score of 8 respond to the prompt successfully, using at least three sources from the prompt. They take an effective position that defends, challenges, or qualifies the claim that the effects of online education are beneficial to students and the school system. They effectively argue their position and support the argument with appropriate and convincing evidence. The prose demonstrates an ability to control an extensive range of the elements of effective writing but may not be entirely flawless.
7	Satisfactory	Essays that earn a score of 7 fit the description of the essays that score a 6 but provide more complexity in both argumentation and explanation and/or demonstrate more distinguished prose style.
6	Satisfactory	Essays that earn a score of 6 respond to the prompt satisfactorily, using at least three of the sources from the prompt. They take an adequate position that defends, challenges, or qualifies the claim that the effects of online education are beneficial to students and the school system. They adequately argue their position and support it with appropriate evidence, although without the precision and depth of the top-scoring essays. The writing may contain minor errors in diction or syntax, but the prose is generally clear.

Scoring Guide

Score	Description	Criteria
5	Plausible	Essays that earn a score of 5 take a position that defends, challenges, or qualifies the claim that the effects of online education are beneficial to students and the school system. They support the position with generally satisfactory evidence, but they may not sufficiently use three sources from the prompt. These essays may be inconsistent, uneven, or limited in their development of the argument. While the writing usually conveys the student's ideas, it may demonstrate lapses in diction or syntax or an overly simplistic style.
4	Inadequate	Essays that earn a score of 4 respond to the prompt inadequately. They may have difficulty taking a position that defends, challenges, or qualifies the claim that the effects of online education are beneficial to students and the school system. The evidence may be particularly insufficient or may not use enough sources from the prompt. The prose may basically convey the student's ideas but suggest immature control over the elements of effective writing.
3	Inadequate	Essays that earn a score of 3 meet the criteria for a score of 4 but reveal less ability to take a position that defends, challenges, or qualifies the claim that the effects of online education are beneficial to students and the school system. The presentation of evidence and argumentation is likely to be unconvincing. The writing may show less control over the elements of effective writing.
2	Little success	Essays that earn a score of 2 demonstrate little success at taking a position that defends, challenges, or qualifies the claim that the effects of online education are beneficial to students and the school system and show little ability to present it with appropriate evidence from the sources in the prompt. Students may misunderstand the prompt, may fail to establish a position with supporting evidence, or may substitute a simpler task by replying tangentially with unrelated, erroneous, or unsuitable explanations, arguments, and/or evidence. The prose frequently demonstrates consistent weaknesses in the conventions of effective writing.
1	Little success	Essays that earn a score of 1 meet the criteria for a score of 2 but are undeveloped, especially simplistic in their explanations, arguments, and/or evidence, or weak in their control of writing.

Note: The following sample essays were not written by the student who brainstormed the above ideas.

High-Scoring Essay

Online education is one of the fastest-growing segments of education today; indeed, the rapid rise of online education is unprecedented in the American Education system. There is no question that online education is growing exponentially; as more and more school districts offer online options, many more students are enrolled in such online programs than ever before, and these numbers grow larger with the beginning of every school year. However, one must question if such growth is justified. Many experts who have studied online education have come to the same conclusion: online education does have the potential to offer many benefits, but because of the way it is currently implemented, its overall effect on the participating students, and on their school districts, is detrimental.

One cannot deny that the explosive growth of online education is well-documented. One example is the report "Keeping Pace with K–12 Digital Learning" (Source A), a very extensive report on the state of online education throughout the country. One of the report's two major conclusions is that "Students have more online learning options than ever before . . ." The report documents the rapid rise in the use of online education across America, but it also reports on one of the many problems that are related to this phenomenon, namely lack of inclusiveness. This issue can be seen in the dramatic geographic disparity; depending on where they live, students in some districts do not have any opportunities to enroll in online education, and yet students in other districts have no adequate option for traditional schooling. As is well documented in "Keeping Pace with K–12 Digital Learning," ". . . wide gaps remain in how these options are distributed among schools." Online learning will not truly serve students well until all students have the same opportunities.

The other disturbing problem in online education is the lack of diversity in the student population. The executive summary of the National Education Policy Center (Source C) explicitly states that, "relative to national public school enrollment, virtual schools had substantially fewer minority students, fewer low-income students, fewer students with disabilities, and fewer students classified as English language learners." Thus, students enrolled in most online education programs lose the opportunity to interact with students who come from different backgrounds; they lose the opportunity to learn and grow and mature in important ways. Furthermore, another major downside of online education is that students lose the opportunity for daily personal contact with other students. This problem is mentioned in Source A that acknowledges elementary school online classes are "deliberately designed to exclude" collaboration with others. Elementary-age students particularly need social interaction; it is an age when kids learn how to work, play, and cooperate appropriately with others. Going even further, Source D reports, "Considering that a large part of a student's life revolves around this personal contact, removing this valuable part of students' lives would be a loss that not only the students themselves would feel, but the faculty as well." Clearly, the isolation that online students face, including few interactions with students of different backgrounds, is a serious issue that weakens the appeal of online education.

Other criticisms of the online education movement are serious enough to warrant questioning the movement's effectiveness for students and school districts. Complaints include the lack of accountability (Source A), the extremely high student-teacher ratio (Source C), the lack of separation of church and state (Source E), and huge percentage of online schools' budgets that is spent on for-profit curriculum materials (Source E). However, of all the criticisms of online education, perhaps most damning of all is that they simply do not do a very good job of educating their students; their students' test performance is sub-par and their graduation rates are dismal. As is evident from the data in Source C, the performance of students in ". . . full-time virtual schools continued to lag significantly behind traditional brick-and-mortar schools." Also, the statistics in Source F show a clear difference in students' outcomes; the average graduation rate for traditional high schools is 85%, but for virtual schools, the average graduation rate is a miserable 40%. Collectively, the data show that online education, especially in full-time virtual schools, needs dramatic improvement before it can be considered beneficial.

While it is certainly true that there are a host of potential benefits that could be gleaned from properly run online education programs, benefits for both the students and for the school districts, this opportunity is unfortunately being squandered. The education establishment in this country must rise to the occasion; they must somehow help the nascent online education industry to overcome these deleterious effects, and thus, begin to use online education as an effective tool to benefit students and districts everywhere in America.

Analysis of the High-Scoring Essay

This student's essay begins with an enticing hint of praise for online education, acknowledging the intense growth in the field. However, the student then takes a turn and strongly states that online education is detrimental over-all, given its current flawed implementation. This introduction is engaging and well developed, and it provides a concise thesis. The AP Reader has no doubt which side of the argument this student's essay will develop.

The first body paragraph, similar to the opening of the introduction, presents specific evidence of the tremen-dous growth in online education, citing Source A. Then, also akin to the introduction, the student transitions into some of the "many problems" that online education faces. The student discusses the issues of lack of inclusive-ness and geographic disparity in online schools, and then concludes the paragraph well with the criticism that students will not be served well until they all have the same online opportunities. This paragraph only includes one source, but it explores the ideas from that source quite well and it provides ample analysis of that source.

The second body paragraph examines a different objection to online education: the lack of diversity in the stu-dent population. The student articulates strong objections to this disparity of representation, acknowledging that without adequate interaction with low-income students, minority students, disabled students, and English lan-guage learners, these online participants lose many opportunities "to learn and grow and mature in important ways." This paragraph expands this theme and examines how isolated some online students can become. Particularly troubling to the student is the notion that elementary students' online learning experiences are "'deliberately designed to exclude'" collaboration. The student expresses a valid point about the need for elemen-tary-age students to interact socially with others, to "learn how to work, play, and cooperate appropriately with others"; this is a point that AP Readers will appreciate. The paragraph continues to expand on this point by including another source, one that laments the lack of personal contact in online education and acknowledges that this isolation is a "serious issue" for the overall effectiveness of online education. This paragraph is very impressive in its development, synthesizing three sources effectively and adding ample analysis of the information in those sources. This student does much more than merely restate what the sources have to say, and it is refreshing for an AP Reader to watch a student process ideas so effectively, as he or she writes under time constraints.

Next, the essay presents another well-developed body paragraph that focuses on other serious criticisms of the online education movement. Masterfully condensing four sources into one sentence, the student outlines pressing concerns about accountability, student-teacher ratio, separation of church and state, and questionable spending of for-profit organizations that make money from buying curriculum materials that they write. If this student had much more time, a Reader can easily imagine what further insightful analysis the student would present regarding these problems. However, the items on this list all effectively and collectively add to the pool of difficulties facing online education. The student continues the paragraph with stronger outcry about the "sub-par" test performance and "dismal" graduation rates in virtual schools. Citing two sources to back up the student's opinion convinces the Reader that the student is on solid ground.

The conclusion begins by circling back to an idea in the opening paragraph: acknowledging the potential of online education, if only it were properly run. Then, instead of merely restating what has been discussed in the essay, the student looks to the future and explains what education must do: rise to the occasion and begin to use online education to benefit all students and all districts.

The student earns praise for clearly addressing the topic throughout the essay and exploring a serious issue with integrity. The essay's organization is clear and logical, with each paragraph focusing on a strong criticism of online education. The development of ideas is stellar throughout, successfully integrating the source material with the student's own observations and commentary. The student manages to appropriately incorporate five of the six sources, which is highly admirable. Finally, the student demonstrates a command of language and a style of composition that is pleasing and free of error. A high score of 8 or 9 is certainly warranted and well deserved.

Low-Scoring Essay

One of the fastest-growing segments of Education today is the growth of Online Education (OE), which is out-pacing the growth of traditional Education. OE is obviously beneficial to both the students and to their school districts, otherwise, why would it be growing so fast?

A typical example of the benefits of OE is in the reference to the Howard-Winn Community School District in Iowa, Source B. In this case, just one man, Superintendent John Carver, saved an entire school district from inevitable decline. The district faced declining enrollment, they couldn't meet the standards of the No Child Left Behind Act, and half the students were so poor that they qualified for a subsidized school lunch program. Plus, they had a lack of funding and no community support. But John Carver, all by himself, instituted a technology revolution, with 1,300 laptop computers and lots of OE opportunities. The District's statistics went through the roof after everyone realized that OE could save the District.

Another good example of the benefits of OE is found in Source A. The new report is extensive, at 176 pages, and it comes to the conclusion that "Online schools and courses are meeting needs for students in those cases where students do not have access to adequate physical school and course options." This is clear proof that OE is beneficial.

Finally, the writer in Source E, who has been teaching in an online environment for many years says, "This is good news, it means that online learning is "working."

Obviously, all of this evidence points in the same direction, that the growth of Online Education is good, it is beneficial for all students and all districts.

Analysis of the Low-Scoring Essay

AP Readers are instructed to reward the students for what they do well, and upon reading this essay, one can see the student's attempt to discuss the topic and organize paragraphs with some degree of cohesion. However, this essay lacks sufficient development of logical ideas, misreads the sources, and includes some sloppy language and distracting grammatical errors.

The introduction begins poorly, combining weak language with faulty logic. It is far from impressive to read "the fastest-growing segments of Education today is the growth of Online Education (OE), which is outpacing the growth . . . " with its repetition and circular logic. The student continues to demonstrate fallacious logic by essentially claiming that if something is growing quickly, it must be advantageous. The student appears to have latched onto the idea that online education is beneficial without thinking about it very much.

The first body paragraph suffers from a fairly significant misread of the passage. The student claims that Superintendent John Carver individually saved the Howard-Winn Community School District in Iowa, but Source B clearly states that Carver worked together with teachers, the school board, and the district. It is also a stretch to say that he "instituted a technology revolution" or that he provided "lots of OE opportunities." While the student is accurate as to the number of computers provided, 1,300, the passage does not address specific online opportunities. The student then engages in hyperbole by claiming that the "District's statistics went through the roof after everyone realized that OE could save the District," which is another factually erroneous claim. Source B states that "The district also has seen a 17 percent increase in students meeting and exceeding summative assessment benchmarks," but the report fails to identify which subjects saw such growth, and this gain, while indeed admirable, can hardly be described as "going through the roof." The student needs to slow down and read the passage more carefully before building a paragraph around such sloppy reading.

In the next paragraph, the student is again reaching for any phrase that will support his or her essay's thesis, regardless of its accuracy. The student bases a global claim of "clear proof that OE is beneficial" on one sentence that is cherry-picked from a lengthy report. Once again, the student is ignoring qualifying evidence in the source and jumping to pre-determined conclusions. In addition, this paragraph, only three sentences long, is quite undeveloped.

The final body paragraph, just one single sentence, is anorexic in its development, and, like the two preceding paragraphs, suffers from ignoring much of the original source. The student extracts one quote from Source E that fits the thesis; however, the student fails to acknowledge that the rest of the source presents some serious questions about online education, especially in its funding. The student should not ignore evidence that qualifies his or her point.

The conclusion is a run-on, one-sentence summary, which merely repeats what we have read before. By this point in the essay, the Reader is neither convinced nor impressed.

Overall, this student needs to pay closer attention to details while reading the sources, and make sure that they do indeed support what the student is presenting. This student does include the required minimum of three sources; however, the presentation is so rife with erroneous arguments and inaccuracies, in addition to being undeveloped and peppered with grammatical errors, that it definitely deserves a very low score. Some Readers will reward it with a 4 because of its content, brief as it is; other Readers will lower it to a 3 because of its logical and grammatical errors.

The Rhetorical Strategies Essay

In your rhetorical strategies essay, be sure to accurately identify rhetorical strategies and figurative language the author uses, and then examine *how* they create effects and help build the author's point. In your AP English classes, you will likely be introduced to terminology appropriate to rhetorical analysis; this book also offers a glossary of terms you can use (see Appendix A). However, high-scoring essays never merely provide a list of the devices an author uses. Instead, an intelligent analysis must explore the author's ideas in depth and describe how the author's presentation enhances those ideas. Dive into the depths of the author's thoughts and enjoy exploring how such good writing enhances interesting ideas.

You'll want to use the text liberally, both implicitly and explicitly. Sophisticated writers embed phrases from the text into their own sentences during discussion. Avoid copying complete sentences from the text. Rather, you should quote only the exact word or phrase that suits your purpose and analyze it within your own sentences. You do not need to cite or refer to any line numbers provided in the margin of the text.

Here are some specific strategies for writing the rhetorical strategies essay.

- Consider the implications of any information you may be given before the passage's text about the author: the time period in which the passage was written, the author's purpose, the intended audience, and what form of writing the passage presents (letter, speech, book excerpt, and so forth).
- Know what the passage is about and understand its overall message.
- Be sure you understand the author's rhetorical purpose. Is it to persuade? To satirize some fault in society? To express ideas?
- Be familiar with common rhetorical strategies authors use to develop their ideas: description, comparison/contrast, argumentation, exemplification, narration, cause and effect, and so forth.
- Use any terminology given in the prompt to help focus your reading, while looking for examples you can analyze in your essay.
  - If the prompt mentions *syntax,* examine the sentence structure, sentence length, parallel constructions, and any unusual sentence constructions such as inverted word order.
  - If the prompt mentions *diction,* look for words and phrases you can analyze, especially pleasing or unusual ones, that help establish the author's tone, attitude, and purpose.
  - If the prompt mentions *figurative language,* look for examples of literary devices you can analyze, such as metaphor, simile, personification, irony, or allusion.
  - If the prompt does not mention any specific terminology, understand that you still want to look for examples of the elements mentioned above—specific items that you can analyze and connect to the author's point. Remember, the passage will be well-written, and it will contain some things that you can discuss.
- Always analyze *how* your examples help create the author's intended effect.
- Use transitions effectively to help your analysis. To introduce examples, use phrases such as "for instance," "for example," or "additionally." Then use appropriate transitions to move your discussion into analysis, such as "consequently," "resulting in," or "accordingly."

A Few Words about Satire

Recent language and literature exams have sometimes included prompts that are from satiric and/or comedic works. Students who are not practiced in writing about satire and recognizing the devices of the satirist may be at a disadvantage compared with those who are comfortable with such tools. The subtleties and nuances of satire can sometimes go unnoticed. Some students may find it hard to know how to analyze the rhetorical strategies that satirists use. Although, of course, satirists can employ all of the devices of rhetoric, quite often they make use of caricature, hyperbole, understatement, irony, wit, sarcasm, allusion, and juxtaposition. (These terms are defined in "Terms for the Multiple-Choice and Free-Response Sections" in Appendix A.)

Frequently, satire is characterized as one of two types.

- *Horatian satire* is gentle, urbane, smiling; it aims to correct with broadly sympathetic laughter. Based on the works of the Roman lyrical poet Horace, its purpose may be "to hold up a mirror" so readers can see themselves and their world honestly. The vices and follies satirized are not destructive. However, they reflect the foolishness of people, the superficiality and meaninglessness of their lives, and the barrenness of their values. Alexander Pope's mock-epic poem "The Rape of the Lock" is a prime example of Horatian satire.

- *Juvenalian satire* is biting, bitter, and angry; it points out the corruption of human beings and institutions with contempt, using *saeva indignatio,* a savage outrage based on the style of the Roman poet Juvenal. Sometimes perceived as enraged, Juvenalian satire sees the vices and follies in the world as intolerable. Juvenalian satirists use large doses of sarcasm and irony. Jonathan Swift's famous essay "A Modest Proposal" is an example of Juvenalian satire.

If you do receive a piece of satire to discuss in your essay prompt, be aware of the rhetorical devices of the satirist and use them to your advantage.

- Use verbs that lead you into analysis, such as "the author suggests," "implies," "reveals," "reflects," or "emphasizes." Avoid using verbs that lead you into paraphrasing, such as "the author says," "claims," "mentions," "states," "tells," or "writes."

Example

William Hazlitt was a 19th-century British author, noted for being a literary critic, essayist, philosopher, and painter. The following excerpt comes from his *Lectures on the English Comic Writers,* which was delivered at the Surrey Institution in 1819.

Read the passage carefully, and then write a well-developed essay in which you analyze the rhetorical strategies Hazlitt uses to make his point about mankind's sense of humor. You might want to consider such elements as tone, point of view, and stylistic devices.

Man is the only animal that laughs and weeps; for he is the only animal that is struck with the difference between what things are, and what they ought to be. We weep at what thwarts or exceeds our desires in serious matters: we laugh at what only disappoints our expectations in trifles. We shed tears from sympathy with real and necessary distress; as we burst into laughter from want of sympathy with that which is
(5)   unreasonable and unnecessary, the absurdity of which provokes our spleen or mirth, rather than any serious reflections on it.

To explain the nature of laughter and tears, is to account for the condition of human life; for it is in a manner compounded of these two! It is a tragedy or a comedy—sad or merry, as it happens. The crimes and misfortunes that are inseparable from it, shock and wound the mind when they once seize upon it, and when
(10)   the pressure can no longer be borne, seek relief in tears: the follies and absurdities that men commit, or the odd accidents that befall them, afford us amusement from the very rejection of these false claims upon our sympathy, and end in laughter. If every thing that went wrong, if every vanity or weakness in another gave us a sensible pang, it would be hard indeed: but as long as the disagreeableness of the consequences of a sudden disaster is kept out of sight by the immediate oddity of the circumstances, and the absurdity or
(15)   unaccountableness of a foolish action is the most striking thing in it, the ludicrous prevails over the pathetic, and we receive pleasure instead of pain from the farce of life which is played before us, and which discomposes our gravity as often as it fails to move our anger or our pity!

Now let's explore both the prompt and the passage, using the specific strategies suggested and jotting down a few of the ideas that are asked for in the prompt.

- **What information can you use from the introductory material?** Hazlitt wrote criticism, essays, and philosophy; the passage is a lecture from 1819. Therefore, it sounds "old and formal." The passage is philosophical, exploring the things that make mankind laugh and cry.
- **What is the passage about? What is Hazlitt's point? His purpose?** It points out how mankind's ability to cry and laugh at disaster and absurdity in life help us to make sense of the world and keep our balance. Hazlitt wants us to understand why we react to extreme events the way we do, why we cry at tragedy and laugh at ridiculousness.
- **What rhetorical strategies does Hazlitt use?** Comparison/contrast, description, philosophical discussion, and persuasion all appear in this passage.
- **What terminology from the prompt can help in analyzing the passage?** "Tone" = animated (exclamation points), reflective, instructive. "Point of view" = mankind needs both tears and laughter. "Stylistic devices" = varied syntax with lots of colons and semicolons, juxtaposition, parallel construction.

Now let's review some key portions of the passage, noting some observations a student might make while reading.

- The first sentence of paragraph 1 shows how man is different from animals. "Struck" is a strong word.
- The second and third sentences of paragraph 1 have parallel construction that creates a fast pace ("we" + verb, followed by a prepositional phrase).

- The first sentence of paragraph 2 expresses a universal idea, and the exclamation point adds emphasis. The short second sentence reinforces this idea. The third and fourth sentences of paragraph 2 are long, exploring the idea in depth.

- The long last sentence compounds negative ideas ("vanity," "weakness," "pang," "hard") but then ends with philosophical balance: When the "sudden disasters" of life are seen in light of their oddity and absurdity, "we receive pleasure instead of pain." The exclamation point is surprising because one does not expect such an exaggerated punctuation mark.

- The phrase "the ludicrous prevails over the pathetic" is memorable.

Scoring

Scoring Guide

Score	Description	Criteria
9	Successful	Essays that earn a score of 9 meet the criteria for essays that receive a score of 8; in addition, they are especially sophisticated in their explanation and argument. They may also present particularly impressive control of language.
8	Successful	These well-written essays successfully demonstrate an understanding of Hazlitt's purpose in his discussion of comedy and its nature. In addition, they reveal a thorough comprehension of how Hazlitt's tone, point of view, and use of stylistic devices reflect that purpose. The thesis is thoughtful and articulate. Strong and relevant evidence from Hazlitt's essay supports intelligent insights concerning Hazlitt's purpose. Thoroughly convincing, these essays show a clear command of essay-writing skills. Although they need not be without errors, these essays show a mature style and use of language.
7	Satisfactory	These essays fit the description of an essay that scored a 6, but they provide a more complete explanation and clarity of thought. Also, they demonstrate a more mature prose style.
6	Satisfactory	These essays satisfactorily comprehend Hazlitt's purpose, but the thesis may be less explicit than that of the top-scoring essay. The evidence offered may be less convincing, but these papers still demonstrate clear thinking. The connection between the evidence and Hazlitt's purpose may not be as clear as in the top-scoring essays. Although well written, these essays may show some errors while maintaining satisfactory control over diction and the essay's requirements.
5	Plausible	These plausible essays show some understanding of Hazlitt's purpose but may not clearly comprehend the relationship between his language and his purpose. The student may merely list the devices Hazlitt uses without relating them to his purpose. The thesis may be simplistic and the evidence insufficient to prove the student's assertions. Acceptable organization and development may be evident, but the style may not be as sophisticated as that of higher-scoring essays.
4	Inadequate	These low-scoring essays fail to convince the AP Reader. The inadequate presentation may not demonstrate a clear understanding of Hazlitt's purpose. Comprehension of how Hazlitt's manipulation of language reflects his purpose may be lacking. The thesis may be unsubstantiated, paragraph development may be weak, and superficial thinking may be evident. Frequent errors in composition that distract the Reader may be present.
3	Inadequate	These essays meet the criteria for a score of 4 but show more weakness in developing the thesis and supporting arguments with sufficient evidence. These essays may fail to complete all the tasks given. These essays may simply catalog the devices and the resources of language used, without analysis or comment on the connection between the author's purpose and language. Weak control of the essay format and/or language may be evident, and mechanical errors may be frequent.

continued

Scoring Guide

Score	Description	Criteria
2	Little success	These poorly written essays lack coherence and clarity. They may attempt to state Hazlitt's purpose without any mention of how his language reflects his purpose. The thesis may be overly obvious or absent. Little or no evidence may be offered, and any connection between the evidence and the thesis may be shallow or nonexistent. These essays may substitute a simpler task by replying to the question with irrelevant information. Persistent weaknesses in grammar and organization may be evident. These essays may be unusually short.
1	Little success	These essays meet the criteria for an essay earning a score of 2, but lack evidence and connections between the evidence and thesis. These essays show a weak control of language and weakness in understanding Hazlitt's purpose.

Note: The following sample essays were not written by the student who brainstormed the above ideas.

High-Scoring Essay

Two masks symbolize the theater, the one merry and joyful, the other weeping and forlorn. In its turn, the theater acts as a microcosm of life, its twin emblems representative of life's paramount elements: comedy coupled with tragedy.

William Hazlitt explores the relationship of comedy and tragedy, tears and laughter, in Lectures on the English Comic Writers. Hazlitt proposes that, like love and hate, mirth and sadness are not really the opposites that some assume them to be. Apathy is perhaps the true opposite of all four emotions. Both comedy and tragedy are intensely concerned with the human condition. Responses to comedy and tragedy are perhaps our most profound reflexive reactions to the world around us, so it is instructive to examine, as Hazlitt does, the similar foundations of the two.

Hazlitt's enthusiastic tone fits his purpose of persuasion. He writes as if he has just made an amazing discovery and cannot wait to tell readers about his find. The eureka tone of amazed discovery is in part achieved by a liberal smattering of exclamation points throughout the essay, such as "it is in a manner compounded of these two!" and "it fails to move our anger or our pity!" which emphasizes this glee. Exploring the nature of the two responses, comedy and tragedy, to the world, Hazlitt writes that both are spurred by man's perception of possibilities, and disappointment or joy results when these are not met, depending on the gravity or ludicrousness of the situation. The more reflective tone at this point serves Hazlitt's purpose well. Indeed, comedy often issues from the wellsprings of tragedy and hurt. Laughter can be a defense mechanism, a protective response to the realities of the world and an opportunity to mock the frightening rather than cower before it.

Hazlitt's point of view has arguably become a part of the conventional wisdom these days. Comedy and tragedy are two sides of the same coin, he asserts. Comedy is made up of trifling tragedies. Not serious enough to wound, they instead inspire ridicule and heckling. Confusion can exist between the emotions: People often cry tears of joy on happy occasions or laugh inappropriately in the face of despair. Hazlitt successfully persuades readers of the inexorable relationship between the emotions.

Hazlitt's prose is brisk, almost breathless. Even though compounded with prepositional phrases and the like, the first paragraph of his essay speeds along with emphasized repetition: "We weep . . . we laugh . . . we shed tears . . . we burst into laughter." Hazlitt keeps the reader to a relentless pace with a series of phrases and clauses separated by commas and semicolons, filling long complex sentences. His last sentence in the essay effectively uses technique as it builds to a crescendo. It piles many negative ideas on top of one another before leaving us with the pleasing idea that we need laughter to give us "pleasure instead of pain from the farce of life." This technique of building negativity and then balancing it helps persuade the reader that Hazlitt's conclusions are valid.

Hazlitt's skillful, rhythmic writing seems capable of lulling readers into believing anything he asserts. He accomplishes his purpose with an enthusiastic passage that clearly demonstrates the inseparable connection between laughter and tears. Understand that, and we are well on our way to understanding life.

Analysis of the High-Scoring Essay

This well-written essay begins with two paragraphs that immediately spark the reader's interest, mentioning the comic and tragic masks of the theater and then effectively relating the theater, as a "microcosm of life," to the essay's content and to the topic question. The introduction has no thesis statement, but that isn't an absolute requirement. This student is definitely on the right track, addressing the issue of Hazlitt's purpose and his means of achieving it.

The next two paragraphs explore Hazlitt's point of view, his success in achieving his purpose, and his perception of comedy and tragedy, relating that perception to contemporary society's ideas. Some textual evidence is presented in the paragraph that discusses tone, for example noting that Hazlitt's use of exclamation points produces a "tone of amazed discovery." However, no specific examples are used in the brief point-of-view paragraph. In any case, both of these paragraphs serve the student's purpose well; they clearly analyze Hazlitt's ideas.

The fifth paragraph presents an analysis of Hazlitt's technique and style, noting the use of repetition and aptly describing the essay's pace as "breathless . . . relentless." This student demonstrates an accurate understanding of how a writer's technique can produce a specific effect on the Reader, especially in the analysis of Hazlitt's last sentence, which the student aptly notes "builds to a crescendo."

The concluding paragraph reiterates the relationship of Hazlitt's "rhythmic writing" to his purpose but doesn't stop at mere summary. It points to the essay's wider implication—that through understanding laughter and tears, we can broaden our understanding of life. This student, like Hazlitt, demonstrates both lively style and discriminating diction. The essay would likely receive a score of 7; it is not as thorough as a top-scoring essay.

Medium-Low-Scoring Essay

William Hazlitt begins by describing the differences between humans and animals. He writes that man has the emotions of humor and sadness that animals don't because men see that things aren't always as good as they could be.

Sometimes people laugh, and sometimes people cry about life, depending on the situation. Through Hazlitt's use of tone and stylistic devices he achieves his purpose to convince the reader that comedy and tragedy spring from the same well of emotion and essentially help mankind to cope with the vicissitudes of life. People just react to life in different ways.

Depending on people and situations, this can be true. "It is a tragedy or a comedy—sad or merry, as it happens," Hazlitt wrote, showing that people can and do react in a different way to the same event. One of Hazlitt's reasons for writing is to prove that mankind needs different reactions; it is part of man's defense mechanism.

Hazlitt's tone tries to educate people about laughing and crying. Perhaps this is so people can feel less self conscious and work together better in the future without worrying whether their response is right or not, since there isn't a lot of difference between comedy and tragedy. So where one person might see one thing as tragic, the other person may not.

Hazlitt uses many literary devices so readers can picture the differing details of comedy and sadness he discusses. He says tragedy can "shock and wound the mind." He describes tears of relief about comedy or happy times without tragedy. He also uses repetition and exclamation to achieve his purpose. Readers now understand the relationship of comedy and tragedy, and agree with his conclusions.

Analysis of the Medium-Low-Scoring Essay

This essay clearly demonstrates areas in which a student writing under time pressure can make mistakes. This paper has a variety of problems in coherence, organization, diction, and proof.

The first paragraph fails to elicit much excitement. A good AP essay doesn't necessarily have to grab attention, but this one is particularly uninteresting, merely paraphrasing Hazlitt's opening comment on humans and animals. The second paragraph improves somewhat. The student attempts to identify Hazlitt's purpose. But while the statement is well worded, it does not yet deal with one of the assigned tasks, a discussion of Hazlitt's technique.

The third and fourth paragraphs discuss Hazlitt's contentions, but perfunctorily and without great insight. Although Hazlitt's tone is mentioned at the beginning of the fourth paragraph, no analysis or examples follow. Weaknesses of this sort usually arise from inadequacies in planning and organization.

The last paragraph finally addresses literary devices and lists "repetition and exclamation," but once again, no evidence follows proving the connection between literary devices and purpose. Here, the student seems to be grasping for ideas and unsure of his or her point.

While this essay shows some understanding of Hazlitt's purpose, which is to be commended, attempts at proof, analysis, and discussion produce confused sentences with murky ideas. In addition, the student's language, while occasionally sophisticated, is more often than not simplistic. Overall, the essay fails to convince the Reader. It deserves a score of 4.

The Argument Essay

Keep in mind that the argument and the synthesis essays are similar in intent; they both give you the opportunity to present your stance on an issue. In this section, we'll exclusively examine the argument essay.

The argument essay will be based on one brief passage or statement from an author. Occasionally, you might be presented with opposing statements from two authors, or even a brief summary of ideas from three authors. You will usually be given some information about the author, the passage source, the audience, or other relevant material. The passage itself may be a short paragraph, a single quotation, an anecdote, or some other brief work. In that regard, this will be the fastest of the three topics to read, but it provides you with the least material to support your essay. You therefore have to garner examples from your own reading, observation, and experience.

Your task is to evaluate the argument's point(s) and then take a stance that either defends, challenges, or qualifies that point, using concrete examples and clear logic to make your case. In this essay, demonstrate your awareness of culture, history, philosophy, and politics. Establish that you are in touch with your own society and with the larger world around you. These topics give you the opportunity to intelligently discuss issues; seize that opportunity and make the most of it.

Here are some specific strategies for writing the argument essay.

- Read carefully the introductory information about the author, the passage's source, and so forth. Note items that you can use to your advantage in your essay.
- Clarify precisely what the issue is and what the author's stance is.
- Articulate clearly your stance on the issue. Of course, it's acceptable to agree with an issue in some circumstances and disagree in others, but do not be wishy-washy. Take your stance and make it clear.
- Use concrete examples from your own readings, observations, and experiences. You can select examples from world history to current events; you can draw from everything you have ever read, known of, or experienced. Organize your thoughts coherently and integrate your examples with style.
- Demonstrate your logical reasoning skills. Avoid logical fallacies such as circular reasoning, non sequitur arguments, or begging the question.
- Be fair in your essay. Use undistorted language and avoid hyperbole. Avoid using absolute words that may be inaccurate, such as "never," "only," "all," "must," "will," or "everyone." Instead, use more general qualifying terms that are likely to be more accurate, such as "some," "often," "frequently," "might," "occasionally," or "likely."
- Be sincere. Show that you find the topic interesting and worthy of intelligent discussion.
- Know your audience. All AP Readers are high school English teachers or college professors.

Example

The British author Fanny Burney (1752–1840) was noted for being a novelist, diarist, and playwright. She became Mme d'Arblay upon her marriage to a French exile in 1793. Known for her social commentary, she wrote in her novel *Camilla* (1796), "There is nothing upon the face of the earth so insipid as a medium. Give me love or hate! a friend that will go to jail for me, or an enemy that will run me through the body!"

In a well-thought-out essay, evaluate the validity of Burney's assertion about extremes. Use appropriate evidence to make your argument convincing.

Now let's explore the prompt and Burney's quotation, using the first four specific strategies listed above, and jot down a few ideas. (The remaining four strategies will help more with writing the essay, not with the brainstorming portion of your planning.)

- **How can the introductory material help guide your ideas?** Fanny Burney was known for social commentary. Although the quotation is more than 200 years old, it is still relevant today.
- **What is the issue in the prompt?** The author dislikes things that are middle-of-the-road, calling them "insipid." She prefers people who show extremes such as love and hate. It is likely that she is referring to people being honest with others and to the way people are drawn to things at the far end of any spectrum.
- **What is your stance on the issue?** I agree that people are attracted by extremes.
- **What concrete examples can you use?** Now's the time to brainstorm from your observations, readings, and/ or experiences.
  1. Extreme personalities get publicity: Lord Byron, Charles Manson, Kanye West, Lady Gaga.
  2. Extreme events are remembered: French and American revolutions, Japanese earthquake and tsunami, Hurricane Harvey.
  3. Extreme feats are remembered: Kirk Gibson's improbable home run in the 1988 World Series, a student protester stands up to tanks in Tiananmen Square, the attacks of 9/11. Maybe use the quote, "It was the best of times, it was the worst of times. . . ."
  4. Humanity is "attracted" to extreme things: car crashes or fights, "extreme" TV shows like *Deadliest Catch,* big weddings like Meghan Markle and Prince Harry's.
  5. I'm a teenager! We're known for extremes in clothing, emotions, language, music. We like to be thought of as "out there."
- **How is it best to organize?** I like my five categories, but I can't write it all in a timed essay. I'll use the ideas from (1), (3), and (4), in that order.

Scoring

Scoring Guide

Score	Description	Criteria
9	Successful	Essays earning a score of 9 meet the criteria for essays that are scored an 8 and, in addition, are especially full or apt in their analysis or reveal particularly remarkable control of language.
8	Successful	Essays scoring an 8 successfully and substantially evaluate Burney's assertion that there is "nothing . . . so insipid as a medium." They present a well-articulated argument that offers ample and appropriate evidence to support the essay's ideas. The development is thorough, the organization clear and logical. The high-scoring essays present language usage and style that show sophistication, although the writing may contain some minor errors.
7	Satisfactory	Essays earning a score of 7 fit the description of essays that are scored a 6 but provide more complete analysis and a more mature prose style.
6	Satisfactory	Essays earning a score of 6 satisfactorily evaluate Burney's assertion in a generally interesting fashion. The arguments are usually logically reliable and offer sufficient support. These essays are often developed quite well, but not to as great an extent as the highest-scoring essays. In general, these essays may show a few lapses in control over language usage but demonstrate such a clear command over diction and syntax that meaning is clear to the reader.

continued

Scoring Guide

Score	Description	Criteria
5	Plausible	Essays earning a score of 5 understand the task and attempt to evaluate Burney's ideas. The argument is generally clear, but frequently too narrow in scope or superficial in its concept. Development is often too limited and ideas too simplistic. Evidence offered may be only tangentially relevant or may not be adequately or logically examined, leaving the reader to question the validity of examples. Although some lapses in grammar and mechanics may be present, they generally do not interfere with meaning, and the Reader can follow the student's ideas.
4	Inadequate	These low-scoring essays inadequately evaluate the topic. They may misunderstand, misrepresent, or oversimplify Burney's assertion. They may use inappropriate examples or fail to develop them in a convincing manner. Development and organization are frequently flawed. Even though the meaning is usually clear, the writing may demonstrate immature control of English conventions.
3	Inadequate	Essays earning a score of 3 meet the criteria for a score of 4 but demonstrate a less clear understanding of Burney's ideas. The essays may show less control over the elements of writing.
2	Little success	Essays earning a score of 2 achieve little success in evaluating Burney's ideas. The student may completely misread the passage or substitute a simpler task instead of developing a cohesive argument. Lack of relevant or convincing evidence typically characterizes the lowest-scoring essays, and weak, simplistic logic or nonexistent explanations of any evidence often compound the essays' problems. The prose frequently reveals consistent weaknesses over diction and syntax.
1	Little success	These poorly written essays meet the criteria for a score of 2 but are undeveloped, especially simplistic in their analysis, and weak in their control of language.

Note: The following sample essays were not written by the student who brainstormed the above ideas.

High-Scoring Essay

Our fascination with extremes is a phenomenon that is unexplainable by any biological method—we have no genuine need for it, and yet Fanny Burney is accurate; this purely human condition is prevalent in nearly all of us. Burney implies a psychological explanation, simple yet multifaceted. In essence, we simply find the extreme to be more interesting. We cannot rely on any scientific techniques to measure such an abstract concept. But perhaps the most effective way to relate Burney's assertion to current public opinion is to look at the press's choices in content. When considering the stories covered by the press, while we are actually looking at events or people which an editorial staff deems newsworthy, in the interest of sales and advertising profits, we can assume that the media caters to the public's interests. Clearly, news about the best or the worst in our world sells. Clearly, the major headlines generating the most interest have all been the result of some sort of extreme. Plane crashes involving hundreds of lives lost, baseball players booming baseballs farther and more frequently, stock market jumps that affect everyone—these are the most readable, most interesting stories. Not the car crash that injured a twenty-five-year-old man (though it may be just as heart-wrenching); not the consistent .330 batting average of a seasoned baseball veteran (though it may be just as difficult to achieve); and certainly not the steady conglomerate (though it may be just as profitable). Certainly, our hearts and minds gravitate to stories and people that pique our interest.

Hollywood, especially, gears its entertainment to fulfilling this interest. We love to watch the over-the-top, clever, and cruel arch-villains who plot to take over the universe, and the overly saccharine brave young heroes who valiantly stop their plans (and win the damsel in distress while they're at it). Even ordinary Clark Kent became the strong Superman, perhaps convincing us that we too, would be able to fly, have x-ray vision, and save the world from any evil nemesis. It appears we want movies to represent extremes of good and evil, not just some "insipid" everyman. And certainly, this interest in the extreme is not a recent phenomenon. If we go back to Shakespeare's work, considered by many to be the archetypal settings and characters for so many stories to come, we see that Burney's comment holds no less truth. For instance, in *Hamlet,* we have Horatio, "a friend that will go to jail for me" and Polonius, "an enemy that will run me through the body," occupying different extremes. There can be no medium in effective drama, for our imaginations and emotions feed off characters and conflicts that are more grandiose than our daily lives. It's what the audience wants; it's what the playwright delivers.

Our insistent need for the extreme serves no harmful purpose. Indeed, it has shaped our modern conceptions of drama, comedy, and news, helping us define our psychological boundaries and sparking the imaginations of generations to come.

Analysis of the High-Scoring Essay

The student who wrote this high-scoring essay has a firm grasp of the topic and a clear view of the world. He or she appropriately uses examples from the news media, Hollywood cinema, and Shakespearean drama to prove that Fanny Burney's quotation is an accurate perception of humanity; we do relish extremes over the mediocre.

The first paragraph blends the introductory material and its effective thesis into a body paragraph that explores the current state of print journalism. Although the student does not use specific existing headlines or news stories as examples, he or she does not need to—the universal point here is that the news media depicts the extremes in life, and the "generic" examples that are presented here work very well. Plane crashes, unthinkable baseball achievements, and the excessive ups and downs of the stock market are all examples that the Reader can relate to and easily connect to the student's point. The student also slips in a legitimate business rationale for these types of stories: Not only does the public crave them, but the paper also profits by them. This paragraph, nicely on topic, focuses on observations of our modern life and convinces the Reader that the media does present extremes in the news, which in turn reflects humanity's desire for such sensationalism.

The next paragraph explores Hollywood movies and Shakespearean drama, again effectively using both to prove that humanity craves extremes in fictional characters. Everyone knows so well the "cruel arch-villain" and the "brave young hero" that Hollywood exaggerates. The student's declaration that we would all like to become a Superman and "save the world from any evil nemesis" both rings true and helps prove Burney's assertion. Middle-of-the-road personalities do not save the world; extreme ones do.

The student's use of *Hamlet* gives the essay a sophisticated and cultured flair, not merely because it is an accurate Shakespearean reference but because it also proves the student is well read and well rounded. It helps to balance the previous contemporary examples in the essay. Perhaps the *Hamlet* discussion could be developed more, explaining how Horatio and Polonius exemplify these extremes in character, but an essay that is written under timed pressure cannot always elaborate as much as an untimed one. Remember that the AP Reader will reward the student for what he or she does well, and this student proves his or her point admirably.

This essay earns its high score through the development of its clear and relevant ideas, as well as its abundant examples, strong organization, and commendable control of written English. The sense of rhythm found in parallel construction that is so pleasing to the ear can be observed in such areas as the repetition of the word "clearly" to begin two sentences, the parenthetical "though it may be . . ." phrasing in the first paragraph, and in the sentence, "It's what the audience wants; it's what the playwright delivers" in the second paragraph. Although parallelism is never a specific requirement, any student who effectively uses such sophisticated devices will demonstrate a sense of style that shines through to the Reader. The essay's strong style propels it to a score of 9.

Low-Scoring Essay

We can't help but be interested by extremes. They represent both the bad and the good of life and are interesting simply because they differ from the typical person. Like scientists who also are interested in differences from the standard, we classify and thus notice these differences. For example, the world records in running have, time and time again, deserved media coverage while the average speed of a typical healthy males may perhaps be an obscure fact. Our societies focus on the individual inevitably results in the few strongest, smartest, quickest being not only isolated but at times revered. The opposite side of the spectrum is similarly true. The publics fascination with, for example, a cereal killer, is only rivaled by its fascination with the fireman who saved twenty lives. Everything in between (with varying degrees), is ordinary and, as Fanny Burney wrote, "insipid."

Perhaps our dedication to seeking out the extremes in life represents our own struggle to find who we are. Extremes provide a watermark to our own situation. Are we that "friend that will go to jail for me" or the "enemy that will run me through the body?" We are most likely in between. But are fascination with this scale is a symbol of our dreams. We certainly cannot achieve such heights (or such lows) but we can often live vicariously through these extreme individuals.

Analysis of the Low-Scoring Essay

This essay attempts to agree with Burney's assertion. However, it does not make a strong point in doing so, nor does it actually convince the Reader. Simply stated, because of its brevity, the essay is not fulfilling. The example with which the student begins, that of track-and-field world records, does not work particularly well; it appears that the student has not thought it through. After all, it *does* make sense that a new world record would "deserve media coverage," while at the same time the "average speed of a typical, healthy male" would not. This average statistical information can be obtained, but it is not particularly newsworthy, so the example does not make much sense to the Reader. The later example of the public's fascination with murderers and heroes is more logically sound, but it is not enough to save the entire paragraph from mediocrity.

The second paragraph appears to be a hastily drawn conclusion; it certainly offers no new examples or ideas to support the student's thesis. Although it may be philosophically interesting to ponder how "seeking out the extremes in life represents our own struggle to find who we are," it does not persuade the Reader of the validity of Burney's assertion, and therefore falls flat. This paragraph does not meet the requirement in the directions, namely using "appropriate evidence" to support ideas. It needs stronger organization and development.

The large number of diction and grammatical mistakes also hurt this essay's score. Although the Readers want to reward the student for what he or she does well, they simply cannot ignore so many errors. Notice the first two sentences. The student claims we are interested "*by*" extremes (an unidiomatic expression to start), then claims "they differ from the typical person," which is not possible. One cannot logically compare "extremes" to "people." Notice also the number agreement problem in the phrase "speed of *a* typically healthy *males.*"

The student also has many diction and/or punctuation mistakes, such as "societies" instead of "society's," "publics" without its apostrophe, and "cereal" instead of "serial." The homophone confusion of using "are" instead of "our" strikes the Reader as yet another careless error. Although an AP Reader can disregard minor mistakes here and there, this essay is riddled with far too many errors to disregard without affecting the score. Giving it a score of 3 would be appropriate.

The essay earns a low score because of its combination of being barely on topic, having weak development, displaying ineffectual organization, and exhibiting numerous mechanical errors.

Chapter 3

Diagnostic Mini-Test

Answer Sheet

Section I: Multiple-Choice Questions

1	Ⓐ	Ⓑ	Ⓒ	Ⓓ	Ⓔ
2	Ⓐ	Ⓑ	Ⓒ	Ⓓ	Ⓔ
3	Ⓐ	Ⓑ	Ⓒ	Ⓓ	Ⓔ
4	Ⓐ	Ⓑ	Ⓒ	Ⓓ	Ⓔ
5	Ⓐ	Ⓑ	Ⓒ	Ⓓ	Ⓔ
6	Ⓐ	Ⓑ	Ⓒ	Ⓓ	Ⓔ
7	Ⓐ	Ⓑ	Ⓒ	Ⓓ	Ⓔ
8	Ⓐ	Ⓑ	Ⓒ	Ⓓ	Ⓔ
9	Ⓐ	Ⓑ	Ⓒ	Ⓓ	Ⓔ
10	Ⓐ	Ⓑ	Ⓒ	Ⓓ	Ⓔ

CUT HERE

Section II: Free-Response Question

CUT HERE

CUT HERE

CUT HERE

CUT HERE

CUT HERE

Questions

Section I: Multiple-Choice Questions

Time: 12 minutes

10 questions

Directions: This section contains a selection from a prose work and questions on its content, style, and form. Read each section carefully. For each question, choose the best answer of the five choices.

This excerpt is taken from a 1981 book that explores specific American communities.

On Route 301 south of Tampa, billboards advertising Sun City Center crop up every few miles, with pictures of Cesar Romero and slogans that read FLORIDA'S RETIREMENT COMMUNITY OF
(5) THE YEAR, 87 HOLES OF GOLF, THE TOWN TOO BUSY TO RETIRE. According to a real-estate brochure, the town is "sensibly located . . . comfortably removed from the crowded downtown areas, the highway clutter, the tourists, and the traffic." It is
(10) 25 miles from Sarasota, and 11 miles from the nearest beach on the Gulf Coast. Route 301, an inland route—to be taken in preference to the coast road, with its lines of trucks from the phosphate plants—passes through a lot of
(15) swampland, some scraggly pinewoods, and acre upon acre of strawberry beds covered with sheets of black plastic. There are fields where hairy, tough-looking cattle snatch at the grass between the palmettos. There are aluminum warehouses,
(20) cinder-block stores, and trailer homes in patches of dirt with laundry sailing out behind. There are Pentecostal churches and run-down cafes and bars with rows of pickup trucks parked out front.
(25) Turn right with the billboards onto Route 674, and there is a green-and-white, suburban-looking resort town. Off the main road, white asphalt boulevards with avenues of palm trees give onto streets that curve pleasingly around
(30) golf courses and small lakes. White, ranch-style houses sit back from the streets on small, impeccably manicured lawns. A glossy, four-color map of the town put out by a real-estate company shows cartoon figures of golfers on the
(35) fairways and boats on the lakes, along with drawings of churches, clubhouses, and curly green trees. The map is a necessity for the visitor, since the streets curve around in a maze fashion, ending in culs-de-sac or doubling back on
(40) themselves. There is no way in or out of Sun City

Center except by the main road bisecting the town. The map, which looks like a child's board game (Snakes and Ladders or Uncle Wiggily), shows a vague area—a kind of no-man's-land—
(45) surrounding the town. As the map suggests, there is nothing natural about Sun City Center. The lakes are artificial, and there is hardly a tree or shrub or blade of grass that has any correspondence in the world just beyond it. At
(50) the edges of the development, there are houses under construction, with the seams still showing in the transplanted lawns. From there, you can look out at a flat, brown plain that used to be a cattle ranch. The developer simply scraped the
(55) surface off the land and started over again.

Sun City Center is an unincorporated town of about 8,500 people, almost all of whom are over the age of 60. It is a self-contained community, with stores, banks, restaurants, and doctors'
(60) offices. It has the advertised 87 holes of golf; it also has tennis courts, shuffleboard courts, swimming pools, and lawn-bowling greens. In addition to the regular housing, it has a "life-care facility"—a six-story apartment building
(65) with a nursing home in one wing. "It's a strange town," a clinical psychologist at the University of South Florida, in Tampa, told me before I went. "It's out there in the middle of nowhere. It has a section of private houses, where people go
(70) when they retire. Then it has a section of condos and apartments, where people go when they can't keep up their houses. Then it has a nursing home. Then it has a cemetery." In fact, there is no cemetery in Sun City Center, but the doctor was
(75) otherwise correct.

Sun City Center has become a world unto itself. Over the years, the town attracted a supermarket and all the stores and services necessary to the maintenance of daily life. Now,
(80) in addition, it has a golf-cart dealer, two banks, three savings and loan associations, four restaurants, and a brokerage firm. For visitors, there is the Sun City Center Inn. The town has a

post office. Five churches have been built by the
(85) residents and a sixth is under construction. A
number of doctors have set up offices in the
town, and a Bradenton hospital recently opened
a satellite hospital with 112 beds. There is no
school, of course. The commercial establishments
(90) all front on the state road running through the
center of town, but, because most of them are
more expensive than those in the neighboring
towns, the people from the surrounding area
patronize only the supermarket, the Laundromat,
(95) and one or two others. The local farmers and the
migrant workers they employ, many of whom are
Mexican, have little relationship to golf courses
or to dinner dances with organ music. Conversely,
Sun Citians are not the sort of people who would
(100) go to bean suppers in the Pentecostal churches
or hang out at raunchy bars where gravel-voiced
women sing "Satin Sheets and Satin Pillows."
The result is that Sun Citians see very little of
their Florida neighbors. They take trips to
(105) Tampa, Bradenton, and Sarasota, but otherwise
they rarely leave the green-and-white developments,
with their palm-lined avenues and artificial lakes.
In the normal course of a week, they rarely see
anyone under sixty.

1. In the first paragraph, the author refers to the
   "fields where hairy, tough-looking cattle snatch
   at the grass between the palmettos" in order to

   A. deny the area any pastoral attractiveness
   B. underscore the loss when farmland is
      subdivided for retirement homes
   C. suggest the savagery of the natural world
      that can be ordered and made beautiful by
      human projects
   D. juxtapose the image of the cattle with that
      of swampland and scrawny pinewoods
   E. compare the cattle to those who live in the
      trailer homes that are surrounded by dirt

2. In the last three sentences of the first paragraph
   ("There are fields . . . parked out front"), the
   author uses all of the following EXCEPT

   A. parallel structure
   B. periodic sentences
   C. specific details
   D. direct statements
   E. subject-verb inversions

3. In the University of South Florida clinical
   psychologist's quotation at the end of the third
   paragraph (lines 68–73), the use of two
   sentences with "where" clauses and three
   sentences beginning with "then" has which of
   the following effects?

   A. It requires the reader to supply the "where"
      clauses for the last two sentences that begin
      with "then."
   B. It provides a rhetorical parallelism for an
      unspoken chronological progression.
   C. It includes a series of transitions that direct
      the reader's attention to the speaker.
   D. It implies the psychologist has studied the
      Sun City Center residents closely.
   E. It emphasizes why retirees would be
      attracted to Sun City Center.

4. In the last paragraph, the list of services
   available in Sun City Center itemized in the
   sentence in lines 79–82 ("Now, in addition . . .
   brokerage firm") primarily suggests the
   residents' concern with

   A. avoiding the idea of death
   B. physical comforts
   C. impressing one another
   D. relaxation
   E. money

5. Which of the following does NOT accurately
   describe this sentence from the fourth
   paragraph: "Conversely, Sun Citians are not the
   sort of people who would go to bean suppers in
   the Pentecostal churches or hang out at raunchy
   bars where gravel-voiced women sing 'Satin
   Sheets and Satin Pillows'" (lines 98–102)?

   A. It reinforces the idea of the preceding
      sentence.
   B. It effectively contrasts Sun City Center
      residents and their neighbors.
   C. It recalls details of the description at the
      end of the first paragraph.
   D. It attacks the values of the people who live
      in the area near Sun City Center.
   E. It presents an image that is amusing in its
      incongruity.

6. The overall effect of the last paragraph of the passage is to call attention to the

    A. age of Sun City Center's residents

    B. convenience of life in Sun City Center

    C. political indifference of Sun City Center's residents

    D. isolation of Sun City Center's residents

    E. wealth of Sun City Center's residents

7. Which of the following best describes the diction of the passage?

    A. formal and austere

    B. informal and documentary

    C. abstract

    D. artless and colloquial

    E. highly metaphorical

8. Which of the following quotations from the passage best sums up the author's main point about Sun City Center?

    A. "As the map suggests, there is nothing natural about Sun City Center." (lines 45–46)

    B. "The developer simply scraped the surface off the land and started over again." (lines 54–55)

    C. "Sun City Center is an unincorporated town of about 8,500 people, almost all of whom are over the age of 60." (lines 56–58)

    D. "In fact, there is no cemetery in Sun City Center, but the doctor was otherwise correct." (lines 73–75)

    E. "The result is that Sun Citians see very little of their Florida neighbors." (lines 103–104)

9. A principal rhetorical strategy of the passage as a whole is to

    A. depict a small city by presenting information in a chronological narrative

    B. portray a place by comparison and contrast

    C. raise and then answer questions about the nature of a place

    D. progressively narrow the focus from a larger area to a smaller one and its residents

    E. develop a discussion of a unique location by using multiple points of view

10. All of the following are characteristics of the style of this passage EXCEPT

    A. variety in the length of its sentences

    B. infrequent use of the first person

    C. infrequent use of adjectives

    D. infrequent use of simile

    E. frequent use of specific details

IF YOU FINISH BEFORE TIME IS CALLED, CHECK YOUR WORK ON THIS SECTION ONLY. DO NOT WORK ON ANY OTHER SECTION IN THE TEST.

Section II: Free-Response Question

Time: 40 minutes

1 question

The following passage comes from J. Hector St. John de Crèvecoeur's *Letters from an American Farmer* (1782).

Directions: Read the selection carefully, and then write an essay in which you analyze Crèvecoeur's attitude toward Europeans and Americans, concentrating on how his rhetorical strategies reflect his opinions.

In this great American asylum, the poor of Europe have by some means met together, and in consequence of various causes; to what purpose should they ask one another what countrymen they are? Alas, two thirds of them had no country. Can a wretch who wanders about, who works and starves, whose life is a continual scene of sore affliction or pinching penury; can that man call England or any other kingdom his country? A country that had no bread for him, whose fields procured him no harvest, who met with nothing but the frowns of the rich, the severity of the laws, with jails and punishments; who owned not a single foot of extensive surface of this planet? No! Urged by a variety of motives, here they came. Everything has tended to regenerate them; new laws, a new mode of living, a new social system; here they are become men: in Europe they were as so many useless plants, wanting vegetative mold and refreshing showers; they withered, and were mowed down by want, hunger, and war; but now by the power of transplantation, like all other plants they have taken root and flourished! Formerly they were not numbered in any civil lists of their country, except in those of the poor; here they rank as citizens. By what invisible power has this surprising metamorphosis been performed? By that of the laws and that of their industry. . . .

What then is the American, this new man? He is either a European, or the descendant of a European, hence that strange mixture of blood, which you will find in no other country. I could point out to you a family whose grandfather was an Englishman, whose wife was Dutch, whose son married a French woman, and whose present four sons have now four wives of different nations. *He* is an American, who leaving behind him all his ancient prejudices and manners, receives new ones from the new mode of life he has embraced, the new government he obeys, and the new rank he holds. He becomes an American by being received in the broad lap of our great *Alma Mater.* Here individuals of all nations are melted into a new race of men, whose labors and posterity will one day cause great changes in the world. Americans are the western pilgrims, who are carrying only with them that great mass of arts, sciences, vigor, and industry which began long since in the east; they will finish the great circle.

IF YOU FINISH BEFORE TIME IS CALLED, CHECK YOUR WORK ON THIS
SECTION ONLY. DO NOT WORK ON ANY OTHER SECTION IN THE TEST.

Answer Key

Section I: Multiple-Choice Questions

1. A
2. B
3. B
4. E
5. D

6. D
7. B
8. A
9. D
10. C

Section II: Free-Response Question

An essay scoring guide, student essays, and analysis appear beginning on p. 64.

Answer Explanations

Section I: Multiple-Choice Questions

The passage referred to in questions 1–10 is from *Cities on a Hill* (1981) by Frances Fitzgerald.

1. **A.** The passage presents the area around Sun City Center as ugly: "scraggly pinewoods" and "a lot of swampland." Although the land is used for cattle ranching, the prose denies it any charm or beauty. The passage has no concern with making a case for the subdivision as ecologically bad (B) or good (C). In the passage, ecology is not an issue. The description in the first paragraph contains a series of images, but nothing suggests the cattle image is supposed to juxtapose against any other image (D). Rather, all of the images combine to create a unified effect. Similarly, the cattle are never compared to those who live in the trailer homes (E); both are just separate images.

2. **B.** These are all loose, not periodic, sentences. Each of the sentences could end after just three or four words, whereas a periodic sentence makes its point in a main clause at the end. Parallel structure (A) exists in the repeated sentence beginnings, "There are." The sentences are direct statements (D) chiefly made up of specific details (C). All three sentences place the verbs ("are") before the subjects ("fields," "warehouses," "churches") (E).

3. **B.** The repetition of "it has" and "then it has" is an example of parallel structure, and the chronology progresses from the time when the people first move to Sun City Center to a later time when their health begins to fail, to a time of greater weakness, to death (B). Although the two "where" clauses invite us to add two more "where" clauses into the last two sentences, thus mentally completing the implied parallel construction, the reader is not required to do so (A). The series does not call attention to the speaker (C). The passage offers no evidence that the psychologist has studied the residents closely (D). The psychologist's quotation hardly makes Sun City Center attractive (E); in fact, the doctor calls it a "strange town."

4. **E.** There are five services listed, and three of the five (banks, savings and loan associations, and a brokerage firm) are specifically related to money. A fourth, the golf-cart dealer, is at least tangentially related to affluence. Choice A is not related to the list of services. Choices B, C, and D are plausible, but E, although it may seem obvious, is the best choice.

5. **D.** The sentence reinforces the idea of the sentence before—the alienation of the Sun Citians from their neighbors (A and B). The bars and Pentecostal churches were mentioned in the last sentence of the first paragraph (C). The notion of a group of middle-class senior citizens sitting in a run-down café listening to country-western music is amusing in its incongruity (E). The passage is not satiric. Its point is not that Sun Citians or their neighbors are flawed, but that they have nothing in common.

6. **D.** Although the paragraph begins with an account of the stores and services of Sun City Center, even the first sentence insists on this development as "a world unto itself." And the last two-thirds of the paragraph (beginning with "There is no school, of course") supports the notion of the residents' isolation from the rest of the world. The age of the residents (A) and their wealth (E), along with the convenience of life in Sun City Center (B), are all mentioned in the passage, but these are not the thrust of the final paragraph. The residents' political indifference (C) is never mentioned or hinted at in the passage.

7. **B.** Although other words may also describe the passage, choice B is the best of the five choices here; the diction is informal (relaxed and casual) and documentary (factual). The passage is not formal and austere (A), not abstract (C), not artless (although a few phrases could be called colloquial) (D), and not at all metaphorical (E).

8. **A.** Choices B, C, and D don't really sum up a central idea of the passage. Both A and E are good answers, but A can include the idea of E, while E is more narrow and not the focus of the whole passage. The whole passage is about the unnaturalness of Sun City Center, its oddness in this geographical area, and the segregation of its residents from their neighbors and from a world where many people are still under 60.

9. **D.** The best choice here is D. The passage begins with the geography of the central west coast of Florida but narrows to Sun City Center ("Turn right with the billboards onto Route 674"). The second paragraph maps out the town, while the third and fourth paragraphs describe its residents. The passage is not a chronological narrative (A). It uses contrast only in the last paragraph (B), asks no questions (C), and has only one point of view and one additional quoted comment (E).

10. **C.** The passage varies its sentence length (A), uses the first person only once in paragraph three (B), contains only one simile (D), and uses a large number of specific details (E). It is very dependent on adjectives; without its adjectives, it would be barren and would lose its purpose.

Section II: Free-Response Question

Scoring Guide

Score	Description	Criteria
9	Successful	Essays earning a score of 9 meet the criteria for essays that are scored an 8 and, in addition, are especially full or apt in their analysis or reveal particularly remarkable control of language.
8	Successful	Essays earning a score of 8 successfully and clearly demonstrate understanding of Crèvecoeur's attitude toward Americans and a thorough comprehension of how his rhetorical strategies reflect his attitude. The thesis is articulate and thoughtful. Strong and relevant evidence from Crèvecoeur's essay is included. Thoroughly convincing, these essays show a clear command of essay-writing skills. Although it need not be without errors, these essays show a mature style and use of language.
7	Satisfactory	Essays earning a score of 7 fit the description of essays that are scored a 6 but provide more complete analysis and a more mature prose style.
6	Satisfactory	These essays show a satisfactory comprehension of Crèvecoeur's ideas, but the thesis may be less explicit than that of the top-scoring essays. The evidence offered may not be as convincing or thorough, making the essay less persuasive. Still, the essay is fairly convincing and shows clear thinking. The connection between the evidence and Crèvecoeur's attitude may not be as clear as in top-scoring essays. Although well written, these essays may demonstrate some errors while still showing satisfactory control over diction and the essay requirements.

Score	Description	Criteria
5	Plausible	These adequately written essays show some understanding of Crèvecoeur's attitude but may not show clear comprehension of the relationship between rhetorical strategies and his attitude. The thesis may be simplistic and predictable, while the evidence offered may be uneven or insufficient to prove the student's points. Evidence presented for Crèvecoeur's attitude may be too brief or understated. Although the presentation of ideas may be acceptable, the essay as a whole is not strongly convincing. Acceptable organization and development may be evident, but the style may not be as sophisticated as that of higher-scoring essays.
4	Inadequate	These low-scoring essays fail to convince the AP Reader because of their inadequate response to the prompt. The weak presentation may not demonstrate a clear understanding of Crèvecoeur's ideas. Comprehension of how Crèvecoeur's rhetorical strategies communicate his attitude may be minimal. The thesis may be unsubstantiated, paragraph development may be weak, and superficial thinking may be evident. The connection between Crèvecoeur's rhetorical strategies and the essay's thesis may be nonexistent or trite. Frequent mechanical errors that distract the Reader may be present.
3	Inadequate	Essays earning a score of 3 meet the criteria for a score of 4 but demonstrate a less clear understanding of Crèvecoeur's ideas. The essays may show less control over the elements of writing.
2	Little success	These poorly written essays lack coherence and clarity. They may present only a brief synopsis of Crèvecoeur's attitude with no mention of how his rhetorical strategies reflect that attitude. The thesis may be overly obvious or nonexistent. Little or no evidence may be offered, and the connection between the evidence and the thesis may be shallow or missing. These essays may misunderstand the task, may fail to articulate Crèvecoeur's attitude, or may substitute a simpler task. These essays may be unusually short and exhibit poor fundamental writing skills. Weak sentence construction may persist, and frequent weaknesses in mechanics may be present.
1	Little success	These poorly written essays meet the criteria for a score of 2 but are undeveloped, especially simplistic in their analysis, and weak in their control of language.

High-Scoring Essay

Many foreigners came to America during the republic's formative years to explore life in the new nation. The writings of de Tocqueville and Charles Dickens commented on the new American character and government in the nineteenth century. J. Hector St. John de Crèvecoeur, who wrote Letters from an American Farmer in 1782, was not alone in his endeavor, though he was one of the first to visit the new United States. His writing generally reflects a positive image of Americans. While taking note of their humble origins and lack of cultural refinement, he praises the resilience of American citizens. Crèvecoeur's diction, and the positive connotations of the words he uses to describe Americans, clearly present his positive, though occasionally paternal and superior, attitude toward Americans.

Americans are defined by Crèvecoeur largely in terms of the land they left. Their new nation is a haven from a Europe of severe laws, "with jails and punishments." The common folk in England are faced by the "frowns of the rich." The new Americans have left the "refinement" of Europe behind, along with the class system and much else which had restricted them. These images tell as much about Crèvecoeur's attitude toward Europeans as it does toward Americans. The negativity attached to Americans' backgrounds perhaps emphasizes their ultimate determination and drive once they arrived on new soil. Crèvecoeur deliberately uses negative phrases in describing Americans' pasts so that their change in the new country will be even more dramatic.

Crèvecoeur emphasizes the newness of the United States, thus implying a positive impression of the land. While he may look down somewhat on the breeding and manners of the Americans, noting that they come from the lower rungs of European social hierarchy, he certainly believes the new land is good for them. America is a place of regenerative powers, with "new laws, a new mode of living, a new social system." Crèvecoeur credits America with encouraging the flourishing of the world's poor and unwanted. Might he then be looking down on America, as the "asylum" he describes in the opening sentence, a refuge suitable only for the wretches of sophisticated European life? Perhaps. But he leaves no doubt about the successful attainment of such a goal, lauding it by writing that the "surprising metamorphosis" from wretches to citizens is thanks to American "laws and . . . industry."

Although Crèvecoeur generally presents Americans in laudable terms, a trace of condescension appears in some phrases. America was made up of "wretches" who had previously wandered about. They had endured lives of "sore affliction or pinching penury." But despite the seeming elitism of Crèvecoeur's description, his word choices elicit sympathy rather than scorn in the attentive reader because he is referring to the Americans' previous lives in Europe. Crèvecoeur makes a careful point of the work ethic of these derelict new countrymen, essentially homeless among the world's nations. Such attention clearly shows that Crèvecoeur is sensitive to the plight of the new Americans.

Crèvecoeur writes as if America has surpassed his expectations as a melting pot of undesirables. He has an optimistic view of the country's role in the future. Compared to crusaders, the Americans he praises are the "western pilgrims" full of the "great mass of arts, sciences, vigor, and industry" that once issued from the east. It is important to note that Crèvecoeur ends his essay on a positive tone, with phrasing that emphasizes greatness. Here, in his conclusion, Crèvecoeur's attitude toward Americans really shines with enthusiasm. They are the nation of the future, he believes, and they will deeply influence the future of the world with their newborn splendor.

Analysis of the High-Scoring Essay

This thorough and well-written essay succeeds both in covering the topic and in convincing the Reader. The student demonstrates a clear comprehension of the passage and does not merely present a one-sided view of Crèvecoeur. The first paragraph introduces and relates other foreign authors who also addressed the personality of the new Americans. Ultimately, it presents a thoughtful thesis that shows a full understanding of Crèvecoeur's attitude while also mentioning his rhetorical strategies, especially diction and connotation.

In the second paragraph, the student addresses Crèvecoeur's negative statements about the Americans' background in Europe and does a nice job of placing this negativity in context by pointing out that it will be balanced with the "dramatic" changes that take place once the new citizens have become Americans. This paragraph, like those that follow, is thoughtful and articulate, presenting an ample number of specific examples for the student's points and providing a connection to the thesis.

The next paragraph addresses the transformation that took place in the Americans after they arrived in the new country. This unified paragraph uses quotations from the passage well and presents interesting ideas from the student. This student shows the ability to think about and interpret Crèvecoeur's ideas, not simply to present them.

The fourth paragraph describes the "condescension" in some of Crèvecoeur's phrasing; again, the student does an admirable job of presenting Crèvecoeur's attitude while remembering that the topic asks for an analysis of rhetorical strategies. The student clearly sees that, although Crèvecoeur presents many negative ideas about the Americans' background, essentially, he praises Americans.

The essay ends positively, just as Crèvecoeur's does. The student's wording, like Crèvecoeur's, shows optimism and provides a clean ending to a fairly long essay. Influencing the future with "newborn splendor" sums up both Crèvecoeur's attitude and the student's ideas very nicely. Overall, the essay uses sophisticated wording and contains many intelligent ideas. It reads well because it's clear that the student has ideas of his or her own and is not merely listing Crèvecoeur's. It deserves to be rewarded with a score of 8.

Medium-Low-Scoring Essay

Crèvecoeur was a French writer who wrote about life in the rural parts of America. He has a partly negative attitude about America, and cuts down the Americans many times in his essay. He also gives them some praise for starting over and doing something new. He also praises them for succeeding at something new.

He uses diction to obtain these results. A careful use of diction shows readers that he sometimes doesn't think much of the American people as a whole. He points out that they were "the poor of Europe" who, as wretches, lived a life of "sore affliction." He also says that "two thirds of them had no country." This hardly sounds like Crèvecoeur admires the Americans background. He stereotypes Americans to all be like this.

Crèvecoeur continues his diatribe against Americans as he calls them "useless plants" in Europe. But finally, he has something more generous to say about Americans as he claims these plants have "taken root and flourished" here in American soil. So, although these Americans were low-life Europeans, once they became Americans they became "new." They became "citizens." Crèvecoeur also notices that Americans work hard and have good laws. I find it interesting that even though he has some good things to say about Americans, he still claims negative things; he believes that once the new Americans arrived, they left behind them all their "ancient prejudices . . . receiving new ones. . . ." We in America today like to believe that we hold no prejudices; at least that's one of the principles that our country was founded on.

Thus it can be seen that Crèvecoeur seemed to have some good thoughts about Americans, but that he was by no means entirely impressed by them. He uses his diction to present his opinions, and very strong diction at that. His wording is surprisingly harsh at times, considering that he seems to want to praise Americans for what they have accomplished, yet he spends so much time degrading their background. His attitude toward Americans is best described as guarded; he certainly does not show Americans in nothing but glowing terms.

Analysis of the Medium-Low-Scoring Essay

This essay, although well organized, clearly shows the student's problems in both reading and writing skills. It begins by attempting to address the topic, but it does so with such a vague thesis that all it essentially sets forth is the simplistic idea that Crèvecoeur is both positive and negative about Americans. How Crèvecoeur's rhetorical strategies establish that attitude is not yet addressed.

The student then devotes a paragraph to proving how negatively Crèvecoeur viewed the Americans' backgrounds by supplying a fair amount of evidence from Crèvecoeur's text. The student cites several examples of negative wording but also makes mistakes. First, the student borders on a misreading of the passage. In explaining the despair that Americans felt before coming to this country, Crèvecoeur's purpose seems to be to show how much the Americans had to overcome, thus emphasizing their strength. However, this student concentrates on only the negative European experience and transfers that negativity to the Americans *after* they became Americans. The student's second mistake is failing to address the topic clearly, failing to comment on exactly *how* Crèvecoeur's attitude is presented through his diction. This student simply gives the evidence and leaves it to the Reader to make the connection.

The next paragraph tries to establish Crèvecoeur's positive attitude toward Americans, but the evidence presented is weak; the student offers little more than that the country is "new" and that people are now "citizens." The student turns again to a negative reading of the text, focusing on Crèvecoeur's claim that Americans have prejudices. Because of this change in direction, the paragraph lacks unity.

The concluding paragraph finally mentions diction again, but again it makes no connection between Crèvecoeur's word choice and the attitude it reflects. Unfortunately, this paragraph is merely summary. Overall, the essay's weaknesses stem from a cursory reading of the passage, weak presentation of evidence, and a lack of attention to the topic of the thesis. Simplistic thinking and simplistic diction combine here to produce a bland essay that fails to convince the Reader. Some Readers might give it a score of 5, but most would likely score it a 4.

Chapter 4

Practice Exam 1

Answer Sheet

Section I: Multiple-Choice Questions

1 Ⓐ Ⓑ Ⓒ Ⓓ Ⓔ		21 Ⓐ Ⓑ Ⓒ Ⓓ Ⓔ		41 Ⓐ Ⓑ Ⓒ Ⓓ Ⓔ
2 Ⓐ Ⓑ Ⓒ Ⓓ Ⓔ		22 Ⓐ Ⓑ Ⓒ Ⓓ Ⓔ		42 Ⓐ Ⓑ Ⓒ Ⓓ Ⓔ
3 Ⓐ Ⓑ Ⓒ Ⓓ Ⓔ		23 Ⓐ Ⓑ Ⓒ Ⓓ Ⓔ		43 Ⓐ Ⓑ Ⓒ Ⓓ Ⓔ
4 Ⓐ Ⓑ Ⓒ Ⓓ Ⓔ		24 Ⓐ Ⓑ Ⓒ Ⓓ Ⓔ		44 Ⓐ Ⓑ Ⓒ Ⓓ Ⓔ
5 Ⓐ Ⓑ Ⓒ Ⓓ Ⓔ		25 Ⓐ Ⓑ Ⓒ Ⓓ Ⓔ		45 Ⓐ Ⓑ Ⓒ Ⓓ Ⓔ
6 Ⓐ Ⓑ Ⓒ Ⓓ Ⓔ		26 Ⓐ Ⓑ Ⓒ Ⓓ Ⓔ		46 Ⓐ Ⓑ Ⓒ Ⓓ Ⓔ
7 Ⓐ Ⓑ Ⓒ Ⓓ Ⓔ		27 Ⓐ Ⓑ Ⓒ Ⓓ Ⓔ		47 Ⓐ Ⓑ Ⓒ Ⓓ Ⓔ
8 Ⓐ Ⓑ Ⓒ Ⓓ Ⓔ		28 Ⓐ Ⓑ Ⓒ Ⓓ Ⓔ		48 Ⓐ Ⓑ Ⓒ Ⓓ Ⓔ
9 Ⓐ Ⓑ Ⓒ Ⓓ Ⓔ		29 Ⓐ Ⓑ Ⓒ Ⓓ Ⓔ		49 Ⓐ Ⓑ Ⓒ Ⓓ Ⓔ
10 Ⓐ Ⓑ Ⓒ Ⓓ Ⓔ		30 Ⓐ Ⓑ Ⓒ Ⓓ Ⓔ		50 Ⓐ Ⓑ Ⓒ Ⓓ Ⓔ
11 Ⓐ Ⓑ Ⓒ Ⓓ Ⓔ		31 Ⓐ Ⓑ Ⓒ Ⓓ Ⓔ		51 Ⓐ Ⓑ Ⓒ Ⓓ Ⓔ
12 Ⓐ Ⓑ Ⓒ Ⓓ Ⓔ		32 Ⓐ Ⓑ Ⓒ Ⓓ Ⓔ		52 Ⓐ Ⓑ Ⓒ Ⓓ Ⓔ
13 Ⓐ Ⓑ Ⓒ Ⓓ Ⓔ		33 Ⓐ Ⓑ Ⓒ Ⓓ Ⓔ		53 Ⓐ Ⓑ Ⓒ Ⓓ Ⓔ
14 Ⓐ Ⓑ Ⓒ Ⓓ Ⓔ		34 Ⓐ Ⓑ Ⓒ Ⓓ Ⓔ		54 Ⓐ Ⓑ Ⓒ Ⓓ Ⓔ
15 Ⓐ Ⓑ Ⓒ Ⓓ Ⓔ		35 Ⓐ Ⓑ Ⓒ Ⓓ Ⓔ		55 Ⓐ Ⓑ Ⓒ Ⓓ Ⓔ
16 Ⓐ Ⓑ Ⓒ Ⓓ Ⓔ		36 Ⓐ Ⓑ Ⓒ Ⓓ Ⓔ		
17 Ⓐ Ⓑ Ⓒ Ⓓ Ⓔ		37 Ⓐ Ⓑ Ⓒ Ⓓ Ⓔ		
18 Ⓐ Ⓑ Ⓒ Ⓓ Ⓔ		38 Ⓐ Ⓑ Ⓒ Ⓓ Ⓔ		
19 Ⓐ Ⓑ Ⓒ Ⓓ Ⓔ		39 Ⓐ Ⓑ Ⓒ Ⓓ Ⓔ		
20 Ⓐ Ⓑ Ⓒ Ⓓ Ⓔ		40 Ⓐ Ⓑ Ⓒ Ⓓ Ⓔ		

CUT HERE

Section II: Free-Response Questions

Question 1

CUT HERE

CUT HERE

CUT HERE

CUT HERE

CUT HERE

Question 2

CUT HERE

CUT HERE

CUT HERE

CUT HERE

Question 3

CUT HERE

CUT HERE

CUT HERE

CUT HERE

Section I: Multiple-Choice Questions

Time: 1 hour

55 questions

Directions: This section consists of selections from prose works and questions on their content, style, and form. Read each selection carefully. For each question, choose the best answer of the five choices.

Questions 1–11 refer to the following passage from a 1989 book of essays about writing.

The written word is weak. Many people prefer life to it. Life gets your blood going, and it smells good. Writing is mere writing, literature is mere. It appeals only to the subtlest senses—the (5) imagination's vision, and the imagination's hearing—and the moral sense, and the intellect. This writing that you do, that so thrills you, that so racks and exhilarates you, as if you were dancing next to the band, is barely audible to (10) anyone else. The reader's ear must adjust down from loud life to the subtle, imaginary sounds of the written word. An ordinary reader picking up a book can't yet hear a thing; it will take half an hour to pick up the writing's modulations, its ups (15) and downs and louds and softs.

An intriguing entomological experiment shows that a male butterfly will ignore a living female butterfly of his own species in favor of a painted cardboard one, if the cardboard one is (20) big. If the cardboard one is bigger than he is, bigger than any female butterfly ever could be, he jumps the piece of cardboard. Over and over again, he jumps the piece of cardboard. Nearby, the real, living butterfly opens and closes her (25) wings in vain.

Films and television stimulate the body's senses too, in big ways. A nine-foot handsome face, and its three-foot-wide smile, are irresistible. Look at the long legs on that man, as high as a (30) wall, and coming straight toward you. The music builds. The moving, lighted screen fills your brain. You do not like filmed car chases? See if you can turn away. Try not to watch. Even knowing you are manipulated, you are still as (35) helpless as the male butterfly drawn to painted cardboard.

That is the movies. That is their ground. The printed word cannot compete with the movies on their ground, and should not. You can describe (40) beautiful faces, car chases, or valleys full of Indians on horseback until you run out of words, and you will not approach the movies' spectacle.

Novels written with film contracts in mind have a faint but unmistakable, and ruinous, odor. I (45) cannot name what, in the text, alerts the reader to suspect the writer of mixed motives; I cannot specify which sentences, in several books, have caused me to read on with increasing dismay, and finally close the books because I smelled a (50) rat. Such books seem uneasy being books; they seem eager to fling off their disguises and jump onto screens.

Why would anyone read a book instead of watching big people move on a screen? Because a (55) book can be literature. It is a subtle thing—poor thing, but our own. In my view, the more literary the book—the more purely verbal, crafted sentence by sentence, the more imaginative, reasoned, and deep—the more likely people are (60) to read it. The people who read are the people who like literature, after all, whatever that might be. They like, or require, what books alone have. If they want to see films that evening, they will find films. If they do not like to read, they will (65) not. People who read are not too lazy to flip on the television; they prefer books. I cannot imagine a sorrier pursuit than struggling for years to write a book that attempts to appeal to people who do not read in the first place.

1. Which of the following best describes how the second and third paragraphs are related?

A. The second paragraph makes an assertion that is qualified in the third paragraph.

B. The second paragraph asks a question that is answered in the third paragraph.

C. The second paragraph describes a situation that is paralleled in the third paragraph.

D. The second paragraph presents as factual what the third paragraph presents as only a possibility.

E. There is no clear relationship between the two paragraphs.

2. The "nine-foot handsome face" (lines 27–28) refers to

A. the female butterfly
B. literary creativity
C. a visual distraction
D. an image in the movies
E. how the imagination of a reader may see a face

3. The sentence "Such books . . . onto screens" (lines 50–52) contains an example of

A. personification
B. understatement
C. irony
D. simile
E. syllogism

4. According to the passage, literature is likely to be characterized by all of the following EXCEPT

A. colloquial language
B. imagination
C. verbal skill
D. moral sense
E. intelligence

5. In the last sentence of the last paragraph, the phrase "sorrier pursuit" can be best understood to mean

A. more regretful chase
B. poorer occupation
C. more sympathetic profession
D. sadder expectation
E. more indifferent striving

6. In the last paragraph, the phrase "a subtle thing—poor thing, but our own" (lines 55–56) is adapted from Shakespeare's "a poor . . . thing, sir, but mine own." The change from Shakespeare's singular pronoun to the author's plural pronoun is made in order to

A. avoid the use of the first person
B. include all readers of this passage who prefer literature
C. avoid direct quotation of Shakespeare and the appearance of comparing this work to his
D. suggest that the number of readers is as great as the number of moviegoers
E. avoid overpraising literature compared to films, which are more popular

7. The sentences "The written word is weak" (line 1), "An ordinary reader . . . and softs" (lines 12–15), and "The printed word . . . should not" (lines 37–39) have in common that they

A. concede a limitation of the written word
B. assert the superiority of film to writing
C. do not represent the genuine feelings of the author
D. deliberately overstate the author's ideas
E. are all ironic

8. With which of the following statements would the author of this passage be most likely to disagree?

A. Life is more exciting than writing.
B. People who dislike reading should not be forced to read.
C. Good books will appeal to those who do not like to read as well as to those who do.
D. The power of film is irresistible.
E. Novels written for people who hate reading are folly.

9. The passage in its entirety is best described as about the

A. superiority of the art of writing to the art of film
B. difficulties of being a writer
C. differences between writing and film
D. public's preference of film to literature
E. similarities and differences of the novel and the film

10. Which of the following best describes the organization of the passage?

A. a five-paragraph essay in which the first and last paragraphs are general and the second, third, and fourth paragraphs are specific
B. a five-paragraph essay in which the first two paragraphs describe writing, the third and fourth paragraphs describe film, and the last paragraph describes both writing and film
C. five paragraphs, with the first about literature; the second about butterflies; and the third, fourth, and fifth about the superiority of film
D. five paragraphs, with the first and last about writing, the third about film, and the fourth about both film and writing
E. five paragraphs of comparison and contrast, with the comparison in the first and last paragraphs and the contrast in the second, third, and fourth

11. All of the following rhetorical devices are used in the passage EXCEPT

A. personal anecdote
B. extended analogy
C. short sentence
D. colloquialism
E. inverted syntax

Questions 12–23 refer to the following passage from an 18th-century political pamphlet.

These are the times that try men's souls. The summer soldier and the sunshine patriot will, in this crisis, shrink from the service of their country; but he that stands it now deserves the (5) love and thanks of man and woman. Tyranny, like hell, is not easily conquered; yet we have this consolation with us, that the harder the conflict, the more glorious the triumph. What we obtain too cheap, we esteem too lightly: it is dearness (10) only that gives everything its value. Heaven knows how to put a proper price upon its goods; and it would be strange indeed if so celestial an article as freedom should not be highly rated. Britain, with an army to enforce her tyranny, has (15) declared that she has a right not only to tax, but "to bind us in all cases whatsoever," and if being bound in that manner is not slavery, then is there not such a thing as slavery upon earth. Even the expression is impious; for so unlimited a power (20) can belong only to God. . . .

I have as little superstition in me as any man living, but my secret opinion has ever been, and still is, that God Almighty will not give up a people to military destruction, or leave them (25) unsupportedly to perish, who have so earnestly and so repeatedly sought to avoid the calamities of war, by every decent method which wisdom could invent. Neither have I so much of the infidel in me as to suppose that He has (30) relinquished the government of the world, and given us up to the care of devils; and as I do not, I cannot see on what grounds the King of Britain can look up to heaven for help against us: a common murderer, a highwayman, or a (35) housebreaker has as good a pretense as he. . . .

I once felt all that kind of anger, which a man ought to feel, against the mean principles that are held by the Tories: a noted one, who kept a tavern at Amboy, was standing at his door, with (40) as pretty a child in his hand, about eight or nine years old, as I ever saw, and after speaking his mind as freely as he thought was prudent, finished with this unfatherly expression, "Well!

Give me peace in my day." Not a man lives on the (45) continent but fully believes that a separation must some time or other finally take place, and a generous parent should have said, "If there must be trouble, let it be in my day, that my children may have peace"; and this single reflection, well (50) applied, is sufficient to awaken every man to duty. Not a place upon earth might be so happy as America. Her situation is remote from all the wrangling world, and she has nothing to do but to trade with them. A man can distinguish (55) himself between temper and principle, and I am as confident, as I am that God governs the world, that America will never be happy till she gets clear of foreign dominion. Wars, without ceasing, will break out till that period arrives, and the (60) continent must in the end be conqueror; for though the flame of liberty may sometimes cease to shine, the coal can never expire. . . .

The heart that feels not now is dead: the blood of his children will curse his cowardice who shrinks (65) back at a time when a little might have saved the whole, and made them happy. I love the man that can smile in trouble, that can gather strength from distress, and grow brave by reflection. 'Tis the business of little minds to shrink; but he whose (70) heart is firm, and whose conscience approves his conduct, will pursue his principles unto death. My own line of reasoning is to myself as straight and clear as a ray of light. Not all the treasures of the world so far as I believe, could have induced me to (75) support an offensive war, for I think it murder; but if a thief breaks into my house, burns and destroys my property, and kills or threatens to kill me, or those that are in it, and to "bind me in all cases whatsoever" to his absolute will, am I to suffer it? (80) What signifies it to me, whether he who does it is a king or a common man; my countryman or not my countryman; whether it be done by an individual villain, or an army of them? If we reason to the root of things we shall find no (85) difference; neither can any just cause be assigned why we should punish in the one case and pardon in the other.

12. When the author addresses the "summer soldier and the sunshine patriot" (line 2), he is most likely referring to

A. the American army's reserve soldiers
B. those citizens who are infidels
C. the British soldiers stationed in America
D. those who support the revolution only when convenient
E. the government's specialized forces

13. The author's style relies on heavy use of

    A. allegory and didactic rhetoric

    B. aphorism and emotional appeal

    C. symbolism and biblical allusion

    D. paradox and invective

    E. historical background and illustration

14. Which of the following does the author NOT group with the others?

    A. common murderer

    B. highwayman

    C. housebreaker

    D. king

    E. coward

15. The "God" that the author refers to can be characterized as

    A. principled

    B. vexed

    C. indifferent

    D. contemplative

    E. pernicious

16. According to the author, freedom should be considered

    A. that which will vanquish cowards

    B. one of the most valuable commodities in heaven

    C. that which can be achieved quickly

    D. desirable but never attainable

    E. an issue only governments should negotiate

17. The author's purpose in using the phrase "with as pretty a child in his hand . . . as I ever saw" (lines 39–41) is most likely to

    A. prove that the tavern owner has a family

    B. display his anger

    C. add emotional appeal to his argument

    D. symbolically increase the tavern owner's evil

    E. dismiss traditional values

18. Which of the following would NOT be considered an aphorism?

    A. "Tyranny, like hell, is not easily conquered . . ." (lines 5–6)

    B. ". . . the harder the conflict, the more glorious the triumph" (lines 7–8)

    C. "What we obtain too cheap, we esteem too lightly . . ." (lines 8–9)

    D. "Not a place upon earth might be so happy as America" (lines 51–52)

    E. ". . . though the flame of liberty may sometimes cease to shine, the coal can never expire . . ." (lines 61–62)

19. As seen in lines 51–62, the author feels that, in an ideal world, America's role in relation to the rest of the world would be

    A. only one of commerce

    B. one of aggressive self-assertion

    C. more exalted than Britain's

    D. sanctified by God

    E. one of complete isolationism

20. The rhetorical mode that the author uses can best be classified as

    A. explanation

    B. description

    C. narration

    D. illustration

    E. persuasion

21. Which of the following best describes the rhetorical purpose in the sentence "The heart that feels . . . made them happy" (lines 63–66)?

    A. It suggests that children should also join the revolution.

    B. It plants fear in people's hearts.

    C. It pleads to the king once again for liberty.

    D. It encourages retreat in the face of superior force.

    E. It encourages support by an emotional appeal to all American patriots.

22. All of the following rhetorical devices are particularly effective in the last paragraph of the passage EXCEPT

    A. aphorism

    B. simile

    C. deliberate ambivalence

    D. parallel construction

    E. analogy

23. The main rhetorical purpose in the passage can best be described as

    A. a summons for peace and rational thinking
    B. overemotional preaching for equality
    C. a series of unwarranted conclusions
    D. a patriotic call to duty and action
    E. a demand for immediate liberty

Questions 24–36 refer to the following passage.

When Charles Lamb was seven years old in 1782, his father's employer, Samuel Salt, obtained for him admission to the famous school in London for poor boys, called Christ's Hospital. In the same year, young Samuel Taylor Coleridge also came to the school, and between the future author of "The Rime of the Ancient Mariner" and the gentle, nervous, stammering Charles Lamb there sprang up a friendship that lasted more than 50 years and was one of the happiest influences in their lives. Lamb wrote of the old schooldays in Christ's Hospital Five-and-Thirty Years Ago[1]. For the sake of innocent mystification, he chose to write as if he were Coleridge.

    In Mr. Lamb's "Works,"[2] published a year or two since, I find a magnificent eulogy on my old school, such as it was, or now appears to him to have been, between the year 1782 and 1789. It
(5) happens, very oddly, that my own standing at Christ's was nearly corresponding with his; and, with all gratitude to him for his enthusiasm for the cloisters, I think he has contrived to bring together whatever can be said in praise of them,
(10) dropping all the other side of the argument most ingeniously.

    I remember L. at school; and can well recollect that he had some particular advantages, which I and others of his schoolfellows had not. His
(15) friends lived in town, and were near at hand; and he had the privilege of going to see them, almost as often as he wished, through some invidious distinction, which was denied to us. The present worthy sub-treasurer to the Inner Temple[3] can
(20) explain how that happened. He had his tea and hot rolls in a morning, while we were battening upon our quarter of a penny loaf—our *crug*—moistened with attenuated small beer, in wooden piggins, smacking of the pitched leathern jack it
(25) was poured from. Our Monday's milk porritch, blue and tasteless, and the pease soup of Saturday, coarse and choking, were enriched for him with a slice of "extraordinary bread and butter," from the hot-loaf of the Temple. The
(30) Wednesday's mess of millet, somewhat less than repugnant—(we had three banyan[4] to four meat

days in the week)—was endeared to his palate with a lump of double-refined, and a smack of ginger (to make it go down the more glibly) or
(35) the fragrant cinnamon. In lieu of our *half-pickled* Sundays, or *quite fresh* boiled beef on Thursdays (strong as *caro equina*[5]), with detestable marigolds floating in the pail to poison the broth—our scanty mutton scrags on Fridays—
(40) and rather more savoury, but grudging, portions of the same flesh, rotten-roasted or rare, on the Tuesdays (the only dish which excited our appetites, and disappointed our stomachs, in almost equal proportion)—he had his hot plate
(45) of roast veal, or the same tempting griskin (exotics unknown to our palates), cooked in the paternal kitchen (a great thing), and brought him daily by his maid or aunt! I remember the good old relative[6] (in whom love forbade pride)
(50) squatting down upon some odd stone in a by-nook of the cloisters, disclosing the viands (of higher regale[7] than those cates[8] which the ravens ministered to the Tishbite[9]); and the contending passion of L. at the unfolding. There was love for
(55) the bringer; shame for the thing brought, and the manner of its bringing; sympathy for those who were too many to share in it; and, at top of all, hunger (eldest, strongest of the passions!) predominant, breaking down the stony fences of
(60) shame, and awkwardness, and a troubling over-consciousness.

[1] *London Magazine, November 1820.*

[2] The first collection of Lamb's writings representing this period of his literary work was published in 1818. Among this material was an essay entitled "Recollections of Christ's Hospital," in which Lamb paid a fine tribute of praise to this charitable institution for the education and support of the young. In the present essay, however, he presents another side of the picture, showing the grievances, real and imaginary, of the scholars, together with some of the humorous aspects of the regulations and traditions of the school. Coleridge, in *Biographia Literaria*, has drawn a companion picture of the better side of Christ's Hospital discipline, and Leigh Hunt, who was a scholar two or three years later than Lamb, has also described in his *Autobiography* the life and ideals of the famous school.

[3] Randall Norris, a family friend

[4] Vegetable days

[5] Horseflesh

[6] In a letter to Coleridge, January 1797, Lamb writes, "My poor old aunt, whom you have seen, the kindest, goodest creature to me when I was at school; who used to toddle there to bring me good things, when I, school-boy like, only despised her for it, and used to be ashamed to see her come and sit herself

down on the old coal-hole steps as you went into the grammar school, and open her apron, and bring out her bason, with some nice thing she had caused to be saved for me."

[7] Banquet

[8] Dainties

[9] The prophet Elijah; see I Kings xvii

24. In the first paragraph, the speaker suggests that

    A. Lamb's recollections are an accurate depiction of the school

    B. Lamb has chosen to ignore negative memories from his school years

    C. Coleridge remembers the school years exactly as Lamb did

    D. Coleridge would write a very different reminiscence of his school days

    E. Coleridge concurs with the accuracy of Lamb's account of the school

25. The speaker implies that the specific reason Lamb enjoyed the privilege of visiting his friends in town was because

    A. his aunt secured him special favors

    B. he was a favorite of the schoolmaster

    C. Lamb's affluent financial standing influenced someone at the Inner Temple

    D. he crept off the school grounds against the rules

    E. Lamb's friends gave special treatment to the sub-treasurer

26. The speaker's description of Lamb's food serves to

    A. juxtapose Lamb's relative wealth with the other boys' poverty

    B. enhance fond memories in all of the boys

    C. explain why his aunt had to deliver extra victuals

    D. exemplify how superior he felt toward the other boys

    E. dispel common myths about British boarding schools

27. The passage contains all of the following EXCEPT

    A. alliteration

    B. complex sentences with clarifying clauses

    C. revolting gustatory imagery

    D. extraneous incidental remarks

    E. historical allusion

28. The italics in *"quite fresh"* (line 36) serve the rhetorical purpose of

    A. establishing how carefully the boys' meals were prepared

    B. reinforcing the speaker's genuine feelings

    C. carefully balancing the positive and negative aspects of their meals

    D. emphasizing how stale the beef was

    E. highlighting the need for Lamb's aunt to bring food

29. The image of the "marigolds floating" (line 38) emphasizes

    A. the beauty and comfort that nature can offer in uncomfortable situations

    B. a feeble attempt to hide the horror of the meal

    C. a pleasant table complement to the meal

    D. the cook's creativity in presenting meals

    E. the need to cover ugliness in the world with natural images

30. The speaker's rhetorical purpose in describing the food of every day of the week is to

    A. emphasize the consistency of the inedible food

    B. ensure a thorough and complete picture of daily life

    C. contradict the idea that the boys were poorly fed

    D. establish Lamb's superior social standing

    E. intimate the inequities of the school system

31. The "contending passion of L." (lines 53–54) suggests that Lamb

    A. showed unbounded enthusiasm for his aunt's gifts

    B. willingly shared the food with those less fortunate

    C. demonstrated indisputable affection for his aunt

    D. suffered a conflict between embarrassment and affection that his aunt's actions caused

    E. knew all the students were aware of his conflicted feelings

32. The description of Lamb's aunt implies that

    A. her love for her nephew outweighed her embarrassment at crouching and waiting for him with food in her apron

    B. she brought her nephew food solely because the school was too stingy to feed him well

    C. she provided him with the food his own family could not afford

    D. she wished she could have brought food for all the boys

    E. she had made previous arrangements with the school officials to deliver Lamb's food

33. Which of the following emotions does Lamb NOT experience when his aunt brings him gifts?

    A. ignominy
    B. affection
    C. compassion
    D. discomfiture
    E. antipathy

34. Lamb's letter to Coleridge (footnote #6) implies that

    A. he remains steadfast in his reaction to her deeds

    B. he and his aunt were only close while he was at school

    C. Lamb and Coleridge both enjoyed the victuals that his aunt delivered

    D. he now better understands his conflicted reactions to her kindness

    E. Coleridge had inquired about Lamb's behavior toward his aunt

35. Footnote #2 presents the perception that

    A. the three authors collaborated on their memoirs

    B. Leigh Hunt disagrees with Lamb's and Coleridge's recollections

    C. the three authors mainly recall the benefits of attending Christ's Hospital

    D. the three authors were equally mistreated while at school

    E. Coleridge and Hunt had more advantages while at school

36. Which of the following phrases most clearly contradicts the rhetorical purpose of the passage as a whole?

    A. "... my old school, such as it was, or now appears to him to have been ..." (lines 2–4)

    B. "... he has contrived to bring together whatever can be said in praise ..." (lines 8–9)

    C. "... can well recollect that he had some particular advantages ..." (lines 12–13)

    D. "... (the only dish which excited our appetites, and disappointed our stomachs, in almost equal proportion) ..." (lines 42–44)

    E. "... the good old relative (in whom love forbade pride) ..." (lines 48–49)

Questions 37–46 refer to the following passage from a 17th-century essay.

Studies serve for delight, for ornament, and for ability. Their chief use for delight is in privateness and retiring; for ornament, is in discourse; and for ability, is in the judgment and
(5) disposition of business; for expert men can execute, and perhaps judge of particulars, one by one; but the general counsels, and the plots and marshaling of affairs come best from those that are learned. To spend too much time in
(10) studies is sloth; to use them too much for ornament is affectation; to make judgment wholly by their rules is the humor of a scholar. They perfect nature, and are perfected by experience; for natural abilities are like natural
(15) plants, that need pruning by study; and studies themselves do give forth directions too much at large, except they be bounded in by experience. Crafty men condemn studies, simple men admire them, and wise men use them; for they teach not
(20) their own use; but that is a wisdom without them and above them, won by observation. Read not to contradict and confute, nor to believe and take for granted, nor to find talk and discourse, but to weigh and consider. Some books are to be
(25) tasted, others to be swallowed, and some few to be chewed and digested; that is, some books are to be read only in parts; others to be read but not curiously; and some few to be read wholly, and with diligence and attention. Some books
(30) also may be read by deputy, and extracts made of them by others; but that would be only in the less important arguments and the meaner sort of books; else distilled books are, like common

(35) distilled water, flashy things. Reading maketh a full man; conference a ready man; and writing an exact man. And therefore, if a man write little, he had need have a great memory; if he confer little, he had need have a present wit; and if he read little, he had need have much cunning,
(40) to seem to know that he doth not. Histories make men wise; poets, witty; the mathematics, subtle; natural philosophy, deep; moral, grave; logic and rhetoric, able to contend: *Abeunt studia in mores!*[1] Nay, there is no stand or
(45) impediment in the wit but may be wrought out by fit studies; like as diseases of the body may have appropriate exercises. Bowling is good for the stone and reins, shooting for the lungs and breast, gently walking for the stomach, riding
(50) for the head, and the like. So if a man's wit be wandering, let him study the mathematics; for in demonstrations, if his wit be called away never so little, he must begin again. If his wit be not apt to distinguish or find differences, let him
(55) study the schoolmen; for they are *cymini sectores!*[2] If he be not apt to beat over matters, and to call up one thing to prove and illustrate another, let him study the lawyers' cases. So every aspect of the mind may have a special receipt.

[1] "Studies form character," Ovid.

[2] Literally, "cutters of cumin seed," or hair splitters.

37. The audience that might benefit the most from the author's ideas is likely to be those who

   A.   have returned to university study
   B.   think studies are unnecessary
   C.   are poor readers
   D.   already have university degrees
   E.   are successful in business

38. Within context, the phrase "the humor of a scholar" (line 12) refers to

   A.   the mirth that scholars enjoy
   B.   the benefit of proper studies
   C.   the excuse for improper studies
   D.   the aspiration of scholars
   E.   the potential mistakes of scholars

39. According to the passage, reading is beneficial when supplemented by

   A.   academic necessity
   B.   literary criticism
   C.   personal experience
   D.   brief discussion
   E.   historical background

40. A prominent stylistic characteristic of the sentence "Read not to . . . weigh and consider" (lines 21–24) is

   A.   understatement
   B.   metaphor
   C.   hyperbole
   D.   parallel construction
   E.   analogy

41. The sentence "They perfect nature . . . bounded in by experience" (lines 13–17) most probably means that

   A.   a professor should emphasize reading over personal experience
   B.   the message in some books is too complex to be understood by the common person
   C.   the ideas in books are readily accessible to one who reads widely
   D.   people misspend valuable time in the pursuit of evasive knowledge
   E.   learning and experience must balance and complement each other

42. In context, the word "observation" (line 21) is analogous to

   A.   "experience" (line 14)
   B.   "directions" (line 16)
   C.   "studies" (line 18)
   D.   "wisdom" (line 20)
   E.   "believe" (line 22)

43. What paradox about studies does the speaker present?

   A.   Crafty men may be tempted to ignore studies.
   B.   Those who are too consumed by studies become indolent.
   C.   Some books can never be completely understood.
   D.   Not all books are approached the same way.
   E.   Some "defects of the mind" can never be remedied.

44. Which of the following does the speaker imply is the greatest error a reader can commit?

A. reading voluminously
B. reading only excerpts
C. reading only what professors recommend
D. reading without thinking
E. reading only for pleasure

45. In context, the phrase "not curiously" (line 28) means

A. with questions in mind
B. with great interest
C. without much scrutiny
D. without strong background
E. with personal interpretation

46. Stylistically, the sentence "Reading maketh a full man . . . writing an exact man" (lines 34–36) is closest in structure to

A. "To spend too much time . . . the humor of a scholar" (lines 9–12)
B. "They perfect nature, and are perfected by experience . . . bounded in by experience" (lines 13–17)
C. "Some books also may be read by deputy . . . flashy things" (lines 29–34)
D. "Nay, there is no stand or impediment . . . exercises" (lines 44–47)
E. "So if a man's wit be wandering . . . begin again" (lines 50–53)

Questions 47–55 refer to the following passage from a 19th-century travel memoir.

Animals talk to each other, of course. There can be no question about that; but I suppose there are very few people who can understand them. I never knew but one man who could. I
(5) knew he could, however, because he told me so himself. He was a middle-aged, simple-hearted miner who had lived in a lonely corner of California, among the woods and mountains, a good many years, and had studied the ways of
(10) his only neighbors, the beasts and the birds, until he believed he could accurately translate any remark which they made. This was Jim Baker. According to Jim Baker, some animals have only a limited education, and use only very simple
(15) words, and scarcely ever a comparison or a flowery figure; whereas, certain animals have a large vocabulary, a fine command of language and a ready and fluent delivery; consequently these latter talk a great deal; they like it; they are
(20) conscious of their talent, and they enjoy "showing off." Baker said, that after long and careful observation, he had come to the conclusion that the blue jays were the best talkers he had found among the birds and beasts. Said he:—
(25) "There's more *to* a blue jay than any other creature. He has got more moods, and more different kinds of feelings than any other creature; and mind you, whatever a blue jay feels, he can put into language. And no commonplace
(30) language, either, but rattling, out-and-out book-talk—and bristling with metaphor, too—just bristling! And as for command of language—why *you* never see a blue jay stuck for a word. No man ever did. They just boil out of him! And another
(35) thing: I've noticed a good deal, and there's no bird, or cow, or anything that uses as good grammar as a blue jay. You may say a cat uses good grammar. Well, a cat does—but you let a cat get excited, once; you let a cat get to pulling fur
(40) with another cat on a shed, nights, and you'll hear grammar that will give you the lockjaw. Ignorant people think it's the *noise* which fighting cats make that is so aggravating, but it ain't so; it's the sickening grammar they use. Now I've never
(45) heard a jay use bad grammar but very seldom; and when they do, they are as ashamed as a human; they shut right down and leave.
"You may call a jay a bird. Well, so he is, in a measure—because he's got feathers on him, and
(50) don't belong to no church perhaps; but otherwise he is just as much a human as you be. And I'll tell you for why. A jay's gifts, and instincts, and feelings, and interests, cover the whole ground. A jay hasn't got any more principle than a
(55) Congressman. A jay will lie, a jay will steal, a jay will deceive, a jay will betray; and four times out of five, a jay will go back on his solemnest promise. The sacredness of an obligation is a thing which you can't cram into no blue jay's
(60) head. Now on top of all this, there's another thing: a jay can out-swear any gentleman in the mines. You think a cat can swear. Well, a cat can; but you give a blue jay a subject that calls for his reserve-powers, and where is your cat? Don't talk
(65) to *me*—I know too much about this thing. And there's yet another thing: in the one little particular of scolding—just good, clean, out-and-out scolding—a blue jay can lay over anything, human or divine. Yes, sir, a jay is
(70) everything that a man is. A jay can cry, a jay can laugh, a jay can feel shame, a jay can reason and plan and discuss, a jay likes gossip and scandal, a

jay has got a sense of humor, a jay knows when he is an ass just as well as you do—maybe better."

47. Which of the following best describes the organization of the first paragraph?

    A. It presents a claim and provides examples to prove it.

    B. It begins with an assertion, followed by an introduction to Jim Baker and his observations, and then it presents Baker's thesis.

    C. It transitions from general to specific, introducing animals' ability to talk and focuses at the end on the author's idea about blue jays.

    D. It states a hypothesis about animals' communication and establishes a metaphorical connection to humanity.

    E. It claims that animals talk to each other and then clarifies the differences in their communication.

48. Which of the following is an unstated assumption embedded in the fourth sentence, "I knew . . . so himself" (lines 4–6)?

    A. Careful observation of birds can reveal their personalities.

    B. Jim Baker's lifestyle puts him in a good position to study birds.

    C. People who live alone know themselves well.

    D. Jim Baker is confident of his ability to understand animals' language.

    E. Jim Baker's accuracy might be suspect.

49. One purpose of the fifth sentence in the first paragraph, "He was . . . they made" (lines 6–12), is to

    A. suggest Jim Baker prefers the company of animals over humanity

    B. discount other people's theories about animal communication

    C. reinforce common stereotypes about miners

    D. establish Jim Baker's credentials as an observer of animal communication

    E. suggest Jim Baker is more qualified than anyone else to comment on animal behavior

50. Which of the following is NOT an idea stated or implied by Jim Baker?

    A. Blue jays are the most eloquent creatures.

    B. Cats are more grammatically correct when they are calm.

    C. Congressmen are more analogous to blue jays than they are to cats.

    D. Some animals are very fluent; others are more reticent.

    E. Animals' education contributes to their eloquence with language.

51. Jim Baker's diction can best be described as a series of

    A. allegorical musings

    B. hyperbolic invectives

    C. didactic aphorisms

    D. paradoxical comparisons

    E. colloquial ramblings

52. The last sentence, "A jay can . . . maybe better" (lines 70–74), contains which of the following stylistic features?

    A. parallel constructions

    B. multiple predicate nominatives

    C. metaphorical conceits

    D. a series of understatements

    E. multiple subordinate clauses

53. Which of the following identifies an irony between Jim Baker and blue jays?

    A. Blue jays are more talkative than Jim Baker.

    B. Blue jays apparently have better grammar than Jim Baker.

    C. Both can give a "good, clean, out-and-out scolding" (lines 67–68) when deserved.

    D. Jim Baker is more observational than blue jays.

    E. Blue jays' emotions are less varied than Jim Baker's.

54. It can be inferred that the author's rhetorical purpose in this passage is to

    A. show that humans should learn lessons from animals

    B. demonstrate that "simple-hearted" loners (line 6) understand animals better than they understand other people

    C. suggest subtle and humorous analogies about humanity

    D. establish how animals communicate with each other

    E. criticize politicians for being unprincipled

55. The last phrase of the passage, "a jay knows when he is an ass just as well as you do—maybe better" (lines 73–74) is intended to imply that

    A. people are not always aware when they are making a fool of themselves

    B. blue jays are more introspective than people

    C. people are foolish more often than blue jays

    D. blue jays are more honest than people

    E. blue jays are always aware when they are being foolish

IF YOU FINISH BEFORE TIME IS CALLED, CHECK YOUR WORK ON THIS SECTION ONLY. DO NOT WORK ON ANY OTHER SECTION IN THE TEST.

STOP

Section II: Free-Response Questions

Time: 2 hours, 15 minutes

3 questions

Question 1

(Suggested writing time—40 minutes. This question counts for one-third of the total free-response section score.)

The media has been influential in the world's reaction to natural disasters, terrorist attacks, and school shootings since the advent of radio and television. What exactly has this influence been and how has it affected the number of people who help or care for the victims of these disasters? Has it encouraged people to help or has it merely shown them that they are the lucky ones who were not involved in each particular disaster?

Considering the influence of the media during disasters, read the following six sources (including any introductory information) carefully. Then, synthesizing at least three of the sources for support, write a coherent, well-written essay in which you take a position that defends, challenges, or qualifies the notion that the media has had a positive influence on the effects of disasters.

Always remember that your argument should be central; the sources should be used to support this argument. Therefore, avoid merely summarizing sources. Clearly cite which sources you use, both directly and indirectly. Refer to the sources by their titles (Source A, Source B, etc.) or by the descriptions in parentheses.

    Source A (ISDR)

    Source B (Cockburn)

    Source C (Floroiu)

    Source D (Maron)

    Source E (Pujol)

    Source F (Shah)

Source A

"ISDR Joins Asia-Pacific Broadcasting Union to boost information, education on disasters." *UNESCAP News Services,* 10 June 2005. Web. 25 Sept. 2005.

The following excerpt is from an online article that introduces new radio and television programs that will educate and prepare people for natural disasters in the Asia-Pacific countries.

ISDR (International Strategy for Disaster Reduction) considers media an essential partner to enhance public safety and adverse impacts of natural disasters. "Media are not only part of the early warning chain; they are the best channel to prepare communities for disasters. They can help educate people on the need to reduce risk by regularly informing on the hazards and social vulnerabilities that may lead to disasters. Media also play an important role in convincing Governments and citizens to invest in disaster reduction," says Salvano Briceño, Director of the ISDR secretariat.

"It is just the beginning of a new collaboration. We are planning to promote educational programmes like the ones we are already developing in Africa, in Latin America and the Caribbean, and incite broadcasters to invest more in disaster reduction. Education and preparedness are the key to reduce the number of affected people by natural hazards every year. If people know what to do, they can save their own life. Education on disasters should be part of the school's curriculum like it is in Japan and Cuba, for instance. The more people are aware of the risks they face, the better chance they have to save their lives when hazards strike," says Mr. Briceño.

"Broadcasters have a responsibility to educate people and raise their awareness of the dangers of natural disasters. They can do this by airing public service announcements, producing special programmes to mark the anniversaries of previous disasters and creating other content," says David Astley, Secretary-General of the ABU. "The ABU is well positioned to both coordinate the improvement of emergency warning systems through television and radio among broadcasters across the Pacific region and to assist in the development of content designed to educate audiences in advance on how to respond in the event of emergencies and natural disasters."

Source B

Cockburn, Patrick. "Catastrophe on camera: Why media coverage of natural disasters is flawed." *The Independent.* 20 Jan. 2011. Web. 29 Nov. 2017.

The following is an excerpted online article discussing the accuracy and impact of media coverage of disasters.

Media coverage of natural disasters—floods, blizzards, hurricanes, earthquakes and volcanoes—is largely accepted as an accurate reflection of what really happened. But in my experience, the opposite is true: the reporting of cataclysms or lesser disasters is often wildly misleading. Stereotyping is common: whichever the country involved, there are similar images of wrecked bridges, half-submerged houses and last-minute rescues.

The scale of the disaster is difficult to assess from news coverage: are we seeing or reading about the worst examples of devastation, or are these the norm? Are victims in the hundreds or the millions? Most usually the extent of the damage and the number of casualties are exaggerated, particularly in the developed world. I remember covering floods on the Mississippi in the 1990s and watching as a wall of cameras and cameramen focused on a well-built house in a St Louis suburb which was slowly disappearing under the water. But just a few hundred yards away, ignored by all the cameramen, a long line of gamblers was walking unconcernedly along wooden walkways to board a river boat casino.

The reporting of natural disasters appears easy, but it is difficult to do convincingly. Over the past year, a series of calamities or, at the least, surprisingly severe weather, has dominated the news for weeks at a time. [In 2010], Haiti had its worst earthquake in 200 years, which killed more than 250,000 people. In [2010], exceptionally heavy monsoon rain turned the Indus river into a vast dangerous lake, forcing millions of Pakistani farmers to flee their homes and take refuge on the embankments. Less devastating was unexpectedly heavy snow in Britain in December and the severe blizzard which struck New York at Christmas. In the first half of January [2011], the news was once again being led by climatic disasters: the floods in Queensland and the mudslides in Brazil.

All these events are dramatic and should be interesting, but the reporting of them is frequently repetitious and dull. This may be partly because news coverage of all disasters, actual or forecast, is delivered in similarly apocalyptic tones. Particularly in the US, weather dramas are so frequently predicted that dire warnings have long lost their impact. This helps to explain why so many people are caught by surprise when there is a real catastrophe, such as Hurricane Katrina breaking the levees protecting New Orleans in 2005 and flooding the city. US television news never admits the role it plays in ensuring that nobody takes warnings of floods and hurricanes too seriously because they have heard it all before.

Once the initial drama of a disaster is over, coverage frequently dribbles away because nothing new is happening. I remember how bizarre the foreign editor of the newspaper I was then working for found it that I should want to go back to Florida a month after Hurricane Andrew to see what had happened to the victims. "I am not sure that is still a story," he responded sourly to what he evidently considered a highly eccentric request.

Source C

Floroiu, Ruxandra. "Alerting America: Effective Risk Communication." Washington, D.C.: The National Academic Press, 2002. Print.

The following excerpt is from a book discussing communications to the public about the risk associated with various kinds of hazards and disasters.

The sixth Natural Disasters Roundtable (NDR) forum, "Alerting America: Effective Risk Communication," was held on October 31, 2002, at the National Academies in Washington, D.C. Approximately 140 participants from government, academia, business, industry and civil society attended the one-day forum. The objective of the forum was to provide the opportunity for researchers, decision-makers, practitioners and other stakeholders to exchange views and perspectives on communicating risk information to the public about various kinds of hazards and disasters.

Effective and consistent risk communication is vital to disaster reduction and response. Formal and informal groups and the media are important channels for risk communication. And technology is playing an increasingly crucial role, making it possible to track potential disaster agents, alert authorities, and educate and warn the public in a more timely manner. However, underlying the public response to risk communication are other factors such as social structure, norms, resources and risk perception, which are embedded in past experience and group interaction.

Source D

Maron, Dina Fine. "How Social Media Is Changing Disaster Response." *Scientific American.* 7 June 2017. Web. 12 Sept. 2017.

The following excerpt examines the degree to which social media has helped improve disaster response and offers suggestions for improvement.

The Federal Emergency Management Agency (FEMA) wrote in its 2013 National Preparedness report that during and immediately following Hurricane Sandy, "users sent more than 20 million Sandy-related Twitter posts despite the loss of cell phone service during the peak of the storm." New Jersey's largest utility company, PSE&G, said at the subcommittee hearing that during Sandy they staffed up their Twitter feeds and used them to send word about the daily locations of their giant tents and generators. "At one point during the storm, we sent so many tweets to alert customers, we exceeded the [number] of tweets allowed per day," PSE&G'S Jorge Cardenas, vice president of asset management and centralized services, told the subcommittee.

Following the Boston Marathon bombings, one quarter of Americans reportedly looked to Facebook, Twitter and other social networking sites for information, according to The Pew Research Center. The sites also formed a key part of the information cycle: when the Boston Police Department posted its final "CAPTURED!!!" tweet of the manhunt, more than 140,000 people retweeted it. Community members via a simple Google document offered strangers lodging, food or a hot shower when roads and hotels were closed.

Each disaster sparks its own complex web of fast-paced information exchange. That's a good thing, says Mark Keim, associate director for science in the Office of Environmental Health Emergencies; it can both improve disaster response and allow affected populations to take control of their situation as well as feel empowered.

Drawing up an effective social media strategy and tweaking it to fit an emergency, however, is a crucial part of preparedness planning, says disaster sociologist Jeannette Sutton, a senior research scientist at the University of Colorado at Colorado Springs who studies social media in crises and disaster. For the Boston Marathon incident, she found no consistent hashtag on Twitter, which can make tracking relevant information difficult. Even searching for the word "Boston" may fall short, she says, because it could lead to unrelated matter like Boston tourism or fail to capture relevant tweets that did not include the word Boston.

As part of disaster preparedness, she says, it would be useful to teach the public how to use social media effectively, how to get information from the Web and also how to put out useful information. "Tweets flow so quickly it's like a fire hose where you're trying to extract bits of information that are relevant."

Source E

Pujol, Frances. "Fukushima as a Chernobyl Nuclear Disaster: Media References by Countries." *Reputation-Metrics.* Newsreputation.com. 16 March 2011. Web. 16 Sept. 2017.

The Fukushima Daiichi Nuclear Power Plant disaster was an energy accident that was primarily initiated by the tsunami following the Tōhoku earthquake on March 11, 2011. The following charts present how much of the news coverage about the Fukushima disaster referred to the previous nuclear disaster at Chernobyl, which had occurred in 1986 in the Ukrainian Soviet Socialist Republic of the Soviet Union (USSR). Each chart explores individual countries in different locations of the world.

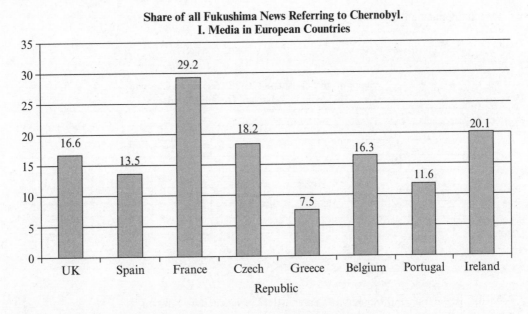

**Share of all Fukushima News Referring to Chernobyl.
I. Media in European Countries**

Media, Reputation and Intangibles Center, MRI Universidad de Navarra

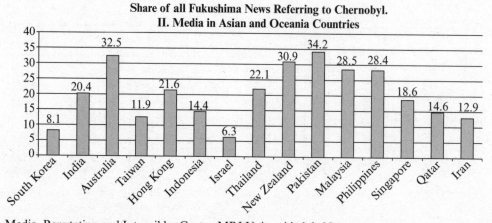

Share of all Fukushima News Referring to Chernobyl.
II. Media in American Countries

Media, Reputation and Intangibles Center, MRI Universidad de Navarra

Share of all Fukushima News Referring to Chernobyl.
II. Media in Asian and Oceania Countries

Media, Reputation and Intangibles Center, MRI Universidad de Navarra

---

Source F

Shah, Anup. "Hurricane Katrina—Rejuvenating the Mainstream Media?" *Global Issues.* 9 Sept. 2005. Web. 12 Dec. 2005.

The following is an online article about the effects of Hurricane Katrina on the media.

It has not gone unnoticed by many that the American mainstream media has become more critical of power in the wake of Hurricane Katrina and the poor response of authorities and George Bush in its aftermath. Many have wondered if this finally means the mainstream media will do what it is supposed to: provide a quality service, critiquing claims rather than simply reporting them, and fundamentally, allowing people to make informed decisions.

Media watchdog *FAIR* is guarded in its optimism, noting that not all reporting has been that good. In addition:

In the aftermath of Hurricane Katrina, a more aggressive press corps seems to have caught the White House public relations team off-balance—a situation the White House has not had to face very often in the last five years. Many might wonder why it took reporters so long; as Eric Boehlert wrote in Salon.com (9/7/05):

"It's hard to decide which is more troubling: that it took the national press corps five years to summon up enough courage to report, without apology, that what the Bush administration says and does are often two different things, or that it took the sight of bodies floating facedown in the streets of New Orleans to trigger a change in the press's behavior."

Question 2

(Suggested writing time—40 minutes. This question counts for one-third of the total free-response section score.)

In the following two passages, Virginia Woolf describes two different meals she was served during a university visit. The first meal was served at the men's college, while the second meal was served at the women's college.

Read the two passages carefully, then write an essay in which you analyze Woolf's underlying attitude toward women's place in society as she describes the two meals. Discuss how rhetorical strategies such as narrative structure, manipulation of language, selection of detail, and tone contribute to the overall effect of the passages.

Passage 1

It is a curious fact that novelists have a way of making us believe that luncheon parties are invariably memorable for something very witty that was said, or for something very wise that was done. But they seldom spare a word for what was eaten. It is part of the novelist's convention not to mention soup and salmon and ducklings, as if soup and a salmon and ducklings were of no importance whatsoever, as if nobody ever smoked a cigar or drank a glass of wine. Here, however, I shall take the liberty to defy that convention and to tell you that the lunch on this occasion began with soles, sunk in a deep dish, over which the college cook had spread a counterpane of the whitest cream, save that it was branded here and there with brown spots like the spots on the flanks of a doe. After that, came the partridges, but if this suggests a couple of bald, brown birds on a plate you are mistaken. The partridges, many and various, came with all their retinue of sauces and salads, the sharp and the sweet, each in its order; their potatoes, thin as coins but not so hard; their sprouts, foliated as rosebuds but more succulent. And no sooner had the roast and its retinue been done with than the silent serving-man, the Beadle himself perhaps in a milder manifestation, set before us, wreathed in napkins, a confection which rose all sugar from the waves. To call it pudding and so relate it to rice and tapioca would be an insult. Meanwhile the wineglasses had flushed yellow and flushed crimson; had been emptied; had been filled. And thus by degrees was lit, halfway down the spine, which is the seat of the soul, not that hard little electric light which we call brilliance, as it pops in and out upon our lips, but the more profound, subtle and subterranean glow, which is the rich yellow flame of rational intercourse. No need to hurry. No need to sparkle. No need to be anybody but oneself. We are all going to heaven . . . in other words, how good life seemed, how sweet its rewards, how trivial this grudge or that grievance, how admirable friendship and the society of one's kind, as, lighting a good cigarette, one sunk among the cushions in the window-seat.

Passage 2

Here was my soup. Dinner was being served in the great dining-hall. Far from being spring it was in fact an evening in October. Everybody was assembled in the big dining-room. Dinner was ready. Here was the soup. It was a plain gravy soup. There was nothing to stir the fancy in that. One could have seen through the transparent liquid any pattern that there might have been on the plate itself. But there was no pattern. The plate was plain. Next came beef with its attendant greens and potatoes—a homely trinity, suggesting the rumps of cattle in a muddy market, and sprouts curled and yellowed at the edge, and bargaining and cheapening, and women with string bags on Monday morning. There was no reason to complain of human nature's daily food, seeing that the supply was sufficient and coal-miners doubtless were sitting down to less. Prunes and custard followed. And if any one complains that prunes, even when mitigated by custard, are an uncharitable vegetable (fruit they are not), stringy as a miser's heart and exuding a fluid such as might run in miser's veins who have denied themselves wine and warmth for eighty years and yet not given to the poor, he should reflect that there are people whose charity embraces even the prune. Biscuits and cheese came next, and here the water-jug was liberally passed round, for it is the nature of biscuits to be dry, and these were biscuits to the core. That was all. The meal was over. Everybody scraped their chairs back; the swing-doors swung violently to and fro; soon the hall was emptied of every sign of food and made ready no doubt for breakfast next morning.

Question 3

(Suggested writing time—40 minutes. This question counts for one-third of the total free-response section score.)

Read the following excerpt from Ralph Waldo Emerson's speech, "The American Scholar," which was delivered at Cambridge on August 31, 1837. Then write a well-reasoned essay that defends, challenges, or qualifies Emerson's ideas about books and their usefulness. Use appropriate evidence to develop your essay.

The theory of books is noble. The scholar of the first age received into him the world around; brooded thereon; gave it the new arrangement of his own mind, and uttered it again. It came into him—life; it went out from him—truth. It came to him—short-lived actions; it went out from him—immortal thoughts. It came to him—business; it went from him—poetry. It was—dead fact; now, it is quick thought. It can stand, and it can go. It now endures, it now flies, it now inspires. Precisely in proportion to the depth of mind from which it issued, so high does it soar, so long does it sing.

Each age, it is found, must write its own books; or rather, each generation for the next succeeding. Yet hence arises a grave mischief. The sacredness which attaches to the act of creation—the act of thought—is instantly transferred to the record. The poet chanting, was felt to be a divine man. Henceforth the chant is divine also. The writer was a just and wise spirit. Henceforth it is settled, the book is perfect; as love of the hero corrupts into worship of his statue. Instantly, the book becomes noxious. The guide is a tyrant. . . . Colleges are built on it. Books are written on it by thinkers, not by Man Thinking; by men of talent, that is, who start wrong, who set out from accepted dogmas, not from their own sight of principles. Meek young men grow up in libraries, believing it their duty to accept the views which Cicero, which Locke, which Bacon, have given, forgetful that Cicero, Locke, and Bacon were only young men in libraries when they wrote these books.

Hence, instead of Man Thinking, we have the book-worm. . . .

Books are the best of things, well used; abused, among the worst.

IF YOU FINISH BEFORE TIME IS CALLED, CHECK YOUR WORK ON THIS SECTION ONLY. DO NOT WORK ON ANY OTHER SECTION IN THE TEST.

105

Answer Key

Section I: Multiple-Choice Questions

1. C	12. D	23. D	34. D	45. C
2. D	13. B	24. B	35. C	46. A
3. A	14. E	25. C	36. B	47. B
4. A	15. A	26. A	37. B	48. E
5. B	16. B	27. E	38. E	49. D
6. B	17. C	28. D	39. C	50. C
7. A	18. D	29. B	40. D	51. E
8. C	19. A	30. A	41. E	52. A
9. C	20. E	31. D	42. A	53. B
10. D	21. E	32. A	43. B	54. C
11. E	22. C	33. E	44. D	55. A

Section II: Free-Response Questions

Essay scoring guides, student essays, and analyses appear beginning on p. 112.

Answer Explanations

Section I: Multiple-Choice Questions

The passage referred to in questions 1–11 is from *The Writing Life* (1989) by Annie Dillard.

1. **C.** The first sentence of the third paragraph makes clear the relevance of the second paragraph. As the butterfly automatically responds to size, so humans respond to the larger-than-life stimuli of films. The last sentence of the third paragraph makes the comparison explicit with its simile, comparing audiences being manipulated by film images to the male butterfly being drawn to the painted cardboard. The third paragraph does not qualify the second paragraph (A). The second paragraph doesn't ask why butterflies behave as they do (B), nor does the third paragraph answer this question. Choice D is questionable. First it claims that the second paragraph presents an idea as factual, but the paragraph refers to what one experiment shows, not what is proven as fact. Additionally, it claims the third paragraph presents only a possibility, when the paragraph strongly states how movies lure in viewers with their large size. Choice E is unreasonable; the relationship between the ideas in the two paragraphs is stated at the end of the third paragraph.

2. **D.** The nine-foot handsome face with its three-foot-wide smile refers to an image on the movie screen to which we cannot help responding. Since the point of the paragraph is the irresistible appeal of size, the reference is to the larger-than-life film image. Choice C incorrectly uses the word "distraction." The passage deals with the way large visual images draw viewers in; they do not distract. The remaining incorrect answer choices are simply unreasonable.

3. **A.** The sentence contains an example of personification. The metaphor compares books to people who can be "uneasy," "eager," and wear "disguises." The metaphor is neither understated (B) nor ironic (C). It is a personified metaphor, not a simile (D) nor a syllogism (E).

4. **A.** The question uses the phrase "according to the passage," and although the writer uses colloquial language ("smell a rat"), she doesn't call such language a characteristic of literature, making choice A the exception. The qualities the author uses to characterize literature (B, C, D, and E) are cited in the first paragraph ("the imagination's vision . . . the moral sense . . . the intellect") and the last ("the more purely verbal, crafted sentence by sentence, the more imaginative").

5. **B.** The phrase means something like "a greater waste of time." The best of the five choices here is "poorer occupation." Within the context of the excerpt, "sorry" means "sad" or "pathetic" (as in a sorry excuse), and "pursuit" means "occupation," not "chase" (A). The word "sympathetic" (C) is inaccurate; it has multiple definitions such as "caring," or "likable," but none of its meanings fits the context of the last sentence in the passage. The word "expectation" (D) is incorrect; the author is not referring to a future achievement. Choice E is incorrect because of the word " indifferent," which refers to a lukewarm or uninterested feeling.

6. **B.** The author uses the plural pronoun "our" to refer to all readers who prefer literature. In the Shakespeare allusion, the speaker is referring only to himself. Choice A can't be right, since "our" is the first-person plural possessive pronoun. The phrase, like most of the passage, makes only modest claims for literature, based on the greater subtlety of the verbal appeal. The move from the first-person singular ("I") of the fourth paragraph to the plural here seems intended to assert a solidarity with the people "who like literature." Choice C is unlikely; it is hard to believe that the author is trying to avoid quoting Shakespeare or that she worries about appearing to compare her work to his. Choice D is untrue and irrelevant; the author never implies that readers are greater in number than moviegoers, and the very idea does not address the question. Choice E explains the phrase "a poor thing," but the question asks about the plural "our."

7. **A.** Throughout the passage, the author frankly admits the limitations of the written word and concedes advantages to film in certain areas. All three of these sentences admit that writing is not powerful, or not immediately so, or not as effective in some areas as other forms of expression. The first two phrases in the question don't deal with film (B). Choices C, D, and E are all untrue. The passage is genuine (C) and doesn't use overstatement (D) or irony (E).

8. **C.** The passage makes no claim of universal appeal for even the best books. Literature, it calmly argues, will appeal to those who like literature. The first paragraph supports the idea that life is more exciting than writing (A). The whole passage suggests that reading is a special taste that some people have acquired, but it makes no case for forcing literature upon those who prefer film or television (B). In fact, the last sentence contends that the attempt to win over nonreaders is foolish (E). The third paragraph calls film "irresistible"(D).

9. **C.** The focus of the passage is on the nature of writing and film and their differences. Although the author may agree with the ideas of choices A and D, neither is the central concern of this passage. The passage ignores the difficulties of being a writer (B). The only mention of the novel is of the book written to be made into a film (E).

10. **D.** The first and last paragraphs are primarily about writing. The second paragraph, about the butterfly, is an analogy for the appeal of the big—the film as opposed to literature—and the third and fourth paragraphs are about films and novels written to become films. Choice A misrepresents the entire passage. Choice B is wrong because it erroneously claims the second paragraph is about writing. Choice C has more than one error: the first paragraph is about writing, not literature, and the last three paragraphs do not present the superiority of film over writing. Choice E misrepresents the first, second, and final paragraphs.

11. **E.** The passage doesn't demonstrate any inverted syntax; the grammatical elements in the sentences—the subject, verb, and direct object—all appear in their normal order. There is a personal anecdote (A) in the description of the author's reading novels written for film (paragraph 4), an extended analogy (B) in paragraphs 2 (the butterfly) and 3 (the film), short sentences (C) throughout the passage, and colloquialism (D) in a phrase such as, "I smelled a rat."

The passage referred to in questions 12–23 is from *The American Crisis* (1776) by Thomas Paine.

12. **D.** The "summer soldier" and the "sunshine patriot" serve their country only when conditions are favorable to themselves, a behavior akin to that of the proverbial "fair-weather friend." These conditionally patriotic citizens, who want to get involved only on their own terms, are the target of the author's criticism in this sentence. Choices A and E are unreasonable; neither army reserves (A) nor special forces (E) existed at this time. Choice B also makes no sense; while the word "infidel" is used in the second paragraph, it has nothing to do with the quotation given. Choice C is contradictory to the meaning of the quotation given; if the professional British soldiers were instead "summer soldiers," the Revolution would be easier to accomplish.

13. **B.** The essay is filled with aphorisms—brief, witty sayings—and emotional appeals. Examples of aphorisms here are "the harder the conflict, the more glorious the triumph" (lines 7–8) and "What we obtain too cheap, we esteem too lightly" (lines 8–9). The author appeals to emotions in his claim that a man's children will curse his cowardice if he fails to act now. Choice A is inaccurate because, although it can be argued that parts of the

essay are allegorical, it does not use didactic rhetoric. The author's purpose is clearly to persuade, not to teach, and the rhetoric is too highly charged with emotion to be described as didactic. Choice C is only partially correct. An argument can be made that the essay uses symbolism; for example, the man who runs the tavern at Amboy may be a symbol for all that the author considers to be wrong with American citizens. But this lone example does not constitute "heavy use." Although God is mentioned in three of the four paragraphs, those references are not technically biblical allusion. The author does not use paradox and invective (highly critical language) as in choice D, or historical background and illustration (E).

14. **E.** The author groups the king (D) of Britain with murderers (A), highwaymen (B), and housebreakers (C) (lines 32–35) but not with cowards (E). The line "the blood of his children will curse his cowardice" (lines 63–64) refers to Americans who fail to support the revolution, not to the king.

15. **A.** God, as characterized here, is a just and principled deity who will not let a people perish through military destruction because they have "so earnestly and so repeatedly sought to avoid the calamities of war" (lines 25–27). Nor, the author suggests, will this God abandon humans, giving them up "to the care of devils" (line 31). None of the references to God are negative, so choice B, "vexed" (angry), choice C, "indifferent," and choice E, "pernicious" (extremely destructive) are inappropriate answers. Choice D ("contemplative") implies merely that God meditates, but the author suggests a more active God.

16. **B.** In lines 10–13, the author claims, "Heaven knows how to put a proper price upon its goods; and it would be strange indeed if so celestial an article as freedom should not be highly rated." Choice A is inaccurate because the author never addresses the relationship between freedom and cowardice. Choice C contradicts the passage; the author states strongly that freedom does not come easily. Choice D also contradicts the passage; the author hopes that one day Americans will know true freedom. Choice E is not addressed in the passage.

17. **C.** The image of the tavern owner holding the hand of his child is likely designed to increase the emotional appeal of this essay, appealing to every man's desire to protect his family, even if he has to fight to save it. As the author says, it is "sufficient to awaken every man to duty." Choice A is too simplistic. True, the mention of the child shows that this man has a family, but introducing that fact is not the purpose of the reference. Choice B is incorrect because it isn't the image of the child that provokes the author's anger, but the image of the child's complacent father. The author may feel that the tavern owner is "evil," but the child's image doesn't symbolically increase the evil (D). Choice E contradicts the passage. The author appeals to the traditional values of family and freedom.

18. **D.** Since aphorisms are short, proverbial sayings of general truth, choice D doesn't fit the definition but rather may be more accurately considered a cliché.

19. **A.** The author states that America's "situation is remote from all the wrangling world, and she has nothing to do but to trade with them" (lines 52–54). The author does picture America as the "conqueror" but only with regard to winning its freedom from Britain, which makes choice B too strong a statement to be correct. The author never implies that America should be greater than Britain (C) or sanctified by God (D). Choice E contradicts the passage; if a country conducts trade, its stance is not one of "complete isolationism."

20. **E.** The author hopes to encourage his readers to take action, and he writes persuasively to achieve that aim. In order to achieve that overall goal, the author employs many modes, but his overriding rhetorical mode is persuasion. Remember that the question asks for the "best" classification of the passage's mode, and the incorrect responses do not identify the author's main purpose.

21. **E.** There is a strong emotional appeal as the author warns American men that their children will think them cowards and, as he claims, that the heart of a reader who does not feel as he does is "dead." Choice A, that children should also join the revolution, has no support in the essay. Choice B isn't his purpose, the outcome he desires. He wants men to join the revolution, to take action, not simply to be afraid. Choice C is inaccurate because the sentence quoted in this question is not directed to the king, but to American citizens. There is no mention of the superiority of either American or British forces and no mention of the advisability of retreat (D).

22. **C.** The author demonstrates no ambivalence in this paragraph. He takes a strong stand without vacillation. The paragraph does include the other devices listed. For example, aphorism ("'Tis the business of little minds to shrink," lines 68–69), simile ("My own line of reasoning is . . . as straight and clear as a ray of light," lines 71–73), parallel construction ("What signifies it to me . . . an army of them?", lines 80–83), and analogy (the comparison of the king to common thieves, lines 81–87).

23. D. Clearly, this author hopes his readers will feel that it is their patriotic duty toward America to join in supporting the revolution. While the author might value "peace and rational thinking" (A), he also clearly suggests that revolution now is necessary to produce later peace. The negative "overemotional" and "unwarranted" in choices B and C should alert you to the fact that these are not likely answers. The passage contradicts choice E. The author suggests that "Tyranny, like hell, is not easily conquered"—that is, freedom will not come immediately. In addition, the essay's primary purpose is to persuade Americans to join in the struggle to win their liberty, not simply to demand that the British government grant it to them.

The passage referred to in questions 24–36 is from *The Complete Letters of Charles Lamb* (1820).

24. B. The final sentence of the first paragraph verifies that Lamb "contrived to bring together whatever can be said in praise of them, dropping all the other side of the argument. . . ." This paragraph offers no evidence of Coleridge's opinion of Lamb's recollections (A, C, and E), or any hint of what Coleridge would have written differently (D).

25. C. The passage states that the "present worthy sub-treasurer to the Inner Temple can explain how that happened" and that Lamb had "particular advantages," which all appear to be related to money. Thus, one can infer that Lamb's family finances had likely influenced a member of the Inner Temple to obtain Lamb's special privileges. The passage offers no evidence that Lamb's aunt was the one who secured the favors (A). Choice B suggests that Lamb was a favorite of the schoolmaster, but no schoolmaster is ever mentioned. The idea that Lamb crept off the school grounds against the rules (D) contradicts the passage, which states that Lamb "had the privilege of going to see [his friends], almost as often as he wished." Choice E is incorrect for two reasons: No evidence is offered that his friends were the ones who gave any special treatment, and the passage does not explicitly clarify that the sub-treasurer was the one who was bribed.

26. A. The speaker extensively describes Lamb's daily food to provide a sharp contrast to the other boys' meals, thereby emphasizing their class differences. Choice B does not make sense; the speaker's description of Lamb's food does not enhance fond memories in the other boys; indeed, they were "invidious" (envious) of "that which was denied to us." Choice C is incorrect because the description of the food does not explain why his aunt brought it in the first place, and the word "had" is inaccurate; she brought the food out of love, not necessity. The idea that Lamb felt superior to the other boys (D) contradicts the speaker's claim that Lamb felt sympathy for the other boys. Choice E is incorrect because the passage reinforces common myths about British boarding schools instead of dispelling them.

27. E. The passage contains no references to any historical events, but all other answer choices can be found. Alliteration (A) appears in phrases like "rotten-roasted or rare." Examples of complex sentences (B) are present throughout the second paragraph, as are the negative descriptions of the boys' food (C). Finally, the speaker includes numerous parenthetical remarks that are extraneous and incidental (D), such as "(to make it go down more glibly)," "(the only dish which excited our appetites, and disappointed our stomachs, in almost equal proportion)," and "(exotics unknown to our palates)."

28. D. The decision to italicize the phrase *quite fresh* emphasizes that the phrase is a tongue-in-cheek, inaccurate description of the beef. In addition, comparing the beef to horseflesh (*caro equina*) in the same sentence reinforces the sarcastic tone and ironic negativity. Choice A contradicts the passage; the description of the food preparation for the boys is consistently negative and implies scant preparation. Phrases claiming the Monday meal was "blue and tasteless," while the "pease soup of Saturday, coarse and choking," and "Wednesday's mess of millet, somewhat less than repugnant," all reinforce the lack of careful preparation that would make their meals palatable. Choice B ignores that the speaker is being ironic and sarcastic, misreading the italicized phrase "*quite fresh*" as portraying the speaker's genuine feelings. Choice C is unreasonable; the italicized phrase hardly balances the positive and negative aspects of the boys' meals. The negative far outweighs the positive. Choice E is irrelevant; Lamb's aunt chooses to bring her nephew home-cooked food, but that fact does not address the question about the italicized phrase.

29. B. This answer choice is the only one that conveys the speaker's negative reaction to the marigolds, emphasizing how feeble this use of flowers is with wording like "detestable" and "floating in the pail to poison the broth." The passage provides no evidence that the marigolds, an image of nature, offer comfort (A) or cover for the ugliness of the world (E). Choice C misreads the passage when it claims the marigolds are a table complement; they are not sitting on the table in a flower vase, but floating in the broth. Choice D is unreasonable; according to the passage, the cook showed no creativity in the meals by placing the "detestable marigolds" in the broth.

30. **A.** The descriptive phrases that accompany each meal's presentation overstate how the food so horrified the boys' palates. Phrases such as "blue and tasteless" and "floating in the pail to poison the broth" are surely exaggerated, making the overall experience more intense. Choice B overstates the case; only the boys' meals are described, not all that encompasses "daily life." Choice C contradicts the passage; the boys were indeed fed very poorly. Lamb's superior social standing (D) is irrelevant to the question, which asks about the rhetorical purpose of the food descriptions. Choice E is too much of a stretch; describing the boys' food does not hint at inequalities in the school system itself.

31. **D.** The "contending passion" is the ambivalence that Lamb felt over his aunt's actions. This is clarified in the last sentence of the passage, with the use of sharply contrasting words such as "love" and "shame." Choice A is too strong; Lamb does not have unbounded enthusiasm; indeed, he is conflicted about the gifts he receives. Choice B contradicts the passage, which clearly states that Lamb felt "sympathy for those who were too many to share in it." He did not have enough food to share with so many hungry students. Choice C, like choice A, is too strong and absolute; Lamb does not demonstrate indisputable affection for his aunt, but is torn in his emotions. Nothing in the passage supports whether or not Lamb knew the other students were aware of his conflicted feelings (E).

32. **A.** The passage describes Lamb's aunt as one "in whom love forbade pride," thus her familial love overcame any potential indignity she may have felt. Choice B is inaccurate because the phrase "school was too stingy" is too strong; the passage does not support that this is the reason why his aunt brought food. Choices C, D, and E also have no evidence in the passage.

33. **E.** Lamb does not feel antipathy, an extreme hatred, toward his aunt. Do not be deceived by Lamb's use of the word "despised" in footnote #6; he clearly shows that he did not feel hostility toward his aunt's actions, but he was immature in his shame at seeing her bring him food. All the other choices, such as choice A, ignominy, which is a synonym for embarrassment, describe emotions that Lamb does feel. He does feel affection for her (B) as evidenced in the phrase "love for the bringer." His compassion for her (C) and his discomfort (D) can be seen in the phrase that he had "shame for the thing brought, and the manner of its bringing."

34. **D.** Footnote #6 clarifies that, in retrospect, Lamb views his aunt's actions far differently from the way he did at the time; with hindsight, he understands that he was acting in a "school-boy like" manner, and he now better comprehends his mixed feelings about gaining extra food while watching his aunt lose her dignity. Choices B and E have no evidence in the passage; choices A and C are contradicted in the passage.

35. **C.** Footnote #2 states that "Lamb paid a fine tribute of praise," Coleridge "has drawn a companion picture of the better side," and Hunt "also described . . . the life and ideals of the school." Choices A, B, D, and E have no evidence in the footnote.

36. **B.** The phrase "contrived to bring together whatever can be said in praise" is clearly contradicted in the passage, as the speaker repeatedly describes the horribly unappetizing and inedible food. Since choice B deals with praise, it opposes the rhetorical purpose of the passage as a whole.

The passage referred to in questions 37–46 is from "Of Studies" (1625) by Francis Bacon.

37. **B.** Most of these comments explain the benefits of studies (for pleasure, discussion, business, and so forth). Thus, the audience that would most benefit from this essay's message is likely to be those who think they don't need studies. Choices A, D, and E name audiences who are probably already aware of the benefits of studies. Poor readers (C) don't necessarily need to be convinced of the benefits of studies, but rather may need to improve their reading skills.

38. **E.** The author explains how students may focus on their studies incorrectly. One may spend too much time in studies and thus be guilty of sloth, or one may use them only to impress others (displaying affectation). Also, one may make judgments based solely upon studies, failing to consider real-life experience. These potential misuses of studies, the author claims, are "the humor of a scholar." He describes what scholars should not do with their studies. The phrase does not have a positive connotation, which eliminates choices A, B, and D. Choice C makes no sense, as the phrase does not refer to an excuse for improper studies.

39. **C.** The author claims, in lines 13–14, that studies "are perfected by experience" and, in line 17, that they are "bounded in by experience." Choices A, B, D, and E are not stated in the passage.

40. **D.** The sentence in this question reads, "Read not to contradict and confute, nor to believe and take for granted, nor to find talk and discourse, but to weigh and consider." Parallel construction is evident—"to contradict and confute," "to believe and take," "to find talk and discourse," "to weigh and consider." The ideas are not understated (A) or hyperbolic (C) but quite straightforward and clear. The sentence is not metaphorical (B); the words and concepts are literal. Finally, the sentence has no analogy (E).

41. E. The author, in this sentence, discusses how people need to "prune" their natural abilities by study. At the same time, however, studies need to be "bounded in by experience." The message is one of moderation and inclusion—neither studies nor experiences should be relied on exclusively or predominantly. The passage never mentions professors (A), and the meaning of this incorrect response also contradicts the passage. Choices B, C, and D have no evidence in the passage; all three equate to a misreading of the passage.

42. A. The wisdom "won by observation" (line 21) is analogous to that "perfected by experience" (lines 13–14). In both instances, the author recommends reading to gain knowledge but also incorporating life's observations and experiences to obtain wisdom. The act of observing is not analogous to the way studies "give forth directions too much at large" (B). In line 18, the word "studies" refers to something that "crafty men condemn," which is also not analogous (C). Choice D is not analogous because wisdom is the end result of combining observation and experience. Choice E is incorrect because the context of the word "believe" deals with what readers should *not* do, namely "read to believe and take for granted"; it is not analogous to combining observation and experience to gain wisdom.

43. B. "To spend too much time in studies is sloth" (lines 9–10) paradoxically suggests that too much work on studies can lead to laziness and lack of work. In other words, overemphasis on studies avoids work in the outside world. Choices A, D, and E are not paradoxes. Although choice C might have paradoxical elements, it is not mentioned in the essay.

44. D. In lines 21–24, the author claims that one should read "not to contradict and confute, nor to believe and take for granted, nor to find talk and discourse, but to weigh and consider." A reader should think. Reading voluminously or only for pleasure, choices A and E, are not necessarily "errors." Choices B and C are perhaps reading mistakes, but the nonthinking reader is presented as the greater problem.

45. C. This sentence discusses how readers might adapt their reading style to the subject matter and their purpose. By reading "not curiously," the author means reading without great care or scrutiny, reading cursorily. Choices A, B, and E directly contradict the idea of reading without considerable scrutiny. The idea that readers do not need a strong background (D), is not mentioned in this portion of the passage.

46. A. The sentence in the question contains parallel construction, in which three ideas make up the sentence. Only choice A uses the same structure, presenting three similarly phrased ideas that make up the sentence.

The passage referred to in questions 47–55 is from *A Tramp Abroad* (1880) by Mark Twain.

47. B. The opening paragraph begins with an assertion that "animals talk to each other," before it introduces Jim Baker and his observations about animals' ability to communicate with one another. The paragraph then concludes with Baker's personal thesis "that the blue jays were the best talkers . . . among the birds and beasts." The paragraph provides no examples to prove a claim (A). Choice C is wrong for two reasons: first, it erroneously claims that the thesis is the author's idea when it is actually Jim Baker's; second, it only transitions from general to specific on the surface level, whereas choice B accurately identifies all of the ideas in the paragraph. Although the opening paragraph may state a hypothesis (D), it does not establish a metaphorical connection to humanity. Choice E is too narrow; this answer only describes a portion of the first paragraph's organization.

48. E. The tongue-in-cheek remarks and the comical tone of the passage help to establish that the author might question Jim Baker's accuracy about blue jays. The only corroboration the author has is that Jim Baker "told me so himself," so he might presume that Baker's assertions are not entirely accurate. At first glance, choice D may seem like the best response. Jim Baker does tell the author openly that he knows how to understand animals' language, but this is actually a direct statement from the passage; therefore, it cannot be an assumption. None of the other answer choices correctly identify assumptions related to this fourth sentence.

49. D. The fifth sentence works to establish Jim Baker's credentials as an observer of animal communication. It clarifies that he lived in a lonely corner of California, with only beasts and birds for neighbors, and that he studied them so much that he truly believed he could accurately understand their language. Choice A is too strong to define the purpose; this sentence does not necessarily indicate that Jim Baker prefers animals over humans. Choices B and C have no evidence in the sentence. Choice E is too strong of a statement; the fifth sentence does not suggest that Jim Baker is more qualified than anyone else to comment on animal behavior.

50. C. Congressmen are compared to blue jays in the third paragraph, but they are never compared to cats; thus choice C is the correct exception. The ideas in all of the other answer choices are, indeed, found in this passage. Choice A, that blue jays are the most eloquent creatures, is imbedded throughout the entire passage. The idea that cats use grammatically correct language when they are calm (B) is implied in lines 39–41, which claim that when cats get excited "you'll hear grammar that will give you the lockjaw." The ideas in both choices D and E are found in the first paragraph.

51. E. Jim Baker's language is colorfully colloquial and it rambles informally, making choice E the best answer. Each of the incorrect answer choices has an inappropriate word that does not accurately describe Baker's language: "allegorical" in choice A, "invectives" in choice B, "didactic" in choice C, and "paradoxical" in choice D are all imprecise. Note that all of these terms are defined in Appendix A.

52. A. The last sentence of the passage includes many examples of parallel construction. For example, it repeats the phrase "a jay can . . ." a total of four times. On the other hand, this sentence contains no predicate nominatives (eliminating choice B) because the sentence has no linking verbs. This sentence does not contain a metaphorical conceit (C), nor does it contain understatements (D), and it includes only a single subordinate clause, not multiple ones (E).

53. B. It is ironic that, while Jim Baker gives high praise to blue jays' grammar, he displays flawed grammar himself. For example, among other errors, he consistently uses double negatives ("don't belong to no church" and "can't cram into no blue jay's head"). Other answer choices are either not evidenced in the passage (D and E) or they are not ironic (A and C).

54. C. One can infer that the author intends for this comic passage to establish comparisons between blue jays and humanity. He directly states that blue jays are like congressmen, but he also implies that there are connections between animal behavior and the whole of humanity. Choice A is too strong to be a viable inference; the author does not go so far as to show that humanity should learn from the animals. Choice B is incorrect because the passage does not demonstrate that loners understand animals better than they do people, and this idea is surely not the author's rhetorical purpose. Choice D is inaccurate because the passage does not establish *how* animals communicate with each other; it merely states that they do. Choice E may be tempting on first glance, but it can be eliminated for two reasons: The author directly states that congressmen are unprincipled, and a direct statement cannot be an inference; plus, this answer is too limited, too narrow, to encompass the rhetorical purpose of the entire passage.

55. A. The phrase, stating that a blue jay knows when he is being foolish "maybe better" than people do, implies that people are not always self-aware when they are being foolish. Thus, choice A is the most plausible of these answer choices. Choices B and C are simply not reasonable inferences that can be drawn from this phrase. Choice D is incorrect because of the word "honest"; the passage does not imply that blue jays are particularly honest, only that they show awareness. Choice E, similarly, is wrong because of the word "always"; the passage does not imply that a blue jay is always aware of his foolishness, only that he "maybe" knows it "better" than people.

Section II: Free-Response Questions

Question 1

Scoring Guide

Score	Description	Criteria
9	Successful	Essays that earn a score of 9 meet the criteria for essays that receive a score of 8. In addition, they are especially sophisticated in the use of language, explanation, and argument.
8	Successful	These essays respond to the prompt successfully, incorporating ideas from at least three sources from the prompt. They take an effective position that defends, challenges, or qualifies the claim that the media has had a positive influence on the effects of natural disasters. They effectively argue the position and support the argument with appropriate evidence. The control of language is extensive and the writing errors are minimal.

Score	Description	Criteria
7	Satisfactory	These essays meet the criteria for essays that receive a score of 6 but provide more depth and strength to the argument and evidence. The prose style is mature and shows a wide control over language.
6	Satisfactory	These essays respond to the prompt satisfactorily. Using at least three sources from the prompt, these essays take an adequate position that defends, challenges, or qualifies the claim that the media has had a positive influence on the effects of natural disasters. The position is adequately argued with support from appropriate evidence, although without the precision and depth of top-scoring essays. The writing may contain minor errors in diction or syntax, but the prose is generally clear.
5	Plausible	These plausible essays take a position that defends, challenges, or qualifies the claim that the media has had a positive influence on the effects of natural disasters. They support the position with generally appropriate evidence, but may not adequately quote, either directly or indirectly, from at least three sources in the prompt. These essays may be inconsistent, uneven, or limited in the development of their argument. Although the writing usually conveys the student's ideas and perspectives, it may demonstrate lapses in diction or syntax, or an overly simplistic style.
4	Inadequate	These essays respond to the prompt inadequately. They have difficulty taking a clear position that defends, challenges, or qualifies the claim that the media has had a positive influence on the effects of natural disasters. The evidence may be insufficient or may not use at least three sources from the prompt. The prose conveys the student's ideas but suggests immature control over the elements of effective writing.
3	Inadequate	These essays meet the criteria for a score of 4 but reveal less success in taking a position that defends, challenges, or qualifies the claim that the media has had a positive influence on the effects of natural disasters. The presentation of evidence and arguments is unconvincing. The prose shows little or no control over the elements of effective writing.
2	Little success	These essays demonstrate little success at taking a position that defends, challenges, or qualifies the claim that the media has had a positive influence on the effects of natural disasters and show little success in presenting it clearly and with appropriate evidence from the sources in the prompt. These essays may misunderstand the prompt, may fail to establish a position with supporting evidence, or may substitute a simpler task by replying tangentially with unrelated, erroneous, or unsuitable explanation, argument, and/or evidence. The prose frequently demonstrates consistent weaknesses in the conventions of effective writing.
1	Little success	These essays meet the criteria for a score of 2 but are undeveloped; especially simplistic in their explanation, argument, and/or evidence; or weak in their control of writing.

High-Scoring Essay

The media has assumed a reputation of candor, coupled with benevolence for the media links desperate people in desperate situations to magnanimous audiences, who, theoretically, are only too eager to help. In a media-perpetuated myth, newspapers, radio, internet, and television supposedly serve the distinct purpose of objectively presenting adversity while respecting victims. Thus, the media has tailored for itself an image of an entity that respects victims of disastrous situations, yet simultaneously provides the public with objective reporting. This is not so. The media simply is not able to live up to its self-created reputation. Rather than providing a service to the public and victims following a disaster, the media compromises the integrity of its broadcasts, disregards victims, and alienates audiences, ultimately doing a disservice to the public.

It becomes difficult to regard the traditional media in a favorable light when one considers the information in Patrick Cockburn's article "Catastrophe on camera: Why media coverage of natural disasters is flawed" (Source B). His thesis examines something that we take for granted, namely that "Media coverage of natural disasters . . . is largely accepted as an accurate reflection of what really happened." The author asserts that assumption is clearly misleading, ". . . in my experience, the opposite is true: the reporting of cataclysms or lesser disasters is often wildly misleading." He recounts details of the deceptive reporting of a string of natural disasters, ranging from the floods in Mississippi in the 1990s to the devastation wrought in New Orleans in 2005. In every case, similar patterns emerge: first comes stereotypical reporting, followed by huge exaggeration of the toll, finally ending in a dull, repetitive monotone. Out of this storm of coverage, very little serves to enlighten their viewers or to help to ease the burden for the victims or the responders. Furthermore, Source F details what the media should be doing, namely "provid[ing] a quality service, critiquing claims rather than simply reporting them, and fundamentally, allowing people to make informed decisions." Instead of inadequate and sensationalist coverage such as the Las Vegas mass shooting, the media should be striving for the objective and complete coverage it pretends to present.

In October of 2002, some of America's brightest minds convened for a seminar on effective risk communication (Source C). Effective risk communicators include different aspects of the media; for instance, television and radio. The media is an "important channel for risk communication," an asset to authorities, and a source of public information, yet Source C explicitly states that society's "social structure, norms, resources and risk perception" undermine media's post-disaster effectiveness. Meanwhile, Source D focuses on the future, arguing that social media channels are likely to subsume the role of traditional media in disaster relief efforts. Indeed, social media has already played a role in recovery efforts following some recent American disasters. However, as disaster sociologist Jeannette Sutton points out, social media needs to find a way to be more effective and consistent in communicating information about disasters. It is clear that the media has much room for improvement when covering disasters. Thus, in spite of the media's disaster education in Latin America (Source A) and roundtable discussions (Source C), media coverage of disasters does a disservice. Reporting on disasters in an incomplete manner, while intrusively disregarding victims' welfare, and failing to effectively reach the public, the media displays the hallmarks of a public service gone awry.

Analysis of the High-Scoring Essay

This very thorough essay demonstrates just how much argumentation a thoughtful writer can include. Freely synthesizing the sources and contemporary events, this student presents an intelligent discussion of the shortcomings of the media regarding its reporting of disasters. Taking a negative stand, the essay systematically criticizes the media's intrusive nature and poor reporting. The student demonstrates a strong command of diction and syntax, presenting sophisticated phrasing such as "candor coupled with benevolence" and "links desperate people in desperate situations to magnanimous audiences." Additionally, the simple sentence, "This is not so," packs a punch because of its brevity and its being surrounded by longer, more complex sentences.

The first body paragraph examines a negative aspect of the media's reporting of disasters: Viewers are only shown selected images of devastation, knowing that such coverage sells. This touches on a universal truth: Humanity is compelled to watch images of horror while simultaneously being repelled by them. The student implicitly understands this concept and uses it to further the essay's argument. By citing multiple examples from Source B and from contemporary incidents, the student makes as thorough a case as one can expect in any 40-minute essay. All of the examples are relevant and demonstrate that the student is not merely repeating the information from the sources, but instead is digesting the ideas, mulling them over, and then producing an intelligent, albeit one-sided, argument against the media. The inclusion of information from Source F regarding the role that the media should ideally play in a society adds depth, both by synthesizing multiple sources in the same paragraph and by bringing this particular one to a logical conclusion.

The next paragraph is interesting in its organizational scheme. It chooses to discuss Sources C and D, both of which are more favorable toward the media than other sources. But, keeping in line with the essay's theses, the student chooses to highlight the negative ideas from each source. The purpose is well-fulfilled. The student points out that the media tries to encourage effective risk communication, but follows it up with Source C's criticism that society is not inclined to heed such ideas. This analysis is not terribly strong, as it mainly just reports what Source C has to say. However, it does expand the essay's critique of the media. The inclusion of Source D helps the paragraph's development, but, again, the student could do more critical thinking; it reads a bit too much like mere reporting.

The conclusion, too, is brief, basically just a summary, but it does bring in another source from the prompt, which highlights the student's overall attention to detail. The essay ends with a very poignant phrase: By stating that the media is a "public service gone awry," the student reasserts the essay's thesis with finality and conviction. Indeed, this essay truly earns its high score; it should receive an 8.

Medium-Scoring Essay

Media has a powerful influence upon our lives. Not only does it provide us with news; it subtly shapes our opinions. Media, be it television, magazines, or radio, has demonstrated the ability to affect a broad audience. Recent natural disasters and terrorist attacks have been thoroughly reported by the media. When the media portrays a natural disaster it serves one distinct purpose. Over and over, the media has shown that it chooses to consistently display world tragedy in such a way as to convey feelings of closeness and empathy to its audience. Thus, the effects of the media are great, and media attention is beneficial for victims of disasters because it shares their plight with a sympathetic world audience.

The 21st century is an age of technology. Television, radio, and the internet are mediums of media that can convey news quickly and effectively. Source C, an excerpt from a seminar on risk communication, clearly viewed media as an important method to limit the effects of a natural disaster. Media can help limit a disaster's immediate effects, "[media can] track potential disaster agents, alert authorities, and educate and warn the public in a more timely manner" (Source C). Media effectively helps victims of a disaster while helping educate the public in order to limit damage and death in future incidents. The seminar's participants from businesses, industry, and civil services (Source C) exemplified the interest in effectively utilizing media to help in disaster situations.

While Source A acknowledges the importance of media immediately following a disaster, the article emphasizes the importance of educational media that limits the effects of future. The article states, "If people know what to do, they can save their own life." Mr. Briceño, the chairman of the committee that held the forum on disasters, asserted, "The more people are aware of the risks they face, the better chance they have to save their lives when hazards strike" (Source A).

Source F acknowledges that Hurricane Katrina, while a horrible event, at least caused the media to question the administration's ability to help those in need, and in the process of showing the world the devastation from the hurricane, brought tremendous sympathy for those victims of the storm. If we had not seen the images of the people who suffered, we would not have felt for them so much. Therefore, the media helped the victims.

Media has proved itself to be an integral component in disaster relief. Helping people immediately after a disaster and in the ensuing months, media has aided authorities, raised money, and educated potential future victims. Thus, media is a valuable tool in disaster relief.

Analysis of the Medium-Scoring Essay

This essay tries to present a coherent argument about the benefits the media provides after disasters, but it is not terribly convincing because of its simplistic approach. For instance, one sentence in the introduction claims that the media serves "one distinct purpose" in reporting disasters: drawing out the audience's sympathy. Surely this naïve thinking exposes an unwarranted assumption; surely the media has many purposes in reporting "world tragedies." A student who displays such one-dimensional thinking early on frequently produces an essay that oversimplifies. Although it is true that media exposure may indeed evoke a sympathetic reaction in the viewers, that alone does not necessarily produce any tangible benefit for the victims. Viewer sympathy alone will not house or feed victims.

The first body paragraph addresses the potential good works that the media can do, such as helping to limit the damage from natural disasters by providing warnings to the public and officials of imminent danger. However, the student seems to have forgotten the thesis of the essay; this paragraph includes no evidence for the concept that the media elicits sympathy in a viewing audience. Although this body paragraph does address some good that the media can do, it does not really relate to the introductory paragraph. Unfortunately, this poor organization does not bode well for the essay.

The second body paragraph suffers from similar organizational problems; it does not support the thesis about eliciting sympathy. Just like the previous paragraph, this one focuses on ways in which the media can help circumvent negative effects of disasters with pre-planning. Perhaps the student would have been better served had he or she changed the thesis to fit what the body paragraphs actually discuss. Furthermore, the weak development of this paragraph is apparent because it contains only three sentences, two of which are merely quotations from the source. In other words, the student barely hints at any interesting ideas and barely develops them.

The last body paragraph attempts to get back on track and address how the media elicited sympathy for Hurricane Katrina victims. However, the writer uses Source F, which does not really present that idea; this source centers on the concept of how, after the hurricane, the media moved to a more aggressive stance in presenting discrepancies between the administration's statements and actions. Therefore, the student's leap of logic, jumping from an article that criticizes the administration to the idea that photos of hurricane victims elicit sympathy in the viewers, is a flaw no AP Reader can ignore. It appears that the student is grasping at straws, searching for any phrase in the sources that might somehow support the thesis, but he or she falls far short of composing a convincing argument.

The essay concludes too quickly with the concept that "helping people immediately after a disaster and in the ensuing months, media has aided authorities, raised money, and educated potential future victims." Unfortunately, these ideas are simply not proven in this essay.

Overall, the essay demonstrates the logical flaws that occur when a student jumps in and begins writing too quickly, without thinking through his or her positions and how the sources can help establish them. The essay's organization would also benefit from greater sophistication. Instead of using the facile "one-source-per-paragraph" method, the essay could successfully demonstrate more complexity if the writer integrated more sources into each paragraph. Always keep in mind that this is the synthesis essay. Keep your focus on the concept of synthesis and use it to your advantage as you think deeply about the topic and navigate your way, exploring a variety of ideas. It deserves no better than a score of 5.

Question 2

Scoring Guide

Score	Description	Criteria
9	Successful	These essays meet the criteria for essays that receive a score of 8, and in addition, they are deeper in their analysis and frequently reveal an exquisite use of language.
8	Successful	These well-written essays clearly and successfully demonstrate an understanding of Woolf's attitude about women in society, while also analyzing how the author's rhetorical strategies, such as structure, diction, tone, and detail, convey that attitude. These essays present a clear, relevant thesis supported by strong evidence from the passage. Analysis of the evidence and how it reflects the author's attitude about women in society is insightful. Not necessarily without flaws, these essays still show maturity in their use of language and sentence structure.
7	Satisfactory	These essays meet the requirements for essays that score a 6, and in addition, provide a more complete and deeper analysis of Woolf's attitude and a more mature prose style.
6	Satisfactory	Well presented, these essays satisfactorily describe Woolf's attitude about women in society, but perhaps less explicitly than do the high-scoring essays. Discussion of the author's rhetorical strategies may be less thorough, or evidence presented may be less specific. Connection between the evidence and the thesis may be less insightful. Although some errors may be present, the essay, overall, shows satisfactory control of format and language.
5	Plausible	These average essays may recognize the author's attitude about women in society but may be less precise in discussing that attitude. Attempts to analyze the author's rhetorical strategies may be simplistic, or evidence offered may be insufficient to prove the thesis adequately. Organization may be clear but not as effective as that of the better-written essays. There may be inconsistencies in the command of language.
4	Inadequate	These essays attempt to address the essay question but inadequately address the author's attitude. They may not complete all of the tasks of the question. Not having enough evidence for the student's ideas may be a problem. Insights may be inaccurate or superficial. These essays may convey ideas, but their weak control over language may distract the AP Reader's attention. There may be frequent errors in mechanics.
3	Inadequate	Essays earning a score of 3 meet the criteria for a score of 4 but demonstrate less understanding of Woolf's attitude and show a lack of depth in analysis of rhetorical strategies. These essays may show little control over the elements of writing.
2	Little success	These essays fail to respond sufficiently to the question or the passage and therefore demonstrate little success in responding to the prompt. They may fail to recognize the author's attitude or may misread the passage so as to distort it. With little or no evidence offered, these essays have little success in persuading the Reader, and the connection between the evidence and the thesis may be shallow or nonexistent. Persistent weaknesses may be evident in the basic elements of composition or writing skills.
1	Little success	These poorly written essays meet the criteria for a score of 2 but are undeveloped, especially simplistic in their analysis, and weak in their control of language.

High-Scoring Essay

The differences between men's and women's colleges were considerable in Virginia Woolf's day. Rather than assert this in a pedestrian, expository way, Woolf uses the respective meals served at each college to illustrate the discrepancies between the schools. The meals are a metaphorical device, akin to a poetic conceit; Woolf makes a far more forceful, profound distinction between the male and female schools through such juxtaposition than if she had merely enumerated their inconsistencies. Woolf details the relative poverty of the women's school, and therefore women's position in society, through varied sentence structure, diction, and imagery between the descriptions of the meals.

Fundamentally different premises underlie each meal. The men's meal is a luxury to be enjoyed, the women's a metabolic necessity to be endured. Woolf, in describing the men's meal, dismisses the notion that ". . . soup and a salmon and ducklings were of no importance whatsoever, as if nobody ever smoked a cigar or drank a glass of wine." She offers a breathless explanation of the sensual joy the meal affords. Diction and sensory detail showcase the piquant pleasure to be taken in foods "spread . . . of the whitest cream," "Sharp and sweet . . . succulent." The men's meal is a catalyst for the "profound, subtle and subterranean glow . . . of rational intercourse." Of course, no similar premium is put on rational intercourse among women, judging by the amenities of the women's meal. They drink not wine "flushed crimson," but rather eat "plain gravy soup . . . transparent liquid." Dry biscuits and water replace partridges, and such victuals provide no stimulus for enlightened conversation; when the eating is done, the women rise and that is all.

Woolf describes the women's meal in plain language, in blunt, staccato, repetitive bursts: "Here was my soup . . . Dinner was ready. Here was the soup. It was a plain gravy soup . . . The plate was plain." All the eloquent wordiness has vanished. The images are those of poverty and ugliness, and the meal is only justified as being superior to that of a coal miner. The prunes are ". . . stringy as a miser's heart and exuding a fluid such as might run in miser's veins . . ." In contrast, the other meal's imagery is that of opulence. The potatoes are "thin as coins," the sprouts "foliated as rosebuds." This is a meal fit for kings, and the diction is suggestive of royalty: "The partridges . . . came with all their retinue . . ." The men are reassured by the meal that they are all going to heaven; the women's meal is a hurried "homely trinity."

As a metaphor for the chasm separating male and female education, and society as a whole, Woolf's piece is mordantly effective. Her point is made with more economy and vivacity through anecdote than it would be through explanation or a propounding of evidence about the inferiority of female schools. By painting the male university as lavish and its female counterpart as lowly, Woolf succeeds in crystallizing her attitude for readers.

Analysis of the High-Scoring Essay

This student addresses the question; he or she also demonstrates a deep understanding of the subtle differences between the two passages. This thesis is relevant and on topic. The body paragraphs provide ample evidence for ideas, and the quotations are used effectively to prove this student's points. This essay does not merely dwell on the obvious aspects of the passages, but probes more deeply into the ramifications of the two meals. Especially effective is the section in which the student demonstrates how Woolf's diction suggests the meaning of each meal. For example, reread the end of the third paragraph as this student connects the word "retinue" with royalty and goes on to suggest what that royal meal does for the men (it reassures them that they are going to heaven). This type of thinking demonstrates the level of analysis necessary for a high score; the student understands how the language of the essay helps to create an effect.

The vocabulary and sentence structure are also very sophisticated, as they should be in top-scoring essays. The phrasing is creative and pleasing. Wording such as "akin to a poetic conceit," "a metabolic necessity," "piquant pleasure," and "mordantly effective" are just a few of the phrases that sing to the Reader's ear. In addition, this student demonstrates a keen sense of sentence structure and thus adds sufficient variety in both sentence pattern and length.

Although very well written, this essay could be improved by providing a stronger connection between ideas, evidence, and thesis. Also, a more profound point could be made about the deeper issues involved in the "chasm separating male and female education." In addition, the student could concentrate more on Woolf's attitude as he or she presents the evidence. However, these criticisms are not significant enough to lower the essay's score. Essays that are this thorough, organized, and well presented, indeed, earn a high score. It should earn a score of 8.

Low-Scoring Essay

Meals are important, but they are often ignored or not thought of much. People often eat in a hurry, and often they don't pay much attention to the details of what they are actually eating.

Virginia Woolf calls readers' attention to this in the selection about two meals which she had when she was at the university. She had one of these at the men's college and the other at the women's college. They were very different in the food but also in the whole atmosphere of the place where she ate.

Woolf says that though people don't often notice it, the food we eat tells us important things about where we are. She compares the two parts of the university with the different meals. She uses narrative structure, details, and tone to present her attitude about the two meals and inform readers of which one she likes better, and why.

The first meal she describes, which is at the men's college, is the one which Woolf likes better. The reasons become obvious for this, because the food is far more appetizing and the atmosphere is just nicer generally. Woolf uses lots of details and metaphors to describe this meal, and often her descriptions are full of imagery. It is all very fancy, with a uniformed waiter serving roast, and Woolf drinks a lot of wine, which sends a glow down her spine. She comments that all the other eaters were very friendly and everything seemed nice and happy after the meal. "We are all going to heaven" she says after the meal. It is almost a religious experience for them.

The second meal is at the women's college, and Woolf's attitude toward it is not as positive. That is understandable, but the food is not even close to as good. Woolf uses lots of metaphors to make the food seem gross and very repulsive. The beef is like "the rumps of cattle in a muddy market, and sprouts curled and yellowed at the edge" she says. The prunes are stringy and miserly, and instead of the good pudding that she ate at the men's college, she has to eat custard that is not nearly so good. The biscuits are dry and unappetizing, which makes for a meal that is not very appealing. She doesn't talk about friends or smoking at this meal, which makes it far more homely than the men's meal.

Thus, through her metaphors and affective descriptions of the food at the two meals, Woolf compares them and strongly shows her attitude to the readers. She makes one realize that even though we don't often think about meals, they are important. The differences are something to realize, and Woolf's excellent description helps you do just that.

Analysis of the Low-Scoring Essay

This essay earns a low score because it recognizes some of the differences between the two meals. However, it doesn't merit a higher score because it fails to address Woolf's underlying attitude toward women's place in society as displayed through her description of the meals. The introductory remarks go on far too long (for three paragraphs). When the thesis is finally stated, it's bland and obvious, as is the entire essay. This student mentions that Woolf presents her attitudes but never clarifies what he or she thinks these attitudes are. Basically, the thesis merely restates a portion of the prompt.

This student has chosen to discuss the two meals separately, in two paragraphs, a technique that doesn't allow for strong comparison. This student does accurately present some evidence, but in many cases it is not sufficient. For example, where are the metaphors to which the student refers? Since they aren't included in the essay, the Reader is left guessing. The student does see some interesting description in the passages but fails to make an intelligent point about it, and the analysis offered is shallow and obvious. Also, no connection is made between the evidence presented and the major topic of Woolf's attitude.

In addition, this essay demonstrates some stylistic and grammatical problems and is not helped by the use of unsophisticated words and phrases such as "things," "a lot," and "not . . . as good." Some awkward sentences tend to distract the Reader's attention from this student's ideas. Incorrect word choices, such as "affective" instead of "effective," show that this student doesn't have a strong command of the language. This difficulty is further demonstrated by pronoun problems such as the improper use of the second person pronoun "you" in the last sentence and "them" at the end of the fourth paragraph, which also has no antecedent.

The positive aspects of this essay are few. It does try to make a point, and it follows many of the conventions of proper writing style. However, its numerous errors and uninteresting, obvious ideas that ignore part of the prompt prevent the essay from achieving a higher score. It should receive a score of 3 or 4.

Question 3

Scoring Guide

Score	Description	Criteria
9	Successful	These essays meet the criteria for essays that receive a score of 8, and in addition, they present deeper understanding of Emerson's ideas and frequently reveal an exquisite use of language.
8	Successful	These well-written essays successfully take a stand concerning Emerson's ideas about the usefulness of books and substantially support it. The thesis is well thought out and relevant to the topic. These essays provide ample evidence to prove the ideas and clearly connect the evidence to the thesis. Thoroughly convincing, these essays demonstrate a significant understanding of the needs of the essay. Although they need not be without errors, these essays show a mature command of style and language.
7	Satisfactory	These essays meet the requirements for essays that score a 6, and in addition, demonstrate a thorough understanding of the author's ideas, while providing stronger and more relevant evidence. The prose style is generally more mature.
6	Satisfactory	These essays demonstrate a satisfactory understanding of Emerson's ideas but produce a less explicit thesis than that of higher-scoring essays. Perhaps less relevant evidence is offered, making these essays less persuasive. Still, they are fairly convincing and show clear thinking. The connection between the evidence and the thesis may not be as articulate as in top-scoring essays. Although well written, these essays may demonstrate some errors while still showing satisfactory control over diction and the essay requirements.
5	Plausible	These essays show some plausible understanding of Emerson's ideas but produce a thesis that may be weak or predictable. The opinions may be too hastily conceived after a cursory reading of Emerson's concepts. Overall, the argument, although acceptable, may not be persuasive or thought-provoking. It may appear opinionated without sufficient evidence to support the opinions. Acceptable organization may be evident, but the style may not be as sophisticated as that of higher-scoring essays.
4	Inadequate	These low-scoring, inadequate essays fail to convince the Reader. The weak presentation may show an unsubstantiated thesis or no thesis at all, weak paragraph development and/or weak organization, insufficient evidence for points made, or superficial thinking. Confusion about Emerson's ideas may be evident, and frequent mechanical errors may be present.
3	Inadequate	These essays earning a score of 3 meet the criteria for a score of 4 but demonstrate little understanding of the ideas. Frequently, these essays suffer from a lack of evidence to support the arguments made. These essays may show little control over the elements of writing.
2	Little success	These poorly written essays lack coherence and clarity and therefore show little success in addressing the prompt. The thesis may be overly obvious or absent. Little or no evidence may be offered for the thesis, and the connection between the evidence and the thesis may be shallow or nonexistent. These essays may be unusually short and exhibit poor fundamental essay skills. Weak sentence construction may be seen, and persistent weaknesses in command of the language may be present.
1	Little success	These poorly written essays meet the criteria for a score of 2 but are undeveloped, especially simplistic in their analysis, and weak in the control of language.

High-Scoring Essay

Ralph Waldo Emerson is perhaps overly strident in his speech, "The American Scholar." But such zeal serves to make a trenchant point about the tendency toward rigid reverence of Great Works, as if each were the Holy Grail itself. He asserts: "Books are the best of things, well used; abused, among the worst." Emerson delivers a stinging indictment of "book-worms." He argues that even the greatest thinkers were once humble students. The danger, Emerson claims, is that of transferring our respect from the venerable acts of creation, of thought, to that endeavor's imperfect product. He believes scholars must not so prostrate themselves before the majesty of profound <u>works</u> that they forget their <u>creators</u>, whom they should emulate in creative thought. They should not idolize the books themselves in a sort of cult of inferiority, Emerson says, but rather write their own books, their own truths, undertake their own sacred acts of creation.

In a strict sense, these points are valid. But Emerson goes beyond these points; he overstates his case. He is treading the ground between the good scholar and the singular genius. Perhaps, given his own stature, it is only fitting that he should hold us to such lofty standards. Nevertheless, his warnings against showing too much respect for books are not altogether true. Such arguments, about the paramount importance of individual thought, can readily be misused to justify a dismissal of the past. Often such self-indulgent, arrogant arguments are used by those less gifted than Emerson as an excuse to disregard the wisdom that has come before them.

A social critic recently said, "It's fine to learn how to think, but what's the point if you have nothing to think about?" The modern education system has sought to shoulder the burden of "teaching students how to think," often elevating such a subjective goal to status superior to teaching facts and sharing insights about past generations. In short, it focuses more on method and process than what students actually learn.

Some students graduate from American high schools ignorant of when the Civil War occurred or the difference between the Preamble and the Constitution and <u>Das Kapital</u>. Reading and digesting the thoughts of the past is as essential as learning the rules of grammar so as to intelligently violate them. In light of today's high illiteracy rate, society's problems hardly include too many people being "book-worms" or attempting to follow the doctrines of Plato or John Locke or Mahatma Gandhi.

We as Americans share a heritage of ideas. Common assumptions must be examined so that we understand where such "conventional wisdom" came from, for it is only then that we may change the portions of it which may be unjust or clouded by bias. Certainly great books should not be locked away, immune from criticism. Neither, however, should they be lambasted out of visceral ignorance, in the name of "individuality."

Studying and learning from the works of the past, and creating new original writing and thought in the present, are not mutually exclusive propositions. Most scholars lack Emerson's genius, but they will be hard-pressed to find a spark of creativity by meditating in the dark.

Emerson implies that ideas are not great <u>in and of themselves</u>. But ideas <u>can</u> be great. Proof resides in the overwhelming numbers of anonymous poems that fill anthology books. How many aphorisms are repeated daily by speakers who know not whether they generated from the tongue of Winston Churchill or Will Rogers? This is not to suggest that great ideas cannot be proved wrong. That Emerson denies perfection to any ideas is hardly a danger. Since no writer, however brilliant, is perfect, it is perfectly safe to acknowledge certain ideas as great, without granting them perfection and immunity.

When people do not know the past, they face the peril of perpetually re-inventing the wheel—blissfully ignorant of their tendency toward trite alliteration or insipid clichés.

Analysis of the High-Scoring Essay

This thorough, thoughtful, and well-written essay deserves a high score. It begins with the topic and promptly takes a relevant position on the issue of studying from books and ideas of the past. The student shows a clear understanding of Emerson's ideas by examining and elaborating on the major points.

The student then points out a major dilemma inherent in a facile acceptance of Emerson's ideas—that of dismissing the past and the wisdom that has come before.

The essay proceeds with a two-paragraph discussion of the state of education today, pointing out the dual needs of teaching both facts and the thinking process. These paragraphs are particularly relevant to the topic, and the examples are presented with insight. The student also acknowledges our American heritage and the necessity of using books to understand that heritage so that the country's great ideas are not hidden away. These paragraphs demonstrate a deep-thinking student, one who is aware of the world and presents complex ideas with clarity and sophistication.

The next paragraph counters Emerson's position with optimism—the student claims that we can have it all; we can learn from the past and still become clear, independent thinkers who create new ideas. The essay points out that great new ideas do exist and cites anonymous poems as examples of these new ideas. The student also acknowledges that ideas can be great while being imperfect and that such imperfection is no reason to dismiss them entirely.

The essay's brief conclusion reminds the Reader that humans may be doomed to repeat their mistakes and to reinvent the wheel unless they learn from the great ideas of the past. Overall, this essay's points are valid. Without dismissing Emerson lightly, the student intelligently discusses his or her concepts. It should earn a score of 8 or 9.

Medium-Scoring Essay

The process of finding meaningful things in life is not always clear. It is not simple to discover what is true and what is just fancy rhetoric or skirting of the issues. Ralph Waldo Emerson, considered one of our best writers and speakers, gave a speech in Cambridge in 1837, where he talked about books and how they can help us to find the truth which we are seeking in our life.

Emerson said in his speech that books are noble and age-old scholars gave arrangement to the life they saw and organized it. Then they put it into the books that they wrote, and produced a new truth for people to refer to. But he also says that each new generation of Americans has to write their own books. They have to discover their own versions of the truth, and what that truth actually means to them.

He was right. He was also right when he said that we can't just go by what was said then, because the ones who wrote the books that fill our libraries were just young and naïve when they authored those books. How can we be sure they are right, just because they are old? Why are they elevated to the status of classics as if they are perfect?

He says you shouldn't spend all your time in the library, however, I know some people who do just this. The result is that instead of having their own ideas, they just listen to all the old ones, and their creativity is stifled. I agree that it is more important to be a thinking man than one who just accepts everything. You need to have the freedom to have your own ideas, to let them flow without being influenced by principles and underlying ideas already presented in books. These ideas might be right, but if everyone only reads them without thinking for themselves, the country will be full of brainwashed people. They might be well educated, but what will be the price of that education?

He said that books can be best if they are used well, but among the worst of things if they are abused. What this actually encourages is for one to be intelligent about reading and not to believe everything that you read. Also, he says that we should not be bookworms, so caught up in the details of what people said in the past that we don't bother to think our own thoughts about the present or concerning issues of the future that are important to our society. This is the centerpiece of his speech. He means that books have a noble "theory." He also means that in practice we must live up to that theory. We must live up to that theory by not being blind or gullible. Instead, we must be Thinking Men and not thinkers only. He talked about how what we observe has to be filtered in to the truth by our own original ideas. We have to use books wisely, Emerson believed, and I agree wholeheartedly.

Analysis of the Medium-Scoring Essay

This essay would score at the low end of the medium range. It begins with a vague introduction that essentially restates a few points from Emerson's speech. The student does not yet state a thesis or take a position.

The second paragraph continues this trend, merely paraphrasing Emerson's speech without thinking critically about those ideas. An essay that only paraphrases the passage will never score in the upper range.

Finally, the third paragraph presents an opinion and takes a position, although it is repetitively worded. The student seems to have finally started thinking, as he or she questions the validity of older books and the pedestal on which the classics have been placed.

The fourth paragraph is probably the best in this essay and saves the score from sinking even lower. The student uses personal experience as an example, citing other friends who have become "stifled" in their creativity by spending too much time in the library, consuming old books and old ideas without thinking while they read. The student apparently understands the need for everyone to become an individual thinker, an analyzer of ideas.

However, the next paragraph reverts to simple paraphrasing. It offers no additional commentary and, therefore, falls flat.

The essay reaches an adequate conclusion, explaining the need to read wisely and not be gullible. Ultimately, the student manages to insert enough of his or her own commentary about Emerson's concepts to salvage the score. However, this essay could be greatly improved by reducing the paraphrasing and including much more analysis and evidence. Remember that this topic specifically directs students to "use appropriate evidence" to develop the essay. This student has barely accomplished that goal, and thus, the score suffers. It should earn a score of 5.

Scoring

Use the following worksheet to arrive at a probable final AP grade on Practice Exam 1. Because being objective enough to estimate your own essay score is sometimes difficult, you might give your essays (along with the sample essays) to a teacher, friend, or relative to score, if you feel confident that the individual has the knowledge necessary to make such a judgment and that he or she will feel comfortable doing so.

Section I: Multiple-Choice Questions

$$\underline{\hspace{2cm}} - (\underline{\hspace{2cm}}) = \underline{\hspace{2cm}}$$

right answers　　wrong answers　　multiple-choice raw score

$$\underline{\hspace{2cm}} \times 1.2272 = \underline{\hspace{2cm}} \text{ (of possible 67.5)}$$

multiple-choice raw score　　multiple-choice converted score

Section II: Free-Response Questions

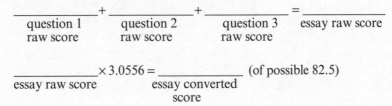

$$\underline{\hspace{2cm}} + \underline{\hspace{2cm}} + \underline{\hspace{2cm}} = \underline{\hspace{2cm}}$$

question 1 raw score　　question 2 raw score　　question 3 raw score　　essay raw score

$$\underline{\hspace{2cm}} \times 3.0556 = \underline{\hspace{2cm}} \text{ (of possible 82.5)}$$

essay raw score　　essay converted score

Final Score

$$\underline{\hspace{2cm}} + \underline{\hspace{2cm}} = \underline{\hspace{2cm}} \text{ (of possible 150)}$$

multiple-choice converted score　　essay converted score　　final converted score

Probable Final AP Score

Final Converted Score	Probable AP Score
150–114	5
113–98	4
97–81	3
80–53	2
52–0	1

Chapter 5

Practice Exam 2

Answer Sheet

Section I: Multiple-Choice Questions

1 Ⓐ Ⓑ Ⓒ Ⓓ Ⓔ	21 Ⓐ Ⓑ Ⓒ Ⓓ Ⓔ	41 Ⓐ Ⓑ Ⓒ Ⓓ Ⓔ
2 Ⓐ Ⓑ Ⓒ Ⓓ Ⓔ	22 Ⓐ Ⓑ Ⓒ Ⓓ Ⓔ	42 Ⓐ Ⓑ Ⓒ Ⓓ Ⓔ
3 Ⓐ Ⓑ Ⓒ Ⓓ Ⓔ	23 Ⓐ Ⓑ Ⓒ Ⓓ Ⓔ	43 Ⓐ Ⓑ Ⓒ Ⓓ Ⓔ
4 Ⓐ Ⓑ Ⓒ Ⓓ Ⓔ	24 Ⓐ Ⓑ Ⓒ Ⓓ Ⓔ	44 Ⓐ Ⓑ Ⓒ Ⓓ Ⓔ
5 Ⓐ Ⓑ Ⓒ Ⓓ Ⓔ	25 Ⓐ Ⓑ Ⓒ Ⓓ Ⓔ	45 Ⓐ Ⓑ Ⓒ Ⓓ Ⓔ
6 Ⓐ Ⓑ Ⓒ Ⓓ Ⓔ	26 Ⓐ Ⓑ Ⓒ Ⓓ Ⓔ	46 Ⓐ Ⓑ Ⓒ Ⓓ Ⓔ
7 Ⓐ Ⓑ Ⓒ Ⓓ Ⓔ	27 Ⓐ Ⓑ Ⓒ Ⓓ Ⓔ	47 Ⓐ Ⓑ Ⓒ Ⓓ Ⓔ
8 Ⓐ Ⓑ Ⓒ Ⓓ Ⓔ	28 Ⓐ Ⓑ Ⓒ Ⓓ Ⓔ	48 Ⓐ Ⓑ Ⓒ Ⓓ Ⓔ
9 Ⓐ Ⓑ Ⓒ Ⓓ Ⓔ	29 Ⓐ Ⓑ Ⓒ Ⓓ Ⓔ	49 Ⓐ Ⓑ Ⓒ Ⓓ Ⓔ
10 Ⓐ Ⓑ Ⓒ Ⓓ Ⓔ	30 Ⓐ Ⓑ Ⓒ Ⓓ Ⓔ	50 Ⓐ Ⓑ Ⓒ Ⓓ Ⓔ
11 Ⓐ Ⓑ Ⓒ Ⓓ Ⓔ	31 Ⓐ Ⓑ Ⓒ Ⓓ Ⓔ	51 Ⓐ Ⓑ Ⓒ Ⓓ Ⓔ
12 Ⓐ Ⓑ Ⓒ Ⓓ Ⓔ	32 Ⓐ Ⓑ Ⓒ Ⓓ Ⓔ	52 Ⓐ Ⓑ Ⓒ Ⓓ Ⓔ
13 Ⓐ Ⓑ Ⓒ Ⓓ Ⓔ	33 Ⓐ Ⓑ Ⓒ Ⓓ Ⓔ	53 Ⓐ Ⓑ Ⓒ Ⓓ Ⓔ
14 Ⓐ Ⓑ Ⓒ Ⓓ Ⓔ	34 Ⓐ Ⓑ Ⓒ Ⓓ Ⓔ	54 Ⓐ Ⓑ Ⓒ Ⓓ Ⓔ
15 Ⓐ Ⓑ Ⓒ Ⓓ Ⓔ	35 Ⓐ Ⓑ Ⓒ Ⓓ Ⓔ	55 Ⓐ Ⓑ Ⓒ Ⓓ Ⓔ
16 Ⓐ Ⓑ Ⓒ Ⓓ Ⓔ	36 Ⓐ Ⓑ Ⓒ Ⓓ Ⓔ	
17 Ⓐ Ⓑ Ⓒ Ⓓ Ⓔ	37 Ⓐ Ⓑ Ⓒ Ⓓ Ⓔ	
18 Ⓐ Ⓑ Ⓒ Ⓓ Ⓔ	38 Ⓐ Ⓑ Ⓒ Ⓓ Ⓔ	
19 Ⓐ Ⓑ Ⓒ Ⓓ Ⓔ	39 Ⓐ Ⓑ Ⓒ Ⓓ Ⓔ	
20 Ⓐ Ⓑ Ⓒ Ⓓ Ⓔ	40 Ⓐ Ⓑ Ⓒ Ⓓ Ⓔ	

CUT HERE

Section II: Free-Response Questions

Question 1

CUT HERE

CUT HERE

CUT HERE

CUT HERE

Question 2

CUT HERE

CUT HERE

CUT HERE

CUT HERE

Question 3

CUT HERE

CUT HERE

CUT HERE

Section I: Multiple-Choice Questions

Time: 1 hour
55 questions

Directions: This section consists of selections from prose works and questions on their content, form, and style. Read each selection carefully. For each question, choose the best answer of the five choices.

Questions 1–14 refer to the following passage from a 20th-century essay.

Here then was I (call me Mary Beton, Mary Seton, or Mary Carmichael or by any name you please—it is not a matter of any importance) sitting on the banks of a river a week or two ago (5) in fine October weather, lost in thought. That collar I have spoken of, women and fiction, the need of coming to some conclusion on a subject that raises all sorts of prejudices and passions, bowed my head to the ground. To the right and (10) left bushes of some sort, golden and crimson, glowed with the colour, even it seemed burnt with the heat, of fire. On the further bank the willows wept in perpetual lamentation, their hair about their shoulders. The river reflected (15) whatever it chose of sky and bridge and burning tree, and when the undergraduate had oared his boat through the reflections they closed again, completely, as if he had never been. There one might have sat the clock round lost in thought. (20) Thought—to call it by a prouder name than it deserved—had let its line down into the stream. It swayed, minute after minute, hither and thither among the reflections and weeds, letting the water lift it and sink it, until—you know the little (25) tug—the sudden conglomeration of an idea at the end of one's line: and then the cautious hauling of it in, and the careful laying of it out? Alas, laid on the grass how small, how insignificant this thought of mine looked; the (30) sort of fish that a good fisherman puts back into the water so that it may grow fatter and be one day worth cooking and eating. I will not trouble you with that thought now, though if you look carefully you may find it for yourselves. . . .

(35) But however small it was, it had, nevertheless, the mysterious property of its kind—put back into the mind, it became at once very exciting and important; and as it darted and sank, and flashed hither and thither, set up such a wash (40) and tumult of ideas that it was impossible to sit still. It was thus that I found myself walking with extreme rapidity across a grass plot. Instantly a man's figure rose to intercept me. Nor did I at first understand that the gesticulations of a (45) curious-looking object, in a cut-away coat and evening shirt, were aimed at me. His face expressed horror and indignation. Instinct rather than reason came to my help; he was a Beadle; I was a woman. This was the turf; there was the (50) path. Only the Fellows and Scholars are allowed here; the gravel is the place for me. Such thoughts were the work of a moment. As I regained the path the arms of the Beadle sank, his face assumed its usual repose, and though turf is (55) better walking than gravel, no very great harm was done. The only charge I could bring against the Fellows and scholars of whatever the college might happen to be was that in protection of their turf, which has been rolled for 300 years in (60) succession, they had sent my little fish into hiding.

What an idea it had been that had sent me so audaciously trespassing I could not now remember. The spirit of peace descended like a (65) cloud from heaven, for if the spirit of peace dwells anywhere, it is in the courts and quadrangles of Oxbridge on a fine October morning. Strolling through those colleges past those ancient halls the roughness of the present (70) seemed smoothed away; the body seemed contained in a miraculous glass cabinet through which no sound could penetrate, and the mind, freed from any contact with facts (unless one trespassed on the turf again), was at liberty to (75) settle down upon whatever meditation was in harmony with the moment. As chance would have it, some stray memory of some old essay about revisiting Oxbridge in the long vacation brought Charles Lamb to mind. . . . Indeed, (80) among all the dead . . . Lamb is one of the most congenial. . . . For his essays are superior . . . because of that wild flash of imagination that lightning crack of genius in the middle of them which leaves them flawed and imperfect, but (85) starred with poetry. . . . It then occurred to me that the very manuscript itself which Lamb had looked at was only a few hundred yards away, so that one could follow Lamb's footsteps across the quadrangle to that famous library where the treasure is kept. Moreover, I recollected, as I put (90) this plan into execution, it is in this famous library that the manuscript of Thackeray's Esmond is also preserved . . . but here I was actually at the door which leads to the library (95) itself. I must have opened it, for instantly there issued, like a guardian angel barring the way with a flutter of black gown instead of white wings, a deprecating, silvery, kindly gentleman, who regretted in a low voice as he waved me back (100) that ladies are only admitted to the library if accompanied by a Fellow of the College or furnished with a letter of introduction.

That a famous library has been cursed by a woman is a matter of complete indifference to a (105) famous library. Venerable and calm, with all its treasures safe locked within its breast, it sleeps forever. Never will I wake those echoes, never will I ask for that hospitality again.

1. According to the passage, the narrator uses several names (lines 1–2) in order to

A. make a universal statement about all humankind
B. deemphasize her personal identity
C. introduce her many pseudonyms as an author
D. attempt to impress the reader with her literacy
E. mask her true identity from the reader

2. The dominant literary device used to describe the narrator's contemplation, "Thought—to call it by a prouder name . . . one day worth cooking and eating" (lines 20–32) is

A. a simile
B. a metaphor
C. personification
D. an apostrophe
E. hyperbole

3. In the phrase "you know the little tug" (lines 24–25), the narrator refers in the abstract to

A. a fish's pull on a fishing line
B. the Beadle's insisting she move off the lawn
C. the annoying loss of a thought
D. the sudden awareness of an idea
E. the pull of her guilty conscience

4. The effect the Beadle has on the narrator is to

A. encourage her pursuit of knowledge
B. cause her thoughts to retreat
C. assure her of correct directions
D. condemn the women's movement
E. inquire if she needs additional assistance

5. It can be inferred that the narrator realizes that she initially cannot remember her thought because

A. it passes so quickly
B. the student rowing by interrupts it
C. it is too undeveloped
D. it does not compare to a great author's ideas
E. it is so carefully and slowly thought out

6. The lawn and library serve the purpose of

A. symbolizing the obstacles that women face
B. reminding readers of the rigors of university study
C. contrasting relaxation with research
D. introducing the existence of equality for women
E. minimizing the author's point about women's roles

7. The passage contains all of the following rhetorical devices EXCEPT

A. personification
B. metaphor
C. simile
D. literary allusion
E. allegory

8. The narrator's purpose in the passage is to

A. explain her anger at the Beadle
B. personify nature's splendor
C. illustrate how men can inhibit women's intellectual pursuits
D. recall the enticing glory of university study
E. preach her beliefs about women's roles in society

9. The organization of the passage could be best characterized as

A. stream of consciousness mixed with narration of specific events
B. comparison and contrast of two incidents
C. exposition of the women's movement and the narrator's opinions
D. description of both the physical setting and the narrator's thoughts
E. flowing smoothly from general ideas to specific statements

10. The pacing of the sentence "But however small it was . . . it was impossible to sit still" (lines 35–41)

A. reflects the acceleration of her thoughts
B. represents a continuation of the pace of the description of the river
C. contrasts with the fish metaphor
D. suggests a sluggishness before the Beadle's interruption
E. parallels that of the description of the library doorman

11. The narrator's description of the Beadle and the library doorman serves to

A. confirm the horror of what she has done
B. frighten women away from universities
C. encourage women to rebel against men
D. contrast the men's manners
E. satirize the petty men who enforce the rules

12. The phrase "for instantly there issued . . . waved me back" (lines 95–99) can best be characterized as containing

A. obvious confusion from the doorman
B. metaphorical reference to a jailer
C. awed wonder at the man's position
D. humorous yet realistic description
E. matter-of-fact narration

13. Overall, at the time of the occurrences she describes, the narrator probably felt all of the following EXCEPT

A. indignation
B. bewilderment
C. delight
D. exasperation
E. repression

14. The narrator's stylistic technique in the passage can best be described as

A. alternating depictions of what she sees, what she does, and what she ponders
B. the presentation of a social problem followed by its resolution
C. general statements followed by illustrative detail
D. presentation of a theory followed by exceptions to that theory
E. comparison and contrast of great authors' ideas

Questions 15–26 refer to the following passage from an 18th-century collection of biographies.

[Alexander Pope] professed to have learned his poetry from Dryden, whom, whenever an opportunity was presented, he praised through his whole life with unvaried liberality; and (5) perhaps his character may receive some illustration if he be compared with his master.

Integrity of understanding and nicety of discernment were not allotted in a less proportion to Dryden than to Pope. The rectitude of Dryden's (10) mind was sufficiently shown by the dismission of his poetical prejudices, and then rejection of unnatural thoughts and rugged numbers. But Dryden never desired to apply all the judgment that he had. He wrote, and professed to write, merely (15) for the people, and when he pleased others, he contented himself. He spent no time in struggles to rouse latent powers; he never attempted to make that better which was already good, nor often to mend what he must have known to be faulty. He (20) wrote, as he tells us, with very little consideration; when occasion or necessity called upon him, he poured out what the present moment happened to supply, and, when once it had passed the press, ejected it from his mind: for when he had no (25) pecuniary interest, he had no further solicitude.

Pope was not content to satisfy; he desired to excel, and therefore always endeavored to do his best: he did not court the candor, but dared the judgment of his reader, and, expecting no (30) indulgence from others, he showed none to himself. He examined lines and words with minute and punctilious observation, and retouched every part with indefatigable diligence, till he had left nothing to be forgiven. . . .

(35) His declaration that his care for his works ceased at their publication was not strictly true. His parental attention never abandoned them; what he found amiss in the first edition, he silently

corrected in those that followed. He appears to
(40) have revised the *Iliad,* and freed it from some of its
imperfections, and the *Essay on Criticism* received
many improvements after its first appearance. It
will seldom be found that he altered without
adding clearness, elegance, or vigor. Pope had
(45) perhaps the judgment of Dryden; but Dryden
certainly wanted the diligence of Pope.

In acquired knowledge, the superiority must be
allowed to Dryden, whose education was more
scholastic, and who before he became an author
(50) had been allowed more time for study, with better
means of information. His mind has a larger
range, and he collects his images and illustrations
from a more extensive circumference of science.
Dryden knew more of man in his general nature,
(55) and Pope in his local manners. The notions of
Dryden were formed by comprehensive
speculation, and those of Pope by minute
attention. There is more dignity in the knowledge
of Dryden, and more certainty in that of Pope.

(60) Poetry was not the sole praise of either; for
both excelled likewise in prose; but Pope did not
borrow his prose from his predecessor. The style
of Dryden is capricious and varied; that of Pope
is cautious and uniform. Dryden obeys the
(65) motions of his own mind; Pope constrains his
mind to his own rules of composition. Dryden is
sometimes vehement and rapid; Pope is always
smooth, uniform, and gentle. Dryden's page is a
natural field, rising into inequalities, and
(70) diversified by the varied exuberance of abundant
vegetation; Pope's is a velvet lawn, shaven by the
scythe, and leveled by the roller.

Of genius, that power which constitutes a poet;
that quality without which judgment is cold, and
(75) knowledge is inert, that energy which collects,
combines, amplifies, and animates; the superiority
must, with some hesitation, be allowed to Dryden.
It is not to be inferred that of this poetical vigor
Pope had only a little, because Dryden had more;
(80) for every other writer since Milton must give place
to Pope; and even of Dryden it must be said, that,
if he has brighter paragraphs, he has not better
poems. Dryden's performances were always hasty,
either excited by some external occasion, or
(85) extorted by domestic necessity; he composed
without consideration, and published without
correction. What his mind could supply at call, or
gather in one excursion, was all that he sought, and
all that he gave. The dilatory caution of Pope
(90) enabled him to condense his sentiments, to multiply
his images, and to accumulate all that study might
produce or chance might supply. If the flights of
Dryden therefore are higher, Pope continues longer

on the wing. If of Dryden's fire the blaze is brighter,
(95) of Pope's the heat is more regular and constant.
Dryden often surpasses expectation, and Pope
never falls below it. Dryden is read with frequent
astonishment, and Pope with perpetual delight.

15. The passage's organization could best be
described as

A. exposition of a thesis followed by
illustrations
B. chronological presentation of each poet's
works
C. presenting ideas based on their order of
importance
D. basing each paragraph on a different
argument
E. comparison of and contrast between the
two poets

16. In context, "candor" (line 28) can be interpreted to
mean

A. acceptance
B. criticism
C. excellence
D. sincerity
E. indifference

17. In each of the following pairs of words, the first
refers to Dryden, the second to Pope. Which
pair best describes their prose style?

A. dignified vs. simplistic
B. passionate vs. lyrical
C. unsystematic vs. harmonious
D. punctilious vs. careless
E. pedantic vs. impetuous

18. Which of the following best describes Pope's
attitude toward his own writing?

A. "[He] dared the judgment of his reader"
(lines 28–29).
B. "His parental attention never abandoned
them" (line 37).
C. "It will seldom be found that he altered
without adding clearness" (lines 42–44).
D. "Pope is cautious and uniform" (lines
63–64).
E. "Pope continues longer on the wing" (lines
93–94).

19. The passage's points could be more convincing if the author were to offer

- **A.** less emphasis on Pope's writing and editing diligence
- **B.** more direct language to present his ideas about the poets
- **C.** more discussion of Dryden's editing theories
- **D.** more point-by-point comparisons of each poet's prose
- **E.** specific examples from each poet's work to support his opinions

20. Which of the following is NOT found in the passage?

- **A.** For Pope, good writing meant rewriting.
- **B.** Both authors were productive.
- **C.** Dryden is the superior prose writer.
- **D.** Dryden follows his own mind more than Pope does.
- **E.** Pope's writing is like a manicured lawn.

21. Which of the following best characterizes Dryden's method of writing?

- **A.** "when he pleased others, he contented himself" (lines 15–16)
- **B.** "he poured out what the present moment happened to supply" (lines 21–23)
- **C.** "when he had no pecuniary interest, he had no further solicitude" (lines 24–25)
- **D.** "His mind has a larger range" (lines 51–52)
- **E.** "the superiority must, with some hesitation, be allowed to Dryden" (lines 76–77)

22. Although Pope did not have as strong a scholastic background as Dryden, the author implies that Pope

- **A.** chose subjects unrelated to Dryden's
- **B.** had great familiarity with his subject matter
- **C.** feigned completing university study
- **D.** compensated by emulating Dryden
- **E.** undermined any effort on his behalf

23. According to the passage, genius can invigorate which of the following in an author?

- **A.** power and prestige
- **B.** insight and cunning
- **C.** judgment and knowledge
- **D.** skepticism and caution
- **E.** idealism and ambition

24. What does the author suggest as the main reason that Dryden's writing style labels him a genius?

- **A.** the apparent effortlessness of his writing
- **B.** the fact that he "continues longer on the wing" (lines 93–94)
- **C.** the fact that his prose is a "natural field" (line 69)
- **D.** the fact that his academic studies prepare him so well
- **E.** the fact that the age he lived in was noted for intelligence

25. In lines 68–72 ("Dryden's page is a natural field . . . leveled by the roller"), which of the following literary devices is used to summarize the differences between Dryden's and Pope's prose?

- **A.** syllogism
- **B.** personification
- **C.** understatement
- **D.** metaphor
- **E.** simile

26. Of the following, which is NOT a major distinction the speaker draws between Dryden and Pope?

- **A.** their educational foundation
- **B.** their prose style
- **C.** their skill in writing
- **D.** their vigor in writing
- **E.** their editing practice

Questions 27–41 refer to the following passage from a 19th-century essay.

It is remarkable that there is little or nothing to be remembered written on the subject of getting a living; how to make getting a living not merely honest and honorable, but altogether
(5) inviting and glorious; for if *getting* a living is not so, then living is not. One would think, from looking at literature, that this question had never disturbed a solitary individual's musings. Is it that men are too much disgusted with their
(10) experience to speak of it? The lesson of value which money teaches, which the Author of the Universe has taken so much pains to teach us, we are inclined to skip altogether. As for the means of living, it is wonderful how indifferent men of
(15) all classes are about it, even reformers, so called,—whether they inherit, or earn, or steal it. I think that Society has done nothing for us in this respect, or at least has undone what she has

(20) done. Cold and hunger seem more friendly to my nature than those methods which men have adopted and advise to ward them off.

The title *wise* is, for the most part, falsely applied. How can one be a wise man, if he does not know any better how to live than other men?—if he is (25) only more cunning and intellectually subtle? Does Wisdom work in a tread-mill? or does she teach how to succeed *by her example*? Is there any such thing as wisdom not applied to life? Is she merely the miller who grinds the finest logic? Is it pertinent (30) to ask if Plato got his living in a better way or more successfully than his contemporaries,—or did he succumb to the difficulties of life like other men? Did he seem to prevail over some of them merely by indifference, or by assuming grand airs? Or find it (35) easier to live, because his aunt remembers him in her will? The ways in which most men get their living, that is, live, are mere makeshifts, and a shirking of the real business of life,—chiefly because they do not know, but partly because they do not (40) mean, any better.

The rush to California, for instance, and the attitude, not merely of merchants, but of philosophers and prophets, so called, in relation to it, reflect the greatest disgrace on mankind. (45) That so many are ready to live by luck, and so get the means of commanding the labor of others less lucky, without contributing any value to society! And that is called enterprise! I know of no more startling development of the (50) immorality of trade, and all the common modes of getting a living. The philosophy and poetry and religion of such a mankind are not worth the dust of a puffball. The hog that gets his living by rooting, stirring up the soil so, would (55) be ashamed of such company. If I could command the wealth of all the world by lifting my finger, I would not pay *such* a price for it. Even Mahomet knew that God did not make this world in jest. It makes God to be a moneyed (60) gentleman who scatters a handful of pennies in order to see mankind scramble for them. The world's raffle! A subsistence in the domains of Nature a thing to be raffled for! What a comment, what a satire, on our institutions! The (65) conclusion will be, that mankind will hang itself upon a tree. And have all the precepts in all the Bibles taught men only this? And is the last and most admirable invention of the human race only an improved muck-rake? Is this the ground (70) on which Orientals and Occidentals meet? Did God direct us so to get our living, digging where we never planted,—and He would, perchance, reward us with lumps of gold?

(75) God gave the righteous man a certificate entitling him to food and raiment, but the unrighteous man found a *facsimile* of the same in God's coffers, and appropriated it, and obtained food and raiment like the former. It is one of the most extensive systems (80) of counterfeiting that the world has ever seen. I did not know that mankind was suffering for want of gold. I have seen a little of it. I know that it is very malleable, but not so malleable as wit. A grain of gold will gild a great surface, but not so much as a grain of wisdom.

(85) The gold-digger in the ravines of the mountains is as much a gambler as his fellow in the saloons of San Francisco. What difference does it make whether you shake dirt or shake dice? If you win, society is the loser. The gold-digger is the enemy of (90) the honest laborer, whatever checks and compensations there may be. It is not enough to tell me that you worked hard to get your gold. So does the Devil work hard. The way of transgressors may be hard in many respects. The humblest observer (95) who goes to the mines sees and says that gold-digging is of the character of a lottery; the gold thus obtained is not the same thing with the wages of honest toil. But, practically, he forgets what he has seen, for he sees only the fact, not the principle, and (100) goes into trade there, that is, buys a ticket in what commonly proves another lottery, where the fact is not so obvious.

27. In his opening sentence, the author asserts that "getting a living" should be both

- A. moral and pious
- B. ethical and admirable
- C. accessible and sensible
- D. desirable and attainable
- E. humble and profitable

28. According to the author, although man must earn money, he is indifferent to

- A. religion
- B. society
- C. cold and hunger
- D. lessons of value
- E. laborers

29. The author asserts that

- A. we have forgotten the proper value of money
- B. good, hard work will save mankind
- C. the world operates solely on luck
- D. religion fails to address the merit of labor
- E. gold-digging is acceptable under certain conditions

30. The "Author of the Universe" (lines 11–12) can be interpreted as a

   A.   symbol for cosmic consciousness
   B.   metaphor for a contemporary writer
   C.   symbol for judgment
   D.   metaphor for all artists
   E.   metaphor for God

31. The author's rhetorical purpose in referring to Plato is to

   A.   make the point about gold-digging more universal and timeless
   B.   qualify the assertions about gold-diggers and their luck
   C.   question whether ancient philosophers faced the same dilemmas that others do
   D.   consider the ancient philosopher's premises about morality in society
   E.   create an authoritative tone to lend credence to the argument

32. What is the antecedent for "it" (line 57)?

   A.   "immorality" (line 50)
   B.   "philosophy" (line 51)
   C.   "hog" (line 53)
   D.   "wealth" (line 56)
   E.   "world" (line 56)

33. Which of the following is the best example of aphorism?

   A.   "The ways in which most men . . . any better." (lines 36–40)
   B.   "Nature a thing to be raffled for!" (line 63)
   C.   "A grain of gold . . . a grain of wisdom." (lines 82–84)
   D.   "What difference does it make . . . shake dice?" (lines 87–88)
   E.   "So does the Devil work hard." (lines 92–93)

34. An unstated assumption of the author is that

   A.   philosophers should work harder to apply their teachings
   B.   a pig would be mortified by some men
   C.   society is gradually improving
   D.   true wisdom comes only through hard work
   E.   what appears honest to one can be harmful to society

35. The author's comments about the California gold rush serve the purpose of

   A.   comparing gold-diggers to the ancient Greeks
   B.   illustrating how immorally men are earning a living
   C.   explaining the relationship of Orientals to Occidentals
   D.   sensationalizing a topical and popular occupation
   E.   criticizing those who think gold-digging is romantic

36. Which of the following negative phrases is, in context, a qualified negative?

   A.   "men are . . . disgusted with their experience" (lines 9–10)
   B.   "Cold and hunger" (line 19)
   C.   "the greatest disgrace on mankind" (line 44)
   D.   "the unrighteous man" (line 75)
   E.   "society is the loser" (line 89)

37. The passage contains all of the following rhetorical devices EXCEPT

   A.   simile
   B.   historical allusion
   C.   rhetorical question
   D.   syllogistic reasoning
   E.   religious reference

38. The sentence "A grain of gold . . . a grain of wisdom" (lines 82–84) can best be restated as

   A.   knowledge is more valuable than gold
   B.   gold-diggers must work harder than philosophers
   C.   gold will last longer than knowledge
   D.   erudition takes longer to achieve than money
   E.   money has no practical purpose

39. The tone of the passage can best be described as

   A.   condescending
   B.   skeptical
   C.   worried
   D.   indignant
   E.   pedestrian

40. Which of the following is NOT part of the author's argument against gold-digging?

    A. "The hog . . . would be ashamed of such company." (lines 53–55)

    B. "digging where we never planted" (lines 71–72)

    C. "I know that it is very malleable" (lines 81–82)

    D. "the enemy of the honest laborer" (lines 89–90)

    E. "of the character of a lottery" (line 96)

41. Which of the following is NOT discussed in the passage?

    A. Man can learn to improve his lot in life.

    B. Authors have not addressed "getting a living."

    C. Gamblers have damaged society.

    D. The title "wise" may be misapplied.

    E. Men are too easily lured by monetary rewards.

Questions 42–55 refer to the following passage.

This excerpt describes a daring and dangerous long-distance flight by Igor Sikorsky in his new flying machine, the Il'ya Muromets. This gigantic four-engine biplane was emblematic of the opulence and contradictions of Imperial Russia at the zenith of its power and glory. The Muromets' appointments bespoke luxury, yet her aerodynamics were of the most primitive order. She boasted unprecedented size and payload, yet she was severely under-powered. After only a few test flights, Sikorsky's confidence and patriotic courage overcame his doubts and the risky flight took off at 1:00 a.m. on June 30, 1914.

Sikorsky determined to fly from St. Petersburg to Kiev, the city of his birth, a distance of 1,200 kilometers. . . . The heavily loaded plane staggered along at about 400 feet of altitude.
(5) Then, disaster struck. The right inboard engine fractured a fuel line, and the exhaust immediately ignited it, triggering a blowtorch of flame jetting back 12 feet behind the engine, playing on the wing surface and wing struts.[1] Without hesitation
(10) pilot-navigator Lieutenant Lavrov and mechanic Vladimir Panasiuk went out on the wing; the quick-thinking Lavrov leaned over the roaring jet of flame, reached down, and closed a fuel valve, shutting off the flow. Then the two men,
(15) using their greatcoats, smothered the flame.

[Days later,] after conferring with the crew, Sikorsky decided to climb. . . . Just above 5,000 feet they broke out into the clear, into a brilliant blue sky above the puffy, white, sunlit clouds. It
(20) was a Jules Verne moment, one that Sikorsky must have recognized and desired ever since as a child he had avidly read *Robur-le-conquérant* with its imaginary open-air promenade above the clouds. Sikorsky turned the plane over to Prussis,
(25) had a cup of coffee, put on his greatcoat, and then stepped out on the upper bridge, keeping his position by holding the rails. "Only a few times in my life have I seen such a majestic and beautiful spectacle as I did then," he recalled
(30) later. "Our ship was gliding along a few hundred feet above a sparkling white surface. The air was calm and the plane seemed motionless with its huge yellow wings. . . . All around me there was a fairyland, formed by clouds."[2]

(35) Cold finally forced Sikorsky indoors, where he rested in his cabin. Two hours later, when it was time to descend into Kiev, Sikorsky took over, and the plane plunged into a gloomy, dark, and turbulent world of clouds . . . it began to thin and
(40) finally, at about 900 feet, they broke out, and there, dead ahead, miraculously, were the domes of Kiev's famed cathedral. Sikorsky throttled the four faithful Argus engines back and set up a straight-in gliding approach, landing on the
(45) muddy field without further ado, tired and worn, but understandably jubilant at having proven the practicality of the long-range airplane. . . . Only one dignitary, the secretary of the Kiev Aeronautical Society, was there to greet them. He
(50) did not offer the reception they might have expected; after only the briefest of perfunctory congratulations, he told them the latest news: the archduke Franz Ferdinand and his wife had been assassinated by Serbian terrorists in the little
(55) Balkan city of Sarajevo.[3] An extraordinary lack of security that lead to a near-fatal bombing earlier in the day; the inexplicable (and suspicious) misdirection of the motorcade off Appel Quay, requiring it to reverse course so that the archduke's
(60) car halted directly in front of Gavrilo Princip; the assassin himself—a trained, fanatical 19-year-old Bosnian Serb gunman, "tiresome, ego, mare eyed, consumptive looking"[4]—all this culminated in two well-aimed shots from Princip's Browning
(65) pistol that irretrievably shattered and reshaped not only European life but the entire course of subsequent world history.[5]

The airplane—the "annihilator of time and space," the embodiment of speed, even more than
(70) the locomotive—promised to create a world of convenient travel. Thus Sikorsky's flight from St. Petersburg to Kiev had an innocence about it that captured at once the romance, the hope,

and—yes—the naiveté of early flying. A young
(75) man reveling in his creation, he stood outside as
his machine droned along above the clouds,
drinking in the bright sky and sun, living in the
fictional adventures of his childhood, seeing the
beauty of the cavernous vista around him, and
(80) like the world he was in, not thinking of the dark,
turbulent storm hidden within all that beauty.
Fellow aviators generally behaved the same. They
flew in competitions, crossed frontiers, admired
the vistas, flung their aircraft about with increasing
(85) abandon, seemingly oblivious that soon they
would participate in a far more deadly
international competition, crossing into each
other's frontiers, observing troop movements
below, and flinging their aircraft about in
(90) desperate attempts to evade or destroy.

[1] Sikorsky, *Winged-S*, 108. Finne, *Igor Sikorsky: The Russian Years*, 49, asserts that it was the left inboard engine that fractured its fuel line and caught fire, but I have relied on Sikorsky's own account, which states that it was the right inboard engine.

[2] Ibid., 113

[3] Ibid., 115.

[4] British minister of trade Alan Clark's evocative reflection upon seeing a photograph of the young assassin in the Princip Museum, Sarajevo, in October 1986. He added, "Something between Seventies CND and Baader-Meinhof." CND refers to leftist anti-nuclear Campaign for Nuclear Disarmament, and Baader-Meinhof is a reference to one of the more murderous leftist terrorist organizations of the late Cold War. Alan Clark, *Diaries* (London: Phoenix, 1993), 146.

[5] There is an excellent summary of the events leading to assassination in Edward Crankshaw's *The Fall of the House of Hapsburg* (New York: Popular Library, 1963 ed.), 402–406. Earlier in the day, Franz Ferdinand himself had to deflect a potentially fatal hand grenade hurled at his car; enormously (if foolishly) brave, he pressed on with the visit, and was in the second car of the motorcade, which was forced to halt and back up when the mayor's car made a wrong right-hand turn. "Security precautions," Crankshaw has rightly concluded, "were practically nil" (403).

42. Considering the passage as a whole, one can conclude that early aviation

　A. was a moderately successful means of mass transportation

　B. was rarely successful until the impetus of World War I

　C. was very dangerous but worth the effort

　D. was never pleasurable for the pioneers of early flight

　E. usually ended in disaster that was unavoidable

43. The effect of the short, three-word sentence, "Then, disaster struck," in line 5 is to

　A. modify details in the preceding sentences

　B. sound like a direct quote from Sikorsky

　C. paraphrase a famous quotation from an earlier work

　D. diminish the crew's surprise

　E. add emphasis to the stark reality of the near-catastrophe

44. The description of the actions of Lavrov and Panasiuk in lines 9–15 implies that the author believes Lavrov and Panasiuk

　A. were the only members of the crew who were brave enough to act decisively

　B. took an unnecessary chance

　C. should not have acted without orders

　D. did not follow proper procedures

　E. proved, through their own actions, the value of quick and effective action, even at the risk of one's own life

45. The author's reference to Jules Verne serves the rhetorical purpose of

　A. establishing that, only a few years before this extraordinary flight, the very idea that man could fly was science fiction

　B. establishing that Sikorsky was a Jules Verne fan who lived in a fantasy world

　C. suggesting that the author shares Sikorsky's fascination with Jules Verne

　D. paying homage to the legions of Jules Verne fans

　E. showing that aviation had not really advanced since Sikorsky was a child

46. The most important intended rhetorical effect of Sikorsky's quotation "Only a few times . . . formed by clouds" in lines 27–34 is

　A. to emphasize that this spectacle is unprecedented in human history

　B. to allow the reader to appreciate the excellent weather

　C. to explain exactly how high over the clouds the aircraft is flying

　D. to describe the ethereal view with vivid imagery

　E. to show how the author feels the need to use direct quotes in his writing

47. An unstated rhetorical purpose for the author's use of the word "faithful" in referring to the aircraft's four engines in line 43 is most likely

A. to refer to Sikorsky's religious faith
B. to allude to the great cathedral in Kiev
C. to chronicle the "four faithful" Russian Orthodox Saints
D. to create the image of the engines as living beings and as obedient servants
E. to acknowledge the name of the engine manufacturer

48. Following Alan Clark's quote (lines 62–63), the author's rhetorical purpose in adding footnote #4 is to

A. reinforce the physical description of Princip through comparisons to later terrorists
B. provide a first-hand description of the Princip Museum in Kiev
C. provide concrete documentation of Sikorsky's log of the flight
D. provide a contrasting perspective of the motives of Gavrilo Princip and other terrorists
E. reference an excellent summary of the events leading to the assassination

49. The image of Sikorsky standing outside his aircraft "drinking in the bright sky and sun . . . living in the fictional adventures . . . seeing the beauty . . . [but] not thinking of the dark, turbulent storm hidden within all that beauty" (lines 76–81) is a metaphor for

A. the bad weather below, where they must eventually return to Earth
B. the coming Great War, in which the opening shots had already been fired
C. Sikorsky's as-yet-unacknowledged loss of faith in his own creation
D. the symbolic return to the homeland that all adventurers must make
E. Sikorsky turning his back on the old world

50. The phrase that most clearly identifies the author's symbolic impression of Sikorsky's specific successful flight is

A. "The airplane—the 'annihilator of time and space'" (lines 68–69)
B. "Sikorsky's flight . . . had an innocence about it that captured . . . the naiveté of early flying" (lines 71–74)
C. "A young man reveling in his creation" (lines 74–75)
D. ". . . living in the fictional adventures of his childhood" (lines 77–78)
E. ". . . the dark, turbulent storm hidden within all that beauty" (lines 80–81)

51. The passage contains all of the following literary devices EXCEPT

A. character development
B. literary allusions
C. vivid descriptions of action
D. primary-source quotations
E. metaphorical allusions

52. The following phrases all refer to the inadequate security precautions for Franz Ferdinand EXCEPT

A. "An extraordinary lack of security" (lines 55–56)
B. "the inexplicable (and suspicious) misdirection of the motorcade" (lines 57–58)
C. "the archduke's car halted directly in front of Gavrilo Princip" (lines 59–60)
D. "tiresome, ego, mare eyed, consumptive looking" (lines 62–63)
E. "'Security precautions,' Crankshaw has rightly concluded, 'were practically nil.'" (footnote #5)

53. Considering the information in footnote #1, one can infer that the author

    A. concludes that it was really the left inboard engine that caught fire

    B. concludes that it was really the right outboard engine that caught fire

    C. has researched his subject; he relies on Sikorsky's own account, which contradicts Finne's conclusion

    D. relies on the information in a book by Finne, *Igor Sikorsky: The Russian Years*

    E. has trouble deciding the facts because he is confronted with differing historical narratives

54. One can gather all of the following facts or inferences from footnote #5 EXCEPT

    A. another assassination attempt occurred earlier that same day

    B. Franz Ferdinand himself repelled a hand grenade, but he pressed on with the visit

    C. a wrong turn by the mayor's car may have contributed to the assassination

    D. Franz Ferdinand's bravado in the face of danger may have contributed to his own assassination

    E. security precautions in Sarajevo were particularly stringent that day

55. Considering the passage as a whole, the author's primary rhetorical purpose is to

    A. establish a strong argument against manned flight

    B. juxtapose the danger and excitement of a history-making flight with a simultaneous history-changing event in Sarajevo

    C. establish the author's condescending attitude toward the early aviation pioneers

    D. criticize the negligent security surrounding Archduke Ferdinand

    E. explain the intricacies of aircraft maneuverability

IF YOU FINISH BEFORE TIME IS CALLED, CHECK YOUR WORK ON THIS SECTION ONLY. DO NOT WORK ON ANY OTHER SECTION IN THE TEST.

STOP

Section II: Free-Response Questions

Time: 2 hours, 15 minutes
3 questions

Question 1

(Suggested writing time—40 minutes. This question counts for one-third of the total free-response section score.)

The National Endowment for the Arts (NEA) is an independent federal agency that has been awarding grants to contemporary visual and performing artists since 1965. This grant money comes from American taxpayers. Much of the visual art that is funded by federal grants has been labeled controversial. Should such controversy continue being funded by unsure taxpayers? How does society today look at art as a contribution to American culture and how does it affect the public's view of the spending habits of the United States government?

Considering the pros and cons of NEA funding, read the following six sources (including any introductory information) carefully. Then, synthesizing at least three of the sources for support, write a coherent, well-written essay in which you take a position that defends, challenges, or qualifies the claim that the United States government should continue to award grants to artists through the National Endowment for the Arts.

Always remember that your argument should be central; the sources should be used to support this argument. Therefore, avoid merely summarizing sources. Clearly cite which sources you use, both directly and indirectly. Refer to the sources by their titles (Source A, Source B, etc.) or by the descriptions in parentheses.

Source A (Brooks)

Source B (Cole)

Source C (Walters)

Source D (Horwitz)

Source E (NEA chart)

Source F (Knochel)

Source A

Brooks, Arthur C. "Do Public Subsidies Leverage Private Philanthropy for the Arts?" Nonprofit and Voluntary Sector Quarterly. Mar. 1999: 28: 32–45. Print.

The following passage is excerpted from an article about the relationship between government funding and private donations to the arts.

The idea that private philanthropy depends positively on public subsidies has commonly been heard of late in the debate over the need for government participation in the provision of the arts in the United States. According to the American Arts Alliance (1995), "Last year [1994], $123 million in [National Endowment for the Arts (NEA)] grants leveraged more than $1.3 billion." This statement imputes causality to the NEA grants: They were in some way responsible for the generation of more than 10 times as much in non-NEA donations.

This argument relies principally on the assumption that donors respond to the added incentives that matching funds from government grants provide: Because NEA dollars require at least equal matching from other sources, these dollars must have elicited at least that amount in donations from the private sector. Other explanations are also commonly heard as to why there should be a positive relationship between public funding and private philanthropy. For example, it has been argued that grants from the government to an organization can bring that organization to the attention of private donors as the object of support. Similarly, being a recipient of government funding requires a certain level of financial accountability and responsibility, which private donors find attractive.

Is it reasonable to claim that government funding to the arts will have this leveraging effect? Some might say not and make the argument that just the opposite effect should obtain: Public funds should tend to "crowd out" private donations, so private donations are likely made in spite of the NEA subsidies rather than because of them. There are three general reasons why this crowding out might occur.

First, the sense of responsibility and public enthusiasm to support a social cause might be diminished if the government takes responsibility for its funding.

Second, subsidies to arts firms may indeed be a signal of quality but not good quality: They might appear to be a bailout of arts firms in dire straits. Although this may attract some donors, others may be driven away by the prospect of a failed project.

Finally, to the extent that higher government subsidies are paid for with higher taxes, individuals have less disposable income and hence do not donate as much as they otherwise might. This is probably insignificant in the United States, where tax revenues (at all levels of government) allocated to the arts in 1987 amounted to just $3.30 per person.

Source B

Cole, David. "The Culture War; When the Government Is a Critic." *Los Angeles Times*. 3 Oct. 1999, home ed.: pg. 1. Print.

The following article discusses the government's role in funding controversial art.

New York City Mayor Rudolph W. Giuliani, who threatened in true New York fashion to bring the Brooklyn Museum to its knees if it went ahead with an art exhibition that he finds "sick," is only the latest in a none-too-distinguished line of government officials who decide to become art critics. The mayor's most prominent precursor is Sen. Jesse Helms (R-N.C.), who, in 1989, objected vociferously to federal funding of a Robert Mapplethorpe exhibition on the ground that it was homoerotic, thereby launching a decade-long cultural battle over the National Endowment for the Arts. Five years earlier, Rep. Mario Biaggi of New York objected to NEA funding of a Metropolitan Opera production of Verdi's "Rigoletto," which he considered denigrating to Italians. Long before that, there was the Inquisition, which tried the painter Paolo Veronese in 1573 for his allegedly sacrilegious depiction of the Last Supper.

This cast of characters should be enough to illustrate why we need to limit government officials' ability to mandate "politically correct" art. Giuliani's heavy-handed tactics underscore the point. His objection apparently focuses on a single painting in a Brooklyn Museum exhibit that opened yesterday, Chris Ofili's "Holy Virgin Mary," a representation of the Virgin Mary with elephant dung on her breast. The mayor objects that the painting is anti-Catholic, which it may or may not be. (Ofili is himself a Catholic who attends church.) When ordinary people decide they don't like such a painting, they generally stay away or turn away. But that's not enough for the mayor. He dislikes this painting so much he doesn't want anyone else to see it.

In light of the prevalence of government subsidies, if the state were free to deny funds to those whose speech it finds disagreeable, freedom of expression would be rendered meaningless. The postmaster could deny subsidies to newspapers that criticized the president. Broadcast stations could be put off the air, nonprofit groups denied their tax exemptions and university faculty fired for expressing controversial views.

This is not a hypothetical concern. Such arguments were widely advanced in the 1950s and 1960s to justify legislative efforts to exclude suspected communists from public universities. The Supreme Court, however, ruled that such claims could not be squared with the principle of academic freedom protected by the 1st Amendment. As a result, even though no professor has a right to be on the government payroll, the court struck down as unconstitutional efforts to deny jobs to those who declined to take an oath against communism.

Two years ago, the Supreme Court had an opportunity to make clear that the same principle applied to public funding of the arts, in National Endowment for the Arts vs. Finley, which challenged a law that required the NEA to "take into consideration general standards of decency" in allocating arts grants. The lower courts held the law unconstitutional. But the Supreme Court ducked the issue, interpreting the statute not to bar funding of indecent or offensive art to be merely advisory. In doing so, however, the majority rejected the view, adopted by Justices Antonin Scalia and Clarence Thomas, that the government has a free hand when subsidizing speech.

Source C

Walters, Scott E. "Some observations on NEA grants." Theatreideas.blogspot.com. Theatre Ideas. 19 May 2011. Web. 3 June 2011.

The following excerpt, written by a professor who teaches drama and theater history at UNC Asheville and serves as the director of the Center for Rural Arts Development and Leadership Education, discusses inequalities in NEA funding.

Last night and this morning, I posted some number crunching of the latest theatre grants given by the NEA. I'd like to do more, and maybe I will, but the next step—examining the populations of the places where grants were given—requires a great deal more time, and I'm not certain it is worth the effort. A quick glance through the list ought to make it pretty clear that most of the grants went to metropolitan areas. But if I get the urge, maybe I'll pull that information together.

Nevertheless, the listing of the grants in a geographic list does make a pretty clear point: five states pulled down over 50% of the theatre grant money. Again. The average grant size is substantially larger for those places, to the tune of about 25%.

As is usually the case when confronted with actual data that confirms an inequality, there is a quick rush to, well, demand more data. How many applications came from each state? We don't know. The NEA says in its press release "Through the Access to Artistic Excellence category, 789 grants out of 1,415 eligible applications are recommended for funding for a total of $24.9 million." That doesn't break it down according to discipline, nor does it indicate where the other eligible applications were from. But given the 55.7% funding rate, let's assume that the proportion of submitted applications was probably pretty similar to those funded. "Aha!" the theatrical birthers pounce, "So that's not really geographical bias, but just the reality of who submitted grants!" Perhaps so. But that's not the point. I'm not claiming, say, bias on the part of the peer review panels—although I suspect that bias is there. What I am claiming is much simpler.

The point is that the theatre has become increasingly centralized (the top five states that received money are also the top five states that have the highest number of TCG-member theatres, for instance), and the NEA is simply reinforcing that centralization through its funding patterns. The question is not whether "that's the way things are," but rather whether "that's the way things ought to be." And if you answer, as I do, that it is not the way things ought to be, if you believe that the arts ought to reflect the diversity of the nation, a diversity which includes not only race but also things like class and geography, then the next question is what the NEA ought to be doing to change the map.

The "N" in NEA stands for "national," but to have more than one-third of the states in the nation receiving no theatre funding at all undermines that claim. Perhaps those states are cleaning up in the other categories, but I doubt it. Regardless, a centralized theatre scene diminishes the theatre's scope, influence, and overall health. It is something we, as theatre people, ought to be concerned about. It reinforces the disconnect between the populace and the arts, and gives credence to those who would claim that the arts are an urban elitist pastime serving a small portion of the nation and therefore unworthy of government funding.

Source D

Horwitz, Andy. "Who Should Pay for the Arts in America?" *The Atlantic*. 31 Jan. 2016. Web. 19 Sept. 2017.

The following excerpt examines the need for diversity in NEA-funded art projects.

One morning last August I visited Williams College in Massachusetts to teach a workshop on "building a life in the arts" with a group of racially, geographically, and economically diverse young people working at the Williamstown Theatre Festival. Later that night I attended a show at the theater, where I saw these idealistic apprentices taking tickets from, ushering, and selling merchandise to an overwhelmingly white audience—mostly over 60 and, judging by appearances, quite well-off. The social and cultural distance between the aspiring artists at Williamstown and their theater-going audience couldn't have been more pronounced. This gulf is quite familiar to most producers and practitioners of the performing arts in America; it plays out nightly at regional theaters, ballets, symphonies, and operas across the country.

The current state of the arts in this country is a microcosm of the state of the nation. Large, mainstream arts institutions, founded to serve the public good and assigned non-profit status to do so, have come to resemble exclusive country clubs. Meanwhile, outside their walls, a dynamic new generation of artists, and the diverse communities where they live and work, are being systematically denied access to resources and cultural legitimation.

Fifty years ago, the National Endowment for the Arts was created to address just such inequity. On September 29, 1965, President Lyndon B. Johnson signed the National Endowment for the Arts into existence, along with a suite of other ambitious social programs, all under the rubric of the Great Society. Johnson imagined these programs as ways to serve "not only the needs of the body and the demands of commerce but the desire for beauty and the hunger for community."

Half a century later, the ethos upon which the NEA was founded—inclusion and community—has been eroded by consistent political attack. As the NEA's budget has been slashed, private donors and foundations have jumped in to fill the gap, but the institutions they support, and that receive the bulk of arts funding in this country, aren't reaching the people the NEA was founded to help serve. The arts aren't dead, but the system by which they are funded is increasingly becoming as unequal as America itself.

* * *

The NEA was founded to "nurture American creativity, to elevate the nation's culture, and to sustain and preserve the country's many artistic traditions." In an inclusive, pluralistic society, arts funding should reflect our increasingly diverse communities. Deliberately excluding art made by and for underrepresented communities goes against the spirit on which the NEA was founded.

If you look at the more than 1,000 projects set to receive NEA funding this year, you can see the historical (and present) richness of American culture that all but demands to be preserved and supported. A small literary press in Hawaii that mostly publishes works by Asian American and native Hawaiian authors. A Chicago children's theater that puts on performances that can be enjoyed by visually impaired audiences or those on the autism spectrum. Songwriting workshops to teach Tlingit children in Hoonah, Alaska, about their culture. A New Orleans film festival for Louisiana filmmakers. Art reflects the values, aspirations, and questions of a culture; it's a mechanism for a society to articulate how it imagines itself. The projects funded by the NEA reflect the growing diversity—and beautiful complexity—of America itself.

Source E

"How the United States Funds the Arts." *National Endowment for the Arts*. Nov. 2012. Web. 13 Sept. 2017.

The following chart explores the amount per capita spent on the arts by agencies in different countries.

Comparison of Funding by Selected Arts Councils and Agencies

	Budget per Capita (U.S. Dollars)	Data Year
Arts Council of Wales	$17.80	2012/2013
Arts Council (Ireland)	$16.96	2012
Scottish Arts Council	$14.52	2009/2010
Arts Council of England	$13.54	2010
Arts Council of Northern Ireland	$12.36	2011/2012
Australian Council	$8.16	2010/2011
Canada Council for the Arts	$5.19	2011
Creative New Zealand	$2.98	2009/2010
National Endowment for the Arts	$0.47	2012

Source F

Knochel, Aaron. "Why Do Conservatives Want the Government to Defund the Arts?" *The Conversation.*
5 Feb. 2017. Web. 1 Oct. 2017.

The following excerpt briefly presents the history of the NEA and explores the current controversy over continued funding for the arts.

Recent reports indicate that Trump administration officials have circulated plans to defund the National Endowment for the Arts (NEA), putting this agency on the chopping block—again.

Historically, the relationship between the state and culture is as fundamental as the idea of the state itself. Prior to the formation of the NEA in 1965, the federal government strategically funded cultural projects of national interest. For example, the Commerce Department subsidized the film industry in the 1920s and helped Walt Disney skirt bankruptcy during World War II. The same could be said for the broad range of New Deal economic relief programs, like the Public Works of Art Project and the Works Progress Administration, which employed artists and cultural workers. The CIA even joined in, funding Abstract Expressionist artists as a cultural counterweight to Soviet Realism during the Cold War.

The NEA came about during the Cold War. In 1963, President John F. Kennedy asserted the political and ideological importance of artists as critical thinkers, provocateurs and powerful contributors to the strength of a democratic society. His attitude was part of a broader bipartisan movement to form a national entity to promote American arts and culture at home and abroad. By 1965, President Johnson took up Kennedy's legacy, signing the National Arts and Cultural Development Act of 1964—which established the National Council on the Arts—and the National Foundation on the Arts and Humanities Act of 1965, which established the NEA.

Since its inception, the NEA has weathered criticism from the left and right. The right generally argues state funding for culture shouldn't be the government's business, while some on the left have expressed concern about how the funding might come with constraints on creative freedoms.

But today, it's not about the art itself. It's about limiting the scope and size of the federal government. And that ideological push presents real threats to our economy and our communities.

Organizations like the Heritage Foundation fail to take into account that eliminating the NEA actually causes the collapse of a vast network of regionally controlled, state-level arts agencies and local councils. In other words, they won't simply be defunding a centralized bureaucracy that dictates elite culture from the sequestered halls of Washington, D.C. The NEA is required by law to distribute 40 percent of its budget to arts agencies in all 50 states and six U.S. jurisdictions.

Therein lies the misguided logic of the argument for defunding: It targets the NEA but in effect threatens funding for programs like the Creede Repertory Theatre—which serves rural and underserved communities in states like Colorado, New Mexico, Utah, Oklahoma and Arizona—and Appalshop, a community radio station and media center that creates public art installations and multimedia tours in Jenkins, Kentucky, to celebrate Appalachian cultural identity.

While the present administration and the conservative movement claim they're simply trying to save taxpayer dollars, they also ignore the significant economic impacts of the arts. The Bureau of Economic Analysis reported that the arts and culture industry generated $704.8 billion of economic activity in 2013 and employed nearly five million people. For every dollar of NEA funding, there are seven dollars of funding from other private and public funds. Elimination of the agency endangers this economic vitality.

Ultimately, the Trump administration needs to decide whether artistic and cultural work is important to a thriving economy and democracy.

Question 2

(Suggested writing time—40 minutes. This question counts for one-third of the total free-response section score.)

The following passages contain comments on two places: M. F. K. Fisher on the French port of Marseille and Maya Angelou on the small town of Stamps, Arkansas.

Read both carefully and write an essay exploring how the authors' rhetorical strategies create both similar and different effects in the two passages.

Passage 1

One of the many tantalizing things about Marseille is that most people who describe it, whether or not they know much about either the place or the languages they are supposedly using, write the same things. For centuries this has been so, and a typically modern opinion could have been given in 1550 as well as 1977.

Not long ago I read one, mercifully unsigned, in a San Francisco paper. It was full of logistical errors, faulty syntax, misspelled French words, but it hewed true to the familiar line that Marseille is doing its best to live up to a legendary reputation as world capital for "dope, whores, and street violence." It then went on to discuss, often erroneously, the essential ingredients of a true bouillabaisse! The familiar pitch had been made, and idle readers dreaming of a great seaport dedicated to heroin, prostitution, and rioting could easily skip the clumsy details of marketing for fresh fish. . . .

"Feature articles" like this one make it seem probable that many big newspapers, especially in English-reading countries, keep a few such mild shockers on hand in a back drawer, in case a few columns need filling on a rainy Sunday. Apparently people like to glance one more time at the same old words: evil, filthy, dangerous.

Sometimes such journalese is almost worth reading for its precociously obsolete views of a society too easy to forget. In 1929, for instance, shortly before the Wall Street Crash, a popular travel writer named Basil Woon published *A Guide to the Gay World of France: From Deauville to Monte Carlo* (Horace Liveright, New York). (By now even his use of the word "gay" is quaintly naïve enough for a small chuckle. . . .)

Of course Mr. Woon was most interested in the Côte d'Azur, in those far days teeming and staggering with rich English and even richer Americans, but while he could not actively recommend staying in Marseille, he did remain true to his journalistic background with an expectedly titillating mention of it:

If you are interested in how the other side of the world lives, a trip through old Marseilles—by daylight—cannot fail to thrill, but it is not wise to venture into this district at night unless dressed like a stevedore and well armed. Thieves, cutthroats, and other undesirables throng the narrow alleys, and sisters of scarlet sit in the doorways of their places of business, catching you by the sleeve as you pass by. The dregs of the world are here, unsifted. It is Port Said, Shanghai, Barcelona, and Sydney combined. Now that San Francisco has reformed, Marseilles is the world's wickedest port.

Passage 2

There is a much-loved region in the American fantasy where pale white women float eternally under black magnolia trees, and white men with soft hands brush wisps of wisteria from the creamy shoulders of their lady loves. Harmonious black music drifts like perfume through this precious air, and nothing of a threatening nature intrudes.

The South I returned to, however, was flesh-real and swollen-belly poor. Stamps, Arkansas, a small hamlet, had subsisted for hundreds of years on the returns from cotton plantations, and until World War I, a creaking lumbermill. The town was halved by railroad tracks, the swift Red River and racial prejudice. Whites lived on the town's small rise (it couldn't be called a hill), while blacks lived in what had been known since slavery as "the Quarters."

In my memory, Stamps is a place of light, shadow, sounds and entrancing odors. The earth smell was pungent, spiced with the odor of cattle manure, the yellowish acid of ponds and rivers, the deep pots of greens and beans cooking for hours with smoked or cured pork. Flowers added their heavy aroma. And above all, the atmosphere was pressed down with the smell of old fears, and hates, and guilt.

On this hot and moist landscape, passions clanged with the ferocity of armored knights colliding. Until I moved to California at thirteen I had known the town, and there had been no need to examine it. I took its being for granted and now, five years later, I was returning, expecting to find the shield of anonymity I had known as a child.

Question 3

(Suggested writing time—40 minutes. This question counts for one-third of the total free-response section score.)

The following essay comes from Sir Thomas More's *Utopia* (1516). Read the passage carefully, then write an essay that evaluates the validity of the author's ideas in light of contemporary standards. Use appropriate evidence to develop your essay and convince the Reader of your ideas.

On Communal Property

By this I am persuaded that unless private property is entirely done away with, there can be no fair distribution of goods, nor can the world be happily governed. As long as private property remains, by far the largest and the best part of mankind will be oppressed with an inescapable load of cares and anxieties. This load, I admit, may be lightened somewhat, but cannot be entirely removed. Laws might be made that no one should own more than a certain amount of land nor possess more than a certain sum of money. Or laws might be passed to prevent the prince from growing too powerful and the populace from becoming too strong. It might be made unlawful for public offices to be solicited, or sold, or made burdensome for the officeholder by great expense. Otherwise officeholders are tempted to reimburse themselves by dishonesty and force, and it becomes necessary to find rich men for those offices which ought rather be held by wise men. Such laws, I say, may have as much effect as good nursing has on men who are dangerously sick. Social evils may be allayed and mitigated, but so long as private property remains, there is no hope at all that they may be healed and society restored to good health. While you try to cure one part, you aggravate the disease in other parts. In redressing one evil another is committed, since you cannot give something to one man without taking the same thing from another.

IF YOU FINISH BEFORE TIME IS CALLED, CHECK YOUR WORK ON THIS SECTION ONLY. DO NOT WORK ON ANY OTHER SECTION IN THE TEST.

Answer Key

Section I: Multiple-Choice Questions

1. B	12. D	23. C	34. E	45. A
2. B	13. C	24. A	35. B	46. D
3. D	14. A	25. D	36. B	47. D
4. B	15. E	26. C	37. D	48. A
5. C	16. A	27. B	38. A	49. B
6. A	17. C	28. D	39. D	50. B
7. E	18. B	29. A	40. C	51. A
8. C	19. E	30. E	41. A	52. D
9. D	20. C	31. C	42. C	53. C
10. A	21. B	32. D	43. E	54. E
11. E	22. B	33. C	44. E	55. B

Section II: Free-Response Questions

Essay scoring guides, student essays, and analysis appear beginning on page 167.

Answer Explanations

Section I: Multiple-Choice Questions

The passage referred to in questions 1–14 is from Virginia Woolf's *A Room of One's Own* (1929).

1. **B.** The phrase that follows the list of names explains this answer: "call me . . . by any name you please—it is not a matter of any importance." The narrator is not trying to make any statement about all humankind (A), introduce any pseudonyms (C), attempt to impress (D), or mask her identity (E).

2. **B.** The narrator primarily uses a metaphor as she describes her thought, imagining it to be on a fishing line that "swayed . . . among the reflections." The thought morphs into a metaphorical fish that she hauls to shore on that line. The device is not personification (C) because in this case an abstract idea is given animal characteristics rather than human (her thought is compared to a fish caught on a line). While one may consider her thought to be personified, it is surely not the dominant literary device Woolf uses. The remaining choices are not used in this part of the passage.

3. **D.** The phrase that follows the quotation clearly identifies the answer: "the sudden conglomeration of an idea at the end of one's line." Choice A names not the abstract meaning but the literal meaning on which the metaphor is based. Choices B, the Beadle's interruption, and C, the annoying loss of her thought, mention later occurrences unrelated to this "tug." There is no suggestion that the narrator has a guilty conscience (E).

4. **B.** Being made aware that she is in an area in which only "Fellows and Scholars" are allowed to walk sends her metaphorical "fish into hiding." The Beadle doesn't encourage (A), direct (C), or ask her questions (E). The women's movement (D) is not addressed in the passage.

5. **C.** In the fish metaphor, the narrator points out "how small, how insignificant" her thought is when examined; at this point her thought is undeveloped. Later she realizes that the thought "became at once very exciting and important," and she mulls it over as she walks across the lawn. However, the Beadle's refusing to let her walk on the lawn again sent her "little fish into hiding." There is no evidence that the thought passes very quickly (A), or is carefully thought out (E), or that either has to do with her forgetting. Notice of the rower (B) occurs before mention of the thought and does not cause her to forget. Finally, the passage does not hint that her thought does not compare to a great author's ideas (D).

6. **A.** The lawn, on which the narrator is forbidden to walk, and the library, where she is forbidden to enter, are symbols of the obstructions all women face. Neither choice B nor choice C accurately identifies the intended symbolism. Choice D contradicts the purpose of the passage—to point out inequality. Choice E is incorrect because these two symbols reinforce, and do not distract from, the narrator's point.

7. **E.** There is no allegory (the use of characters to symbolize truths about humanity) in this passage. The passage does use personification ("willows wept in perpetual lamentation," choice A), metaphor (the "fish" sequence, choice B), simile ("like a guardian angel," choice C), and literary allusion (to Thackery's Esmond, choice D).

8. **C.** The vignettes demonstrate how men have told women where they may and may not go. On a deeper level, they suggest that men's attitudes inhibit women in their intellectual pursuits. The narrator is angry (A) and touches on nature (B), but neither fact states the purpose of the passage. Choice D contradicts the passage; women have been kept away from university study. Choice E overstates; the narrator neither preaches nor discusses society and women's roles in general.

9. **D.** The passage presents external reality, such as the descriptions of the environs of the university and the actions of the Beadle and the doorman, while interspersing the narrator's thoughts about the events. The passage is too logical and grammatical to be classified as a stream of consciousness (A), which is a narrative technique, not a structural element. The passage doesn't compare or contrast two incidents (B) or address the women's movement (C). Although choice E might be a method of organization, it is not used in this passage.

10. **A.** The sentence accelerates, as do her thoughts—"it became at once very exciting and important; . . . it darted and sank . . . flashed hither and thither . . . tumult of ideas . . . impossible to sit still." Choice B is incorrect because the sentence describes her thought, not the river. Choice C is incorrect because the sentence is her fish metaphor, not a contrast to it. The speed of the sentence is the opposite of being sluggish (D). Nothing suggests that the pace of this sentence parallels the library doorman (E).

11. **E.** The description of the men, of their pompous behavior and dress, satirically emphasizes how trifling are the narrator's supposed crimes—walking on the grass and attempting to enter the library—and how foolish is the men's self-important enforcement of discriminatory rules. Choices A and B contradict the passage. The narrator doesn't consider what she's done a "horror," nor would she intend to frighten women away from universities. Choice C is not addressed. Choice D is incorrect because the men's manners are similar, not contrasting.

12. **D.** The description of the gentleman is realistic but also takes a humorous turn in describing a simple doorman as "like a guardian angel barring the way with a flutter of black gown instead of white wings . . . deprecating" as he bars the narrator from entering the library. The doorman is not confused (A), and the reference is not to a jailer (B) but to a guardian angel. Both choices C and E are unreasonable.

13. **C.** It is highly unlikely that the events described produced an overall feeling of delight. The events ultimately are described with a negative tone, even though some of the details are definitely pleasing. Notice that all answer choices except choice C are negative.

14. **A.** The narrator blends a presentation of what she sees, what actions she takes, and her thoughts as she walks. For example, she sees the river, the trees, the Beadle, and the library doorman; she walks across the forbidden lawn and to the library; she ponders about such things as the indignity of being shooed off the lawn and refused entrance to the library. Choice B is incorrect because there is no resolution to her problem. The narrator's stylistic technique does not include making a generality and following it with detail (C), presenting a theory and any exceptions to it (D), or comparing and contrasting great authors' ideas (E).

The passage referred to in questions 15–26 is from *The Lives of the English Poets* (1781) by Samuel Johnson.

15. **E.** The passage compares and contrasts the two poets, Dryden and Pope. Johnson begins by explaining that Dryden was a strong influence on Pope. Hence, Johnson sets out to "compare [Pope] with his master." The second paragraph explains Dryden's method of writing. The two paragraphs following discuss the care Pope took in writing and editing. The fifth paragraph explains the differences in the poets' educational backgrounds, and the sixth compares their prose skills. The passage's concluding paragraph continues to draw comparisons and contrasts, ultimately calling Dryden the better poet, while acknowledging both men's strengths. The passage is primarily one of opinion. There is no thesis given and no extensive use of illustrations (A), other than mention of the *Iliad* and the *Essay on Criticism*. Both choices B (chronological) and C (importance) are inaccurate. Johnson does not present a different argument in each paragraph (D), or strictly present arguments at all. The passage is an analysis of the poets' styles.

16. **A.** Within context, the word "candor" most closely means acceptance; this idea is most consistent with Johnson's intent in the passage. Pope did not court his readers' acceptance, but "dared [their] judgment." Because the sentence sets up an opposition, "criticism" (B), "excellence"(C), "sincerity" (D) (the modern meaning of "candor"), and "indifference" (E) make little sense, as they are not good opposites of "judgment."

17. **C.** In the sixth paragraph (lines 60–72), Dryden's prose style is described as "capricious," obeying "the motions of his own mind," sometimes "vehement and rapid," producing prose that is a "natural field, rising into inequalities . . . diversified"—that is, unsystematic, written quickly and without a preconceived order. Pope's prose, on the other hand, is described as "uniform," while he "constrains his mind to . . . rules of composition." Pope's prose is "smooth, uniform, and gentle," a "velvet lawn." If you check the first word of each answer pair, you will see that choices A, D, and E can quickly be eliminated because they are not suggested or are inappropriate to refer to Dryden's prose. Finally, you can eliminate choice B. While Dryden might be considered passionate, there is no suggestion that Pope is lyrical. (*Note:* In answering questions of this sort, you can also begin by checking the second term of each pair.)

18. **B.** Pope's attitude toward his own writing is best seen in line 37, "His parental attention never abandoned them," which suggests a nurturing attitude toward his work; he "silently corrected" anything he "found amiss" in his published work. Choice A shows not so much an attitude toward his writing as an attitude toward his audience. Choice C deals with the outcome of Pope's editing and, therefore, does not address his attitude toward the actual writing. Choices D and E primarily present Johnson's opinions of Pope's work, not Pope's attitude toward his own writing.

19. **E.** A reader might be more convinced that Johnson's opinions are valid if presented with some evidence, some examples. He mentions Pope's editing of the *Iliad* but never explains exactly what was changed. He calls Dryden's prose "vehement and rapid" but, again, offers no proof. A reader might be left to wonder what Johnson had read of Pope's and Dryden's works that led him to reach these conclusions, and some examples would help. Choice A is incorrect because less emphasis would hardly provide a more convincing argument. The language of the passage is direct (B), and point-by-point comparisons (D) are made; more of the same is unlikely to more thoroughly convince the reader. Dryden, it seems, did little editing (C), so additional discussion here would not be helpful, either.

20. **C.** Johnson makes no definitive claim about the superiority of either poet's prose. In the sixth paragraph, they are presented as different in style but not necessarily in quality. It is Dryden's poetry that Johnson says is superior (although with some hesitation). Remember that this question asks for what is NOT found in the passage, so all of the incorrect answers are evidenced. Choice A, that Pope equated good writing with rewriting, can be found in the third paragraph which claims that, "he examined lines and words with minute and punctilious observation, and retouched every part with indefatigable diligence. . . ." The passage as a whole supports choice B, that both authors were productive, both in poetry and prose. Choice D, that claims Dryden follows his own mind more than Pope does, is clearly stated in the sentence "Dryden obeys the motions of his own mind; Pope constrains his mind. . . ." Finally, Pope's prose is described as "a velvet lawn, shaven by the scythe, and leveled by the roller," which supports choice E.

21. **B.** Johnson explains how quickly Dryden wrote: "He spent no time in struggles to rouse latent powers," and "He wrote, as he tells us, with very little consideration." Choice B is the only answer choice that addresses the question. Choice A does not describe a method of writing; instead, it refers to Dryden's being content if he simply pleased others. The remaining answer choices are wrong for similar reasons. Choice C suggests that Dryden only wrote when he had financial interests. Choice D addresses the scope and breadth of Dryden's mind. Choice E comments that Dryden's poetry has some degree of superiority over Pope's.

22. **B.** Johnson claims that even though Pope did not have the same education opportunities that Dryden enjoyed, Pope gave his subjects his "minute attention"; he had "more certainty" than Dryden, suggesting that Pope knew his subjects well. Choices A, C, D, and E are all unreasonable.

23. **C.** The last paragraph claims that genius invigorates judgment (without which it is cold) and knowledge (without which it is inert). Genius does not invigorate power (A); rather, it is the power that constitutes a poet (line 73). Although choices B, D, and E each have at least one idea that may seem accurate, none of the choices are claimed by the author. Choice C is in print.

24. **A.** The author suggests Dryden's ease in writing as a component of his genius in the second paragraph. The fact that Dryden could produce great poetry and admirable prose so quickly and without laborious rewriting and editing attests to Dryden's genius. The quotation given in choice B refers to Pope, not to Dryden. Choice C may be an apt description of Dryden's prose, but Johnson claims Dryden is a genius in his poetry. Although Dryden had a strong educational foundation (D), Johnson does not address Dryden's education in relation to his genius. The passage offers no evidence for choice E.

25. **D.** Johnson uses an effective pair of metaphors to summarize his opinion of the two poets' prose: Dryden's is a "natural field," while Pope's is a "velvet lawn." The remaining choices are not used in this sentence.

26. **C.** Johnson clearly acknowledges that both poets are gifted, skillful, and talented. He levels little criticism at either poet's writing skills. All other distinctions given are addressed in the passage.

The passage referred to in questions 27–41 is from Henry David Thoreau's "Life Without Principle" (1863).

27. **B.** Thoreau insists that "getting a living" should be ethical ("honest and honorable," line 4) and admirable ("altogether inviting and glorious," lines 4–5). All of the other choices contain at least one disqualifying word; Thoreau did not stress aspects such as "pious" (A), nor "accessible" (C), nor "attainable" (D), nor "profitable" (E).

28. **D.** Thoreau explains that "the lesson of value which money teaches . . . we are inclined to skip altogether" (lines 10–13). Although all of the other answer choices are mentioned in the passage, man is not indifferent to these ideas; they do not answer the question.

29. **A.** A major assertion of the passage is that people no longer understand the proper value of money. The author claims that people get money in the wrong way and use it based on the wrong principles. Thoreau never addresses what will "save mankind" (B). And while he acknowledges that gold-digging may be "hard work," "gold thus obtained is not the same thing with the wages of honest toil" and "society is the loser." Although Thoreau believes that gold-diggers rely on luck to find gold, he doesn't believe that the entire world operates this way (C). Neither choice D nor E is suggested in the passage.

30. **E.** To Thoreau, the "Author of the Universe" is God. None of the other choices is a reasonable answer.

31. **C.** The author wonders if Plato had to face the same dilemmas that others do, if Plato lived his life more admirably than did his contemporaries. The author's points about gold-digging—choices A and B—are not addressed in the discussion of Plato. Thoreau doesn't mention Plato's premises about morality (D). Mentioning Plato does nothing to change the tone of the passage (E), and it is highly unlikely that the author uses Plato merely to impress his readers.

32. **D.** Thoreau claims that he would not raise a finger for "all the wealth of the world." The pronoun "it" refers to this wealth.

33. **C.** An aphorism, a brief, pointed statement of fundamental truth, is similar to a proverb. Choice C fits this definition, as it addresses how gold can cover a great surface, but cannot cover one grain of wisdom. Choice A essentially claims that most men get their living through improvised means; it is an opinion, not a statement of truth. Choice B is also not an aphorism; in fact, Thoreau states that choice B's quotation is a "comment. . . a satire." Choice D follows Thoreau's opinion that gamblers and gold-diggers are alike; again, it is an opinion, not an aphorism. Finally, choice E, that claims the Devil works hard, clarifies Thoreau's analogy between gold-diggers and gamblers, but it is not an aphorism.

34. **E.** Thoreau suggests that, although gold-digging may appear to be an honest way to earn "food and raiment" to some, it harms society in the same way that gambling does; it "is not the same thing with the wages of honest toil." The author never implies that philosophers should work harder (A), that society is improving (C), or that hard work produces wisdom (D). In fact, he suggests the opposite: Hard work can be the "enemy." Choice B is not an unstated assumption, but a paraphrase of an explicit statement.

35. **B.** The California gold rush, which some saw as an example of hard-working men diligently trying to get ahead, is used by this author as an example of immorality, of gambling in life. Thoreau doesn't compare gold-diggers to Greeks (A), explore relations of Orientals and Occidentals (C) (that relationship is only touched on), sensationalize (D), or criticize those who saw the gold rush as romantic (E) (he directly criticizes those who participate in the gold-digging).

36. **B.** Thoreau states that "cold and hunger seem more friendly to my nature." Cold and hunger, generally undesirable states, are here seen as better than man's methods of warding them off. The other answer choices are not qualified negative ideas; they are truly negative.

37. **D.** There is no syllogistic reasoning in this passage. The author does use simile (A) ("The gold-digger . . . is as much a gambler as his fellow in the saloons," lines 85–86), historical allusion (B) (to Plato and to the gold rush), rhetorical question (C) (for example, "Does Wisdom work in a tread-mill?"), and religious reference (E) (for example, mention of Mahomet and God). You will find definitions of these terms in Appendix A.

38. **A.** Knowledge is more valuable than gold; wisdom will metaphorically gild more surface than gold. The remaining answer choices are unreasonable.

39. **D.** The author is angry, indignant at humanity's unseemly pursuit of money. The tone is not condescending (A), which means haughty and arrogant. Skeptical (B) is too weak a word for the author's tone, as is worried (C). Choice E, pedestrian, which means humdrum and unimaginative, does not apply to the tone.

40. **C.** This quotation is not part of the argument against gold-digging. It simply states a fact about gold. All of the other answer choices do indeed help further the author's argument.

41. **A.** Thoreau doesn't directly address man's improving his lot in life, although one can infer that he probably believes man should do so. All of the other answer choices are addressed in the passage.

The passage referred to in questions 42–55 is from *Taking Flight* (2003) by Richard P. Hallion.

42. **C.** The author walks a fine line; he includes dangerous elements in his narrative, but he concludes with praise for the overall success of this milestone flight. Choice A is incorrect because aviation had not yet become mass transportation. Choices B, D, and E do restate some of the author's negative points, but they all take his points to an extreme.

43. **E.** The sudden change in cadence focuses the reader's attention on the dramatic change of mood. Choice A is incorrect because the short sentence is a departure from both the content and the style of the preceding sentences. Choices B and C are incorrect; these words are not a quote from Sikorsky or from an earlier work. Choice D is incorrect because the short, three-word sentence does not diminish the crew's surprise, it enhances it.

44. **E.** The inclusion of this incident indicates that the author places a high value on the crewmen's actions, which, indeed, saved the lives of everyone on board. Choices A, B, C, and D are all negative reactions to the incident, which is a reversal of the author's true position.

45. **A.** The idea the author wishes to emphasize is not about Jules Verne, per se. Rather, the author's purpose is to dramatically juxtapose Verne's writing, in which human flight was purely fictional, with this true-life flight of fantasy, which occurred only a few years later. Although Sikorsky was a Jules Verne fan (B), establishing this idea is not the author's rhetorical purpose. Choice B also includes the incorrect phrase "who lived in a fantasy world." Choice C has no evidence in the passage; we do not know whether or not the author shares an interest in Jules Verne. Choice D is too much of a stretch; the passage only mentions Verne in passing as he compares Sikorsky's flight to "a Jules Verne moment," which is hardly an homage to Verne's fans. Choice E contradicts the passage; aviation did indeed advance between Sikorsky's childhood and this historic flight in 1914. Additionally, the reference to Jules Verne does not suggest that aviation had not advanced over the years.

46. D. The most important effect that the author wishes to impart is a vivid description of the unworldly, ethereal view above the clouds that Sikorsky details. At first glance, choice A also appears to have merit, but Sikorsky's own words contradict the idea of the event being unprecedented in human history. He states clearly that he had seen it a few times before. Choices B, C, and E do not address the question, which makes them irrelevant.

47. D. In this context, the author's use of the word "faithful" personifies the engines. He wishes to impart a sense of Sikorsky's empathy with, and gratitude for, these untiring, helpful servants. Choices A, B, C, and E are simply unreasonable.

48. A. The author wishes to emphasize Princip's unsavory physical appearance, so, in footnote #4, he elevates Clark's brief description to an "evocative reflection," and he also includes odious comparisons to later murderous terrorists. The other choices include information that does not appear in footnote #4; choice C refers to footnote #1 and choice E refers to footnote #5.

49. B. The author implies that Sikorsky is truly insulated in his fantastic world of flight, but only for a very brief time, because the coming Great War will wash away all vestiges of the naiveté of these early aviators. Choice A is incorrect because the bad weather below the airship is not a metaphor; it is a literal image. Choice C has no evidence in the passage. Choice D is too much of a stretch; it may be true in fiction and the imagination that adventurers symbolically must return home, but this passage is nonfiction, and the acknowledgment of Archduke Ferdinand's assassination in the previous paragraph makes choice B a more accurate metaphor. Choice E also seems to have merit. However, in the end, it is not Sikorsky's choice to turn his back on the old world, but rather, that the old world will disappear soon enough in flames and chaos of its own making.

50. B. The intent of the author's diction is to emphasize the success of this unprecedented flight, and in retrospect, to symbolically encapsulate the seeming naiveté of the early aviators. Although choices C and D do apply to Sikorsky, they are not the most important message. The quotes in choices A and E are off topic since they do not refer to Sikorsky's specific flight.

51. A. Character development requires a more lengthy narrative than is provided by the format of this brief, yet wide-ranging, passage. The other choices all indicate literary devices that are used in this work. The text refers to Jules Verne in a literary allusion (B). The passage contains vivid descriptions of action (C) when the men go out on the wing to extinguish the engine fire. The passage also presents primary-source quotations (D), from Sikorsky himself, at the end of the second paragraph. The passage contains more than one metaphorical allusion (E). It is historically accurate to identify the airplane engines as Argus engines; the Argus Motoren Company built German aircraft engines beginning in 1906. However, the name Argus itself has many mythological origins that make this a metaphorical allusion, not just an engine manufacture's name. One fitting option, for example, is that Odysseus' dog, named Argus, waited faithfully 20 years for his master's return, and the engines are referred to as "the faithful Argus engines," making them metaphorically similar to Odysseus' dog. Additionally, the "turbulent storm hidden within" is a metaphor that alludes to the coming of World War I.

52. D. This phrase merely describes Gavrilo Princip's appearance; it is not one of the author's many examples of the pathetic security on that fateful day. On the other hand, choices A, B, C, and E do explore the inadequate security.

53. C. The details revealed in Sikorsky's own flight log in footnote #1 are neither well known nor readily available, and they overturn the conventional wisdom. The fact that the author has uncovered these illuminating details clearly indicates the breadth of his research and the depth of his understanding. Choice A contradicts the information in footnote #1. Choice B misstates which right engine caught fire, claiming it was the outboard (farthest) engine, not the inboard engine, the one closest to the airplane fuselage. Choice D is incorrect because footnote #1 does not rely on information from Finne's book, it contradicts it. Choice E is simply a misread; the author has indeed decided which historical narrative to believe.

54. E. On the contrary, rather than being stringent, the author emphasizes that security precautions were particularly lax that day. However, all of the other facts and inferences in choices A, B, C, and D are appropriately drawn from footnote #5.

55. B. The author's rhetorical purpose is well served by his juxtaposition of two seemingly unrelated yet concurrent events, each in its own way both exhilarating and terrifying, each with great perils and great bravery, each finally reaching a dramatic, history-making resolution. All of the other answer choices are not global enough to address the author's primary purpose.

Section II: Free-Response Questions

Question 1

Scoring Guide

Score	Description	Criteria
9	Successful	Essays that earn a score of 9 meet the criteria for essays that receive a score of 8. In addition, they are especially sophisticated in their explanation and argument. They may also present particularly remarkable control of language.
8	Successful	Essays that receive a score of 8 respond to the prompt successfully, using at least three sources from the prompt. They take an effective position that defends, challenges, or qualifies the claim that the government should continue to fund NEA grants to artists. They effectively argue their position and support the argument with appropriate and convincing evidence. The prose demonstrates an ability to control an extensive range of the elements of effective writing, but may not be entirely flawless.
7	Satisfactory	Essays that earn a score of 7 fit the description of the essays that score a 6 but provide more complexity in both argumentation and explanation and/or demonstrate a more distinguished prose style.
6	Satisfactory	Essays that earn a score of 6 respond to the prompt satisfactorily, using at least three sources from the prompt. They take an adequate position that defends, challenges, or qualifies the claim that the government should continue to fund NEA grants to artists. They adequately argue their position and support it with appropriate evidence, although without the precision and depth of the top-scoring essays. The writing may contain minor errors in diction or syntax, but the prose is generally clear.
5	Plausible	Essays that earn a score of 5 take a position that defends, challenges, or qualifies the claim that the government should continue to fund NEA grants to artists. They support the position with generally appropriate evidence, but they may not adequately use at least three sources from the prompt. These essays may be inconsistent, uneven, or limited in the development of their argument. While the writing usually conveys the student's ideas, it may demonstrate lapses in diction or syntax or an overly simplistic style.
4	Inadequate	Essays that earn a score of 4 respond to the prompt inadequately. They may have difficulty taking a position that defends, challenges, or qualifies the claim that the government should continue to fund NEA grants. The evidence may be particularly insufficient or may not use at least three sources from the prompt. The prose may basically convey the student's ideas but suggests immature control over the elements of effective writing.

continued

Score	Description	Criteria
3	Inadequate	Essays that earn a score of 3 meet the criteria for a score of 4 but reveal less ability to take a position that defends, challenges, or qualifies the claim that the government should continue to fund NEA grants. The presentation of evidence and argumentation is likely to be unconvincing. The essay may show less control over the elements of effective writing.
2	Little success	Essays that earn a 2 demonstrate little success at taking a position that defends, challenges, or qualifies the claim that the government should continue to fund NEA grants, and show little ability to present it with appropriate evidence from the sources in the prompt. These essays may misunderstand the prompt, may fail to establish a position with supporting evidence, or may substitute a simpler task by replying tangentially with unrelated, erroneous, or unsuitable explanation, argument, and/or evidence. The prose frequently demonstrates consistent weaknesses in the conventions of effective writing.
1	Little success	Essays that earn a score of 1 meet the criteria for a score of 2 but are undeveloped; especially simplistic in their explanation, argument, and/or evidence; or weak in their control of writing.

High-Scoring Essay

Our world is far from that of Renaissance Florence where all was abuzz with the revival of humanitarian philosophy and a rapidly changing society. This was a time of radical development in art, coupled with major shifts in social values and views. However, much has changed in the five hundred years since this rebirth. The twenty-first century is driven by technological advancement and rational thinking more than any time before; these priorities have the result, whether intended or not, of placing funding for the arts in jeopardy. However, at the heart of mankind lies an appreciation for the arts and all they do to improve our world. Thus, it is necessary for government spending, through the National Endowment for the Arts (NEA), to step in and help provide the arts to a society that has forgotten the importance of art in fostering self-discovery and the progression of mankind.

It is only natural for art to be controversial. Art is often an expression of internal strife, a stinging criticism of society, a challenge to what is accepted, or a dare to humanity to look at our everyday world with a new perspective. Indeed, art is at the very cusp of social change. When Praxiteles sculpted the first female nude sculpture in Ancient Greece it produced as much uproar as Chris Ofili's "Holy Virgin Mary" that Giuliani objected to (Source B). Yet today we look back at the countless nude figures in art as beautiful, not scornful. Art is a necessity that is very rarely accepted without conflict. So it remains today. But, if artists have been under attack for hundreds of years and have continued to persist, why must they still require the support of our government?

The answer is a complex one. Art and government have always been intertwined. Before cameras, television, or the internet, art was a main form of propaganda used by the government and even the church. From the Great Pyramids to the frescos in the Sistine Chapel, from the Nazi recruiting posters to the murals of Diego Rivera, leaders of all times and regions have employed art for political and social purposes. As Aaron Knochel notes, even the CIA funded "Abstract Expressionist artists as a cultural counterweight to Soviet Realism during the Cold War" (Source F). However, government-sponsored propaganda-art was often more subdued, and thus more ethically acceptable, than was non-governmental propaganda-art of the time. No government needed to worry about issuing formal guidelines to control obscenity for the art it sponsored. However, what the NEA seeks to achieve is quite different than any previous government institution and it is this that concerns people. Instead of supporting art that benefits the government they are supporting art that supposedly benefits the people. The NEA claims to be protecting "freedom of expression" (Source B), and generating a "positive relationship between public funding and private philanthropy" (Source A).

What necessitates this fusion of art and government is the changing ethos of the American people. Nowadays, there is very little emphasis placed on the humanities, personal expression, or creativity. Our world is changing rapidly, and many feel there is simply no time for these frivolous pursuits. Math, science, and reason are emphasized as the pathways to success, fortune, fame, and the advancement of humanity.

However, while humans are making huge strides with their minds, they are leaving their hearts and emotions underdeveloped. Many seem as if they are mentally stuck in the Age of Enlightenment, a time when reason was emphasized as the solution to all problems over all other human capabilities. Today people are much more willing to invest their money in economic ventures than in the more intangible experiments of artists. The government has perceived this change and, fortunately, has deemed the arts important enough to be saved, albeit at meager levels. Unfortunately, in the United States, arts funding lags far, far behind other developed countries. If the U.S. were to quadruple arts funding, we'd still fall short of New Zealand's budget, and if we were to multiply it tenfold, we'd still not even reach the funding of Northern Ireland (Source E). Scott E. Walters decries the inequity in funding throughout all the states; clearly the NEA grants help fulfill this need (Source C). Andy Horwitz adds to Walters' worry, noting that "the institutions they support, and that receive the bulk of arts funding in this country, aren't reaching the people the NEA was founded to help serve." However, the fact that the NEA was created to fulfill the "desire of beauty and the hunger for community" (Source D) reminds us that the NEA must adhere to its founding principles.

The NEA must continue to award grants to artists to support the social change we value so much. Perhaps some art works will be better received than others, and perhaps some works will make people "sick" (Source B), while others will delight them. But, no matter what, the work of artists will keep our society awake and changing. It is for this reason that the NEA must strive to "reflect our increasingly diverse communities" so that we can continue to see "the historical (and present) richness of American culture that all but demands to be preserved and supported" (Source D). If we lose our art, we will lose our ability to express ourselves and expand our minds, and we will lose the essence of our humanity. In our bustling modern world, the art supported by the NEA is an essential connection back to our internal experience.

Analysis of the High-Scoring Essay

This thoughtful and insightful essay clearly addresses the prompt and thoroughly develops the idea that the NEA should continue to fund grants for public art. It is far more developed than most essays, but an AP Reader will quickly sense that the student is well-versed in the topic. The student's knowledge of the history of art gives him or her a chance to shine. By using all available sources, the student efficiently integrates both implicit and explicit evidence to bolster his or her position. The introduction blends a historical perspective, noting the Florentine Renaissance, with an examination of 21st-century priorities. The student logically demonstrates that current funding for the arts has become a lower priority than funding for technology. The precept that humanity has a fundamental need for the arts in order to make societal progress sets up the thesis that the NEA should, indeed, continue to fund grants in the arts.

The second paragraph explores the idea that art has always had a component of controversy, and it effectively uses an example from ancient Greek art, comparing the public reception for Praxiteles' sculpture to the objection posed in modern times by Mayor Giuliani to an art exhibit. The student accepts that art will always entail controversy, but acknowledges that art is necessary to bring social advancement. Leaving the Reader with a thought-provoking question, the student wonders why artists need government support, given that their work will be "under attack." This paragraph encourages the Reader to pause and contemplate the answer. By demonstrating both the ability to engage the Reader's intellect and to pose thought-provoking questions, the student is already earning a high score.

The third paragraph readily acknowledges that "the answer is a complex one" and proceeds to demonstrate how intricate the issue really is. The effective use of examples from throughout art history, all of which involve some degree of controversy, demonstrates the student's overall awareness of the world and of how its political history affects the art world; this skill will impress any AP Reader. Although the student acknowledges the role governments have played in funding the arts, he or she also acknowledges that the arts have sometimes been misused by governments as official tools of propaganda. The student then rightfully differentiates NEA funding from previous government-sponsored art by specifying that NEA-funded projects are designed to "benefit the people," not to promulgate government propaganda. This paragraph, although a bit rough in its construction, presents sound ideas while differentiating the purpose of NEA grants from previous government-sponsored art. Given that this essay was written under a time limit, it is easy to overlook minor wording issues that would likely be clarified in a more polished draft. The fact that the student integrates three sources into this paragraph is also an effective demonstration of his or her writing skill.

The next paragraph advances the progress of the argument by exploring contemporary needs for arts funding. The comparison of our current society to the Age of Enlightenment demonstrates this student's grasp of humanity's intellectual development and the similarities between today and an era hundreds of years ago. The idea that humanity is too ensconced in becoming successful at the expense of the arts is an interesting thought; it causes the Reader to ponder this philosophical issue. The essay uses ample evidence from the sources to back up its assertion of the lack of adequate funding for the arts in the U.S. and the inequities of funding distribution. The student's choice to end the paragraph by emphasizing the positive role the NEA should play is also effective.

The student concludes by lobbying on behalf of all humanity, by acknowledging that "we value" the social change that the arts represent. This application works well because it uses the classical rhetorical appeal of ethos, an appeal that makes the Reader appreciate the shared aims of humanity. Overall, this essay truly earns its high score because it is specifically on topic, it demonstrates superior organizational skills, and it has splendid development. The student's command of language is also outstanding; the syntax is varied, and the diction is accurate and concise. It would be hard for any Reader to ask for more success in a timed essay than is displayed here, and it deserves its score of 9.

Medium-Scoring Essay

The National Endowment for the Arts (NEA) must stop awarding grants to artists because it takes society out of the picture, allows the public no say in what is produced, and crowds out public investment.

For as long as art has existed so has the strenuous relationship between art and society. It is a natural part of the production of art—that artists must struggle and search out support in society. The NEA takes the place of society and ruins this relationship: "the sense of responsibility and public enthusiasm to support a social cause might be diminished if the government takes responsibility for its funding" (Source A). Government interference is only hurting the production of art by hindering the centuries-old method of artistic production.

It is dangerous to let a bureaucracy control something as creative as art. This is clear with Mayor Rudolph Giuliani who relied on "a none-too-distinguished line of government officials who decide to become art critics" (Source B) for advice. Our country was founded on the ideas of freedom of expression and no taxation without representation. It is not right that people's money is being used for projects they do not support. Source F is accurate when it argues "state funding for culture shouldn't be the government's business." Politicians are representative of society and its interests. The NEA is headed down a slippery-slope toward too much government control.

Finally, the NEA discourages people to donate to the arts because they think it has already been taken care of by the government. Many might have thought that this was enough. It is not unreasonable to think that "public funds tend to 'crowd out' private donations" (Source A). People no longer feel the moral obligation to support the arts. This separates people from the art of our society, therefore decreasing its power, meaning, and effectiveness.

The National Endowment for the Arts hinders the public's involvement in the development and production of art. Furthermore, it is systematizing a creative progress and allocating funds in an irresponsible manner. The government is responsible for regulating trade, waging war, passing laws, and collecting taxes—not supporting art. That is the job of the people.

Analysis of the Medium-Scoring Essay

This essay makes a few good points, but it is impaired by brevity and logical flaws. Simply put, it does not exhibit the development and clarity of thought that are required to earn a high score. The introductory paragraph takes a clear stand, albeit simplistic, stating that the NEA should simply stop funding all grants. Several of the assumptions underlying this one-sentence paragraph are questionable at best. One example is the assumption that the "public [has] no say" in NEA decisions; no evidence is presented to substantiate this claim. Another questionable assumption is that NEA funding will indeed "crowd out public investment," despite any actual evidence of this. These unsubstantiated assertions indicate that this student is not as aware of the world as one would hope, and they lead the Reader to fear that the essay will merely present an oversimplified view of a very complex issue. Alas, that fear is realized.

The second paragraph simplistically states that artists must struggle, another questionable assertion that is heavily laden with the student's preconceived notions about artists. Next, it claims that NEA funding somehow "ruins" this struggle. Presumably, this student believes that, since the NEA helps an artist to some degree with some form of funding, the artist is free to create art without any other pressures. The student's conclusion is questionable because the logic is full of holes. He or she offers neither concrete examples nor logical explanation; therefore, the paragraph fails to convince the Reader.

The next paragraph is riddled with unfortunate logical errors that distract the Reader's attention from the points the student is trying to make. For example, the student leaps from the idea that bureaucratic control is dangerous to the unrelated idea of "no taxation without representation." This jarring jump in logic leaves the Reader's head spinning, wondering how the student is trying to connect these two ideas. It comes across as if the student suddenly remembered the "no taxation without representation" phrase from a history class and tried to work it into the essay, regardless of its relevance. Although it might be possible to construct a convincing argument for this student's ideas, this oversimplified presentation does not work in the student's favor. The student seems to be composing without considering what he or she had previously stated. For example, in this paragraph, the student claims that "politicians are representative of society." If this were true, then it directly contradicts the student's statements in the first paragraph, which claim that the NEA takes "society out of the picture." If politicians are representative of society, then society is indeed "in the picture." The student's word choices would benefit from clarification and consistency.

The fourth paragraph contains more examples of awkward wording, such as the phrase "discourages people to donate." Perhaps with more time the student might have improved this diction. In addition, the muddled thinking and leaps of logic that the student demonstrated previously crop up again in this paragraph. For example, the student equates "moral obligation" with financial funding, which are not necessarily the same; a moral obligation to the arts does not necessarily include a financial obligation. Additionally, the student never addresses the important questions of how a lack of funding will "separate people from the art of our society" or why a decrease in arts funding would bring a decrease in art's "power, meaning, and effectiveness." The student does not seem to have thought through these positions well enough to understand their logical ramifications.

The concluding paragraph does present a very interesting opinion, that NEA funding of the arts may be "systematizing a creative progress." If the student developed this idea in more detail and explored its implications, the essay might have come out stronger. However, as the essay is presented, it appears that the student thought of this new idea just as time was running out. Overall, this essay demonstrates how a student can begin with potentially good ideas and arguments, but unless they are thought through to their logical conclusions and supported with relevant evidence from the sources, they can fall far short of producing a convincing argument. Finally, the student's repeated problems with diction and poor development definitely hold this essay back from a higher score. It should earn a score of 5.

Question 2

Scoring Guide

Score	Description	Criteria
9	Successful	Essays that earn a score of 9 meet the criteria for essays that receive a score of 8. In addition, they are especially sophisticated in their explanation and argument. They may also present particularly impressive control of language.
8	Successful	These well-written essays successfully demonstrate a clear understanding of the similarities and differences between the effects of the two passages and the authors' handling of rhetorical strategies in producing these effects. These effective essays support their points with specific and cogently presented evidence from the passages. Although these essays may contain a few minor errors, they demonstrate the ability to communicate effectively and precisely.
7	Satisfactory	Essays that earn a score of 7 fit the description of the essays that score a 6 but provide more sophistication in argumentation and explanation and/or demonstrate a more distinguished prose style.

continued

Score	Description	Criteria
6	Satisfactory	These essays, also well written, satisfactorily identify the effects of the two passages but perhaps in a less convincing manner than do top-scoring essays. The discussion of the handling of rhetorical strategies may be less thorough and specific. Connections between the thesis and the evidence may not be as clear as that found in top-scoring essays. Some errors in mechanics may occur, but overall, these essays show satisfactory control over organization, development, and use of language.
5	Plausible	These plausible essays show a general understanding of the effects of the passages but may not present as clear a thesis concerning those effects. The attempt to analyze the authors' use of rhetorical strategies may be simplistic, or evidence offered to support the essay's points may be insufficient and may not be clearly related to the authors' use of the resources of language. These essays may be coherently organized but may show inconsistent control of diction.
4	Inadequate	Essays that earn a score of 4 respond to the prompt inadequately. They may have difficulty identifying and discussing the effects of the passages. The evidence may be particularly insufficient or simplistically presented. The prose may convey the student's ideas but suggest immature control over the elements of effective writing.
3	Inadequate	These essays attempt to identify and discuss the effects of the passages but do so ineffectively, perhaps because of an inaccurate reading or with presentation of inadequate evidence. They may fail to complete all of the tasks given. These essays may simply catalog the rhetorical strategies, without analysis or comment on the connection between effect and language use. Weak control of the essay format and/or language may be evident, and mechanical errors may be frequent.
2	Little success	These essays fail to sufficiently respond to the question or the passages. They may fail to understand the effects of the passages, misreading them in a way that distorts those effects. Little or no attention may be given to the rhetorical strategies used in the passages. These essays fail to convince the Reader of their points, and the thesis may be shallow or nonexistent. These essays may substitute a simpler task by replying to the question with irrelevant information. Persistent weaknesses in grammar and organization may be evident. The prose often demonstrates consistent weaknesses in writing.
1	Little success	Essays earning a score of 1 meet the criteria for a score of 2 but are undeveloped, especially simplistic in their analysis, or show weak control of the language. The evidence is insufficient or may not use many, if any, examples from the prompt.

High-Scoring Essay

Although M. F. K. Fisher's description of Marseille and Maya Angelou's description of Stamps both seek to dispel illusions of their places, they differ in the use of technique, tone, and diction. In the first passage, Fisher uses a satiric style to poke fun at Marseille's misconceived reputation as "the world's wickedest port." In the other passage, Maya Angelou uses fantastic imagery to also reveal a faulty reputation, this time, of the South. Both authors are attempting to reform mistaken opinions of their places, but they both use extremely different techniques.

In her passage, M. F. K. Fisher seeks only to quell Marseille's misrepresentation. By wryly examining articles describing Marseille, Fisher never directly gives her impression of this French port, but instead she reveals the spurious nature of these descriptions. Throughout the passage, a satiric tone is employed. Before introducing Basil Woon's piece on Marseille, Fisher writes "Sometimes such journalese is almost worth reading for its precociously obsolete views." This statement ridicules Woon's work even before it is introduced. Contributing to the tone of the piece, Fisher not only derides the descriptions of Marseille, but also the backgrounds of their writers. Although Woon did not recommend visiting Marseille, "he did remain true to his journalistic background with an expectedly titillating mention of it." Fisher masks an otherwise intense diatribe with the light-hearted, humorous use of satire.

The use of precise and informal diction also contributes to the effects of the first passage. In describing newspaper descriptions of Marseille, the words "mild shockers" are used. The concise image formed by these words contributes to the informal mood of the passage. Also, instead of employing the more conservative and respected word "journalism," Fisher chose to use the word "journalese." This simple substitution embodies the essence of the passage. Like the word journalese, the passage continually ridicules writers' misrepresentations of Marseille.

Using an opposite style of attack, Maya Angelou does not mock the faulty representation of the South. Instead she contrasts both a description of the "American fantasy" of the South with her own vivid impressions. The dream-like tone of the first paragraph is aided by the rich choice of diction. "Women float eternally" among "wisps of wisteria." Like paradise, the word "eternally" allows this scene of gentle alliteration to last forever.

This fantasy is contrasted in the remaining paragraphs with an intense, passionate tone of life. The descriptions, like smells "spiced with the odor of cattle manure, the yellowish acid of the ponds and rivers, the deep pots of greens and beans," are all concrete. These concrete images sharply contrast the ethereal images of women floating eternally. The misrepresentation of the South is easily dispelled by the reality of Maya Angelou's observations. Furthermore, the choice of diction is superb. Angelou's South was "flesh-real and swollen-belly poor." These words easily bring to mind the harshness of black life in the South. Toward the end of the passage, a metaphor is used to change the direction of the passage from concreteness into memories ". . . passions clanged with the ferocity of armored knights colliding." After erasing the erroneous images of the South, the passage prepares to tell Angelou's story.

Though these passages are similar in their goals, their distinct uses of diction and tone drastically differ in their methods of dispelling illusions.

Analysis of the High-Scoring Essay

The essay begins by directly addressing the topic with a relevant comparison of the passages, pointing out that each "seek[s] to dispel illusions" of the perception of a location. This student recognizes that, although the passages have the same purpose, their differences lie in their stylistic choices. Such interesting ideas as these engage the Reader.

The next two paragraphs analyze the Fisher passage on Marseille and, together, demonstrate a clear understanding of Fisher's use of humor and satire to ridicule those who have painted Marseille as "the world's wickedest port." The student supports the point with appropriate quotations from the passage. The second paragraph specifically analyzes and gives evidence for Fisher's purpose—to dispel the myths about Marseille—while the third paragraph explores how the language of the passage contributes to the effect. The student here uses effective organization and sophisticated diction, making this a strong section.

The fourth and fifth paragraphs deal with the Angelou passage, again analyzing the author's effect and the language used to create it. The analysis begins with Angelou's first paragraph, noting its differences from the Fisher passage—specifically, that she "does not mock the faulty representation" as Fisher does and noting that Angelou creates a "dream-like tone" contrasting with her own impressions. The analysis continues with a discussion of diction, noting how effectively Angelou dispels the misrepresentation of the South with her use of concrete images, an exploration of Angelou's use of metaphor, and an explanation of the metaphor's effect in introducing the realistic treatment that follows in the work. A Reader might perhaps wish that the student would explore the effect of racial comments in Angelou's description, but, since it is not mentioned in the prompt, a Reader cannot fault the student for not mentioning it.

The essay concludes with a brief summary of its main point—that the authors have similar goals but different techniques. Although the statement is not itself thought-provoking, it is an adequate end to the essay. Overall, this student makes points clearly while demonstrating a competent command of language. The essay prompt asks specifically for a comparison and contrast of the "effect" of the two pieces, and this essay can be faulted because, to some degree, it confuses effect with purpose. The essay also misreads the tone of the Fisher passage as an "intense diatribe" and could benefit from additional evidence from the passages. On the whole, however, the essay is intelligent, articulate, and substantiated with enough evidence to score in the upper-half range. It earns a score of 7.

Medium-Scoring Essay

Although both passages describe places, their styles are very different. The first passage illustrates how most descriptions of Marseille treat this city unfairly. This is accomplished through the author's humiliation of these articles. The second passage shows how most people's description of the South is wrong. But rather than through satire, this is accomplished through the use of imagery. Thus, both pieces are similar in their effect, but are different in their author's handling of the resources of language.

The first piece by M. F. K. Fisher about the French port of Marseille succeeds in showing that writers about this place only tell the wrong side of the story. Although Marseille like all cities has its attractions and its good points, these writers unfairly give it "a legendary reputation as a world capital for 'dope, whores, and street violence.'" Thus this piece humiliates and satirizes those writers. The tone of this piece is very light and humorous, but it hides the meaning of the author's words. For instance, "The familiar pitch had been made, and idle readers dreaming of a great seaport dedicated to heroin, prostitution, and rioting could easily skip the clumsy detail of marketing for fresh fish." By including the talk of fresh fish in the sentence, this passage is making a parody of the article where dope, whores, and street violence are combined with how to make a true bouillabaisse. The other article that this passage also talks about says "Marseilles is the world's wickedest port." The passage ridicules this piece with the satiric sentence "Sometimes such journalese is almost worth reading for its precociously obsolete views of a society too easy to forget." This piece is sarcastically saying that readers should read this article because it is a great example of something bad. Therefore, this passage is able to use sarcasm, satire, and humiliation to show how Marseille is improperly represented by writers.

The second piece by Maya Angelou about the small town of Stamps, Arkansas, tries to show how this place is also improperly represented. This is done by using imagery. First, that passage describes the South as "a much-loved region in the American fantasy where pale white women float eternally under black magnolia trees." These images show that the American fantasy is a peaceful, relaxed South where white people linger around. In fact, this image is wrong. In the next part of the passage, the South is shown in the harsh light of reality. "The South I returned to, however, was flesh-real and swollen-belly poor." These images succeed in showing the harshness of life the African Americans led in the South. This sentence also shows this point. "And above all, the atmosphere was pressed down with the smell of old fears, and hates, and guilt." The use of atmosphere adds to the depressingly real tone created by these images. Also a metaphor is used "passions clanged with the ferocity of armored knights colliding." This adds to the electrical atmosphere of the passage. By using such strong images to create the electrical atmosphere of the passage, the illusion of the first paragraph is shown for what it truly is. Therefore, this passage is able to use images, words, and atmosphere to show how Stamps, Arkansas, is improperly represented by the American fantasy of the South. The style of this passage is different from the other, which humiliates the improper representation. Therefore, both passages use their authors' handling of the resources of language in a different way to talk about the same effect.

Analysis of the Medium-Scoring Essay

The essay's introduction accurately addresses the topic. However, the student's writing style and depth of thought do not demonstrate the sophistication needed for a high-scoring essay. To claim merely that the two passages are "similar in effect, but . . . different" in their use of language barely touches on the topic.

The second paragraph concentrates on Fisher's article and points out that Fisher humiliates (an inaccurate word in this context) and satirizes the authors who have presented Marseille as the "wickedest port." The student seems to recognize Fisher's effect but doesn't extend the observation, merely stating that Fisher is "making a parody" through use of sarcasm. Some examples from the passage are included, but they are treated perfunctorily and obviously, without depth or strong analysis.

The last paragraph also is accurate in its discussion, but the presentation is simplistic and uninteresting. For example, "This sentence also shows this point" fails to connect the two examples effectively, and the claim that the use of metaphor creates an "electrical atmosphere" doesn't explain in what way "armored knights colliding" does so. The phrase "which humiliates the improper representation" is simply baffling. This paragraph, as those preceding it, makes valid points but doesn't explore them in enough depth to engage or convince the Reader. This essay could be greatly improved with the use of deeper analysis and more sophisticated presentation. This essay is a weak 5.

Question 3

Scoring Guide

Score	Description	Criteria
9	Successful	Essays earning a score of 9 meet the criteria for essays that are scored an 8 and, in addition, are especially full or apt in their analysis or reveal particularly remarkable control of language.
8	Successful	These well-written essays clearly take a stand concerning More's ideas on communal property and successfully support that stand. The thesis is articulate and relevant to the topic. The essays provide strong and relevant evidence that is intelligently connected to the thesis. Although they need not be without errors, these essays show a mature command of style and language.
7	Satisfactory	Essays earning a score of 7 fit the description of essays that are scored a 6 but provide more complete analysis and a more mature prose style.
6	Satisfactory	These essays contemplate More's ideas on communal property in a satisfactory manner but produce a less explicit thesis. Perhaps less relevant or insufficient evidence is offered, and the Reader may not be as thoroughly convinced as with a top-scoring essay. Although well written, they may demonstrate some errors while still showing satisfactory control over diction and the essay requirements.
5	Plausible	The plausible presentation in these essays includes a thesis, but one that is perhaps not as well thought out as in higher-scoring essays. The ideas may be too hastily conceived after a cursory reading of More's concepts. Overall, the argument may not be as strong or convincing. It may appear more opinionated without sufficient evidence to support the opinions. Acceptable organization may be evident, but the style may be much more simplistic than in higher-scoring essays.
4	Inadequate	Essays that earn a score of 4 respond to the prompt inadequately. These low-scoring essays fail to convince the Reader. The weak presentation may include an unsupported or unsubstantiated thesis, weak paragraph development, and/or poor organization. These essays may exhibit confusion in ideas and superficial thinking in the use of evidence. Frequent mechanical errors may be present.
3	Inadequate	Essays earning a score of 3 meet the criteria for a score of 4 but demonstrate a less clear understanding of More's ideas. The essays may show less control over the elements of writing.
2	Little success	These poorly written essays lack clarity and coherence. They may have an overly obvious thesis or no thesis at all. They may contain little or no evidence, and the connection between the evidence and the thesis may be shallow or nonexistent. These essays may misunderstand the task, may fail to articulate More's attitude, or may substitute a simpler task. These essays may be unusually short and exhibit poor fundamental essay skills. Weak sentence construction and consistent weaknesses in mechanics may be present.
1	Little success	These poorly written essays meet the criteria for a score of 2 but are undeveloped, especially simplistic in their analysis, and weak in their control of language.

High-Scoring Essay

Sir Thomas More's Utopia discusses ideas and conflicts still relevant to society today. He manages to perceptively express the nature of wealth and material goods; and although written over 400 years ago, his essay still reveals essential truths about the attitudes in our contemporary society.

More primarily addresses the issue of ownership of private property and its hindrance upon the fair distribution of wealth. More points out that ownership of private wealth hurts those who have little or none themselves, which makes up the majority of the population. More perceives that "As long as private property remains, by far the largest and the best part of mankind will be oppressed with an inescapable load of cares and anxieties." In today's society, More's idea still holds true. The majority of the population does control less than their fair amount of wealth and goods. This is evident not just in America, but also among competing nations of the world. Each day, in countries like Mexico, the poor struggle to keep from getting poorer, while the wealth of many of the rich grows more opulent. Because of this unfair distribution of wealth, the poor have little opportunity to change their worsening situations.

More's concerns also go beyond the poor and encompass another major realm of controversy: politics. More correctly predicts the nature of politics that exists in a society where not everyone is of the same economic class. He suggests that "It might be made unlawful for public offices to be solicited, or sold, or made burdensome for the officeholder by great expense. Otherwise officeholders are tempted to reimburse themselves by dishonesty and force, and it becomes necessary to find rich men for those offices which ought rather be held by wise men." This prediction has certainly come true in contemporary America, where the vast number of politicians tends to come from the upper echelons of society; conversely, one would be hard-pressed to name a top office-holder who rose from the ranks of the poor under-class. In addition, just as Plato saw the needs for wise, rational men to fill the position of philosopher-king, More also realizes the danger of public offices held by rich men rather than wise men, an event fostered by a society in which unequal distribution of goods exists. Both Plato and More have made a valid point here, and the voting public should be constantly cautioned to question a potential leader's wisdom and rational thinking before they vote.

While More's essays define the evils that burden a private property-owning society, More fails to see some of the problems that would follow with completely eradicating the system. More suggests several legal reforms to stop and prevent the amassing of goods by citizens. When this is stopped, however, all incentive to work is taken away. People rarely have the time, the energy, or the interest to work solely for the merit of working. In contemporary society, human nature drives people to work to earn something tangible—be it wealth, or goods, or love. More's reforms are also unfair. While at first glance they may sound fair and equal, in reality they are not. This system would be unfair to hard workers who do deserve a reward, and unfair to lazy workers who don't earn what they receive. Instead of promoting equality, this system would promote laziness and remove the incentive to work. In theory, this would be a good system. But, in reality, Sir Thomas More's Utopia does not work. The breakdown of the Soviet Union alone disproves More's system.

More's essay perceptively observes some of the major injustices and corruptions within a private property-owning society. While these are valid, pertinent issues, More overlooks some of the inherent pitfalls within the system of a society that bans the ownership of private property.

Analysis of the High-Scoring Essay

This thoughtful essay immediately addresses the topic in its first sentence. The student uses contemporary examples to buttress points, and also insightfully comments that More addresses more concepts than money and land distribution.

The student's inclusion of Plato in the third paragraph relevantly extends this idea. In the fourth paragraph, the student acknowledges that More fails to accurately predict all the consequences of his proposals—the problem that the need for reward is inherent in human nature. Showing both advantages and disadvantages of More's proposal demonstrates the skill of close reading and a high degree of maturity in this student.

To improve this essay, the student could have worked on a stronger thesis that more accurately addresses his or her points; notice that the thesis does not allude to any criticism of More's ideas. Some of the vague wording could be made more specific, such as the statements, "More's reforms are also unfair. While at first glance they may sound fair and equal, in reality they are not." In general, the essay's ideas are more sophisticated than their presentation.

This essay is well organized and the ideas are supported by examples from contemporary society. Overall, this essay deserves a high score for pointing out the validity of More's ideas for today's society, as well as their perhaps mistaken assumptions. Its ideas could warrant a score of 8, but its presentation could drop it to a 7.

Medium-Scoring Essay

Sir Thomas More's <u>Utopia</u> discusses fair government and equal social status within our society, and identifies the need for people to give up their private property. His ideas (as written about in the essay) are valid in light of contemporary standards.

More's initial position that private property is an unnecessary evil within our society at first appears to be blatantly Communistic. His desires to redistribute wealth and property and to make laws preventing people from earning too much money seem absurd at first glance. However, on further inspection, the reader realizes that some of More's views are valid and relevant to society. More predicts corruption of the government, something that our nation has been experiencing for several decades. This corruption is a result of politicians feeling obligated to remunerate themselves for the great expense they go through as a part of their job. More sums this up very nicely and accurately as he points out that rich men (instead of wise men) take over the offices of government.

Not only do we see the validity of More's views in our current day and age, but personally speaking, I agree with More's beliefs. The greed and self-interest associated with Capitalism are two symptoms of the sickness that comes with private property. It is wrong for a country's government to allow some people to starve on the streets while others are living like kings. More sympathizes with the great majority of people who do not have much private property.

Throughout his essay More proposes solutions to the problem of private property. He advocates altruism and his ideas are shown to be relevant to our society. His essay is very valid in light of today's social standards.

Analysis of the Medium-Scoring Essay

This medium-scoring essay attempts to address the topic. The first paragraph produces a thesis that claims that More's ideas are valid for contemporary society, but little else is presented here. The thesis is not highly thought-provoking, and it contains some redundancy ("as written about in the essay").

The student devotes almost half of the second paragraph to explaining his or her first impression of More, only to reverse it after a deeper analysis. This student should be commended for looking below the surface, but no evidence is offered to support the student's opinions. This paragraph would be stronger if the student were to include some specific examples of government corruption, rather than merely alluding to them.

The third paragraph becomes a forum for the student's personal beliefs. Once again, the student presents relevant ideas but little evidence for them. The only example included, the idea that the government allows poor people to starve while others live like kings, may indeed be true, but it is not specific. Stronger development of both ideas and examples would improve this paragraph.

The concluding paragraph merely summarizes the essay's only point, that the student finds More's ideas valid. There's not much of substance here, and the conclusion doesn't help to convince the Reader of the validity of the student's opinions.

Although this essay does take a stand, it offers only weak support and sometimes simplistic and redundant wording. This essay would be stronger if the student were to include more of More's ideas and test their validity by today's standards. Overall, this essay is adequate, but it is not persuasive enough to merit a higher score. It should receive a score of 5.

Scoring

Use the following worksheet to arrive at a probable final AP grade on Practice Exam 2. Because being objective enough to estimate your own essay score is sometimes difficult, you might give your essays (along with the sample essays) to a teacher, friend, or relative to score, if you feel confident that the individual has the knowledge necessary to make such a judgment and that he or she will feel comfortable doing so.

Section I: Multiple-Choice Questions

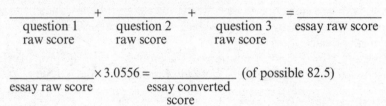

$$\underline{\hspace{3cm}} - (\underline{\hspace{3cm}}) = \underline{\hspace{3cm}}$$

right answers   wrong answers   multiple-choice raw score

$$\underline{\hspace{3cm}} \times 1.2272 = \underline{\hspace{3cm}} \text{ (of possible 67.5)}$$

multiple-choice raw score   multiple-choice converted score

Section II: Free-Response Questions

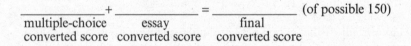

$$\underline{\hspace{2cm}} + \underline{\hspace{2cm}} + \underline{\hspace{2cm}} = \underline{\hspace{2cm}}$$

question 1 raw score   question 2 raw score   question 3 raw score   essay raw score

$$\underline{\hspace{3cm}} \times 3.0556 = \underline{\hspace{3cm}} \text{ (of possible 82.5)}$$

essay raw score   essay converted score

Final Score

$$\underline{\hspace{3cm}} + \underline{\hspace{3cm}} = \underline{\hspace{3cm}} \text{ (of possible 150)}$$

multiple-choice converted score   essay converted score   final converted score

Probable Final AP Score

Final Converted Score	Probable AP Score
150–114	5
113–98	4
97–81	3
80–53	2
52–0	1

Chapter 6

Practice Exam 3

Answer Sheet

Section I: Multiple-Choice Questions

1 Ⓐ Ⓑ Ⓒ Ⓓ Ⓔ	21 Ⓐ Ⓑ Ⓒ Ⓓ Ⓔ	41 Ⓐ Ⓑ Ⓒ Ⓓ Ⓔ
2 Ⓐ Ⓑ Ⓒ Ⓓ Ⓔ	22 Ⓐ Ⓑ Ⓒ Ⓓ Ⓔ	42 Ⓐ Ⓑ Ⓒ Ⓓ Ⓔ
3 Ⓐ Ⓑ Ⓒ Ⓓ Ⓔ	23 Ⓐ Ⓑ Ⓒ Ⓓ Ⓔ	43 Ⓐ Ⓑ Ⓒ Ⓓ Ⓔ
4 Ⓐ Ⓑ Ⓒ Ⓓ Ⓔ	24 Ⓐ Ⓑ Ⓒ Ⓓ Ⓔ	44 Ⓐ Ⓑ Ⓒ Ⓓ Ⓔ
5 Ⓐ Ⓑ Ⓒ Ⓓ Ⓔ	25 Ⓐ Ⓑ Ⓒ Ⓓ Ⓔ	45 Ⓐ Ⓑ Ⓒ Ⓓ Ⓔ
6 Ⓐ Ⓑ Ⓒ Ⓓ Ⓔ	26 Ⓐ Ⓑ Ⓒ Ⓓ Ⓔ	46 Ⓐ Ⓑ Ⓒ Ⓓ Ⓔ
7 Ⓐ Ⓑ Ⓒ Ⓓ Ⓔ	27 Ⓐ Ⓑ Ⓒ Ⓓ Ⓔ	47 Ⓐ Ⓑ Ⓒ Ⓓ Ⓔ
8 Ⓐ Ⓑ Ⓒ Ⓓ Ⓔ	28 Ⓐ Ⓑ Ⓒ Ⓓ Ⓔ	48 Ⓐ Ⓑ Ⓒ Ⓓ Ⓔ
9 Ⓐ Ⓑ Ⓒ Ⓓ Ⓔ	29 Ⓐ Ⓑ Ⓒ Ⓓ Ⓔ	49 Ⓐ Ⓑ Ⓒ Ⓓ Ⓔ
10 Ⓐ Ⓑ Ⓒ Ⓓ Ⓔ	30 Ⓐ Ⓑ Ⓒ Ⓓ Ⓔ	50 Ⓐ Ⓑ Ⓒ Ⓓ Ⓔ
11 Ⓐ Ⓑ Ⓒ Ⓓ Ⓔ	31 Ⓐ Ⓑ Ⓒ Ⓓ Ⓔ	51 Ⓐ Ⓑ Ⓒ Ⓓ Ⓔ
12 Ⓐ Ⓑ Ⓒ Ⓓ Ⓔ	32 Ⓐ Ⓑ Ⓒ Ⓓ Ⓔ	52 Ⓐ Ⓑ Ⓒ Ⓓ Ⓔ
13 Ⓐ Ⓑ Ⓒ Ⓓ Ⓔ	33 Ⓐ Ⓑ Ⓒ Ⓓ Ⓔ	53 Ⓐ Ⓑ Ⓒ Ⓓ Ⓔ
14 Ⓐ Ⓑ Ⓒ Ⓓ Ⓔ	34 Ⓐ Ⓑ Ⓒ Ⓓ Ⓔ	54 Ⓐ Ⓑ Ⓒ Ⓓ Ⓔ
15 Ⓐ Ⓑ Ⓒ Ⓓ Ⓔ	35 Ⓐ Ⓑ Ⓒ Ⓓ Ⓔ	
16 Ⓐ Ⓑ Ⓒ Ⓓ Ⓔ	36 Ⓐ Ⓑ Ⓒ Ⓓ Ⓔ	
17 Ⓐ Ⓑ Ⓒ Ⓓ Ⓔ	37 Ⓐ Ⓑ Ⓒ Ⓓ Ⓔ	
18 Ⓐ Ⓑ Ⓒ Ⓓ Ⓔ	38 Ⓐ Ⓑ Ⓒ Ⓓ Ⓔ	
19 Ⓐ Ⓑ Ⓒ Ⓓ Ⓔ	39 Ⓐ Ⓑ Ⓒ Ⓓ Ⓔ	
20 Ⓐ Ⓑ Ⓒ Ⓓ Ⓔ	40 Ⓐ Ⓑ Ⓒ Ⓓ Ⓔ	

CUT HERE

Section II: Free-Response Questions

Question 1

CUT HERE

CUT HERE

CUT HERE

CUT HERE

Question 2

CUT HERE

CUT HERE

CUT HERE

Question 3

CUT HERE

CUT HERE

CUT HERE

CUT HERE

Section I: Multiple-Choice Questions

Time: 1 hour
54 questions

Directions: This section consists of selections from prose works and questions on their content, form, and style. Read each selection carefully. For each question, choose the best answer of the five choices.

Questions 1–12 refer to the following passage from a 1979 book by a contemporary American female author.

A greater inducement to folly is excess of power. After he had conceived his wonderful vision of philosopher-kings in the *Republic,* Plato began to have doubts and reached the
(5) conclusion that laws were the only safeguard. Too much power given to anything, like too large a sail on a vessel, he believed, is dangerous; moderation is overthrown. Excess leads on the one hand to disorder and on the other to
(10) injustice. No soul of man is able to resist the temptation of arbitrary power, and there is "No one who will not under such circumstances become filled with folly, the worst of diseases."[1] His kingdom will be undermined and "all his
(15) power will vanish from him." Such indeed was the fate that overtook the Renaissance Papacy to the point of half, if not all, of its power; and Louis XIV, although not until after his death; and—if we consider the American Presidency to
(20) confer excess of power—Lyndon Johnson, who was given to speaking of "*my* air force" and thought his position entitled him to lie and deceive; and, most obviously, Richard Nixon.

Mental standstill or stagnation—the main-
(25) tenance intact by rulers and policy-makers of the ideas they started with—is fertile ground for folly. Montezuma is a fatal and tragic example. Leaders in government, on the authority of Henry Kissinger, do not learn beyond the
(30) convictions they bring with them; these are "the intellectual capital they will consume as long as they are in office."[2] Learning from experience is a faculty almost never practiced. Why did American experience of supporting the unpopular
(35) party in China supply no analogy to Vietnam? And the experience of Vietnam none for Iran? And why has none of the above conveyed any inference to preserve the present government of the United States from imbecility in El Salvador?
(40) "If men could learn from history, what lessons it might teach us!" lamented Samuel Coleridge. "But passion and party blind our eyes, and the

light which experience gives us is a lantern on the stern which shines only on the waves behind
(45) us."[3] The image is beautiful but the message misleading, for the light on the waves we have passed through should enable us to infer the nature of the waves ahead. . . .

Aware of the controlling power of ambition,
(50) corruption and emotion, it may be that in the search for wiser government we should look for the test of character first. And the test should be moral courage. Montaigne adds, "Resolution and valor, not that which is sharpened by ambition but
(55) that which wisdom and reason may implant in a well-ordered soul."[4] The Lilliputians in choosing persons for public employment had similar criteria. "They have more regard for good morals than for great abilities," reported Gulliver, "for,
(60) since government is necessary to mankind, they believe . . . that Providence never intended to make management of public affairs a mystery, to be comprehended only by a few persons of sublime genius, of which there are seldom three born in an
(65) age. They suppose truth, justice, temperance and the like to be in every man's power: the practice of which virtues, assisted by experience and a good intention, would qualify any man for service of his country, except where a course of study is
(70) required."[5]

While such virtues may in truth be in every man's power, they have less chance in our system than money and ruthless ambition to prevail at the ballot box. The problem may be not so much a
(75) matter of educating officials for government as educating the electorate to recognize and reward integrity of character and to reject the ersatz. Perhaps better men flourish in better times, and wiser government requires the nourishment of a
(80) dynamic rather than a troubled and bewildered society. If John Adams was right, and government is "little better practiced now than three or four thousand years ago," we cannot reasonably expect much improvement. We can only muddle on as we
(85) have done in those same three or four thousand years, through patches of brilliance and decline, great endeavor and shadow.

[1] Plato, "The worst of diseases": *Laws,* III, 691D.

[2] "Intellectual Capital": Kissinger, 54.

[3] Coleridge, "If men could learn": *Oxford Dictionary of Quotations,* 157, no. 20.

[4] Montaigne, "Resolution and Valor": *Complete Essays,* trans. Donald M. Frame, Stanford, 1965, II, 36.

[5] Lilliputians "Have more regard": Jonathan Swift, *Gulliver's Travels,* Part One, chap. 6.

1. In the discussion of Plato's idea that "laws were the only safeguard" (line 5), the author implies that

   A. Plato's original vision of philosopher-kings is valid
   B. excess always leads to injustice
   C. excess always leads to disorder
   D. rulers can never be trusted with too much power
   E. Plato believed that one should not put too large a sail on a vessel

2. One can infer that Plato would most likely disagree with the idea that

   A. no man can resist totalitarian authority
   B. intellectual idleness causes folly
   C. successful leaders can be trained
   D. good rulers need to have superior ethics
   E. governing effectively will not improve in the future

3. The rhetorical effect of the use of italics in the quotation "*my* air force" (line 21) is that it

   A. emphasizes the corruption of Richard Nixon
   B. emphasizes the heartfelt attention paid by Lyndon Johnson to the war effort
   C. depersonalizes Johnson's use of power
   D. is just another example of the use of power; the italics add nothing
   E. gives depth to Johnson's excesses; his use of power was *personal*

4. The third paragraph can be distinguished from the others because it

   A. discusses traits that are valuable in an effective leader
   B. shifts the emphasis of the essay to literary analysis
   C. explores the positive and the negative aspects of government
   D. questions the practicality of finding a successful ruler
   E. sends a strong message, thus connecting literature to daily life

5. The series of questions posed in lines 33–39 serve the rhetorical purpose of

   A. demonstrating a few contrary examples that modify the author's position
   B. introducing the reference to *Gulliver's Travels*
   C. proving that "Learning from experience is a faculty almost never practiced" (lines 32–33)
   D. exploring 19th-century examples of mankind's folly
   E. exhorting antiwar protestors to rethink their position

6. Which of the following most clearly enunciates the author's position vis-à-vis Coleridge's "lantern on the stern" metaphor (lines 43–44)?

   A. The author believes that Coleridge misstates the importance of the "light" of history.
   B. The author believes that shining a light on the past is an excellent method for divining future events.
   C. The author believes that Coleridge is blinded by "passion and party."
   D. The author believes that the image of the lantern on the stern is visually terrifying.
   E. The author believes Coleridge's metaphor is a powerful summation of the misuse of historical precedents by men blinded by "passion and party."

7. A comparison of the author's description of Plato's philosopher-king to the Lilliputians' ideas about selecting public servants leads to the conclusion that

A. Plato's vision is a more practical idea than the Lilliputians'

B. the Lilliputians believed that all power should reside in one individual

C. Plato's original idea was too fanciful; the Lilliputians' idea was much more pragmatic

D. the Lilliputians believed that many people who are well suited to be rulers were born in every age

E. Plato's ideal of a philosopher-king was one he carried throughout his life

8. Based on the inclusion of such diverse historical examples as Plato, the Renaissance Papacy, Montezuma, and American presidents, one can infer that the author is

A. demonstrating that the same factors arise repeatedly throughout history and always result in the folly of power

B. searching far and wide to find any examples that fit her preconceived notions

C. throwing in everything that she can find, hoping that the reader will be able to relate to at least one of the examples

D. showing the diverse methods these individuals used successfully to wield great power

E. trying to tie these examples together into a coherent narrative, although she ultimately fails

9. What is the primary rhetorical purpose of the third paragraph?

A. It details the folly of the excess of power.

B. It details the folly of mental stagnation.

C. It explains the significance of the "lantern on the stern" metaphor.

D. It clarifies what kind of man actually governs best.

E. It clarifies what type of man governs worst.

10. Considering the passage as a whole, the best description of the author's tone is that it is

A. tentatively optimistic about mankind's future

B. cynical about mankind's ability to overcome the same mistakes

C. reverent toward 19th-century authors

D. credible as to the successful examples of governance

E. hagiographical in its exultation of successful rulers

11. Collectively, the five footnotes demonstrate that the author

A. synthesizes ideas culled from a wide variety of sources

B. specializes in 19th-century philosophers

C. chooses to ignore any author who disagrees with her position

D. admires great philosophers

E. disagrees with Coleridge's positions

12. The author would most likely agree with which of the following ideas?

A. Mankind's predilections are unalterable; the public should never be allowed a direct vote in the selection of its leaders.

B. Although brutal, excesses of power can sometimes be used for the public good and the betterment of mankind.

C. Through proper training, even unsuitable political leaders can govern effectively.

D. It is likely that mankind will manage to overcome its illogical propensities and select better leaders in the future.

E. History provides numerous examples of the folly of political leaders who succumbed to the excesses of power.

Questions 13–23 refer to the following letters exchanged by two 19th-century British authors as they separately toured America.

To Archibald Forbes[1]

[20 January 1882] Arlington Hotel, Washington

Dear Mr. Forbes, I felt quite sure that your
(5) remarks on me had been misrepresented. I
must however say that your remarks about me
in your lecture may be regarded as giving *some*
natural ground for the report. I feel bound to
say quite frankly to you that I do not consider
(10) them to be either in good taste or appropriate
to your subject.

I have something to say to the American
people, something that I know will be the
beginning of a great movement here, and all
(15) foolish ridicule does a great deal of harm to
the cause of art and refinement and civilisation
here.

I do not think that your lecture will lose in
brilliancy or interest by expunging the passage,
(20) which is, as you say yourself, poor fooling
enough.

You have to speak of the life of action, I of the
life of art. Our subjects are quite distinct and
should be kept so. Believe me, yours truly,
(25) OSCAR WILDE

To Archibald Forbes

Monday [23 January 1882] Arlington Hotel,
Washington

Dear Mr. Forbes, Colonel Morse[2], who kindly
(30) manages for me a somewhat bulky
correspondence, tells me that you feel yourself
wronged by something I am supposed to have
said of you in the papers, and that you have
written to me in, natural I acknowledge,
(35) indignation on the subject. He has sent the
letter to Mr. Carte without my reading it, as he
considers that Mr. Carte can best answer those
parts of it relating to my intended visit to
Baltimore. In any case let me assure you that I
(40) have neither spoken of you to anyone except as
I would speak of a man whose chivalry, whose
personal bravery, and whose pluck, have won
him the respect and the admiration of all
honest men in Europe and in America, and
(45) who has given to English journalism the new
lustre of action, of adventure and of courage. I
did not believe what I read in the papers about
you, that you had spoken of me in a sneering

way behind my back. I in fact denied it to a
(50) reporter who came here with the story on
Thursday night late, I do not think you should
have believed it of me. It is true you hardly
know me at all personally, but at least you
know me well enough to come and ask me
(55) personally if, after your generous letter to me, I
had said of you things which seem to you
ungenerous and unfair and untrue. The only
papers I have seen about the subject are the
Herald and *World*. Miss Meigs whom I had the
(60) honour of meeting last night tells me that
some garbled interview appeared in the *Post*
which contained certain foolish things
supposed to have proceeded from me. I have
not seen the paper at all, or I would have
(65) written to you at once about it. [*The rest of this
letter is missing.*]

Forbes had answered Wilde's letters of 20 and
23 January as follows:

26 January 1882 46 West 28 Street, New York

(70) Dear Mr. Wilde, It has a tendency to create
confusion when a man does not read
important letters addressed to himself, and
there is yet greater risk of this when he essays
to reply to them on a summary given him
(75) apparently without a due realisation of their
personal significance to him.

I accept your disclamation of the remarks in
connection with me which your letter states to
have been put into your mouth without
(80) warrant.

But it was not of these remarks which my
letter complained. What the letter protested
against was

First: the claim set up by you in your letter of
(85) Friday last, that I should trim a lecture of mine
to suit your sensitiveness to an inoffensive
effort at humour; and

Secondly and *chiefly*—with the knowledge I
have, and which you know I have, of the utterly
(90) mercenary aim of your visit to America, the
possibility of my accepting your pretensions
put forward in the same letter as follows: 'I
have something to say to the American people,
something that I know will be the beginning of
(95) a great movement; and all foolish ridicule does
a great deal of harm to the cause of art,
refinement and civilisation here.'

It is no affair of mine to whom else you may
choose to advance these pretensions; but I
(100) must utterly decline to allow you to address
them to me, for the reasons given at length in

my letter which you have not thought proper to read.

(105) Your letter of Monday, with its irrelevant expressions of cordiality, cannot affect the situation. What I have to ask is that you withdraw, as obviously offensive to me, the whole of your letter of Friday, and that you do so categorically, and in so many words, with

(110) the exception of the first sentence of it.

As it is irksome to me that the matter should hang over, I must demand that you send me a letter containing the withdrawal specified, by Sunday next. In the event of my non-receipt

(115) thereof, I beg to intimate to you that I will print the whole correspondence in a New York paper of Monday morning. I am faithfully yours,

ARCHIBALD FORBES.

[1] British war correspondent and author (1838–1900). He was also lecturing in the United States at this time, wearing all his medals, and had small sympathy with Wilde's ideas on aesthetics and dress reform. It had been reported that Wilde would attend Forbes's lecture at Baltimore on 19 January, but the two men quarreled on the train from Philadelphia and Wilde went straight on to Washington without stopping at Baltimore. Both Forbes and the leaders of Baltimore Society were offended. The passage in Forbes's lecture to which Wilde objected described a visit to the Czar in war-torn Bulgaria: "I glanced down at my clothes, which I had not changed in a fortnight, and in which I had ridden 150 miles. Now I wish it understood that I am a follower, a humble follower, of the aesthetic ecstasy, but I did not look much like an art object then. I did not have my dogskin knee breeches with me, nor my velvet coat, and my black silk stockings were full of holes. Neither was the wild, barren waste of Bulgaria congenial to the growth of sunflowers and lilies."

[2] D'Oyly Carte's representative in America.

13. Wilde's choice to italicize *"in your lecture"* (line 7) indicates that

A. Wilde is unwilling to disregard Forbes' written correspondence

B. formal presentations deserve accuracy

C. Wilde is determined to retaliate in his own lectures

D. Wilde capriciously decided to chastise Forbes

E. chance meetings can instill misperceptions

14. Wilde suggests that Forbes do all of the following EXCEPT

A. delete the offending passage from his lecture

B. allow each man to speak to the American people

C. use stronger discretion in his lecture remarks

D. continue speaking on subjects he knows well

E. reword the section of his lecture that discusses Wilde

15. All of the following can be inferred about American journalism of the 1880s EXCEPT

A. newspapers published libel

B. newspapers were used as vehicles of personal correspondence

C. journalistic integrity was paramount

D. anyone could easily get something printed quickly

E. the public believed what was published

16. The pronoun "it" in Wilde's remark "I do not think you should have believed *it* of me" (line 52) most likely refers to

A. Forbes' talking about Wilde behind his back

B. the paper's reporting the two men's argument

C. Wilde's supposedly sneering remarks about Forbes

D. Wilde's capacity for chivalry and personal bravery

E. the harm done by "foolish ridicule" (line 15)

17. Forbes' use of the word "essays" as a verb (line 73) serves as a

A. symbolic gesture of support for Wilde's writing

B. hyperbolic display of Forbes' anger

C. metaphor for Wilde's body of work

D. play on words regarding Wilde's correspondence with Forbes

E. demonstration of Forbes' linguistic obfuscation

18. The attitude of each writer can best be described as

  A. condescending to the other and convinced of his own moral superiority
  B. hopeful that they can come to an agreement and put this past misunderstanding behind them
  C. fearful that their reputations will be permanently tarnished
  D. complacent about future encounters they may have
  E. sincere in their effort to mend past disagreements

19. Wilde would most likely object to the quotation from Forbes' lecture in footnote #1 because it

  A. is a direct attack on Wilde's pacifism
  B. is a poorly written description of the countryside
  C. denigrates Wilde's antiwar position
  D. presumes that Wilde would never participate in a war
  E. is a disguised attack on Wilde's notions of dress reform and aesthetics

20. Footnote #1 serves the rhetorical purpose of

  A. summarizing Forbes' argument about the need for war
  B. juxtaposing what Forbes perceives as serious issues, namely "war-torn Bulgaria," with trivial matters, namely Wilde's preoccupation with clothing
  C. providing a logical completion to Forbes' humorous anecdote
  D. acting as an incentive for Wilde to respond
  E. giving Forbes a chance to repeat his criticism of Wilde

21. Wilde's letter of January 23 and Forbes' reply differ in that

  A. Forbes is direct and confrontational; Wilde is conversational and explanatory
  B. Forbes is willing to forget their past disagreement; Wilde insists on bringing it up repeatedly
  C. Wilde takes responsibility for his actions, while Forbes deflects the blame
  D. Wilde anticipates an amicable end to their dispute; Forbes believes it will continue
  E. Wilde makes logical, step-by-step assertions; Forbes meanders to his point

22. Wilde's second letter differs rhetorically from his first in that the second

  A. systematically outlines his points
  B. shows respect for Forbes' ideas
  C. attacks Forbes more directly
  D. becomes less assertive and aggressive
  E. sincerely flatters Forbes

23. Which of the following phrases most clearly displays Wilde's intended ironic condescension?

  A. "I feel bound to say quite frankly to you that I do not consider them to be either in good taste or appropriate to your subject" (lines 8–11)
  B. "You have to speak of the life of action, I of the life of art." (lines 22–23)
  C. ". . . [Y]ou feel yourself wronged by something I am supposed to have said of you in the papers" (lines 31–33)
  D. "I would speak of a man whose chivalry, whose personal bravery, and whose pluck, have won him the respect and the admiration" (lines 41–43)
  E. "It is true you hardly know me at all personally" (lines 52–53)

Questions 24–34 refer to the following passage written by an 18th-century British author.

This single stick, which you now behold ingloriously lying in that neglected corner, I once knew in a flourishing state in a forest; it was full of sap, full of leaves, and full of boughs; but now, in (5) vain, does the busy art of man pretend to vie with nature, by tying that withered bundle of twigs to its sapless trunk; 'tis now, at best, but the reverse of what it was, a tree turned upside down, the branches on the earth, and the root in the air; 'tis (10) now handled by every dirty wench, condemned to do her drudgery, and, by a capricious kind of fate, destined to make other things clean, and be nasty itself; at length, worn to the stumps in the service of the maids, either thrown out of doors, or (15) condemned to the last use, of kindling a fire. When I beheld this, I sighed, and said within myself: *Surely Man is a Broomstick!* Nature sent him into the world strong and lusty, in a thriving condition, wearing his own hair on his head, the (20) proper branches of this reasoning vegetable, until the axe of intemperance has lopped off his green boughs, and left him a withered trunk; he then flies to art, and puts on a periwig, valuing himself upon an unnatural bundle of hairs (all covered (25) with powder) that never grew on his head; but now should this our broomstick pretend to enter the scene, proud of all those birchen spoils it never bore, and all covered with dust, though the sweepings of the finest lady's chamber, we should (30) be apt to ridicule and despise its vanity. Partial judges that we are of our own excellences, and other men's defaults!

But a broomstick, perhaps you will say, is an emblem of a tree standing on its head; and pray, (35) what is a man but a topsy-turvy creature, his animal faculties perpetually mounted on his rational, his head where his heels should be, groveling on the earth! And yet, with all his faults, he sets up to be a universal reformer and corrector (40) of abuses, a remover of grievances, rakes into every slut's corner of nature, bringing hidden corruption to the light, and raises a mighty dust where there was none before; sharing deeply all the while in the very same pollutions he pretends (45) to sweep away; his last days are spent in slavery to women, and generally the least deserving; till, worn out to the stumps, like his brother broom, he is either kicked out of doors, or made use of to kindle flames for others to warm themselves by.

24. All of the following are present in the opening sentence of the passage EXCEPT

    A. syntactically complex structure
    B. parallel construction
    C. a pedantic tone
    D. the narrative of a broomstick's life
    E. subordinate clauses

25. According to the author, both a broomstick and a man

    A. cleanse the world
    B. become corrupted by the evil in society
    C. can be proud of their humble accomplishments
    D. symbolize integrity in the world
    E. were untainted in their natural state

26. According to the passage, the broomstick symbolizes

    A. society's corruption of the youth
    B. the goodness in nature that man uses and discards
    C. the triumph of nature over man's evil tendencies
    D. the evil inherent in man's soul
    E. the tremendous power of nature that man fears

27. The "axe of intemperance" (line 21) can be interpreted as

    A. an understatement of man's dominance over nature
    B. a metaphor for nature's nourishing elements
    C. a simile comparing man and tree
    D. a hyperbole describing man's destruction
    E. a metaphor for man's excesses

28. The author's attitude toward mankind can best be described as

    A. disillusionment at man's deeds
    B. perplexed concern for man's future
    C. guarded optimism for man's soul
    D. anger at the society man has created
    E. sincere praise for man's use of nature

29. Which of the following does NOT demonstrate a negative attitude by this author?

    A. "a flourishing state in a forest" (line 3)
    B. "the axe of intemperance" (line 21)
    C. "an unnatural bundle of hairs" (line 24)
    D. "sweepings of the finest lady's chamber" (line 29)
    E. "sharing . . . the very same pollutions he pretends to sweep away" (lines 43–45)

30. The word referred to by the phrase "this reasoning vegetable" (line 20) is

    A. "Man" (line 17)
    B. "hair" (line 19)
    C. "head" (line 19)
    D. "branches" (line 20)
    E. "green boughs" (lines 21–22)

31. In context, "this our broomstick" (line 26) is a

    A. symbol for the thriving forest
    B. metaphor for man's pretentious character
    C. link between nature and society
    D. demonstration of nature's control
    E. representation of man's intelligence

32. What does the author imply about man's ability to be a "corrector of abuses" (lines 39–40)?

    A. Man easily solves his own problems.

    B. Man effectively improves society.

    C. Man can act as a fair arbitrator in disputes.

    D. Man readily accepts his role as a social reformer.

    E. Man causes problems where none previously existed.

33. The tone of the passage can best be described as

    A. neutral toward society

    B. condescending toward nature

    C. cynical toward mankind

    D. bellicose toward mankind

    E. dogmatic toward society

34. Which of the following represents the strongest statement of the author's theme?

    A. "condemned to do her drudgery" (lines 10–11)

    B. "destined to make other things clean" (line 12)

    C. "the axe of intemperance has lopped off his green boughs" (lines 21–22)

    D. "Partial judges that we are of our own excellences" (lines 30–31)

    E. "his last days are spent in slavery" (line 45)

Questions 35–45 refer to the following passage by a 19th-century American author.

    The time is coming, I hope, when each new author, each new artist, will be considered, not in his proportion to any other author or artist, but in his relation to the human nature, known to us all,

(5) which is his privilege, his high duty, to interpret. "The true standard of the artist is in every man's power" already, as [Edmund] Burke says; Michelangelo's "light of the piazza," the glance of the common eye, is and always was the best light

(10) on a statue; . . . but hitherto the mass of common men have been afraid to apply their own simplicity, naturalness, and honesty to the appreciation of the beautiful. They have always cast about for the instruction of some one who professed to know

(15) better, and who browbeat wholesome common-sense into the self-distrust that ends in sophistication. . . . They have been taught to compare what they see and what they read, not with the things that they have observed and

(20) known, but with the things that some other artist or writer has done. Especially if they have themselves the artistic impulse in any direction they are taught to form themselves, not upon life, but upon the masters who became masters only

(25) by forming themselves upon life. The seeds of death are planted in them, and they can only produce the still-born, the academic. They are not told to take their work into the public square and see if it seems true to the chance passer, but to test

(30) it by the work of the very men who refused and decried any other test of their own work. The young writer who attempts to report the phrase and carriage of every-day life, who tries to tell just how he has heard men talk and seen them look, is

(35) made to feel guilty of something low and unworthy by the stupid people who would like to have him show how Shakespeare's men talked and looked, or Scott's, or Thackeray's, or Balzac's, or Hawthorne's, or Dickens's; he is instructed to

(40) idealize his personages, that is, to take the life-likeness out of them, and put the book-likeness into them. He is approached in the spirit of the wretched pedantry into which learning . . . always decays when it withdraws itself and stands apart

(45) from experience in an attitude of imagined superiority, and which would say with the same confidence to the scientist: "I see that you are looking at a grasshopper there which you have found in the grass, and I suppose you intend to

(50) describe it. Now don't waste your time and sin against culture in that way. I've got a grasshopper here, which has been evolved at considerable pains and expense out of the grasshopper in general; in fact, it's a type. It's made up of wire and cardboard,

(55) very prettily painted in a conventional tint, and it's perfectly indestructible. It isn't very much like a real grasshopper, but it's a great deal nicer, and it's served to represent the notion of a grasshopper ever since man emerged from barbarianism. You

(60) may say that it's artificial. Well, it is artificial; but then it's ideal too; and what you want to do is to cultivate the ideal. You'll find the books full of my kind of grasshopper, and scarcely a trace of yours in any of them. The thing that you are proposing

(65) to do is commonplace; but if you say that it isn't commonplace, for the very reason that it hasn't been done before, you'll have to admit that it's photographic."

    I hope the time is coming when not only the

(70) artist, but the common, average man, who always "has the standard of the arts in his power," will have also the courage to apply it, and will reject the ideal grasshopper wherever he finds it, in science, in literature, in art, because it is not

(75) "simple, natural, and honest," because it is not

like a real grasshopper. But . . . I think the time is yet far off, and that the people who have been brought up on the ideal grasshopper, the heroic grasshopper, the impassioned grasshopper, the (80) self-devoted, adventureful, good old romantic cardboard grasshopper, must die out before the simple, honest, and natural grasshopper can have a fair field. I am in no haste to compass the end of these good people, whom I find in the meantime (85) very amusing. It is delightful to meet one of them, either in print or out of it some sweet elderly lady or excellent gentleman whose youth was pastured on the literature of thirty or forty years ago—and to witness the confidence with which they preach (90) their favorite authors as all the law and the prophets. They have commonly read little or nothing since or, if they have, they have judged it by a standard taken from these authors, and never dreamed of judging it by nature; they are destitute (95) of the documents in the case of the later writers; they suppose that Balzac was the beginning of realism, and that Zola is its wicked end; they are quite ignorant, but they are ready to talk you down, if you differ from them, with an assumption (100) of knowledge sufficient for any occasion. The horror, the resentment, with which they receive any question of their literary saints is genuine; you descend at once very far in the moral and social scale, anything short of offensive personality (105) is too good for you; it is expressed to you that you are one to be avoided, and put down even a little lower than you have naturally fallen.

35. The tone of the passage can best be described as

A. somber
B. ornate
C. didactic
D. critical
E. formal

36. The speaker feels common people make which of the following mistakes?

A. judging a work of art too quickly
B. letting their own interpretation interfere with their reading
C. letting authorities tell them how to interpret literature
D. basing their judgments on appearances only
E. not modeling their tastes after their neighbors

37. The phrase "The seeds of death" (lines 25–26) is a

A. metaphor for imitative art
B. symbol of the destruction of art
C. metaphor for the art of an older age
D. reference to Michelangelo's art
E. symbol of artistic immaturity

38. The author's criticism of those who read only older literature is tempered by the fact that he

A. is certain their ideas will die out quickly
B. finds them entertaining and delightful
C. dismisses them as unimportant
D. alleges they do little harm to the average reader
E. acknowledges that they have great knowledge

39. The idealized grasshopper is a symbol for

A. the quest to merge art and science
B. the human search for perfection
C. art that lasts through the ages
D. artificial rather than realistic art
E. the scientist's folly in trying to describe nature

40. According to the author, the irony of the idealized grasshopper is that

A. it ceases to be realistic
B. scientists will find it useful
C. it blends science and art into one
D. it cannot be distinguished from a real grasshopper
E. it has not been created

41. Which of the following types of grasshopper does the author feel will be the slowest to become integrated into mainstream literature?

A. the heroic grasshopper
B. the ideal grasshopper
C. the simple, honest, natural grasshopper
D. the impassioned grasshopper
E. the good old romantic cardboard grasshopper

42. The story of the grasshopper contains

    A. hidden hyperbole

    B. satiric humor

    C. overstated oxymoron

    D. ruthless criticism

    E. remarkable realism

43. In context, which of the following best represents the author's main idea about art appreciation?

    A. "simplicity, naturalness, and honesty" (lines 11–12)

    B. "people who would like to have him show how Shakespeare's men talked" (lines 36–37)

    C. "an attitude of imagined superiority" (lines 45–46)

    D. "it is artificial; but then it's ideal too" (lines 60–61)

    E. "witness the confidence with which they preach their favorite authors" (lines 89–90)

44. What similarity is suggested between the scientist and artist who discuss the grasshopper?

    A. The models of their studies will both be artificial.

    B. They both love to observe nature.

    C. They both look to old masters for inspiration.

    D. Both of their methods will become obsolete.

    E. They both spend too much time on research.

45. Which of the following devices is NOT used in the passage?

    A. irony

    B. metaphor

    C. caricature

    D. allusion

    E. analogy

Questions 46–54 refer to the following passage by a 19th-century British author during his first trip to America.

Take the worst parts of the City Road and Pentonville,[1] or the straggling outskirts of Paris, where the houses are smallest, preserving all their oddities, but especially the small shops and
(5) dwellings occupied in Pentonville (but not in Washington) by furniture brokers, keepers of poor-eating houses, and fanciers of birds. Burn the whole down; build it up again in wood and plaster; widen it a little; throw in part of St.
(10) John's Wood[2]; put green blinds outside all the private houses, with a red curtain and a white one in every window; plough up all the roads; plant a great deal of coarse turf in every place where it ought *not* to be; erect three handsome
(15) buildings in stone and marble anywhere, but the more entirely out of everybody's way the better; call one the Post Office, one the Patent Office, and one the Treasury; make it scorching hot in the morning, and freezing cold in the afternoon,
(20) with an occasional tornado of wind and dust; leave a brick-field, without the bricks, in all central places where a street may naturally be expected; and that's Washington.

The hotel in which we live is a long row of small
(25) houses fronting on the street, and opening at the back upon a common yard, in which hangs a great triangle. Whenever a servant is wanted, somebody beats on this triangle from one stroke up to seven, according to the number of the house in which his
(30) presence is required; and as all the servants are always being wanted, and none of them ever come, this enlivening engine is in full performance the whole day through. Clothes are drying in this same yard; female slaves, with cotton handkerchiefs
(35) twisted round their heads, are running to and fro on the hotel business; black waiters cross and recross with dishes in their hands; two great dogs are playing upon a mound of loose bricks in the centre of the little square; a pig is turning up his
(40) stomach to the sun, and grunting "That's comfortable!" and neither the men, nor the women, nor the dogs, nor the pig, nor any created creature takes the smallest notice of the triangle, which is tingling madly all the time.

(45) I walk to the front window, and look across the road, upon a long, straggling row of houses, one story high, terminating nearly opposite, but a little to the left, in a melancholy piece of waste ground with frouzy [sic] grass, which looks like a
(50) small piece of country that has taken to drinking, and has quite lost itself. Standing anyhow and all wrong, upon this open space, like something meteoric that has fallen down from the moon, is an odd, lop-sided, one-eyed kind of wooden
(55) building, that looks like a church, with a flagstaff as long as itself sticking out of a steeple something larger than a tea-chest. . . . The three most obtrusive houses near at hand are the three meanest. On one—a shop, which never has
(60) anything in the window, and never has the door open—is painted in large characters, "THE CITY LUNCH." At another, which looks like the back-way to somewhere else, but is an independent building in itself, oysters are procurable in every

(65) style. At the third, which is a very, very little tailor's shop, pants are fixed to order; or, in other words, pantaloons are made to measure. And that is our street in Washington.

It is sometimes called the City of Magnificent
(70) Distances, but it might with greater propriety be termed the City of Magnificent Intentions; for it is only on taking a bird's-eye view of it from the top of the Capitol that one can at all comprehend the vast designs of its projector, an aspiring
(75) Frenchman. Spacious avenues that begin in nothing, and lead nowhere; streets mile-long, that only want houses, roads, and inhabitants; public buildings that need but a public to be complete; and ornaments of great thoroughfares, which
(80) only lack great thoroughfares to ornament—are its leading features. . . .

Such as it is, it is likely to remain. It was originally chosen for the seat of Government as a means of averting the conflicting jealousies and
(85) interests of the different States; and very probably, too, as being remote from mobs: a consideration not to be slighted, even in America. It has no trade or commerce of its own: having little or no population beyond the President and his
(90) establishment: the members of the legislature, who reside there during the session; the Government clerks and officers employed in the various departments; the keepers of the hotels and boarding-houses; and the tradesmen who
(95) supply their tables. It is very unhealthy. Few people would live in Washington, I take it, who were not obliged to reside there; and the tides of emigration and speculation, those rapid and regardless currents, are little likely to flow at any
(100) time towards such dull and sluggish water.

[1] City Road and Pentonville: areas in north central London

[2] St. John's Wood: an upscale neighborhood in northwest London

46. In the passage, the author's overall attitude toward Washington, D.C., can best be described as

A. viciously sarcastic
B. amusingly nonjudgmental
C. strikingly pedantic
D. grudgingly appreciative
E. fundamentally patronizing

47. The stylistic feature most prominent in the sentence "Burn the whole . . . that's Washington" (lines 7–23) is the use of

A. metaphorical description
B. repeated syntactical patterns
C. inaccurate use of the semicolon
D. several adjective clauses
E. a series of prepositional phrases

48. One purpose of the first paragraph is to

A. describe the incongruous patterns that make up Washington
B. suggest the similarity between Washington and Pentonville
C. reinforce the superiority of Pentonville and Paris over Washington
D. suggest possible improvements to the Washington street scheme
E. list ways to augment Washington's appearance

49. Which of the following rhetorical devices is used in the phrase that says the "triangle . . . is tingling madly all the time" (lines 43–44)?

A. antithesis
B. personification
C. euphemism
D. situational irony
E. juxtaposition

50. Which of the following pairs of details in the second paragraph most strongly contrast with each other?

A. the drying clothes and the cotton handkerchiefs on women's heads
B. the female slaves and the black waiters
C. the front of the houses and the common yard
D. the pig and the humans
E. the animals' and the humans' reaction to the sound of the triangle

51. The third paragraph differs from the other paragraphs in its use of

A. allusion
B. metaphor
C. simile
D. colloquialism
E. hyperbole

52. Which of the following images is most ironic in the third paragraph?

    A. The row of houses ends in a "waste ground" (lines 48–49)

    B. The "melancholy . . . waste ground" (lines 48–49) looks "lost itself" (line 51)

    C. The "three most obtrusive houses" (lines 57–58) are the "meanest" (line 59)

    D. The City Lunch shop has nothing in its windows, while the next building has oysters "in every style" (lines 64–65)

    E. The tailor's shop provides "pantaloons . . . made to measure" (line 67)

53. Which of the following does NOT include a degree of comic effect?

    A. "furniture brokers, keepers of poor-eating houses, and fanciers of birds" (lines 6–7)

    B. "a pig is turning up his stomach to the sun, and grunting 'That's comfortable!'" (lines 39–41)

    C. "like a small piece of country that has taken to drinking, and has quite lost itself" (lines 49–51)

    D. "It is sometimes called the City of Magnificent Distances, but it might with greater propriety be termed the City of Magnificent Intentions" (lines 69–71)

    E. "It was originally chosen for the seat of Government as a means of averting the conflicting jealousies and interests of the different States" (lines 82–85)

54. The passage as a whole can best be characterized as

    A. a critical description of Washington's appearance and atmosphere

    B. a scathing review of Washington politics

    C. a personal reminiscence of the author's visit

    D. an ironic homily about Washington's faults

    E. a series of images that are open to varied interpretations

IF YOU FINISH BEFORE TIME IS CALLED, CHECK YOUR WORK ON THIS SECTION ONLY. DO NOT WORK ON ANY OTHER SECTION IN THE TEST.

Section II: Free-Response Questions

Time: 2 hours, 15 minutes

3 questions

Question 1

(Suggested writing time—40 minutes. This question counts for one-third of the total free-response section score.)

Polling has become an integral part of the United States election process. The media, as well as the voting population, take into great consideration the results of various political polls. But are these polls truly accurate? Has the United States been relying too heavily on the often inaccurate data of political polling?

Considering the role that political polls play in U.S. elections, read the following six sources (including any introductory information) carefully. Then, in a coherent, well-written essay that synthesizes at least three of the sources for support, take a position that defends, challenges, or qualifies the claim that political polls do not accurately represent the views of a population.

Always remember that your argument should be central; the sources should be used to support this argument. Therefore, avoid merely summarizing sources. Clearly cite which sources you use, both directly and indirectly. Refer to the sources by their titles (Source A, Source B, etc.) or by the descriptions in parentheses.

> Source A (photo)
> Source B (Triola)
> Source C (Fund)
> Source D (Morgan)
> Source E (Patterson)
> Source F (Ponnuru)

Source A

Dewey Defeats Truman. 5 Nov. 1948. Photograph. Library of Congress, New York World-Telegram and Sun Newspaper Photograph collection. loc.gov. Web. 5 Oct. 2017.

The following photograph, published on November 3, 1948, shows President Truman, jubilant after winning the 1948 election, holding up a copy of the Chicago Daily Tribune *newspaper with the erroneous headline stating that Truman's opponent, New York Governor Thomas Dewey, had won the election. The newspaper relied on political polls to predict the "winner," but in this case the polls were clearly wrong.*

Source B

Triola, Mario F. *Elementary Statistics,* 7th ed. Reading: Addison Wesley Longman, Inc., 1998. Print.

The following passage is taken from a statistics textbook that examines the uses and abuses of statistics.

Abuses of statistics have occurred for some time. For example, about a century ago, statesman Benjamin Disraeli famously said, "there are three kinds of lies: lies, damned lies, and statistics." It has also been said that "figures don't lie; liars figure," and that "if you torture the data long enough, they'll admit to anything." Historian Andrew Lang said that some people use statistics "as a drunken man uses lampposts—for support rather than illumination." These statements refer to abuses of statistics in which data are presented in ways that may be misleading. Some abusers of statistics are simply ignorant or careless, whereas others have personal objectives and are willing to suppress unfavorable data while emphasizing supportive data. We will now present a few examples of the many ways in which data can be distorted.

Loaded Questions: Survey questions can be worded to elicit a desired response. A famous case involves presidential candidate Ross Perot, who asked this question in a mail survey: "Should the president have the line item veto to eliminate waste?" The results included 97% "yes" responses. However, 57% said "yes" when subjects were randomly selected and asked this question: "Should the President have the line item veto, or not?" Sometimes questions are unintentionally loaded by such factors as the order of the items being considered. For example, one German poll asked these two questions:

- Would you say that traffic contributes more or less to air pollution than industry?

- Would you say that industry contributes more or less to air pollution than traffic?

When traffic was presented first, 45% blamed traffic and 32% blamed industry; when industry was presented first, those percentages changed dramatically to 24% and 57%, respectively.

Source C

Fund, John. "Polling Isn't Perfect." *The Wall Street Journal.* 14 Nov. 2002: n. pag. Print.

The following passage is excerpted from an article in a national newspaper about problems facing pollsters.

America has too many political polls, and Americans pay too much attention to them. Many people have believed that for a long time. What's different now is that some pollsters are starting to agree.

"We have falsely raised expectations about polling," says John Zogby, who is famous for having called Bill Clinton's margin in the 1996 presidential race almost exactly and having been virtually the only pollster to give Al Gore a slight popular-vote edge on election eve in 2000. But this year Mr. Zogby saw three of his final 11 statewide polls indicate the wrong winner. He says it would be helpful if people discovered the limitations of polling. In a speech and interview in Washington yesterday he described some of the problems his profession faces:

- The nightly tracking polls that both candidates and reporters fixate on are less reliable than larger polls taken over a longer period of time. "I probably should have used larger samples," admits Mr. Zogby, who thought that Democrat Jeanne Shaheen would win an open New Hampshire Senate seat and that Republican Jim Ryan was tied for the governor's race in Illinois. (She lost by four points and he by seven.)

Dave Winston, a Republican pollster, says one problem with nightly tracking polls is that a pollster doing them doesn't have the time to make innumerable repeat calls to people who won't pick up the phone. Mr. Zogby says that he now has to make an average of seven calls to get just one person willing to spend the 20 minutes or so it takes to answer his polling questions.

- *Pollsters can't poll on Election Day.* Surveys this year found that between 4% and 12% of voters in key states made up their mind who to vote for on Election Day. Although challengers tend to pick up most of the undecided vote, it doesn't always work out that way—making last-minute votes impossible to predict.

- *Answering machines, caller ID and other screening devices make pollsters easier to avoid.* Some phones won't even ring unless they recognize the number of the caller. Scott Adler, University of Colorado political scientist, says pollsters are now concerned that the people who do finally agree to answer a pollster's questions are no longer representative of the voters as a whole.

Whit Ayres, a GOP pollster, told the *Atlanta Journal-Constitution* that "I can't fathom 20 years from now the telephone remaining the primary means of data collection. This industry is in a transition from telephone data collection to Internet data collection." In the meantime, look for polls to be more variable and less reliable than ever. Perhaps it's time that we spend more time listening to the candidates and having people make up their own mind who's doing well.

Source D

Morgan, Lee. "The Disadvantages of Public Polling." *Classroom*. N.D. Web. 17 Sept. 2017.

The following article explores reasons for polls being inaccurate.

Public opinion polls are used to gather information about the attitudes of a population regarding politics and other social issues. While they often prove to be useful in determining outcomes of elections or persuading politicians or business owners to take a particular action on an issue, the public opinion poll is a flawed process that has its own unique set of disadvantages.

The Leading Option

According to Surveys.com.au, one major disadvantage of public opinion polling is the tendency of the person taking the survey to go with "the leading option." The leading option is the answer to a polling question that the researcher suggests is the popular answer while asking someone else. For example, a pollster may tell a person that research has shown that Candidate A is the most common answer when people are asked who they think will win the election between Candidates A, B and C. When the poll question is actually asked, it is phrased, "Among Candidate A, B and C, who do you believe will win the election?" Having already heard what the supposed most popular answer is, those who do not have a strong opinion about the matter are likely to go with Candidate A because most other people have apparently done the same. This leads to inaccurate public opinion and is a way that pollsters with an agenda can help get the results they want.

Sampling Errors

If you've seen poll results on the news, there is usually a disclaimer that lets the viewer know that there is a plus or minus 3 percent margin of error. This may occasionally be the case, but there is no solid way to tell just how big the error margin is, according to PollingReport.com. Sampling errors take place in a number of different ways. If a pollster is conducting a sidewalk survey, there is a strong possibility several people will refuse to take part in it. If the poll was about attitudes toward public opinion polls, for example, a very significant portion of the population may not be represented. And, of course, there is outright dishonesty by pollsters. If the poll is driven by an agenda, little stops them from doctoring the results to fit that agenda or wording questions in a way that is likely to provoke a certain response.

Selection Bias

Selection bias happens when the people intentionally selected to take part in a poll may not be representative of the entire population. If a conservative talk radio station is conducting a call-in opinion poll from its listeners concerning their opinion on a liberal political candidate, the results are fairly predictable. The liberal politician is likely to be viewed as unfavorable to the station's conservative listeners. In addition, in the above example, the people who feel strongly about a subject are likely to call in multiple times to vote. According to the Skeptic's Dictionary website, a poll conducted by Alfred Kinsey about homosexuality showed that 10 percent of the American population is gay. Later studies suggested the number is more like 2 percent. Kinsey's numbers were subject to selection bias because he conducted the survey with people in prisons and those who attended his lectures. Neither was representative of the entire population.

Source E

Patterson, Dan. "Numbers lie all the time: How political polls work." *TechRepublic.* 23 Aug. 2016. Web. 17 Sept. 2017.

The following excerpt is from an article about how political polls are conducted.

Numbers lie all the time. Yet the business of numbers is big business. Big data helps companies make better decisions by extracting key insights from piles of information. Polling does the same for politics.

And like big data for business, though results can be ambiguous and notoriously hard to interpret, polls are essential tools for political campaigns. When pundits and politicos talk about "the polls," they're referring to a bevy of companies and universities that perform specialized research.

Modern political polls are generally conducted through telephone surveys that target population samples based on demographic and psychographic criteria. Poll recipients are run through a barrage of carefully worded questions about personalities, messaging, and policy.

Quality polls use random sampling to determine who is called. Random digit dialing, a widely used tactic, is based on manual selection of the area code and phone number prefix, then picks the last four digits of a phone number at random. This tactics is great at getting usable local responses to questions, but bad because it doesn't exclude business, Skype, and other non-human numbers.

Registration-based sampling, another common polling method, is based on available data, usually voter registration lists and other data provided by the party. These polls can be less expensive, because voter data is already captured.

Tracking, policy, benchmark, and opinion polls are often commissioned by campaigns digging for information about voter segments. The final product, presented to the campaign or client, is typically a document that breaks down recipient responses by age, gender, location, income, and political association.

Big data played a major role in informing the Ted Cruz campaign who to microtarget and poll during the primaries. Computers are prohibited from calling cell phones, but humans can manually dial numbers from spreadsheets generated by computers.

Are polls accurate? Poll results can seem inconsistent because the business of polling is diverse. Gallup, a respected data firm that provides deep analytics to large organizations, routinely publishes a survey on its election polling accuracy.

Data site FiveThirtyEight tracks the accuracy of dozens of polling agencies, ranging from local regional specialists to national firms and large research universities. While accuracy depends on the type of poll and the agency conducting poll research, political polls have been fairly accurate.

A Bloomberg survey seems to confirm that, during the 2016 political cycle campaign, polls have been reliable. Bloomberg used RealClearPolitics aggregate polling data in a month-long survey during the primaries, which showed that 86 percent of polls accurately forecast election winners.

Though polls have been accurate this cycle, the industry appears to be in a period of transition. Mobile devices have had a significant impact on poll response rates. Because many polls are conducted over the phone, consumers are more able to block or dismiss unknown calls. A Vanderbilt survey found that response rates to robocalls are abysmal.

Big data companies are hungry for political dollars and attempting to augment or supplant polling data with web and mobile user data. During the recent Republican National Convention, several polling experts indicated that the polling and big data industries could someday merge. A number of private data companies . . . already provide campaigns with mission critical data. Several political data companies see politics as a stepping-stone to other industries.

Source F

Ponnuru, Ramesh. "Margin of Error." Review of *Mobocracy: How the Media's Obsession with Polling Twists the News, Alters Elections, and Undermines Democracy,* by Matthew Robinson. *National Review.* 6 May 2002: 49. Print.

The following passage is excerpted from a book review of Mobocracy: How the Media's Obsession with Polling Twists the News, Alters Elections, and Undermines Democracy, *by Matthew Robinson.*

Reporters lean on polls because they provide the illusion of numerical certainty amid all the spin. In political campaigns, reporters are torn between the conflicting desires to stay with the herd and to write a new story: Changes in the poll numbers provide the pivot point that lets everyone know when to make the switch together. Now the candidate whose campaign was brilliant last week is revealed as a sad-sack loser. His initiative on health care has bombed. How do we know that? Because he's down in the polls. Why is he down in the polls? Because his health-care initiative has bombed.

The over reliance on polls has the effect of overestimating public support for small policies that seem innocuous to voters. But it kills big ideas in the crib. Voters' initial reaction to any sweeping change is likely to be negative, so the first polls on it will show that it is unpopular. From then on, the idea can be dismissed as such. Polls can interfere with the formation of public opinion.

They can also create the illusion that public opinion exists when it does not. Reports that discuss what the public thinks about stem-cell research, or the Middle East peace process, are pointless because the public has no coherent, consolidated view on these matters, at least at the level of specificity needed to guide action. Polls, and media summaries of them, routinely gloss over the vast public ignorance and apathy that makes them so fluid.

Question 2

(Suggested writing time—40 minutes. This question counts for one-third of the total free-response section score.)

In the following excerpt, John Updike, in his essay "The First Kiss," describes the opening of a new baseball season, including reflecting on the past season and the attitude of the fans as the new season begins.

Read the following narrative carefully. Then, in a well-developed essay, analyze how the author's rhetorical strategies, including metaphor and other devices, convey an audience's attitude toward a sporting event.

The many-headed monster called the Fenway Faithful yesterday resumed its romance with twenty-five youngish men in red socks who last year broke its monstrous big heart. Just showing up on so dank an Opening Day was an act of faith. But the wet sky dried to a mottled pewter, the tarpaulin was rolled off the infield and stuffed into a mailing tube, and we Faithful braced for the first kiss of another prolonged entanglement.

Who can forget the ups and downs of last year's fling? First, the Supersox; then, the unraveling. Our eyeballs grew calluses, watching Boomer swing from the heels and Hobson throw to the stars. Dismal nights watching the Royals play pinball with our heroes on that plastic prairie in Kansas City. Dreadful days losing count of Yankee singles in the four-game massacre. Fisk standing ever more erect and stoic at the plate, looking more and more like a Civil War memorial financed with Confederate dollars. The Noble Lost Cause.

In September, the mini-resurrection, Zimmer's last stand, the miraculous last week of no losses, waiting for the Yankees to drop one. Which they did. And then, the cruelest tease, the playoff game surrendered to a shoestring catch and a shortstop's cheap home run. Enough. You'll never get us to care again, Red Sox.

But monsters have short memories, elastic hearts, and very foolable faculties, as many an epic attests. From natty-looking to nasty-looking, the fans turned out. "We Miss Louis and Bill," one large cardboard complained. "Windsor Locks Loves the Sox!" a bedsheet benignly rhymed. Some fellow behind us exhaled a sweetish smell, but the dragon's breath was primarily flavored with malt.

Governor King was booed royally. Power may or may not corrupt, but it does not win friends. A lady from Dedham not only sang all the high notes in "The Star-Spangled Banner" but put in an extra one of her own, taking "free" up and out of the ballpark. We loved it. Monsters love high notes and hoards of gold.

The two teams squared off against each other in a state of statistical virginity. Every man in both lineups was batting .000. On the other hand, both pitchers had earned-run averages of 0.00. And every fielder there had thus far played errorless ball.

Eckersley looked quick. A moment of sun made some of the windows of the Prudential Center sparkle. The new Red Sox uniforms appeared tight as outfits for trapeze artists but otherwise struck the proper conservative note, for a team of millionaires: buttons on the shirt and a single red pinstripe. Eckersley yielded a double and then struck out two. The first nicks in statistical virginity had been taken. The season had begun.

We witnessed a little by-play at the beginning that may tell it all. After the Cleveland lineup had been called out, the Red Sox roll began with Zimmer. Out he trotted, last year's anti-hero, the manager who watched ninety-nine victories be not quite enough, with his lopsided cheeks and squint, like a Popeye who has let the spinach settle to his middle. The many-headed monster booed furiously, and Zimmer laughed, shaking hands with his opposite manager, Torborg.

That laugh said a strange thing. It said, *This is fun.* Baseball is meant to be fun, and not all the solemn money men in fur-collared greatcoats, not all the scruffy media cameramen and sour-faced reporters that crowd around the dugouts can quite smother the exhilarating spaciousness and grace of this impudently relaxed sport, a game of innumerable potential redemptions and curious disappointments. This is fun.

A hard lesson for a hungry monster to master, but he has six months to work on it. So let's play ball.

Question 3

(Suggested writing time—40 minutes. This question counts for one-third of the total free-response section score.)

In a well-thought-out essay, examine the accuracy of the following aphorism in modern society. Concentrate on appropriate examples from your observations, reading, and experiences to develop your ideas.

Henry David Thoreau wrote, "Many men go fishing all of their lives without knowing that it is not fish they are after."

IF YOU FINISH BEFORE TIME IS CALLED, CHECK YOUR WORK ON THIS SECTION ONLY. DO NOT WORK ON ANY OTHER SECTION IN THE TEST.

Answer Key

Section I: Multiple-Choice Questions

1. D	10. B	19. E	28. A	37. A	46. E
2. C	11. A	20. B	29. A	38. B	47. B
3. E	12. E	21. A	30. A	39. D	48. A
4. A	13. B	22. D	31. B	40. A	49. D
5. C	14. E	23. D	32. E	41. C	50. D
6. E	15. C	24. C	33. C	42. B	51. C
7. C	16. C	25. E	34. D	43. A	52. D
8. A	17. D	26. B	35. D	44. A	53. E
9. D	18. A	27. E	36. C	45. C	54. A

Section II: Free-Response Questions

Essay scoring guides, student essays, and analysis appear beginning on page 222.

Answer Explanations

Section I: Multiple-Choice Questions

The passage referred to in questions 1–12 is from *The March of Folly* (1984) by Barbara Tuchman.

1. **D.** The author juxtaposes Plato's early optimistic vision of an all-powerful yet benevolent philosopher-king with his later jaded conclusion that "laws were the only safeguard." This implies that Plato eventually realized rulers with too much power cannot be trusted. Choice A contradicts the key point of this paragraph. Choices B and C are incorrect because they are stated as facts, not implications. Choice E is Plato's metaphor, not the author's implication.

2. **C.** The author states that Plato "began to have doubts" about the ability to select and nurture a philosopher-king who is carefully chosen and trained in the art of rational decision-making for the good of the community. All other answer choices, although they do appear in the passage, *are* ideas with which one can reasonably infer Plato would agree.

3. **E.** The author's use of italics in "*my* air force" helps to demonstrate the very personal connection that President Johnson felt in his use of power. Choice A is incorrect; the quote is not from Richard Nixon. Choice B is incorrect; the author's intent is not to *praise* Johnson's personal attention to the war. Choice C contradicts the intent of the quotation. The use of "*my*" does not depersonalize Johnson's use of power; rather, it personalizes it. Choice D is unreasonable; authors add italics for a reason, and they always add something.

4. **A.** Paragraph 3 provides many examples of both valuable leadership traits and effective selection methods that can combine to produce a successful leader. Choices C and D are both incorrect because they are too negative to describe this optimistic paragraph. Choices B and E do not accurately relate to the content of this paragraph.

5. **C.** Recognizing the context of the series of queries is essential to understanding their impact, which derives power from placement. These probing questions provide vigorous reinforcement for the preceding statement, "Learning from experience is a faculty almost never practiced."

6. **E.** The author utilizes Coleridge's quotation eloquently to state her own conclusions that history and experience can be misleading when attempting "to infer the nature of the waves ahead. . . ." Choices A and C are incorrect; the author does not hint that Coleridge misspoke or was blinded. Choice B is actually a reversal of the author's conclusion about the worth of shining a light on the past. Choice D is incorrect; the author states, "The image is beautiful. . . ."

7. **C.** Because even Plato himself finally discarded the idea of a benevolent philosopher-king, the author gives greater credence to the Lilliputians, as "They have more regard for good morals than for great abilities." Choice A is a contradiction. Choice E is incorrect; Plato changed his mind and decided his idea of a philosopher-king was impractical. Additionally, Choices B, D, and E are incorrect because they do not answer the question; they do not *compare* Plato's ideas to those of the Lilliputians.

8. **A.** The speaker successfully integrates these disparate historical examples to help illustrate how man's folly throughout the ages displays that the same factors repeatedly lead to abuses of power. It is unrealistic to think that the author is merely grasping for examples that fit her hypothesis (B). Choice C is also unreasonable; the author's use of four historical examples can hardly be described as "throwing in everything she can." Choice D incorrectly claims the author shows what methods the individuals used to gain power; no methods are presented. Choice E has questionable phrasing, with the idea that the passage is a "narrative" in the first place, and that the author "ultimately fails."

9. **D.** The author's purpose in comparing the ideas espoused by such diverse thinkers as Montaigne and the fictional Lilliputians is to illustrate her belief that the *morally righteous* man is best suited to govern. Choice A is simply incorrect; the folly of the abuse of power is discussed in the first paragraph. Choices B and C are likewise incorrect; both mental stagnation and the "lantern on the stern" metaphor are in the second paragraph. Choice E is incorrect; the third paragraph deals exclusively with men who govern best.

10. **B.** The speaker indicates specific ways in which men *can* govern wisely, but she appears unconvinced that this will actually happen. She ends on a sad, cynical note: ". . . we cannot reasonably expect much improvement." Choice A is incorrect because the author is not optimistic. Choice C is too narrow in its scope; the passage as a whole is not about 19th-century authors. The author's tone is not credible (D). Choice E might present a new word, "hagiographical," but in any case, the rest of the answer choice eliminates choice E because the passage does not present any exultation of successful leaders. A hagiography is a biography that paints the subject in a very flattering light; specifically, the term refers to biographies of the saints.

11. **A.** Taken collectively, the five footnotes clearly demonstrate both the breadth of the author's research as well as the depth of her analysis; they reveal her to be a truly qualified expert in this field of study. Choice C is incorrect; she does not dismiss contradictory ideas out of hand. Choices B, D, and E are incorrect because these statements are not supported in the footnotes.

12. **E.** The passage's main theme is the oft-repeated story of political leaders who do not avoid excesses of power and, thus, they fail to avoid folly. Choice A exaggerates the author's position; she has little faith in the public's ability to select successful leaders, but she never intimates that direct elections should be abolished. Choices B and C are incorrect because the author believes that unsuitable leaders will, in the end, remain unsuitable, and that excesses of power are never justified. Choice D is inaccurate; the author does not expect improvement in mankind's skill in the selection of leaders.

The passage referred to in questions 13–23 is from *The Complete Letters of Oscar Wilde*.

13. **B.** Wilde's italicizing the phrase "*in your lecture*" shows that his strong reaction to Forbes' negative remarks is due to the fact that they were made in a public speaking forum, a formal setting that deserves accuracy. Choice A may be an inference, but a very far-fetched one; it barely connects to the italicized phrase in the question. Choice D incorrectly claims that Wilde was capricious in choosing to "chastise Forbes." Choices C and E are not reasonable inferences one can draw from this italicized phrase.

14. **E.** Wilde states that he believes Forbes' lecture will not suffer "by expunging the passage" (line 19) that Wilde finds so offensive (A). Therefore, Wilde will not settle for Forbes' merely rewording it, choice E. Wilde does suggest that Forbes should allow each to speak to American citizens (B), use stronger discretion in his lectures (C), and speak on the subjects he knows well (D).

15. **C.** One can infer that in American journalism in the 1880s, journalistic integrity was a virtue not yet generally practiced, since both writers' libelous accusations toward each other were indirectly published in newspapers. All other answer choices are reasonable inferences.

16. **C.** Wilde's phrase, "I do not think you should have believed *it* of me," is an attempt to persuade Forbes that Wilde did not actually utter the alleged negative remarks about the war correspondent. Choice A contradicts the passage. Choice B is off topic; the word "it" refers to the content of the newspaper report, not to the fact that the newspaper reported on the men's argument. Choice D refers to something Wilde said about Forbes, not about himself. Choice E is inaccurate because the word "it" does not refer to harm done, and in context the phrase "foolish ridicule" refers to the world of "art and refinement," not Wilde's actions or remarks.

17. **D.** Using the word "essays" as a verb is a play on words. Wilde is writing personal letters to Forbes, not essays, but perhaps his letters come across with the formality of an essay. Choice A is a contradiction; Forbes is not supporting Wilde, and his letter is not symbolic. Forbes' use of "essays" as a verb is not hyperbolic (B) or metaphorical (C). Choice E is unreasonable; Forbes hardly exhibits any linguistic prowess (or obfuscation—the act of making obscure or confusing) but instead uses a straightforward, logical presentation.

18. **A.** Each writer's tone is rife with condescension and a feeling that he is morally above the other. Each man feels certain that he has been socially snubbed and accordingly displays a snobbish and patronizing attitude. The passage does not include any evidence for their being hopeful (B), fearful for their reputations (C), complacent about the future (D), or sincere about settling their disagreements (E).

19. **E.** Footnote #1 states that Forbes had "small sympathy with Wilde's ideas on aesthetics and dress reform." Most of the direct quotation details Forbes' own disheveled dress as he arrived in Bulgaria, yet Forbes insists on describing himself as a follower of "aesthetic ecstasy." This becomes a thinly veiled attack on Wilde's ideals of aesthetics and dress reform. None of the incorrect answer choices address clothing or aesthetics.

20. **B.** Forbes points out in his quotation that his reporting is serious; after all, he is meeting with the czar of war-torn Bulgaria. In aiming his slight at Wilde, he points out that his own sub-par clothing after hard and long travel was inconsequential to his purpose. In contrast, Forbes implies that Wilde is only interested in appearances and the trivial fluff of life. Choice A is factually incorrect; footnote #1 does not summarize Forbes' argument for war. Choice C is incorrect because Forbes is not drawing a logical conclusion. The footnote does not suggest that Forbes is trying to bait Wilde into retaliating (D). Although Forbes may indeed repeat his criticism of Wilde (E), it is not the purpose of the footnote.

21. **A.** Forbes' reply is very direct, detailing his grievances against Wilde in an itemized list. Wilde's letter explains how innocent he feels he is in this matter, and he rambles on in a conversational tone. Choice B is inaccurate because both ideas are direct contradictions of the men's letters. Choice C wrongly states that Wilde takes responsibility when he instead claims his innocence. Choice D has no direct support in the letters. Choice E reverses the two men's approaches.

22. **D.** Wilde's first letter begins the fray with a direct attack, stating specifically that Forbes' remarks were not "in good taste or appropriate" (line 10). However, in the second letter Wilde tries to appease Forbes, claiming that he did not and would not say negative remarks about Forbes, and hopes Forbes knows him well enough to believe this claim. Therefore, Wilde becomes more conciliatory and less aggressive in his second letter. Choice A is inaccurate because Wilde never "systematically outlines" his points. He never mentions Forbes' ideas, making choice B incorrect, and he definitely does not attack Forbes at all in the second letter (C). Wilde does not honestly flatter Forbes in his second letter (E); when one considers the overall tone of Wilde's letter, one will see that his words of "praise" are not entirely sincere.

23. D. Wilde's use of the word "chivalry" shows cutting irony as he satirizes Forbes for living in an idealized past. In addition, his phrases such as "personal bravery" and "pluck" are actually tongue-in-cheek comments about Forbes' experience as a war correspondent. The remaining answer choices are sincere, not ironic. Pay particular attention to the letter's negative tone to understand how Wilde is being ironic when he seems to praise Forbes.

The passage referred to in questions 24–34 is from "Meditations upon a Broomstick" (1701) by Jonathan Swift.

24. C. The sentence is not pedantic (overly scholarly). The sentence is syntactically complex (A), and it has parallel construction (B), ". . . full of sap, full of leaves, and full of boughs. . . ." It contains a narrative of the broomstick's life (D), from tree sapling to death in a fireplace. Finally, the sentence has subordinate clauses (E), such as ". . . which you now behold ingloriously lying in that neglected corner. . . ."

25. E. The broomstick began life in nature in a "flourishing state . . . full of sap, full of leaves, and full of boughs." Man began life in youth "strong and lusty, in a thriving condition." Choices A, C, and D contradict the passage. Choice B is not addressed.

26. B. The broomstick starts life as a flourishing tree, but after man uses it up, he throws it away or burns it. Choice A has no support in the passage. Choices C and E contradict the passage. Nature does not triumph over man's evil tendencies, and man does not fear nature, but rather destroys it. The evil inherent in man's soul (D) is not addressed.

27. E. Intemperance is a lack of moderation in behavior, and the "axe of intemperance" is a metaphor for those excesses. It is the "axe" that chops man down like a tree. Before that, man had "green boughs"; after, he has but a "withered trunk." The phrase does not refer to "man's dominance over nature" (A). Nature is not shown as providing much nourishment (B); rather, it is destroyed. "Axe of intemperance" is neither a simile (C) nor hyperbole (D).

28. A. The author is saddened and disillusioned by man's behavior. Choice B is incorrect because man's future is not addressed. Choices C and E contradict the tone of the passage—there is no optimism or praise here. This author is angry with man and his nature, not the society man has created (D).

29. A. The phrase "a flourishing state in a forest" refers to pure, untouched nature (before man chops down trees) and has positive connotations. All other answer choices are negative within the passage's context.

30. A. The phrase "this reasoning vegetable" refers to "Man." Notice how the author claims that "Nature sent him (man) into the world. . .this reasoning vegetable." Do not be confused when the author adds that man was sent into the world "wearing his own hair on his head," because the hair refers to "the proper branches of this reasoning vegetable," and that "reasoning vegetable," who happens to have hair on his head, is man. The head itself (C) is not the reasoning vegetable; man is. The remaining answer choices do not refer to the "reasoning vegetable."

31. B. Man pretends to solve the problems of the world but only makes them worse. Choice A is inaccurate— the broomstick represents decline, not thriving. Choice C is also inaccurate; the broomstick is a metaphor for man, not society. There is no evidence for choice D; nature doesn't exert control in this author's world, man does. Choice E is obviously incorrect; the broomstick is an analogy for man's physical state, not his intellectual state.

32. E. It is only man's presentation that allows him to believe that he can correct abuses. In fact, he "raises a mighty dust where there was none before." All incorrect answer choices are positive ideas; the correct response needs a negative one.

33. C. Swift is cynical toward mankind and all of man's works, believing that mankind is motivated wholly by self-interest and therefore not to be trusted. This author takes a strong position, not a neutral one (A), and while he may be condescending, the condescension is directed toward man, not nature (B). "Bellicose" (D) means quarrelsome and warlike, and is too strong a term to accurately describe the tone here. Finally, "dogmatic" (E) fails to adequately convey the negative, cynical tone of the passage.

34. D. Swift appears to concentrate on how inappropriate it is for man to try to reform nature while thinking of himself in such grand terms while, in reality, being the corrupter of nature. Choices A and E are too narrow in their scope. Choices B and C do not articulate the author's overall theme.

The passage referred to in questions 35–45 is from "Criticism and Fiction" (1891) by William Dean Howells.

35. D. The best term to describe the tone of this passage is "critical." The author's purpose is to criticize those who do not think for themselves, imitating older works in pursuit of art. Some examples of this critical tone include: "men have been afraid to apply their own simplicity," "seeds of death are planted," "spirit of the wretched pedantry," "decays when it withdraws itself," "they are destitute of the documents," "they are quite ignorant," "you descend . . . in the moral social scale," and "you are one to be avoided." "Somber" (A) is too strong, as evidenced by the playful grasshopper analogy and the fun the author pokes at old readers. The sentences are not complex enough or the diction flamboyant enough to be called "ornate" (B). The author's purpose is not "didactic" (C); that is, he does not mean to teach, and his diction is not pedantic. Choice E, "formal," like "ornate," is too strong. The tone is more conversational than formal.

36. C. Howells feels that the common people don't place enough trust in their own abilities to interpret literature, but rather rely on "some one who professed to know better and who browbeat wholesome common-sense" into them (lines 14–16). Choices A and D are not mentioned. Choices B and E contradict the passage. Howells feels that common people should attempt to make their own judgments rather than copy anyone's taste.

37. A. "The seeds of death" is a metaphor for imitative art—art formed from studying older masters who themselves imitated the life of their time. According to Howells, this practice produces dead art, imitative art. The author doesn't deal with the destruction of art (B), but rather, with the imitation of art. The "seeds of death" does not refer to the art of an older age (C), to Michelangelo (D), or to artistic immaturity (E).

38. B. While Howells feels that readers who restrict their reading to older literature are narrow-minded, he also finds them "very amusing . . . delightful." The author claims that these old ideas will die out slowly, not quickly (A), that "the time is yet far off." He doesn't dismiss these readers as unimportant (C), suggesting only that they are far too limited in their approach. Howells does attribute harm to them (D) in their narrow approach, and characterizes their knowledge as assumed rather than great (E).

39. D. The idealized grasshopper, made of cardboard and wire, is symbolic of the artificial. No quest to merge art and science is mentioned (A); the passage presents only an artist talking to a scientist, and no reference is made to the search for perfection—the cardboard grasshopper is far from perfection (B). Although this cardboard grasshopper is said by the artist to be indestructible, it will not last through the ages of art (C) because it is divorced from reality (although the artist seems to think that it will). Choice E is incorrect because the scientist doesn't produce the idealized grasshopper, the artist does.

40. A. In the quest for the ideal, the grasshopper is created out of wire, cardboard, and paint, ironically becoming in the process a lesser thing because it does not resemble reality. Even if true (and there is no evidence that they are), choices B and C are not ironic. Common sense tells us that everyone can tell a cardboard grasshopper from a real one (D), and the passage suggests that the cardboard grasshopper has, indeed, been created (E).

41. C. In lines 69–83, Howells claims that the natural, simple grasshopper will eventually be recognized. The remaining choices are types of grasshoppers that he hopes will disappear as the natural one emerges.

42. B. Howells' satire makes fun of those who believe that they can create an idealized copy of nature when, obviously, nature's product is alive, real, and superior. It is also humorous to think of this silly cardboard grasshopper as a realistic imitation of life. The other answer choices are either stated too strongly (C and D) or are not evident in the passage (A and E).

43. A. The author believes that one should use simplicity, naturalness, and honesty in art and in its appreciation. The remaining answer choices involve attitudes that Howells criticizes.

44. A. Although the artist creates an idealized version of the grasshopper and the scientist's description (version) of the grasshopper will be based on reality, both of their creations remain artificial, both representations rather than reality. It is true that Howells presents the scientist's creation as preferable because it approaches reality more closely, but the fact remains that neither creation is itself reality. There is no evidence in the passage for the remaining answer choices.

45. C. A caricature is an exaggerated depiction of a character's features, and, by extension, the character's personality—a device not found in the passage. The remaining devices are present. Some examples include: Irony (A)—the grasshopper analogy (while the artist professes that the cardboard grasshopper is to be preferred to the real, Howells would have the reader understand that the opposite is true). Metaphor (B)—"The seeds of death" (lines 25–26). Allusion (D)—to Shakespeare, Thackeray, Hawthorne, and others. Analogy (E)—extended analogy in the grasshopper segment.

Questions 46–54 refer to the following passage from *American Notes,* Charles Dickens' observations of Washington, D.C., during his first visit to the United States in 1842.

46. E. The author's attitude toward Washington, D.C., can best be described as "fundamentally patronizing" because of the condescending diction he uses to describe the city. For example, he criticizes the irrational pattern in which the Washington streets are laid out, the way servants pay no attention to the tingling triangle that is supposed to summon them for work, and the incongruous appearance of the buildings. "Viciously sarcastic" (A) is too strong to accurately describe the author's attitude; while the author is sarcastic to a large degree, he is not vicious or spiteful. The word "amusingly" in choice (B) is accurate, but he is certainly not "nonjudgmental." Choice C is inaccurate because of the word "pedantic," which refers to things that are overly academic and formal. Finally, the passage provides no evidence for the idea in choice D that the author has any appreciation for Washington.

47. B. The sentence repeats the same syntactical pattern 11 times, separating each use with a semicolon. Each of these independent clauses begins with an imperative verb, which is followed by a direct object and sometimes additional modifying phrases or clauses. Choice A is incorrect because the sentence is not "metaphorical." The use of the semicolon in this long sentence is grammatically correct, making choice C inaccurate. Choices D and E are both wrong for the same reason; they overstate their idea. The sentence does not have "several" adjective clauses (D), and although it does it have a "series" of prepositional phrases (E), they are not the most prominent stylistic feature of the sentence.

48. A. The first paragraph contains many incongruous details, such as planting "coarse turf in every place where it ought *not* to be," erecting public buildings where they are "out of everybody's way," and leaving "a brick-field, without the bricks, in all central places where a street may naturally be expected." Choice B contradicts the passage; the author discusses the differences between Pentonville and Washington, not their similarities. Although the author likely believes that Pentonville and Paris are superior to Washington (C), this idea is not reinforced in the paragraph and so it does not accurately identify the paragraph's purpose; the author is merely using Pentonville and Paris for comparisons. Choices D and E basically incorporate the same idea, that the paragraph's purpose is to suggest or list ways to improve Washington—and this paragraph does neither.

49. D. The fact that the triangle is "tingling madly all the time" is ironic because, according to the author, the triangle is used to call servants to work and "none of them ever come," so the triangle is constantly being rung while no man, woman, or animal ever pays any attention to its noise. Antithesis (A) is inaccurate because this word indicates a seeming contradiction of ideas within a balanced grammatical structure. Personification (B) is also inaccurate because it means, of course, to endow animals or inanimate objects with human characteristics. Euphemism (C) is likewise inaccurate; the term refers to using more agreeable terms for something unpleasant, which does not apply to the quotation. Juxtaposition (E), the devices of placing dissimilar items side by side, is not evidenced in the quotation. (All of these terms are defined in Appendix A.)

50. D. The juxtaposition of the pig and the humans provides the strongest contrast in the second paragraph because, while the humans are running to and fro and are in constant motion, the pig is lying in a sedentary pose, with his stomach turned to the sun, grunting, "That's comfortable!" The details in all of the other answer choices are similar in their descriptions, not contrasted.

51. **C.** The third paragraph is the only paragraph in the passage that uses similes: the grass "looks like a small piece of country that has taken to drinking"; the wooden building looks "like something meteoric that has fallen down from the moon"; the wooden building also "looks like a church, with a flagstaff as long as itself sticking out of a steeple something larger than a tea-chest"; the shop next to The City Lunch "looks like the back-way to somewhere else." The third paragraph does not contain any of the devices mentioned in the other answer choices. Choices A and B, allusion and metaphor, are not in any of the paragraphs. While one may try to make a case for the paragraph using colloquialism (D), one would have to admit that the entire passage does so; therefore, this term is not limited to the third paragraph. Choice E, hyperbole, is used throughout the first paragraph but not the third paragraph.

52. **D.** Of these various images, the most ironic is the idea of a restaurant with "nothing in its windows," while the building next door, which is not labeled as a restaurant, offers oysters "in every style." None of the images in the remaining answer choices are ironic.

53. **E.** The statement "It was originally chosen for the seat of Government as a means of averting the conflicting jealousies and interests of the different States" is straightforward and not comical. On the other hand, all the other answer choices do have some degree of comic effect, whether it's in the odd pairing (A), the surprising image (B and C), or satire (D).

54. **A.** The passage as a whole criticizes the appearance and atmosphere of Washington (A) because every paragraph chides some aspect of Washington, especially its appearance. Choice B is inaccurate because of the word "politics," which is barely mentioned in the passage. Choice C is wrong because of the word "reminiscence," which refers to the act of recalling past events or experiences; the author is merely describing what he observed on his recent visit. The word "homily" makes choice D inaccurate; a homily is a sermon or a lecture. The last phrase in choice E is off target; the images in the passage are not open to varied interpretations, but rather, they are consistently critical of Washington.

Section II: Free-Response Questions

Question 1

Scoring Guide

Score	Description	Criteria
9	Successful	Essays that earn a score of 9 meet the criteria for essays that receive a score of 8. In addition, they are especially sophisticated in the use of language, explanation, and argument.
8	Successful	These essays respond to the prompt successfully, incorporating ideas from at least three sources from the prompt. They take a position that defends, challenges, or qualifies the claim that political polls do not accurately represent the views of a population. They effectively argue the position and support the argument with appropriate evidence. The control of language is extensive and the writing errors are minimal.
7	Satisfactory	These essays meet the criteria for essays that receive a score a 6 but provide more depth and strength to the argument and evidence. The prose style is mature and shows a wide control over language.
6	Satisfactory	These essays respond to the prompt satisfactorily. Using at least three sources from the prompt, these essays take a position that defends, challenges, or qualifies the claim that political polls do not accurately represent the views of a population. The position is adequately argued with support from appropriate evidence, although without the precision and depth of top-scoring essays. The writing may contain minor errors in diction or syntax, but the prose is generally clear.

Score	Description	Criteria
5	Plausible	These plausible essays take a position that defends, challenges, or qualifies the claim that political polls do not accurately represent the views of a population. They support the position with generally appropriate evidence but may not adequately quote, either directly or indirectly, from at least three sources in the prompt. These essays may be inconsistent, uneven, or limited in the development of their argument. Although the writing usually conveys the student's ideas and perspectives, it may demonstrate lapses in diction or syntax or an overly simplistic style.
4	Inadequate	These essays respond to the prompt inadequately. They have difficulty taking a clear position that defends, challenges, or qualifies the claim that political polls do not accurately represent the views of a population. The evidence may be insufficient, or may not use at least three sources from the prompt. The prose conveys the student's ideas but suggests immature control over the elements of effective writing.
3	Inadequate	These essays meet the criteria for a score of 4 but reveal less success in taking a position that defends, challenges, or qualifies the claim that political polls do not accurately represent the views of a population. The presentation of evidence and arguments is unconvincing. The prose shows little or no control over the elements of effective writing.
2	Little success	These essays demonstrate little success at taking a position that defends, challenges, or qualifies the claim that political polls do not accurately represent the views of a population, and show little success in presenting it clearly and with appropriate evidence from the sources in the prompt. These essays may misunderstand the prompt, fail to establish a position with supporting evidence, or substitute a simpler task by replying tangentially with unrelated, erroneous, or unsuitable explanation, argument, and/or evidence. The prose frequently demonstrates consistent weaknesses in the conventions of effective writing.
1	Little success	These essays meet the criteria for a score of 2 but are undeveloped; especially simplistic in their explanation, argument, and/or evidence; or weak in their control of writing.

High-Scoring Essay

In modern elections, candidates are under constant pressure to stay in the public eye. Long gone are the days when candidates would traverse the country by train, for instance, visiting city after city on a pre-set itinerary. To be competitive today, candidates for national office must crisscross the country many times; their image must be seen and heard relentlessly. One factor that helps modern candidates and their managers decide what route to travel and which issues to highlight is the modern political poll. Recall the 2016 presidential election in the final weeks and days before the voting. Hillary Clinton and Donald Trump traversed the country, showing up at carefully planned rallies to muster more support. Both the locations and attendees were carefully chosen, based on the most up-to-date poll information about likely voters and their ballot choices. Attaining success in any close political contest is difficult; candidates must utilize many voting tactics, and no tactic is more prevalent, albeit less precise, than political polls. These polls theoretically provide candidates with an accurate assessment of public opinion. Unfortunately, political polls tend to be unreliable; their results are sometimes intentionally skewed; they yield inaccurate information and provide a poor indicator of public opinion.

Designed to ascertain general public opinion by querying a small number of individuals, then multiplying the individual's answers to project a population's opinion, polls inherently rely upon statistics. However, Benjamin Disraeli, the famous British Prime Minister, succinctly stated, "'there are three kinds of lies: lies, damned lies, and statistics'" (Source B). Common sense indicates that polls should be taken with the proverbial grain of salt; polls often display a specific margin of error, an explicit admission of fallibility.

Unfortunately, far too many rely on the results of polls while ignoring their potential inaccuracies. Perhaps this stems from mankind's tendency to "trust numbers" as if they are facts that are actually true. Ramesh Ponnuru, in a book review, commented that "reporters lean on polls because they provide the illusion of numerical certainty" (Source F). Indeed, this "illusion" also persuades the public to rely on and trust in polls, simply because they appear to be so accurate. But when the logic behind any political poll is faulty, the integrity of the poll's results is compromised.

Often a poll's accuracy is compromised by its authors. The intentional skewing of questions and audiences is a significant factor that adversely affects a poll's results. For example, identical questions pertaining to Ross Perot's platform resulted in a 40 percent variance between answers when the questions were subtly reworded (Source B). Unfortunately, polls suffer from a "unique set of disadvantages" (Source D). According to Source D, polls' accuracy falls prey to "The Leading Option," plus sampling errors and selection bias. Naturally, those who conduct and write polls are extremely aware of these ways to skew the results and use these techniques to their advantage. Polls exhibiting the aforementioned faults provide inaccurate information for a variety of reasons, only one of which is antagonizing the respondent. "Because many polls are conducted over the phone, consumers are more able to block or dismiss unknown calls. A Vanderbilt survey found that "response rates to robocalls are abysmal" (Source E).

While the published poll results attempt to appear "fair and balanced," for instance, by revealing the number of people polled and what part of the country they live in, etc., the public rarely thinks about the important questions one needs to know about any given poll before judging its accuracy. The public needs to question who wrote the poll, who administered it and under what conditions, how many people were sampled at what time of day, how many questions the poll had, what order they were given in, etc. Regrettably, we do not take the time to even think of these questions, let alone search out the answers; we just accept the numbers.

The advent of modern technology has increasingly enabled target audiences to elude pollsters. Caller ID and answering machines enable people to circumvent time-consuming political polls (Source C), therefore reducing the potential variety of opinions from those who do respond. Additionally, pollsters find that it takes seven calls to find one participant who is "willing to spend the 20 minutes or so it takes to answer his polling questions." (Source C), thus further compromising a poll's accuracy. Similar to the number of people who have opinions about governmental matters but do not take the time to write letters to the editor of their local newspaper, those who do not answer the phone when approached by a pollster can add to the inaccuracy of a poll merely by keeping their opinions to themselves.

Polls are ubiquitous in national publications; however, their value is debatable. Source E asks "Are polls accurate? Poll results can seem inconsistent because the business of polling is diverse." However, "A Bloomberg survey seems to confirm that, during the 2016 political cycle campaign, polls have been reliable" (Source E).

Perhaps the promise and pitfalls of polling are most aptly summarized by Lee Morgan: "While they often prove to be useful in determining outcomes of elections or persuading politicians or business owners to take a particular action on an issue, the public opinion poll is a flawed process that has its own unique set of disadvantages" (Source D). A long track record of unreliability, perpetuated by inherent flaws in the creation and administration of polls, has consistently yielded inaccurate data, thus making polls a poor representation of a population's opinion.

Analysis of the High-Scoring Essay

This essay is praiseworthy for its development and its thoughtful discussion of the role that political polls play in American elections. The introductory paragraph successfully juxtaposes the campaigns of "long gone" elections with the tactics of contemporary politicians. Although this comparison is apt, the presentation could be a bit stronger in drawing connections; as it is, the Reader must implicitly understand the student's point. The thesis follows: "Although candidates in modern elections must rely heavily on political polls, these polls do not provide an accurate assessment of the populace's opinions."

Next, in discussing the reliability of polls, the essay skillfully includes both the humorous quotation from Disraeli and the interesting notion that numbers seem so trustworthy to humanity. This idea is a fascinating one that helps capture the Reader's attention. This idea points out one of the underlying reasons why polls are trusted by politicians and the public alike, which demonstrates that this student is incorporating more than just the information in the sources. This paragraph synthesizes the sources well, presenting more than one reference in the same paragraph to advance the student's points.

The third paragraph discusses the ways in which polls can elicit inaccurate information, based on examples from the sources. Clearly this student understands the problematic nature of polls and data gathering. The student also presents information appropriately and uses logical reasoning to demonstrate a good grasp of human psychology.

Next, the essay explores an additional factor that contributes to inaccurate poll results. This fourth paragraph focuses on the fact that many people simply avoid responding to polls; this factor alone indicates that polls cannot represent all people's opinions. In the sixth paragraph, with the example of those who never write letters to the editor, the student makes an appropriate analogy to those who have opinions but never share them. Then the student extends this logic to show that the accuracy of polls is diminished with fewer respondents. The thinking is sound and the presentation valid.

By the seventh paragraph, this essay seems to lose some of the energy and forcefulness of the beginning paragraphs, almost as if the student is both running out of steam and running out of time to develop ideas thoroughly. This paragraph has only four sentences, and it's hard to understand how they connect. The Reader wonders where the student got the idea about polls being "ubiquitous" in national publications and what connection that has to the inaccurate poll predictions in the recent elections. If the student were to have expanded this paragraph and explored the controversies of the elections in more depth, this paragraph would have more to offer. As written, it falls flat.

The concluding paragraph neatly summarizes the essay. Adding the quotation from Source D works well, as it precisely fits the student's thesis. The Reader may wish the essay's conclusion would have had more to offer than a recapitulation of the essay's main ideas, but again, this issue is most likely due to the limited time, not the student's inability to think. However, overall, the essay is consistently on topic, decently organized, well developed, and appropriate in its use of language. It does deserve a high score of 8.

Medium-Low-Scoring Essay

In the United States, where politics is heavily bank-rolled, political races are tight, and (in the presidential election) the victor becomes the world's most powerful man, candidates seek every advantage. Polls are regarded as a source of information regarding potential voters. After subscribing to a political poll, parties will attempt to tailor their campaigns to reach voters who indicated they were disaffected on the poll. Thus, political campaigns consider polls to be valuable assets that indicate a population's opinion. Unfortunately for the political parties, polls have proved to be unreliable indicators of opinion; effectively rendering them useless.

One major fault of the polls is that they are misleading. According to Source B, a statistics textbook, "survey questions can be worded to elicit . . . desired response[s]." Important factors such as diction and the order of the statements in the question can heavily affect the response. For example, Ross Perot asked, "'should the president have the line item veto to eliminate waste?'" 97 percent of respondents said "yes" (Source B). Conversely when the same question was rephrased to "'should the president have a line item veto, or not?'" only 57 percent of respondents indicated "yes" (Source B). The big difference between the first poll's results and the second's (which asked essentially the same question) indicate that polls are unreliable because of their intentional loaded questions.

Polls are designed by experts in order to establish accurate information. According to Source D, "the public opinion poll is a flawed process that has its own unique set of disadvantages." Also, "one major disadvantage of public opinion polling is the tendency of the person taking the survey to go with "the leading option" (Source D). In addition, "there is usually a disclaimer that lets the viewer know that there is a plus or minus 3 percent margin of error . . . but there is no solid way to tell just how big the error margin is" (Source D). Another problem happens when "Selection bias happens when the people intentionally selected to take part in a poll may not be representative of the entire population" (Source D).

Rather than providing a public service, polls actually limit the infusion of new ideas into society. Source F states that because initial reactions to reform are almost always negative, early polls will present reform as "unpopular" and ultimately "interfere with the formation of public opinion."

Polls do not accurately reflect a population's views for a variety of reasons. First, polls are filled with loaded questions designed to trick the participant and elicit a wrong answer. Secondly, polls suffer from a variety of handicaps such as sampling bias, interview bias, and wording bias. Finally, polls are often used improperly, clouding the true intentions of the poll's subject. Thus, it is fair to conclude that polls do not provide an accurate representation of the population's opinions.

Analysis of the Medium-Low-Scoring Essay

This essay attempts to present an adequate response to the prompt but suffers from simplistic thinking and presentation. In the first paragraph, the student establishes a thesis, that political polls are "useless" and "unreliable indicators of public opinion." However, the writing demonstrates numerous errors that begin to distract the Reader. The first sentence contains a subject-verb error: "politics is bank-rolled." The second sentence includes odd and repetitive diction that essentially says nothing, such as, "Polls are regarded as a source of information regarding potential voters." The third sentence displays additional problems with diction: First, political parties do not "subscribe" to polls; second, the phrase "disaffected on the poll" is simply inaccurate and inexact language. The fourth sentence has no grammatical or diction errors, but the final sentence uses the semicolon inappropriately. The Reader is left with a fairly disappointing introduction, so the first impression from this essay is not a strong one. The student has taken a stand, claiming that political polls are "useless," but failed to provide any details to back it up.

The second paragraph is adequate, but only in restating the facts in Source B. Basically, this paragraph paraphrases Source B but offers no strong ideas that help prove the student's thesis. It does make the point that diction and the order of questions can affect responses to polls, but that information is already in the source. The paragraph would be stronger if the student were to integrate more sources and develop more analytical ideas. Unfortunately, as it reads now, the paragraph is undeveloped and overly simplistic.

The third paragraph gets off to a bad start with an unsubstantiated assumption that the goal of polls is, in fact, to design ones that elicit "accurate information." However, this idea contradicts this essay's overall point, that polls are "useless." The student seems to ignore the first sentence in this paragraph and continues to paraphrase Source D, pointing out the many ways in which polls can be misleading. This paragraph, just like the previous one, would be much stronger were it to contain additional ideas, incorporated from more sources, and more insightful analysis from the student.

The fourth paragraph, containing only two sentences, presents an underdeveloped idea: Polls tend to limit the spread of new ideas in a society. The student basically copies the information in Source F and the paragraph ends clumsily. The Reader cannot avoid the impression that the student felt compelled to produce five paragraphs, focusing a body paragraph on one of the sources, but by now was running out of time.

The essay finishes with simplistic summary of the three body paragraphs; it displays no new insights. Overall, the entire essay is held back from a higher score by the continual lack of analytical depth. The essay would be more impressive if the student were to actually synthesize the information in the sources and then present a more engaging argument.

This essay clearly demonstrates the oversimplification that is typical of medium- to low-scoring essays. Remember, the synthesis essay offers students an open opportunity to truly demonstrate how they think and how well they interact with the world. Every student should try to seize this opportunity and present well-developed ideas in a sophisticated manner. The extra effort will be rewarded with a higher score than this sample essay earns, which currently stands at a score of 4.

Question 2

Scoring Guide

Score	Description	Criteria
9	Successful	Essays earning a score of 9 meet the criteria for essays that are scored an 8 and, in addition, are especially full or apt in their analysis or reveal particularly remarkable control of language.
8	Successful	Essays that score at the top perceptively and successfully analyze how Updike's metaphors and other rhetorical strategies help establish the love-hate relationship an audience has toward sports. These essays appreciate how Updike's language works and wisely use appropriate examples from the text, both implicit and explicit, to support the student's ideas. Top-scoring essays offer thorough development and superior organization. Although these essays may have a few minor flaws, the writing demonstrates solid command of written English and the ability to write with syntactic variety.
7	Satisfactory	Essays earning a score of 7 fit the description of essays that are scored a 6 but provide more complete analysis and a more mature prose style.
6	Satisfactory	Upper-level essays correctly understand how Updike's metaphors work and explore other rhetorical strategies as well, using this understanding in the service of satisfactorily explaining how these devices convey attitude. Characteristically, these essays use the text well, implicitly or explicitly, to support the student's thoughts, although these ideas may not be as perceptive or as sophisticated as those of the top-scoring essays. Usually, these essays are well-developed and organized. Minor errors in writing may be present, but the student's meaning is clear and coherent.
5	Plausible	Essays that score in the middle range attempt to analyze the topic, but frequently do not understand how rhetorical strategies connect to meaning. Their insights are quite often obvious and pedestrian. They may paraphrase the passage instead of analyzing it. Development and organization may be too brief, illogical, or unfulfilled. Although the writing style itself may be adequate to convey meaning, inconsistencies in controlling written English may be present.
4	Inadequate	Lower-scoring essays inadequately respond to the prompt. They may concentrate solely on what the audience feels during a sporting event, or perhaps only discuss the use of metaphor without connecting rhetorical strategies to the audience's attitude. Paraphrasing is frequently used instead of analysis. Development and organization of ideas is often inconsistent and limited. Although the writing may communicate ideas, the writing may have serious or persistent flaws that distract the Reader. These low-scoring essays offer simple ideas that are presented in a simple manner.
3	Inadequate	Essays earning a score of 3 meet the criteria for a score of 4 but demonstrate less understanding of how metaphor and rhetorical strategies connect to attitude. These essays may show less control over the elements of writing.
2	Little success	The lowest-scoring essays demonstrate little or no success at analyzing how Updike's rhetorical strategies create attitude. They may pay scant attention to structural or rhetorical techniques or misunderstand their use. These essays may misunderstand the task, fail to articulate any connection between language and attitude, or substitute a simpler task. These essays may be unusually short and exhibit poor fundamental essay skills. Weak sentence construction and persistent weaknesses in mechanics may be present.
1	Little success	These poorly written essays meet the criteria for a score of 2 but are undeveloped, especially simplistic in their analysis, and weak in their control of language.

High-Scoring Essay

In this passage, John Updike's juxtaposition of two central metaphors, combined with his occasional bellicose diction, allows him to emphasize the vicissitudes and the simple grandeur of baseball and the game's ability to reveal our humanity. Symbolic of our life and love, baseball offers prospective liberation along with possible disillusionment.

Both the monster and romance metaphors are used throughout the passage, creating a sense of continuity and allowing the author to thematically connect all the elements—from opening day to the action of the field to the real significance of the passage. Phrases like "its monstrous big heart," "act of faith," and "the first kiss of another prolonged entanglement" sustain imagery that the monster is altogether human and thus forgiving and loving. The contrast of the typical monster and the one portrayed as the "Fenway Faithful" not only adds interest to the piece, but also mirrors the roller coaster ride experienced by the fans. From "Supersox" to "dreadful days," the metaphors' inherent contrasts allow Updike to emphasize the same in the hearts of the fans. The author relies on us to draw upon our own life experiences, as we know romance, too, is full of disagreements and perfect moments, of triumphs and disappointments, truly a "hard lesson for a hungry monster to master." And yet, by the end of the passage, the author recognizes the simple beauty of baseball. Updike implies the innocent joy and magnificence in the way these "twenty-five youngish men" manipulate the hearts of fans. Indeed, it is so much like a romance, with its simplicity and complexity, perfectly summed up in the words, "You'll never get us to care again." However, Updike's voice clearly implies the opposite, that this game of love and hate will continue.

Indeed, the author seems to use the game of baseball as a microcosm of the outside world. His use of warlike diction elevates the game to a near life-or-death struggle. A four-game sweep by the Yankees becomes a "massacre"; a winning streak becomes a "mini-resurrection"; and players seem to be "Civil War memorial[s]" who are fighting for a "Noble Lost Cause" in "Zimmer's last stand." Interestingly enough, this supposed struggle between life and death that is fought out on the baseball diamond ultimately turns into Updike's commentary on life itself. For, in reality, it is not war, but instead, to quote the manager Zimmer, "This is fun." Ultimately, his metaphors using the monster and romance only seek to simplify the relationship between the game and the fans. Like baseball, life, the author implies, should be fun at its core element, stripped of "solemn money men . . . scruffy media cameramen and sour-faced reporters." It is, in the end, a game of "innumerable potential redemptions and curious disappointments." In our attempts to understand, influence, and record these vicissitudes, perhaps Updike's intention is to leave us with some sense of the here and now. Perhaps it's best that we just jeer, holler, boo, and cheer as we enjoy ourselves in the sun. Perhaps that special moment is a little of what that "many-headed monster" feels that makes it come back again and again.

Analysis of the High-Scoring Essay

This essay does an excellent job of addressing the topic. It thoroughly explores metaphors and the connotation of Updike's "warlike diction," showing in the process how these elements create not only Updike's attitude toward baseball, but toward life itself. The introduction clearly tells the Reader what to expect and ends with a graceful statement of how baseball symbolizes life. Updike would agree that this student truly comprehends his point.

The first body paragraph examines the monster and romance metaphors, showing how the two are intricately connected. The student offers ample examples of each and then ties them together with appropriate logic and interesting ideas. The student makes noteworthy points about how Updike relies on his audience to connect his ideas about baseball to their own life experiences, which we will find to be "full of disagreements and perfect moments, of triumphs and disappointments. . . ." The student's poise in using parallelism in this sentence also demonstrates his or her polish as a writer, which an AP Reader will certainly notice and appreciate. The student's final idea in this paragraph, that baseball is a "game of love and hate" that "will continue," serves effectively not only as a clinching sentence to this paragraph, but also as a transition to the next paragraph, which explores the author's diction.

The second body paragraph scrutinizes how Updike's diction, especially the references to war, emphasizes the "life-or-death struggle" of the game. The student presents virtually every example of "warlike diction" that the excerpt offers, but does not stop at merely listing them. He or she makes a larger point about how this diction helps establish Updike's attitude: that although it may seem like war on the baseball diamond, it is really just a game played for fun. The student has a good perspective on language analysis and on life itself.

Overall, this essay covers the topic very well; it is organized logically and develops ideas substantially. The student also demonstrates a very nice flair for language, as witnessed in the use of parallelism (notice it not only in the first body paragraph, as previously noted, but also in the closing two sentences with the repetition of the word "Perhaps . . ."). The student's sentence structure is varied, vocabulary is sophisticated, and a sense of rhythm is present. This essay indeed deserves a high score of 8.

Medium-Scoring Essay

The author's use of the monster metaphor allows him to paint the fans as having similar hopes and reactions to the Boston Red Sox's at times rocky season.

By incorporating the monster metaphor throughout the passage, the author calls the fans both hopeful and disappointed. He writes that last years had broken its "monstrous big heart," and that showing up was "an act of faith." Clearly, the fans cannot help but come back and watch the Boston Red Sox, despite the multitude of horrifying disappointments, often at the hands of the Yankees. "Monsters," the author writes, "have short memories, elastic hearts, and very foolable faculties." The fans, interestingly, in all their differences, have a singular attitude and wish that unites them. It is this wish for the Boston Red Sox to win that enables the author to group these people into an entity, what he calls the "many-headed monster." What is the focus of much of the passage, however, is a description of the fundamental essence of the game of baseball.

It is decidedly from a baseball fans point of view. It is focused on the fun of baseball, how little things within the game bring so much enjoyment and pleasure. It is, to this author, more than just a game of baseball, but rather a celebration of life and an atmosphere. As the author writes, "Monsters love high notes and hoards of gold," referring to "The Star-Spangled Banner" performance and the governor's appearance. The fans, represented as a whole by the monster, love everything about the atmosphere of baseball. From the pure essence of "statistical virginity" to the manager, "last year's anti-hero," the fans love the effect it has on their lives. They keep coming back, it makes no difference because of the elevation of baseball to a more important level—a staple of their lives. The author may be saying to us that the wonderfulness of baseball is, in itself, good enough.

Analysis of the Medium-Scoring Essay

This essay essentially attempts to tackle the topic, but does not accomplish much more than paraphrasing the original passage. The student recognizes that Updike uses a metaphor, but there is little else in this essay that is praiseworthy. The introduction/thesis is somewhat vague. For example, when the student writes that the fans have "similar hopes and reactions," the Reader wonders exactly what they are similar to; are they similar to the "rocky season"? A clearer thesis statement would certainly help this essay.

The first body paragraph identifies the monster metaphor and correctly identifies that it represents the baseball audience, but the student offers no strong analysis of that metaphor. Instead, the student paraphrases Updike: Yes, the fans are "both hopeful and disappointed"; yes, the fans come back to watch over and over; yes, the fans have a "singular . . . wish that unites them," but the student merely lists these ideas and never analyzes how Updike's metaphor establishes his attitude. It is not convincing to merely state the attitude and drop in a quotation or two from the author.

The second body paragraph, too, is basically accurate in its paraphrasing of Updike; indeed, to Updike the game is a "celebration of life." However, once again, the student offers little more than a string of quotations and examples of the behavior and attitude of fans from the passage. For a stronger essay, the student needs to have a reason for presenting all of this information, an analytical point about how these examples work in this excerpt.

Also compounding the student's weak analytical skills is his or her weak command of written English. Apostrophe errors abound ("last years had broken . . ." and "a baseball fans point of view" to name two), plus run-on sentences ("They keep coming back, it makes no difference . . .") and weak wording ("things," "the author writes," and so on) do not help demonstrate sophistication in the writing. Top-scoring essays address the topic, have clear organization, develop ideas thoroughly, and demonstrate strong control over written English. This essay simply does not show those traits. It deserves a score of 5.

Question 3

Scoring Guide

Score	Description	Criteria
9	Successful	These essays meet the criteria for essays that receive a score of 8, and in addition, they are deeper in their analysis and frequently reveal an exquisite use of language.
8	Successful	These well-written essays thoroughly explore the accuracy of Thoreau's aphorism in modern society. They successfully and clearly substantiate their points with relevant evidence from contemporary life, connecting that evidence to the thesis with meaningful insights about human nature. Although these essays may contain a few flaws, they demonstrate a command of language, sentence structure, and conventions of the essay form.
7	Satisfactory	These essays meet the requirements for essays scored as a 6 and, in addition, demonstrate a thorough understanding of the author's aphorism, while providing stronger and more relevant evidence. The prose style is generally more mature.
6	Satisfactory	These essays satisfactorily explore Thoreau's aphorism but produce a less explicit thesis than that of top-scoring essays. Evidence offered is perhaps less specific or not as clearly connected to the thesis. These essays' ideas may not be as crisply articulated as those in top-scoring essays. Although there may be some errors, these papers are well written and demonstrate mature style and satisfactory command of language.
5	Plausible	These plausible essays have an acceptable thesis and present some evidence concerning the applicability of the aphorism in modern society, but may exhibit flaws in organization, number of examples, or discussion of ideas. In general, these essays are not as effective or convincing because of a pedestrian treatment of the topic, producing commonplace, predictable reading. Inconsistent control of language and sentence structure may be present.
4	Inadequate	These essays fail to convince because of their inadequate presentation. Superficial thinking and weak evidence may be combined with an uninteresting or obvious thesis. Confused or contradictory thinking may be present, and these essays may lack adequate support to prove their points. Weak organization and paragraph development may be present. Frequent grammatical problems may distract the Reader.
3	Inadequate	Essays earning a score of 3 meet the criteria for a score of 4 but demonstrate little understanding of the ideas, frequently coupled with a lack of evidence to support the arguments made. These essays may show little control over the elements of writing.
2	Little success	These essays frequently lack coherence and clarity of thought and may produce an unclear thesis concerning the accuracy of the aphorism. Little or no evidence may be presented for the thesis, and the connection between the evidence and the thesis may be shallow or nonexistent. These essays may exhibit poor organization and paragraph development. Weak syntax and persistent grammatical errors may be present.
1	Little success	Essays that earn a score of 1 meet the criteria for a score of 2 but are undeveloped; especially simplistic in their explanation, argument, and/or evidence; or weak in their control of writing.

Medium-High-Scoring Essay

Henry David Thoreau aptly described the nature of mankind by expressing man's tendency to become lost in unimportant pursuits in today's society. Using fish as a symbol for what people believe they are searching for, Thoreau describes a problem of human nature which is seen in all of society: the problem of continually searching while not recognizing what one truly desires in life.

This problem is clouded by the confusing mist of appearances. This shroud hangs over what society has taught one to see as success: money, fancy cars, large houses, to name a few. In the pursuit of what society deems symbolic of success, one is trapped in the conflict of appearance versus reality. All too often someone craves a material object, only to find it boring shortly after it was acquired. This, of course, causes the person to want more possessions, always with the same result. This endless cycle continues, the result being dissatisfaction; as Thoreau might note, this person looks for still more fish, not knowing that fish will not satisfy.

This conflict leads only to the greater problem of getting lost in the race for success and losing sight of life's full meaning. In a society such as America, it is easy to forget that inner happiness cannot to be bought with material goods. With so many opportunities for one to flaunt wealth, it is not difficult to understand how people get caught up in trivial pursuits which do not satisfy their actual desire for success. The necessity to discern between needs and wants then becomes apparent within society. Today this confusion of true desire and false success is seen as the divorce rate increases, as drug abuse rises, as people continue to look for permanent happiness and inner success in temporary feelings and actions. Thoreau was accurate as he used this aphorism to describe human tendencies. Sad yet true, Thoreau's comment is still truthful in regard to the earnest search for false success.

Analysis of the Medium-High-Scoring Essay

This essay is concisely articulate in its exploration of Thoreau's aphorism in relation to modern society. It clearly takes a stand and buttresses it with discussion and examples. The student is not sidetracked into irrelevance and keeps the commentary specific.

The second paragraph presents its insights with a nice flair. Phrases such as "clouded by the confusing mist of appearances" and the "shroud [that] hangs over" are negative images appropriate to the student's assertions, and reinforce the theme of the deceit of "success" as our society defines it. By returning to Thoreau's symbol of fish, the student completes the paragraph logically and effectively links it to the topic.

The third paragraph continues the philosophical discussion, adding additional relevant, contemporary examples and expanding the notion that people are never satisfied with what they have. Divorce and drugs are especially apt illustrations. The essay would be stronger if it included more such examples, but those used are convincing.

Overall, the essay deserves a fairly high score because it is clearly on topic, is well organized, shows sufficient paragraph development, and demonstrates maturity in style, even if only sporadically. It would earn a higher score if it offered stronger evidence and development and used more precise language. The repetition of ideas is a problem, but one that is sometimes seen when writing on philosophical topics under time pressure. It should score in the 6 range.

Low-Scoring Essay

Thoreau's quote relating to man's futile search for fish is applicable to modern society today. I think this quote especially relates to materialism, which is rampant within our greedy, American, self-centered society. Many values today revolve around selfishness and instant gratification, and the big picture of life isn't really seen. This drive for ownership and power and wealth often materializes itself in the mad rush to buy things. Credit cards only encourage this behavior, and the trip for the fish is not what they need. Materialism is a perfect example of this behavior, since many people feel the need to fill their lives with something, whether it's love or money or things. Thoreau sums up this observation about human nature so well, and this statement related not only to Thoreau's society, but to our society in modern America as well. The difference between needs and wants are easily confused, and those who are consumed by materialism cannot see the forest for the trees. I think Thoreau was reminding people not to forget what the important things in life are, and to express the importance of searching for what really matters in life, not settling for temporary things like material goods.

Analysis of the Low-Scoring Essay

This essay has some merit: It attempts to discuss the topic. The paragraph is acceptable and some of the points are relevant, but the essay falls short of thoroughly convincing the Reader. The student's one-paragraph format leads to a rambling, unfocused result. It isn't necessarily the essay's ideas alone that lower the score, but the presentation. The student uses pertinent examples from contemporary life, such as the use of credit cards and "materialism," but lapses into vague terms like "things."

The student should be commended for trying to connect the essay to Thoreau's "fish" aphorism, but that important connection should be incorporated more smoothly. For example, the sudden jump from "credit cards" to "fish" in the fifth sentence needs a transitional phrase so that the Reader can follow the student's argument. In addition, demonstrating more sophisticated skills in the fundamentals of the essay form and more effective diction would significantly improve this essay. It should score a 3.

Scoring

Use the following worksheet to arrive at a probable final AP grade on Practice Exam 3. Because being objective enough to estimate your own essay score is sometimes difficult, you might give your essays (along with the sample essays) to a teacher, friend, or relative to score, if you feel confident that the individual has the knowledge necessary to make such a judgment and that he or she will feel comfortable doing so.

Section I: Multiple-Choice Questions

$$\underline{} - (\underline{}) = \underline{}$$

right answers   wrong answers   multiple-choice raw score

$$\underline{} \times 1.2272 = \underline{} \text{ (of possible 67.5)}$$

multiple-choice raw score   multiple-choice converted score

Section II: Free-Response Questions

$$\underline{} + \underline{} + \underline{} = \underline{}$$

question 1 raw score   question 2 raw score   question 3 raw score   essay raw score

$$\underline{} \times 3.0556 = \underline{} \text{ (of possible 82.5)}$$

essay raw score   essay converted score

Final Score

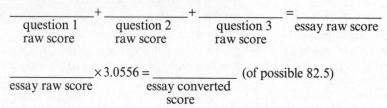

$$\underline{} + \underline{} = \underline{} \text{ (of possible 150)}$$

multiple-choice converted score   essay converted score   final converted score

Probable Final AP Score

Final Converted Score	Probable AP Score
150–114	5
113–98	4
97–81	3
80–53	2
52–0	1

Chapter 7

Practice Exam 4

Answer Sheet

Section I: Multiple-Choice Questions

1 Ⓐ Ⓑ Ⓒ Ⓓ Ⓔ	21 Ⓐ Ⓑ Ⓒ Ⓓ Ⓔ	41 Ⓐ Ⓑ Ⓒ Ⓓ Ⓔ
2 Ⓐ Ⓑ Ⓒ Ⓓ Ⓔ	22 Ⓐ Ⓑ Ⓒ Ⓓ Ⓔ	42 Ⓐ Ⓑ Ⓒ Ⓓ Ⓔ
3 Ⓐ Ⓑ Ⓒ Ⓓ Ⓔ	23 Ⓐ Ⓑ Ⓒ Ⓓ Ⓔ	43 Ⓐ Ⓑ Ⓒ Ⓓ Ⓔ
4 Ⓐ Ⓑ Ⓒ Ⓓ Ⓔ	24 Ⓐ Ⓑ Ⓒ Ⓓ Ⓔ	44 Ⓐ Ⓑ Ⓒ Ⓓ Ⓔ
5 Ⓐ Ⓑ Ⓒ Ⓓ Ⓔ	25 Ⓐ Ⓑ Ⓒ Ⓓ Ⓔ	45 Ⓐ Ⓑ Ⓒ Ⓓ Ⓔ
6 Ⓐ Ⓑ Ⓒ Ⓓ Ⓔ	26 Ⓐ Ⓑ Ⓒ Ⓓ Ⓔ	46 Ⓐ Ⓑ Ⓒ Ⓓ Ⓔ
7 Ⓐ Ⓑ Ⓒ Ⓓ Ⓔ	27 Ⓐ Ⓑ Ⓒ Ⓓ Ⓔ	47 Ⓐ Ⓑ Ⓒ Ⓓ Ⓔ
8 Ⓐ Ⓑ Ⓒ Ⓓ Ⓔ	28 Ⓐ Ⓑ Ⓒ Ⓓ Ⓔ	48 Ⓐ Ⓑ Ⓒ Ⓓ Ⓔ
9 Ⓐ Ⓑ Ⓒ Ⓓ Ⓔ	29 Ⓐ Ⓑ Ⓒ Ⓓ Ⓔ	49 Ⓐ Ⓑ Ⓒ Ⓓ Ⓔ
10 Ⓐ Ⓑ Ⓒ Ⓓ Ⓔ	30 Ⓐ Ⓑ Ⓒ Ⓓ Ⓔ	50 Ⓐ Ⓑ Ⓒ Ⓓ Ⓔ
11 Ⓐ Ⓑ Ⓒ Ⓓ Ⓔ	31 Ⓐ Ⓑ Ⓒ Ⓓ Ⓔ	51 Ⓐ Ⓑ Ⓒ Ⓓ Ⓔ
12 Ⓐ Ⓑ Ⓒ Ⓓ Ⓔ	32 Ⓐ Ⓑ Ⓒ Ⓓ Ⓔ	52 Ⓐ Ⓑ Ⓒ Ⓓ Ⓔ
13 Ⓐ Ⓑ Ⓒ Ⓓ Ⓔ	33 Ⓐ Ⓑ Ⓒ Ⓓ Ⓔ	53 Ⓐ Ⓑ Ⓒ Ⓓ Ⓔ
14 Ⓐ Ⓑ Ⓒ Ⓓ Ⓔ	34 Ⓐ Ⓑ Ⓒ Ⓓ Ⓔ	54 Ⓐ Ⓑ Ⓒ Ⓓ Ⓔ
15 Ⓐ Ⓑ Ⓒ Ⓓ Ⓔ	35 Ⓐ Ⓑ Ⓒ Ⓓ Ⓔ	55 Ⓐ Ⓑ Ⓒ Ⓓ Ⓔ
16 Ⓐ Ⓑ Ⓒ Ⓓ Ⓔ	36 Ⓐ Ⓑ Ⓒ Ⓓ Ⓔ	
17 Ⓐ Ⓑ Ⓒ Ⓓ Ⓔ	37 Ⓐ Ⓑ Ⓒ Ⓓ Ⓔ	
18 Ⓐ Ⓑ Ⓒ Ⓓ Ⓔ	38 Ⓐ Ⓑ Ⓒ Ⓓ Ⓔ	
19 Ⓐ Ⓑ Ⓒ Ⓓ Ⓔ	39 Ⓐ Ⓑ Ⓒ Ⓓ Ⓔ	
20 Ⓐ Ⓑ Ⓒ Ⓓ Ⓔ	40 Ⓐ Ⓑ Ⓒ Ⓓ Ⓔ	

Section II: Free-Response Questions

Question 1

CUT HERE

CUT HERE

CUT HERE

CUT HERE

CUT HERE

Question 2

CUT HERE

CUT HERE

CUT HERE

Question 3

CUT HERE

CUT HERE

Section I: Multiple-Choice Questions

Time: 1 hour

55 questions

Directions: This section consists of selections from prose works and questions on their content, style, and form. Read each selection carefully. For each question, choose the best answer of the five choices.

Questions 1–12 refer to the following passage by a 21st-century British author.

Even though he had finished *The School of Athens* more than a year earlier, Raphael returned to this work in the early autumn of 1511. Using a piece of red chalk, he sketched a

(5) single figure in freehand onto the painted plaster beneath Plato and Aristotle. . . . Raphael then proceeded to paint, in a single *giornata,* the slumped, solitary philosopher known as the *pensieroso,* or "the thinker."[1]

(10) This figure—the fresco's fifty-sixth—is generally thought to represent Heraclitus of Ephesus. Heraclitus was one of the few philosophers in *The School of Athens* to remain outside the teacher-student groups through which,

(15) in Raphael's view, knowledge was transmitted. No eager philosophical apprentices huddle around Heraclitus. A self-absorbed, downcast figure with black hair and a beard, he rests his head on his fist as he scribbles distractedly on a piece of paper,

(20) utterly oblivious to the philosophical debates raging about him. With leather boots and a shirt cinched at the waist, he is dressed in considerably more modern garb than his fellow philosophers, all of whom are barefoot and wrapped in flowing

(25) robes. Most interesting of all, his nose is broad and flattened—a feature that has convinced a number of art historians that the model for him was none other than Michelangelo, whom Raphael added to the fresco as an act of homage

(30) after seeing the Sistine ceiling.[2]

If Michelangelo was in fact the model for Heraclitus, the compliment was double-edged. Heraclitus of Ephesus, known as both Heraclitus the Obscure and "the Weeping Philosopher,"

(35) believed the world to be in a state of constant flux, a proposition summed up in his two most famous sayings: "You cannot step into the same river twice" and "The sun is new every day." But it is not this philosophy of universal change that

(40) seems to have inclined Raphael to lend him the features of Michelangelo; more likely it was Heraclitus's legendary sour temper and bitter

scorn for all rivals. He heaped derision on predecessors such as Pythagoras, Xenophanes,

(45) and Hecataeus. He even abused Homer, claiming the blind poet should have been horse-whipped. The citizens of Ephesus were no more popular with the cantankerous philosopher. Every last one of them, he wrote, ought to be hanged.

(50) The appearance of Heraclitus in *The School of Athens* was, therefore, perhaps both a tip of the hat to an artist whom Raphael greatly admired and a joke at the expense of the surly, remote Michelangelo. Its addition also possibly

(55) carried the implication that the grandeur and majesty of Michelangelo's style on the Sistine ceiling—with its robust physiques, athletic posturings, and vibrant colors—had somewhat overshadowed Raphael's own work in the Stanza

(60) della Segnatura. Put another way, Michelangelo's individualistic and isolated figures from the Old Testament had eclipsed the elegant and congenial classical worlds of Parnassus and the "new Athens."

(65) One way to understand the differing styles of the two artists is through a pair of aesthetic categories developed two and a half centuries later by the Irish statesman and writer Edmund Burke in his *Philosophical Enquiry into the Origin of Our*

(70) *Ideas of the Sublime and Beautiful,* published in 1756. For Burke, those things we call beautiful have the properties of smoothness, delicacy, softness of color, and elegance of movement. The sublime, on the other hand, comprehends the vast,

(75) the obscure, the powerful, the rugged, the difficult—attributes which produce in the spectator a kind of astonished wonder and even terror.[3] For the people of Rome in 1511, Raphael was beautiful but Michelangelo sublime.

---

[1] For Raphael's technique in adding the *pensieroso,* see Nesselrath, *Raphael's School of Athens,* p.20. The *pensieroso* is known to be a later addition because it does not appear in Raphael's cartoon for *The School of Athens,* and because examination of the plaster has proved that it was painted on intonaco, added to the wall at a later date. The exact timing of this addition is speculative, but it seems most likely that Raphael painted it as he finished work in the Stanza della Segnatura, that is, sometime in the summer or autumn of 1511 (ibid., p.21).

[2] This intriguing theory was first suggested by Deoclecio Redig de Campos in *Michelangelo Buonarroti nel IV centenario del "Giudizio universale"* and repeated in his *Raffaello nelle Stanze.* Roger Jones and Nicolas Penny find the argument "implausible" without, however, offering strong counterarguments; see their *Raphael.* Ingrid D. Rowland, on the other hand, states that Heraclitus "presents a simultaneous portrait of Michelangelo's face and Michelangelo's artistic style" in her essay "The Intellectual Background" in Hall's book, *Raphael's "School of Athens,"* and Frederick Hartt claims that his features are "clearly those of Michelangelo" in his *History of Italian Renaissance Art.*

[3] Edmund Burke, *A Philosophical Enquiry into the Origin of Our Ideas of the Sublime and Beautiful,* ed. James T. Boulton (Notre Dame, Ind.: University of Notre Dame Press, 1986), esp. pp. 57–125.

1. What can one infer about Raphael's decision to modify his masterpiece, *The School of Athens,* by adding the "solitary philosopher" at a later date?

    A. He was experimenting with new techniques in figure painting.
    B. He realized the painting needed at least one contemporary figure.
    C. He realized the painting was unbalanced before its addition.
    D. He added it after realizing his admiration for his rival, Michelangelo.
    E. He wanted to show the variety of personalities in the ancient Athenian school.

2. The rhetorical purpose behind the author's description of "the thinker" is to emphasize that it

    A. integrates the philosophers by placing them in the same picture
    B. visually distinguishes the lone figure by distancing him from the other Athenians
    C. shows how Heraclitus was held in disdain by his fellow Athenian philosophers
    D. causes one to ponder Raphael's motive for including the philosopher
    E. demonstrates the author's knowledge of art history

3. All of the following can be inferred from the description of the solitary figure EXCEPT

    A. the figure is alienated physically and intellectually from the other philosophers
    B. the figure is a dark, foreboding character
    C. the figure does not invite empathy in the viewer
    D. the figure rests in a languid pose
    E. the figure may be a self-portrait by Raphael

4. The use of the word "double-edged" (line 32) implies that the speaker feels

    A. the comparison was a compliment to both Michelangelo and Heraclitus
    B. Michelangelo should feel doubly honored to receive the compliment from Raphael
    C. Raphael's comparison to the disputatious Heraclitus was actually a veiled reference to Michelangelo's disputatious disposition
    D. the comparison of Michelangelo to Heraclitus is beyond the edge of reason
    E. Raphael was unsure of his opinion about Michelangelo

5. In considering the structure of the essay as a whole, the most important rhetorical function of the fifth paragraph is to

    A. present new information about how the two artists were regarded in their own time
    B. analyze the styles of the two artists vis-à-vis modern artistic styles
    C. analyze the styles of the two artists using aesthetic categories developed two and a half centuries earlier
    D. reconcile the various positions on the artists; they were equally invaluable because "Raphael was beautiful but Michelangelo sublime"
    E. use Edmund Burke's description of the two artists as his closing line

6. From the lengthy description of Heraclitus, a logical conclusion is that the author

    A. greatly admires Heraclitus for his many contributions to the field of philosophy
    B. considers Heraclitus a great teacher to other philosophers
    C. reveals Heraclitus was really "the laughing philosopher"
    D. believes Heraclitus' dictum "You cannot avoid stepping into the same river twice"
    E. concentrates on Heraclitus' foul disposition and acidic derision for all rivals

7. The author's inclusion of not just one but two direct quotes from Heraclitus (lines 37–38) reveals that

    A. Raphael followed Heraclitus's teachings
    B. Michelangelo followed Heraclitus' teachings
    C. the author followed Heraclitus' teachings
    D. the author understands little of Heraclitus' teachings
    E. Heraclitus' own words add depth and humanity to his portrait

8. The original *School of Athens* does NOT portray philosophers who are

    A. engaged in philosophical debates with one another

    B. engaged in philosophical debates with Heraclitus

    C. surrounded by enthusiastic novices

    D. dressed in open, flowing robes

    E. gathered in teacher-student groupings

9. From his use of metaphorical language in the closing line, one can conclude that the author

    A. confuses the subtle differences between Raphael and Michelangelo

    B. feels the need to properly explain and illuminate his positions

    C. uses the metaphors to provide a powerful summation of his position

    D. believes that these metaphors provide the best summary of Edmund Burke's views regarding Raphael versus Michelangelo

    E. believes that the metaphors add new facts to his argument

10. The most important rhetorical purpose for the addition of footnote #1 is that it provides

    A. conclusive evidence about the exact timing of the addition to *The School of Athens*

    B. a reference for the *pensieroso* appearing in Raphael's cartoon of *The School of Athens*

    C. credibility to the author's views by referencing another source

    D. examples of similar works by Raphael in the Stanza della Segnatura

    E. additional space for the author to express his own conclusions regarding the *pensieroso*

11. As to the question of whether Michelangelo was the model for the *pensieroso,* the information presented in foot #2 implies that the author's position is

    A. probable agreement; he dismisses the only contrary quote as "without . . . offering strong counterarguments"

    B. strong agreement; he feels the *pensieroso* must be Michelangelo because Raphael identified him as such in his painting of *The School of Athens*

    C. complete neutrality; he quotes an equal number of experts on both sides of the issue

    D. strong disagreement; he feels the timing is not correct

    E. probable disagreement; he feels that the figure does not look like Michelangelo

12. The structure of the two sentences in lines 71–77 ("For Burke . . . even terror.") includes which of the following?

    A. simple sentences with substantial imagery

    B. complex sentences with parallel construction

    C. compound sentences with descriptive appositives

    D. varied sentence constructions with participial phrases

    E. compound-complex sentences with adverbial clauses

Questions 13–24 refer to the following passage by a 20th-century American author.

When I was first aware that I had been laid low by the disease, I felt a need, among other things, to register a strong protest against the word "depression." Depression, most people
(5) know, used to be termed "melancholia," a word which appears in English as early as the year 1303 and crops up more than once in Chaucer, who in his usage seemed to be aware of its pathological nuances. "Melancholia" would still
(10) appear to be a far more apt and evocative word for the blacker forms of the disorder, but it was usurped by a noun with a bland tonality and lacking any magisterial presence, used indifferently to describe an economic decline or a
(15) rut in the ground, a true wimp of a word for such a major illness. It may be that the scientist generally held responsible for its currency in modern times, a Johns Hopkins Medical School faculty member justly venerated—the Swiss-
(20) born psychiatrist Adolf Meyer—had a tin ear for the finer rhythms of English and therefore was unaware of the semantic damage he had inflicted by offering "depression" as a descriptive noun for such a dreadful and raging disease.
(25) Nonetheless, for over seventy-five years the word has slithered innocuously through the language like a slug, leaving little trace of its intrinsic malevolence and preventing, by its very insipidity, a general awareness of the horrible intensity of
(30) the disease when out of control.

As one who has suffered from the malady in extremis yet returned to tell the tale, I would lobby for a truly arresting designation. "Brainstorm," for instance, has unfortunately
(35) been preempted to describe, somewhat jocularly, intellectual inspiration. But something along these lines is needed. Told that someone's mood disorder has evolved into a storm—a veritable howling tempest in the brain, which is indeed

(40) what a clinical depression resembles like nothing else—even the uninformed layman might display sympathy rather than the standard reaction that "depression" evokes, something akin to "So what?" or "You'll pull out of it" or "We all have

(45) bad days." The phrase "nervous breakdown" seems to be on its way out, certainly deservedly so, owing to its insinuation of a vague spinelessness, but we still seem destined to be saddled with "depression" until a better, sturdier

(50) name is created.

13. Which of the following clarifies one reason why the author would prefer to use the word "melancholia" instead of the word "depression"?

    A. It suggests a more acceptable condition.

    B. It seems a more gentle word.

    C. It would bring a contemporary lightness to the condition.

    D. It would make the condition more well known.

    E. Its meaning is limited to its reference to a mental condition.

14. In line 14, the word "indifferently" can be best defined as

    A. apathetically

    B. neither particularly well nor badly

    C. indiscriminately

    D. ardently

    E. with no understanding

15. The author objects to the word "depression" to describe the disease because

    A. it has been used for only about 75 years

    B. its other meanings are nondescript and too euphemistic

    C. it evokes an irrational fear in those who hear it

    D. it is applied too strictly to a specific malady

    E. the psychiatrist who coined the term had a tin ear

16. The phrases "wimp of a word" (line 15) and "tin ear" (line 20) are two different examples of

    A. paradox

    B. colloquialism

    C. euphemism

    D. mixed metaphor

    E. parody

17. All of the following words or phrases contribute to creating the same meaning and effect EXCEPT

    A. "semantic damage" (line 22)

    B. "dreadful and raging disease" (line 24)

    C. "intrinsic malevolence" (lines 27–28)

    D. "horrible intensity" (line 29)

    E. "howling tempest in the brain" (line 39)

18. The word "brainstorm" (line 34) can probably not be used to replace the word "depression" because

    A. it does not adequately suggest what depression is like

    B. it is more misleading than the term "depression"

    C. the public is slow to adapt to new terminology

    D. it already has another very different meaning

    E. psychiatrists do not support any such change

19. In the sentence in lines 37–45 ("Told that someone's . . . have bad days"), the author

    A. suggests a possible way of changing the conventional response to a victim of depression

    B. exaggerates the unsympathetic response in order to increase sympathy for the mentally ill

    C. exaggerates the suffering of the victim of depression in order to increase the sympathetic response

    D. suggests possible responses people can use for those who suffer from depression

    E. questions his own idea of a more accurate term

20. In line 45, the speaker refers to the phrase "nervous breakdown" in order to

    A. suggest that the phrase is more evocative that the word "depression"

    B. give an example of an inadequate phrase that is losing its currency

    C. offer a second example of a bland and unevocative phrase

    D. contrast a well-chosen name for mental illness with the ill-chosen word "depression"

    E. show that the uninformed layman is unsympathetic to mental illness

21. Of the following, which would the author probably prefer to use to describe a person suffering from acute depression?

    A. dispirited

    B. down-at-the-mouth

    C. utterly desolated

    D. gloomy

    E. low

22. Of the following, which best describes the author's overall attitude toward the use of the word "depression"?

    A. resigned approval

    B. amused disapproval

    C. casual disinterestedness

    D. cool dislike

    E. strong resentment

23. Which of the following best describes the rhetorical purpose of the passage?

    A. to record the history of the word "depression"

    B. to criticize the inadequacy of the word "depression"

    C. to explain the multiple meanings of the word "depression"

    D. to demonstrate the shortcomings of medical language

    E. to argue for the use of the word "melancholia" in place of the word "depression"

24. Which of the following is a central idea of this passage?

    A. The denotation of a word may not adequately represent what it really means.

    B. The healthy do not properly sympathize with victims of mental illness.

    C. The changes in meanings of words over time are unpredictable.

    D. The scientific understanding of depression is incomplete.

    E. Words are an inadequate means of describing reality.

Questions 25–36 refer to the following passage from a 17th-century British essay.

First, he that hath words of any language, without distinct ideas in his mind to which he applies them, does, so far as he uses them in discourse, only make a noise without any sense or (5) signification; and how learned soever he may seem by the use of hard words, or learned terms, is not much more advanced thereby in knowledge than he would be in learning, who had nothing in his study but the bare titles of books, without (10) possessing the contents of them. For all such words, however put into discourse, according to the right construction of grammatical rules, or the harmony of well turned periods, do yet amount to nothing but bare sounds, and nothing else.

(15) Secondly, he that has complex ideas, without particular names for them, would be in no better case than a bookseller, who had in his warehouse volumes that lay there unbound, and without titles; which he could therefore make known to (20) others only by showing the loose sheets, and communicating them only by tale. This man is hindered in his discourse for want of words to communicate his complex ideas, which he is therefore forced to make known by an (25) enumeration of the simple ones that compose them; and so is fain often to use twenty words to express what another man signifies in one.

Thirdly, he that puts not constantly the same sign for the same idea, but uses the same words (30) sometimes in one, and sometimes in another signification, ought to pass in the schools and conversation for as fair a man as he does in the market and exchange, who sells several things under the same name.

(35) Fourthly, he that applies the words of any language to ideas different from those to which the common use of that country applies them, however his own understanding may be filled with truth and light, will not by such words be (40) able to convey much of it to others, without defining his terms. For however the sounds are such as are familiarly known, and easily enter the ears of those who are accustomed to them; yet standing for other ideas than those they usually (45) are annexed to, and are wont to excite in the mind of the hearers, they cannot make known the thoughts of him who thus uses them.

Fifthly, he that imagined to himself substances such as never have been, and filled his head with (50) ideas which have not any correspondence with the real nature of things, to which yet he gives settled and defined names, may fill his discourse, and perhaps another man's head, with the fantastical imaginations of his own brain, but (55) will be very far from advancing thereby one jot in real and true knowledge.

He that hath names without ideas, wants meaning in his words, and speaks only empty sounds. He that

(60) hath complex ideas without names for them, wants liberty and dispatch in his expressions, and is necessitated to use periphrases. He that uses his words loosely and unsteadily, will either be not minded, or not understood. He that applies his names to ideas different from their common use, (65) wants propriety in his language, and speaks gibberish. And he that hath the ideas of substances disagreeing with the real existence of things, so far wants the materials of true knowledge in his understanding, and hath instead thereof chimeras.

25. As it is used in line 13, the word "periods" may be best defined as

A. sound conclusions
B. complete sentences
C. musical measures
D. marks of punctuation
E. times

26. In line 25, the word "ones" refers to

A. words
B. books
C. ideas
D. discourse
E. names

27. In the second paragraph, the shift from the first sentence (lines 15–21) to the second sentence (lines 21–27) can be best described as one from

A. objective to subjective
B. indicative to interrogative
C. analytical to discursive
D. figurative to literal
E. speculative to assertive

28. The comparison in lines 15–21 ("Secondly . . . only by tale") likens words to

A. the pages of a book
B. the contents of a warehouse
C. complex ideas
D. booksellers
E. the bindings of books

29. In the first and second paragraphs, the author supports his arguments by the use of

A. analogies
B. personifications
C. understatements
D. rhetorical questions
E. hyperbole

30. In line 32, the word "fair" is best understood to mean

A. equitable
B. attractive
C. clement
D. unblemished
E. average

31. In line 48, "substances" are contrasted with

A. shadows
B. ideas
C. imaginings
D. realities
E. names

32. Based on the content of the first five paragraphs, which of the following best clarifies how their ideas are united?

A. paragraph 1; paragraphs 2 and 3; paragraphs 4 and 5
B. paragraph 1; paragraphs 2, 3, and 4; paragraph 5
C. paragraphs 1, 2, and 3; paragraphs 4 and 5
D. paragraphs 1 and 2; paragraph 3; paragraphs 4 and 5
E. paragraphs 1 and 2; paragraphs 3 and 4; paragraph 5

33. Which of the following best describes the relation of the last paragraph to the rest of the passage?

A. It comments on and develops the arguments of the first five paragraphs.
B. It calls into question the arguments of the preceding paragraphs.
C. It raises new issues about language that the preceding paragraphs have not addressed.
D. It sums up the contents of the first five paragraphs.
E. It develops the ideas raised in the fourth and fifth paragraphs.

34. Which of the following is the meaning of the word "chimeras" that can be inferred from its use in the last sentence of the passage (line 69)?

A. fanciful illusions
B. confused conundrums
C. religious revelations
D. logical conclusions
E. philosophical distinctions

35. Which paragraph describes a person who misunderstands the meaning of the word *refuse* and instead uses it to mean *agree*?

- **A.** first paragraph (lines 1–14)
- **B.** second paragraph (lines 15–27)
- **C.** third paragraph (lines 28–34)
- **D.** fourth paragraph (lines 35–47)
- **E.** fifth paragraph (lines 48–56)

36. In which paragraph does the passage deal with a speaker or writer who would use the word "apple" to denote a fruit, an animal, and an article of footwear?

- **A.** first paragraph (lines 1–14)
- **B.** second paragraph (lines 15–27)
- **C.** third paragraph (lines 28–34)
- **D.** fourth paragraph (lines 35–47)
- **E.** fifth paragraph (lines 48–56)

Questions 37–46 refer to the following passage from an early 18th-century British essay.

The talent of turning men into ridicule, and exposing to laughter those one converses with, is the qualification of little ungenerous tempers. A young man with this cast of mind cuts himself
(5) off from all manner of improvement. Everyone has his flaws and weaknesses; nay, the greatest blemishes are often found in the most shining characters; but what an absurd thing it is to pass over all the valuable parts of a man and fix our
(10) attention on his infirmities; to observe his imperfections more than his virtues; and to make use of him for the sport of others, rather than for our own improvement.
We therefore very often find that persons the
(15) most accomplished in ridicule, are those who are very shrewd at hitting a blot, without exerting anything masterly in themselves. As there are many eminent critics who never writ a good line, there are many admirable buffoons that
(20) animadvert upon every single defect in another, without ever discovering the least beauty of their own. By this means these unlucky little wits often gain reputation in the esteem of vulgar minds and raise themselves above persons of much more
(25) laudable characters.
If the talent of ridicule were employed to laugh men out of vice and folly, it might be of some use to the world; but instead of this, we find that it is generally made use of to laugh men
(30) out of virtue and good sense, by attacking everything that is solemn and serious, decent and praiseworthy in human life.

We may observe, that in the first ages of the world, when the great souls and masterpieces of
(35) human nature were produced, men shined by a noble simplicity of behaviour, and were strangers to those little embellishments which are so fashionable in our present conversation. And it is very remarkable, that notwithstanding we fall
(40) short at present of the ancients in poetry, painting, oratory, history, architecture, and all the noble arts and sciences which depend more upon genius than experience, we exceed them as much in doggerel, humour, burlesque, and all the
(45) trivial arts of ridicule. We meet with more raillery among the moderns, but more good sense among the ancients.

37. Lines 8–13 ("but what an absurd . . . our own improvement") are an example of

- **A.** a periodic sentence
- **B.** parallel construction
- **C.** a conditional sentence
- **D.** an extended metaphor
- **E.** an indirect question

38. The simile of the second paragraph compares

- **A.** defects and beauties
- **B.** weakness and blot
- **C.** critics and buffoons
- **D.** fault-finders and archers
- **E.** height and reputation

39. The function of the second paragraph is to

- **A.** develop the idea of the opening sentence of the passage
- **B.** suggest exceptions to the ideas of the opening paragraph
- **C.** shift the focus from personal opinion to a widely held view
- **D.** provide a comic interlude in an otherwise serious passage
- **E.** introduce the ideas to be developed in the third paragraph

40. In line 30, the phrase "virtue and good sense" is contrasted with

- **A.** "vulgar minds" (line 23)
- **B.** "persons of much more laudable characters" (lines 24–25)
- **C.** "vice and folly" (line 27)
- **D.** "solemn and serious" (line 31)
- **E.** "decent and praiseworthy" (lines 31–32)

41. In lines 31–32, the phrase "solemn and serious, decent and praiseworthy in human life" is used to

    A. suggest the author's uncertainty about condemning ridicule

    B. clarify what the author means by "vice and folly" (line 27)

    C. provide an example of the proper use of ridicule

    D. clarify what the author means by "virtue and good sense" (line 30)

    E. introduce the central idea of the paragraph that follows

42. We can infer from the third paragraph that the author would approve of ridicule if it were directed against

    A. youth

    B. foolishness

    C. human weakness

    D. solemnity

    E. raillery

43. In the last paragraph, the contrast between "genius" and "experience" (line 43) can be best understood as the contrast between

    A. spiritual values and physical realities

    B. praise and ridicule

    C. natural aptitude and active participation

    D. instinctive capacity and acquired knowledge

    E. uniqueness and familiarity

44. In the fourth paragraph, all of the following refer to kinds of comic speech or writing EXCEPT

    A. "embellishments" (line 37)

    B. "doggerel" (line 44)

    C. "humour" (line 44)

    D. "burlesque" (line 44)

    E. "raillery" (line 45)

45. According to the passage, in which of the following forms would the modern writer be most likely to surpass the ancient?

    A. lyric poetry

    B. tragedy

    C. satire

    D. epic

    E. prose fiction

46. Of the following literary works, which one would the author of this passage probably regard most highly?

    A. ancient epics

    B. drama of the Middle Ages

    C. religious lyrics of the Renaissance

    D. Elizabethan tragedy

    E. contemporary comedy

Questions 47–55 refer to the following passage from a commencement address by an American author in the late 19th century.

Jefferson Davis[1] was a typical Teutonic[2] hero; the history of civilization during the last millennium has been the development of the idea of the Strong Man of which he was the
(5) embodiment. The Anglo-Saxon loves a soldier—Jefferson Davis was an Anglo-Saxon, Jefferson Davis was a soldier. There was not a phrase in that familiarly strange life that would not have graced a mediaeval romance: from the fiery and
(10) impetuous young lieutenant who stole as his bride the daughter of a ruler-elect of the land[3], to the cool and ambitious politician in the Senate hall. So boldly and surely did that cadaverous figure with the thin nervous lips and flashing eye,
(15) write the first line of the new page of American history, that the historian of the future must ever see back of the War of Succession, the strong arm of one imperious man, who defied disease, trampled on precedent, would not be defeated,
(20) and never surrendered. A soldier and a lover, a statesman and a ruler; passionate, ambitious and indomitable; bold reckless guardian of a people's All—judged by the whole standard of Teutonic civilization, there is something noble in the figure
(25) of Jefferson Davis; and judged by every canon of human justice, there is something fundamentally incomplete about that standard.

I wish to not consider the man, but the type of civilization which his life represented: its
(30) foundation is the idea of the Strong Man—Individualism coupled with the rule of might—and it is this idea that has made the logic of even modern history, the cool logic of the Club. It made a naturally brave and generous man,
(35) Jefferson Davis—now advancing civilization by murdering Indians, now hero of a national disgrace called by courtesy, The Mexican War, and finally, as the crowning absurdity, the peculiar champion of a people fighting to be free in order
(40) that another people should not be free. Whenever this idea has for a moment escaped from the

individual realm, it has found an even more secure foothold in the policy and philosophy of the State. The Strong Man and his mighty Right Arm have
(45) become the Strong Nation with its armies. Under whatever guise, however a Jefferson Davis may appear, as man, as race, or as a nation, his life can only logically mean this: the advance of a part of the world at the expense of the whole: the
(50) overwhelming sense of the I and the consequent forgetting of the Thou. It has thus happened, that advance in civilization has always been handicapped by shortsighted national selfishness. The vital principle of division of labor has been
(55) stifled not only in industry, but also in civilization, so as to render it well nigh impossible for a new race to introduce a new idea into the world except by means of the cudgel. To say that a nation is in the way of civilization is a contradiction in terms,
(60) and a system of human culture whose principle is the rise of one race on the ruins of another is a farce and a lie. Yet this is the type of civilization which Jefferson Davis represented: it represents a field for stalwart manhood and heroic character,
(65) and at the same time for moral obtuseness and refined brutality. These striking contradictions of character always arise when a people seemingly become convinced that the object of the world is not civilization, but Teutonic civilization. Such a
(70) type is not wholly evil or fruitless: the world has needed and will need Jefferson Davises; but such a type is incomplete and never can serve its best purpose until checked by its complimentary ideas.

[1] Jefferson Davis: an American statesman and President of the Confederacy during the American Civil War

[2] Teutonic: having qualities associated with ancient Germanic people of northwest Europe

[3] The daughter of a ruler-elect of the land: Davis's first wife, Sarah Knox Taylor, was the daughter of Zachary Taylor, who later became the 12th U.S. President in 1848. When the couple married in 1835, Mr. Taylor did not approve of their marriage. Sarah died three months after their marriage; Davis and Taylor did not reconcile until 1847.

47. Considering the context of the passage as a whole, the term "Strong Man" refers to those who

   A. display their virtue and virility in their actions

   B. use physical force to command others

   C. boldly conquer others in the name of progress and civilization

   D. convince others of the righteousness of their ideas before taking action

   E. speak up against moral weakness and demonstrate ethical strength

48. In the first paragraph, which of the following phrases represents the speaker's strongest overall criticism of Jefferson Davis and his society?

   A. "from the fiery and impetuous young lieutenant who stole as his bride the daughter of a ruler-elect of the land" (lines 9–11)

   B. "cadaverous figure with the thin nervous lips" (lines 13–14)

   C. "defied disease, trampled on precedent, would not be defeated, and never surrendered" (lines 18–20)

   D. "bold reckless guardian of a people's All" (lines 22–23)

   E. "judged by every canon of human justice, there is something fundamentally incomplete about that standard" (lines 25–27)

49. Which of the following statements demonstrates that the speaker is not merely making a personal attack on Jefferson Davis?

   A. "I wish to not consider the man, but the type of civilization which his life represented" (lines 28–29)

   B. "It made a naturally brave and generous man . . . not be free" (lines 33–40)

   C. "the overwhelming sense of the I and the consequent forgetting of the Thou" (lines 49–51)

   D. "To say that a nation is in the way of civilization is a contradiction in terms" (lines 58–59)

   E. "the world has needed and will need Jefferson Davises" (lines 70–71)

50. The rhetorical purpose of the second paragraph in relation to the first paragraph is to

   A. emphasize why Jefferson Davis is the embodiment of the Strong Man

   B. provide examples of Jefferson Davis' successes

   C. illustrate Jefferson Davis' Teutonic connections

   D. explain what is "fundamentally incomplete" about the standard of Teutonic civilization

   E. modify the first paragraph's criticism of Jefferson Davis

51. The speaker's attitude toward Jefferson Davis may best be described as

A. accepting of Davis' pivotal role in United States' history

B. overly preoccupied with Davis' adherence to slavery

C. a combination of recognition of his achievements and criticism of his actions

D. incredulous that Davis could have misled so many people

E. admiring of that which is noble in Davis

52. Which of the following most accurately describes the tone of the sentence "It made a naturally brave and generous man . . . in order that another people should not be free"? (lines 33–40)

A. vitriolic yet balanced

B. sardonic and sarcastic

C. revengeful and snooty

D. condescending but reverent

E. bitter yet reflective

53. Within its context, which of the following phrases does the speaker intend to be most ironic?

A. "cadaverous figure with the thin nervous lips" (lines 13–14)

B. "defied disease, trampled on precedent" (lines 18–19)

C. "there is something noble in the figure of Jefferson Davis" (lines 24–25)

D. "now advancing civilization" (line 35)

E. "stalwart manhood and heroic character" (line 64)

54. Which of the following clarifies the speaker's overall message about the way civilization advances?

A. The progress of civilization has constantly been thwarted when nations' actions are based solely on their own self-interest.

B. The Jefferson Davises of the world will do less damage if they are recognized early enough to be inhibited by those who think differently.

C. The Strong Man will invariably create a Strong Nation.

D. If some people in a nation are free, others cannot be.

E. Those who are as noble as Jefferson Davis should never surrender.

55. The speaker implies which of the following about America?

A. American society has been fashioned by strong individuals who believe that might makes right.

B. Americans should encourage the development of the "Strong Man."

C. Some Americans still admire the pre–Civil War Southern society.

D. Americans will never again be deceived into following a misguided "Strong Man."

E. American society reached its acme in pre–Civil War Southern society.

IF YOU FINISH BEFORE TIME IS CALLED, CHECK YOUR WORK ON THIS SECTION ONLY. DO NOT WORK ON ANY OTHER SECTION IN THE TEST.

STOP

Section II: Free-Response Questions

Time: 2 hours, 15 minutes
3 questions

Question 1

(Suggested writing time—40 minutes. This question counts for one-third of the total free-response section score.)

Throughout recent years, professional athletes' salaries have skyrocketed. Do you find that today's athletes are overpaid? Or are professional athletes paid an appropriate amount for their physical talents?

Considering the salaries that are paid to professional athletes, read the following six sources (including any introductory information) carefully. Then, in a coherent, well-written essay that synthesizes at least three of the sources for support, take a position that defends, challenges, or qualifies the claim that professional athletes are overpaid.

Always remember that your argument should be central; the sources should be used to support this argument. Therefore, avoid merely summarizing sources. Clearly cite which sources you use, both directly and indirectly. Refer to the sources by their titles (Source A, Source B, etc.) or by the descriptions in parentheses.

Source A (Simmons)
Source B (Henderson)
Source C (Callahan)
Source D (Morss)
Source E (P. K.)
Source F (Hollway)

Source A

Simmons, Mark. "Most Paid Salaries." *Ask Men.* 2005. Web. 2 Oct. 2005.

This online article examines the history of professional sports salaries in the late 20th and early 21st centuries.

Economics theory would suggest that with expansion comes increased supply, which would decrease the price that people would pay for a good or service. What happened was the opposite. Why?

As the number of teams increased, so did the number of jobs. As the number of jobs increased, so did the demand for players.

While the early owners had taken Business 101 and knew that fighting for players would rapidly escalate prices (the not-so-nice term is collusion), the more recent club owners knew that signing the marquee players would not only attract more fans, but also the premium advertisers that end up financing new stadiums and subsidizing players' salaries.

In 1988, the highest earning basketball player was the Los Angeles Lakers' Earvin "Magic" Johnson at $3 million. Ten years later, Shaquille was making $17.14 million, a 472% increase.

In baseball, Ozzie Smith earned $2.34 million from the St. Louis Cardinals for pounding his frame into the dirt and fetching all of those grounders. Ten years later, Pedro Martinez (part of that 1994 Expos team) was getting $11 million from the Boston Red Sox, a 370% increase.

Football was no different. The Denver Broncos' John Elway was paid $1.96 million in 1988. A decade later, Dallas Cowboys Troy Aikman's compensation was $5.87 million, a 200% increase.

Something has got to give. Players making millions is fine by me. Really. No, not because I make millions. I think that players sacrifice a lot to make it to the big show. So many players end up as road kill, as their careers fail to take them to the pros.

Perhaps 1 player out of 100 makes it to the college squad, and 1 college player out of 100 gets drafted. And as you may know, just because you get drafted, that doesn't mean you will make it. It takes an insane amount of dedication, sacrifice, aversion to pain, tenacity, and determination to get to be the king of the hill. If you make it, then you deserve every penny.

My only fear is what will happen when players want $100 million per year. Think it's funny? While the BoSox were paying Martinez $11 million in 1998, the Dodgers are currently paying $15 million for Kevin Brown, a 36% increase within two years. Eleven million would not even crack the top ten.

All in all, this is scary in a time when people are finding it harder and harder to cough up the dough to go to ballgames. Yet corporations are scooping up tickets at high prices, writing off the cost as business expenses. They are increasing ticket demand, thus increasing prices. If that weren't enough, they are simultaneously paying premium dollars to get stadium naming rights and advertising spots, adding to the teams' wallets and allowing them to pay the multi-million-dollar contracts that are increasingly out of whack.

For an idea of baseball players' salaries, check this out:

Player and Team	Yearly Salary
Kevin Brown, L.A. Dodgers	$15,000,000
Shawn Green, L.A. Dodgers	$14,000,000
Mo Vaughn, Anaheim Angels	$13,333,333
Randy Johnson, Arizona Diamondbacks	$13,100,000
Mike Piazza, N.Y. Mets	$13,000,000
Albert Belle, Baltimore Orioles	$13,000,000
Pedro Martinez, Boston Red Sox	$12,500,000
Bernie Williams, N.Y. Yankees	$12,500,000
Larry Walker, Colorado Rockies	$12,500,000
David Cone, N.Y. Yankees	$12,000,000

Source B

Henderson, Audrey. "Who Makes More Money: Athletes, Actors, National Leaders, or CEOs?" *Supermoney*. 26 Aug. 2017. Web. 18 Sept. 2017.

This excerpt from a financial website compares salaries from professions that are perceived as high-paying ones.

The income inequality gap is huge—and growing. Some of the obvious beneficiaries, such as CEOs of major corporations, draw compensation that drives much of the wage gap. But other high-paid individuals, including Hollywood stars and athletes, also make more than any American can dream of. On the other hand, many national government leaders draw surprisingly modest salaries.

Hollywood stars draw amazing salaries, although ponder this: male stars greatly out-earn their female counterparts. Nonetheless, even while they earn far less than male stars, female A-listers are still doing pretty well. This is true whether their annual earnings or per-film salaries are measured, according to the *Hollywood Reporter*. For instance, Dwayne Johnson, perhaps better known as wrestling superstar The Rock, has built a solid action film career, earning an estimated 52 million dollars between June 2013 and June 2014, commanding an average 15 million per picture. Leading man Leonardo DiCaprio earned 45 million dollars between June 2013 and June 2014, but routinely averages 20 million dollars per film, according to the *Hollywood Reporter*.

By contrast, Jennifer Lawrence, the highest-paid female actress mentioned by the *Hollywood Reporter*, earned a not-bad 35 million dollars between June 2013 and June 2014. But the Oscar-winning actress also got a big raise for her most recent films. Lawrence's paycheck jumped from 500,000 dollars to a cool 10 million dollars between the filming of the first two installments of the blockbuster *Hunger Games* franchise.

Superstar athletes draw huge salaries ranging well into seven and even eight figures. But those figures tell only part of the story. Even when those astronomical salaries are broken down into per-game figures as *Business Insider* did in 2013, the totals far exceed what many average workers make in an entire year.

For instance, quarterback Peyton Manning earns a reported 15 million dollars from the Denver Broncos. Manning took a 4 million dollar pay cut for his team in 2015, meaning he made 19 million in 2014. But since football players only play once every week, his weekly salary translates to an eye-popping 937,500 dollars.

By contrast, basketball superstar Kobe Bryant earns 25 million dollars from the Los Angeles Lakers, a pay cut from his 30.4 million in 2014. But since basketball players play many more games each season than football players, Kobe Bryant averages "only" 304,000 dollars per game, according to *Business Insider*.

Baseball star Alex Rodriguez is paid right there with Bryant: 25 million dollars. But baseball players play even more games each season than basketball players—which translates to a per-game average paycheck of only 154,000 dollars for Alex Rodriguez.

The average salary for Chief Executive Officers ranges comfortably into six figures, with many CEOs earning millions in bonuses and shareholdings. And while the compensation of big names such as Larry Ellison of Oracle (more than 78 million in 2013) and Marissa Mayer of Yahoo! (almost 25 million in 2013) is stunning, the highest compensation packages are reserved for executives whose names are virtually unknown. For instance, the very top earning CEO in 2013 was someone named Charif Souki of Cheniere Energy, whose compensation totaled an amazing 141,949,280 dollars.

And while many CEOs log more working hours than the standard 40-hour work week, they are well compensated for their time and efforts. The average CEO earned more than 331 times the salary of everyday workers in 2013. Compare that figure with salaries for rank-and-file employees, which averaged just $16.94 per hour in 2013, or $35,239 annually, according to figures compiled by the AFL-CIO.

With his country sinking into recession in response to intense pressure from international sanctions, Russian Federation president Vladimir Putin cut his own salary by 10 percent, according to CNN Money. His remaining salary is 8.2 million rubles annually, which translates to about 136,000 US dollars. French President François Hollande gave himself a 30 percent salary haircut when he took office in 2012, reducing his annual earnings from 255,600 Euros (274,522 US dollars) to 194,251 dollars.

By contrast, CNN Money reports that German Chancellor Angela Merkel and her cabinet received a 2.2 percent pay rise in March 2015. The raise increased her annual salary to 213,000 Euros, or the equivalent of 234,383 US dollars. China's President Xi Jingping also obtained a raise at the beginning of 2015. But even after a 60 percent boost, his annual salary is still shockingly low—the equivalent of only 22,000 US dollars annually, according to CNN Money.

For the record, United States President Barack Obama is the highest-paid world leader. He earns 400,000 dollars annually, and also has a tax-free 50,000 dollar expense account. Not too shabby.

Source C

Callahan, Gene. "Athletes' Salaries Too High? Sports Fans, Blame Yourselves." *The Foundation for Economic Education.* Fee. 1 July 2007. Web. 29 Sept. 2017.

This excerpt from a financial website presents the idea that high salaries in professional sports are directly caused by sports fans.

It is the very fans who often grumble about the "ridiculous" wages paid to top athletes who in effect set their salaries. That's because in a market economy the price paid for any factor of production (including labor services) arises from the choices consumers make about the items they wish to buy and how much they are willing to pay. Producers face costs in providing a good, and if they estimate that buyers will not pay at least enough for their output to cover their costs plus some profit, the good will not be produced. Those estimates can turn out to be over-optimistic: producers are often mistaken in gauging consumer demand, and many a business has gone under because it spent more to manufacture its offerings than consumers were willing to pay. But competition among entrepreneurs for buyers' dollars rewards those entrepreneurs whose forecasts are generally most accurate with profits that allow them to remain in business and invest even more in the future.

Consumers must bid enough to prompt producers into action, and the price of every good—industrial products as well as consumption items—can be traced to consumer choice. Producers of items needed for the production of consumer goods will find it rewarding to produce those items only if consumers value the final goods enough to pay for the resources and work necessary to create them.

What's more, the costs producers face in their operations are not determined by nonhuman factors such as energy expenditures, chemical transformations, or the abundance or scarcity of various raw materials; rather they are the consequence of the producers' evaluation of alternative ways in which they might earn their livings by meeting consumer demand. Of course, producers must not ignore physical reality in their business decisions: it will clearly require far more time and energy to manufacture skillets from iron mined on Mars than from the same metal mined on earth. However, unless consumers value "Martian skillets" more than the terrestrial variety, expending all that effort to procure otherworldly metal will not result in a higher price being paid for it. It is the preferences of consumers that drive the formation of prices all the way backwards along the production chain. If some resource could be used in the creation of a consumer good, but producers judge that their efforts to acquire it will not add enough to the value of the final product to be worth their while, they simply will choose not to employ it; they have no power to drive up the price of the end product by picking an extravagant way of manufacturing it.

This aspect of the market economy, which has been termed "consumer sovereignty," is entirely independent of how concerned a proprietor is about the welfare of his customers. One entrepreneur may start a firm because of a sincere conviction that the product or service he plans to provide will bring immense benefits to his clientele. Another may be motivated solely by his desire to become fabulously wealthy. But to succeed, both will be equally bound to judge accurately as to how much consumers will value his offerings. Certainly, an unscrupulous businessman may try to deceive consumers about the true nature of what he is selling, but that is more accurately classified as theft rather than commerce and properly is subject to legal sanctions.

Nevertheless, the enormous salaries earned by sports stars are chiefly the result of the willingness of their fans to pay to see them play. If my neighbors in the sports bar are seriously distressed that star athletes make so much more than educators, the power to alter that situation lies with them. They can stop paying so much for ESPN and tickets to ballgames and instead spend the money they save on their children's schooling. I certainly would not complain about such a shift in people's priorities. But it is the only way a free people can address the situation.

Source D

Morss, Elliot. "The Global Economics of Professional Sports." *Global Finance*. 9 May 2012. Web. 17 Sept. 2017.

This chart compares average salaries in different sports around the world.

This table presents data on average salaries by sport and country. US basketball (NBA) tops the list, with Indian Cricket in second place. The National Football League is in a very strong position relative to its players. Not only is the average salary relatively low, but salaries are not guaranteed. That means if you can't play because of an injury, the team does not have to pay you.

Sport/League	Average Salary
Basketball - NBA	**4,375,735**
Cricket - India	**3,612,726**
Baseball - Total	**3,218,840**
Baseball - MLB	3,415,772
Baseball - Japan	841,208
Soccer - Total	**2,338,081**
Soccer - Britain	3,184,110
Soccer - Germany	2,380,330
Soccer - Spain	1,970,263
Soccer - Italy	1,960,080
Soccer - Scotland	446,571
Soccer - Australia	202,291
Soccer - US	192,689
Hockey - NHL	**2,311,733**
Football - Total	**2,188,374**
Football - NFL	2,208,364
Football - Canada	102,812

Source E

P. K. "Athletes Are Underpaid: The Economics of Player Salaries." *Don't Quit Your Day Job . . .* DQYDJ. 26 Sept. 2017. Web. 1 Oct. 2017.

This excerpt examines ways in which athletes' salaries are not as high as many think.

The problem with painting every sports contract with the "overpaid" brush is there is an army of athletes who will never touch the salaries that make us do a double take—we contend that, as a whole, **athletes are underpaid.**

Starting with Pee Wee sports, there is a pretty well-defined route to professional leagues. Kids start from as young as 4 or 5 to learn the fundamentals of the game, and play for the sports teams of their schools or pickup games in their neighborhoods. As athletes progress in age, there are sports camps, AAU teams, college camps, and other competitive travel teams that can get young athletes onto scouting radars. Next up is usually (with the notable exception of baseball, which has two paths to the pros) recruitment to an NCAA school. Finally, a few of those athletes will go on to be drafted by teams—and fewer still will get the huge contracts that we so often dismiss as absurd and obscene.

What am I saying here? The first reason that "athletes" are underpaid is because the odds are so stacked against "athlete" as a career it is reasonable to think that those who make it should draw a large salary. What we are missing out on are the millions of children who grew up dreaming they'd be the next Michael Jordan, Emmitt Smith, or Babe Ruth (or Wayne Gretzky. Or . . . Pelé). It's a bias against the unseen—there has to be a reasonable reward at the end of the road for the number of athletes who actually make it out of the various stages of the game. There are cuts at every stage—it's a pyramid.

How large is the pool that the draft ends up drawing from? In 2006, this CNN article pegged youth participation at 41 million. Athletes (not just the four major sports) in the NCAA number 400,000. As for the pros? Let's look at the four major sports:

Football (NFL): 32 players a round, 7 rounds means 224 players a year from the draft, plus a smattering of free agents—generally place kickers, punters, and the occasional retiree.

Basketball (NBA): 30 players a round, 2 rounds means 60 players a year are drafted.

Baseball (MLB): Baseball is the exception to our draft rule, due to its nicely varied league levels and development teams (Low-A, High-A, AA, AAA, Majors). It's tough to pin down a hard number for draft size, but in 2006, 1,503 players were selected. Most of them will never make a major league roster.

Hockey (NHL): 30 players a round, 7 rounds means 210 players are drafted.

Of the four majors, the NHL comes in with the highest minimum salary at $525,000. Basketball players pull in $490,180 annually. Baseball players pull in a minimum of $414,000. Football players will make at least $375,000 annually. Those numbers are huge—the 2010 median household income in the United States was $49,445. However, when talking about career longevity we tend to cherry pick the most durable players we can think of—Robert Parish (21 seasons in NBA), Brett Favre (20 seasons in NFL), Wayne Gretzky (16 seasons, NHL), or Tim Wakefield (17 seasons and still active, MLB). The truth is most players will see nowhere near the sorts of contracts we see from the Peyton Mannings and the Alex Rodriguezes of the sports world—most will be closer to the minimum, and play out much shorter careers.

From what I can find, NHL players average 5.66 seasons, NFL players 6.86, NBA players 4.81, and MLB players (again, skewed by the minor league system) 5.6. All else being equal, the NBA would pay the highest minimum salary and the NFL the least.

Remember that a college athlete drafted at 21 and out of the league 5 years later is still 26 years old. Even with 5 years of large salaries, his future is not guaranteed. It's one of the reasons so many former players are broke, even some of the ones with salaries near the top of the ranges.

There is no doubt in my mind that some of the contracts in the sports world grate on the nerves of my fellow members of the 9–5 crowd. When we hear of guys making millions a dollar a year on police blotters, it's normal to be a bit disgusted. However, salaries are high but rational—in aggregate, we still argue athletes are underpaid.

The extreme difficulty of developing the skills necessary to be a professional, *staying injury-free* until you can demonstrate those skills at the pro level, then maintaining the skills for a reasonable number of years is so extreme that the salaries we see make a little more sense.

Source F

Hollway, Cameron. "Bargain or Bust?" *St. Louis Post-Dispatch.* 3 Aug. 2005: D2. Print.

This newspaper article questions the validity of professional sports salaries.

Since Bobby Hull became the first reported million-dollar man in 1972, salaries in professional sports have escalated to out-of-control proportions. Tuesday, Shaquille O'Neal's restructured contract worth $100 million over five years was barely a blip on the radar screen in the NBA, where $100 million deals are common. Bryant Reeves makes $7.8 million a year and LeBron James pockets $90 million for wearing Nike skids.

Athlete contracts have become more about "respect" and one-upping a rival player than about the money—seriously, besides Mike Tyson, who can really spend $100 million? Tiger Woods might actually be worth his reported $1-billion-plus bank account, but are any of the other milestone millionaires deserving of their loot?

From Hull to O'Neal, we take a look at a few big-money payouts and whether they were worth the risk.

Alex Rodriguez (baseball)

The money: A-Rod's 10-year, $252-million contract delivered by Texas in December 2000 is the richest in professional sports history. In January, Carlos Beltran became the 10th big-league player to sign a $100 million contract.

Bust: Babe Ruth's $50,000 contract in 1922 was a record that took 25 years to double (Hank Greenberg, $100K, 1947). After Mike Piazza signed for $13 million annually in 1998, it took only two years for A-Rod to pull in more than double at $27 million.

Shaquille O'Neal (NBA)

The money: The game's most dominant big man opted out of his one-year contract for $30.6 million, saying through his agent that he preferred the "stability" of a long-term deal. Five years, $100 million buys a stable of stability.

Bust: Remember when Magic Johnson signed a 25-year deal for $25 million in 1984? Shaq Daddy is too fat, too injury-prone and too dramatic to draw $20 million per, even if he is the most physically dominant player in NBA history.

Question 2

(Suggested writing time—40 minutes. This question counts for one-third of the total free-response score.)

The following passage is excerpted from President Barack Obama's first inaugural address on January 21, 2009. In it, he calls for a new era of responsibility. Read the passage carefully and write an essay in which you analyze how the rhetorical strategies that President Obama uses develop his message. In your analysis, use specific references to the text.

Forty-four Americans have now taken the presidential oath. The words have been spoken during rising tides of prosperity and the still waters of peace. Yet, every so often, the oath is taken amidst gathering clouds and raging storms. At these moments, America has carried on not simply because of the skill or vision of those in high office, but because we, the people, have remained faithful to the ideals of our forebears and true to our founding documents.

So it has been; so it must be with this generation of Americans.

. . .

Today I say to you that the challenges we face are real. They are serious and they are many. They will not be met easily or in a short span of time. But know this America: They will be met.

. . .

In reaffirming the greatness of our nation we understand that greatness is never a given. It must be earned. Our journey has never been one of short-cuts or settling for less. It has not been the path for the faint-hearted, for those that prefer leisure over work, or seek only the pleasures of riches and fame. Rather, it has been the risk-takers, the doers, the makers of things—some celebrated, but more often men and women obscure in their labor—who have carried us up the long rugged path towards prosperity and freedom.

For us, they packed up their few worldly possessions and traveled across oceans in search of a new life. For us, they toiled in sweatshops, and settled the West, endured the lash of the whip, and plowed the hard earth. For us, they fought and died in places like Concord and Gettysburg, Normandy and Khe Sahn.

Time and again these men and women struggled and sacrificed and worked till their hands were raw so that we might live a better life. They saw America as bigger than the sum of our individual ambitions, greater than all the differences of birth or wealth or faction.

. . .

The question we ask today is not whether our government is too big or too small, but whether it works—whether it helps families find jobs at a decent wage, care they can afford, a retirement that is dignified. Where the answer is yes, we intend to move forward. Where the answer is no, programs will end. And those of us who manage the public's dollars will be held to account, to spend wisely, reform bad habits, and do our business in the light of day, because only then can we restore the vital trust between a people and their government.

. . .

Our challenges may be new. The instruments with which we meet them may be new. But those values upon which our success depends—honesty and hard work, courage and fair play, tolerance and curiosity, loyalty and patriotism—these things are old. These things are true. They have been the quiet force of progress throughout our history.

What is demanded, then, is a return to these truths. What is required of us now is a new era of responsibility—a recognition on the part of every American that we have duties to ourselves, our nation and the world; duties that we do not grudgingly accept, but rather seize gladly, firm in the knowledge that there is nothing so satisfying to the spirit, so defining of our character than giving our all to a difficult task.

. . .

So let us mark this day with remembrance of who we are and how far we have traveled. In the year of America's birth, in the coldest of months, a small band of patriots huddled by dying campfires on the shores of an icy river. The capital was abandoned. The enemy was advancing. The snow was stained with blood. At the moment when the outcome of our revolution was most in doubt, the father of our nation ordered these words to be read to the people:

"Let it be told to the future world . . . that in the depth of winter, when nothing but hope and virtue could survive . . . that the city and the country, alarmed at one common danger, came forth to meet [it]."

America: In the face of our common dangers, in this winter of our hardship, let us remember these timeless words. With hope and virtue, let us brave once more the icy currents, and endure what storms may come. Let it be said by our children's children that when we were tested we refused to let this journey end, that we did not turn back nor did we falter; and with eyes fixed on the horizon and God's grace upon us, we carried forth that great gift of freedom and delivered it safely to future generations.

Question 3

(Suggested writing time—40 minutes. This question counts for one-third of the total free-response score.)

The following excerpt is taken from *The Autobiography of Benjamin Franklin* (1791). Read the passage carefully and develop an essay that evaluates the validity of Franklin's assertions about the ability to justify one's actions through reasoning. Use appropriate evidence to make your argument convincing.

I believe I have omitted mentioning that in my first voyage from Boston, being becalmed off Block Island, our people set about catching cod and hauled up a great many. Hitherto I had stuck to my resolution of not eating animal food; and on this occasion I considered with my Master Tryon, the taking of every fish as a kind of unprovoked murder, since none of them had or ever could do us any injury that might justify the slaughter. All this seemed very reasonable. But I had formerly been a great lover of fish, and when this came hot out of the frying pan, it smelled admirably well. I balanced some time between principle and inclination: till I recollected, that when fish were opened, I saw smaller fish taken out of their stomachs: Then, thought I, if you eat one another, I don't see why we mayn't eat you. So I dined upon cod very heartily and continued to eat with other people, returning only now and then occasionally to a vegetable diet. So convenient a thing it is to be a *reasonable creature,* since it enables one to find or make a reason for everything one has a mind to do.

IF YOU FINISH BEFORE TIME IS CALLED, CHECK YOUR WORK ON THIS SECTION ONLY. DO NOT WORK ON ANY OTHER SECTION IN THE TEST.

Answer Key

Section I: Multiple-Choice Questions

1. D	12. B	23. B	34. A	45. C
2. B	13. E	24. A	35. D	46. A
3. E	14. C	25. B	36. C	47. C
4. C	15. B	26. A	37. B	48. E
5. D	16. B	27. D	38. C	49. A
6. E	17. A	28. E	39. A	50. D
7. E	18. D	29. A	40. C	51. C
8. B	19. A	30. A	41. D	52. B
9. C	20. B	31. D	42. B	53. D
10. C	21. C	32. E	43. D	54. A
11. A	22. E	33. D	44. A	55. A

Section II: Free-Response Questions

Essay scoring guides, student essays, and analysis appear beginning on page 274.

Answer Explanations

Section I: Multiple-Choice Questions

The passage referred to in questions 1–12 is from *Michelangelo and the Pope's Ceiling* (2003) by Ross King.

1. **D.** The author states that an examination of the painting ". . . convinced a number of art historians that the model was none other than Michelangelo, whom Raphael added to the fresco as an act of homage after seeing the Sistine ceiling." The passage offers no evidence that Raphael was experimenting with new techniques (A) or that he felt the painting was unbalanced without the new addition (C). Nothing in the passage implies Raphael considered the need for a contemporary figure in the painting (B). Choice E, which claims that Raphael wanted to show a variety of personalities in the ancient Athenian school, may indeed be an inference; however, it is not a reasonable inference to draw when asked why he modified the painting. *The School of Athens* already had a variety of personalities.

2. **B.** The visual details demonstrate the intent of the artist to set the solitary figure apart in every way; his mode of dress, his expression, and his self-absorbed, downcast pose all help to show his lack of connection to his fellow philosophers. No other answer choice addresses the author's rhetorical purpose.

3. **E.** Although the figure does appear to be modeled after a great artist of the day, the likely model is Michelangelo, *not* Raphael. All other answer choices are very reasonable inferences.

4. **C.** The addition of the *pensieroso* figure to *The School of Athens* was both a great compliment to Michelangelo and also a somewhat insulting joke at his expense. Raphael's addition of Michelangelo to his own masterwork was "an act of homage after seeing the Sistine ceiling," but his comparison of Michelangelo to a disputatious, sour-tempered old philosopher was certainly not complimentary. Choice A misreads the phrase "double-edged," which is not complimentary; choice B also misunderstands the phrase. Choice D makes no sense and contradicts the passage; the comparison of Michelangelo to Heraclitus is entirely within reason. Choice E is incorrect because Raphael clearly knew his opinion of Michelangelo.

5. D. The author resolves the disparate portraits of the two artists that he has presented in the preceding paragraphs. He demonstrates that both artists, while quite different from each other, present an artistic vision of inestimable value. Choice A is incorrect because this paragraph does not address how the artists were regarded in their own time. Choice B is incorrect because the paragraph does not address contemporary artistic styles. Choice C misstates the facts (the categories were developed two and a half centuries later, not earlier) and it does not reflect the "most important rhetorical function"; the author does not analyze the two artists' styles but merely labels them. Choice E also misstates the facts; the final line does not contain Burke's description.

6. E. The passage indicates that Raphael portrayed Heraclitus as Michelangelo because ". . . more likely it was Heraclitus's legendary sour temper and bitter scorn for all rivals." Choices A and B are incorrect because the author neither admires Heraclitus nor considers him a great teacher. Choice C is incorrect; he was known as "the Weeping Philosopher." Choice D is incorrect; it misquotes Heraclitus' famous aphorism.

7. E. The author makes good use of the two quotes, as they help to "humanize" and balance the negativity with which he portrays Heraclitus. Choices A, B, and C are all incorrect because none of these individuals followed the teachings of Heraclitus. Choice D is incorrect because the inclusion of the quotes demonstrates that the author *does* understand Heraclitus' true nature.

8. B. The other philosophers are not engaging Heraclitus in discussion. He appears solitary, self-absorbed, and ". . . utterly oblivious to the philosophical debates raging about him." All other answer choices are demonstrated in the painting.

9. C. In his final line, the author succinctly presents his position through the use of metaphor. Choices A and B are both incorrect; the author is quite secure in his conclusions, and he reveals them clearly. Choice D is incorrect; these metaphors give voice to the author's words, not those of Edmund Burke. Choice E is incorrect; these metaphors do not introduce any new facts to the discussion.

10. C. The footnote adds credibility to the author's assertion that the figure was a later addition to the already completed *The School of Athens* by providing additional documentation. Choice A is incorrect because the footnote states "The exact timing of this addition is speculative." Choice B is incorrect; the author cites the cartoon to show that the figure was not originally in *The School of Athens*. Choice D is incorrect; the author does not indicate that Raphael's painting in the Stanza della Segnatura is similar, only contemporaneous. Choice E is incorrect; although this footnote does provide additional space for the author to express his position, this is certainly not the rhetorical purpose of the note.

11. A. It is probable that the author agrees. Throughout his overview of the scholarly writings regarding the identity of the *pensieroso,* it is clear that the majority conclude that Michelangelo was, indeed, the model. Choice B is incorrect for several reasons. The phrase "strong agreement" and the word "must" are too absolute, and the idea that Raphael identified Michelangelo as his subject has no evidence in the footnote or the passage. Choice C is incorrect; the author is not neutral and does not present a balanced number of arguments pro and con. Choice D is incorrect; the phrase "strong disagreement" does not match the author's presentation in the footnote, and the footnote does not address the timing of the addition. Choice E is incorrect because the figure does look like Michelangelo.

12. B. The two sentences in lines 71–77 are both complex sentences and each contains parallel construction. All other answer choices misidentify the sentences' construction.

The passage referred to in questions 13–24 is from the American novelist William Styron's *Darkness Visible* (1990), an autobiographical account of his suffering from clinical depression.

13. E. The first paragraph of the passage explains that the word "depression" has far too many varied definitions and uses; "melancholy" is more specifically appropriate to the mental condition. Choice A contradicts the author's intent; he feels that melancholia is "a far more apt and evocative word for the blacker forms of the disorder" than is depression, but he does not claim that calling the condition melancholia would give it wider acceptance. The author does not want a more gentle word (B); he wants a more accurate one. The phrase "contemporary lightness" makes choice C incorrect; the term "melancholy" was used since the 1300s, so it is not "contemporary," and the disease is anything but "light." The passage offers no evidence that the author thinks changing the term would make it more well known (D).

14. **C.** Though "indifferent" can mean "apathetic" (A) or "average" (B), in this context the word has another of its several meanings: "showing no preference or bias, indiscriminate." The author's point is that a word that can be equally well used to denote a rut or financial hard times should not be used to describe a disease as terrible as depression. Choice D, ardently, means to do something passionately, enthusiastically, which does not fit the context of the passage. Choice E is too much of a stretch; the author's point that the word *depression* is applied to so many different situations does not mean that the word is used without any understanding.

15. **B.** The author objects to using a word with two other commonplace meanings, a "bland tonality," and a euphemistic effect. The author believes the word is less expressive, less shocking than is necessary to denote the condition accurately. Because the passage suggests replacing "depression" with another word, the length of time the word has been in use cannot be held against it. The 75 years mentioned in choice A are too long rather than too short a time. Answer C is flat-out wrong; the author states nothing about people feeling fear when they hear the word "depression." The author does not imply that the term is applies too strictly (D). Finally, the author indeed makes fun of the Swiss-born psychiatrist who coined the term for having a tin ear (E), but that is hardly the reason why he objects to the term.

16. **B.** Both "wimp" and "tin ear" are colloquialisms—that is, words, phrases, or idioms used in conversation or informal writing. Choice A, paradox, is simply not accurate; this term refers to two seemingly contradictory statements that actually do have some truth, and the phrases in this question are not contradictory. Choice C is incorrect because the phrases are not euphemisms, kind phrases for harsh realities. The phrase "wimp of a word" is metaphorical—the word is compared to a type of person—but it is not a mixed metaphor (D), which might compare a word to a person and to a tree at the same time, for example. Finally, choice E is blatantly inaccurate; the phrases are not a parody, nor is the passage as a whole a parody.

17. **A.** The phrase "semantic damage" (A) refers to harm done by the use of the word "depression," but not to the effect of the illness. The phrases in the rest of the answer choices all refer to the fierce power of depression, the disease itself.

18. **D.** The passage says that "brainstorm" describes the disease well, but that it cannot be used because it already has a different established meaning, one of "intellectual inspiration." Choices A and B are both contradictions; the author feels "brainstorm" is a more accurate term for the disease. Choices C and E have no evidence in the passage; it never alludes to how quickly the public may or may not adopt a new term or to psychiatrists' reticence to change terms.

19. **A.** The sentence argues that a better word than "depression" might change the conventional response to the illness. The author insists that he is not exaggerating ("veritable," "indeed," "like nothing else") what the victim suffers (C), and we have no reason to assume his examples of the "standard reaction" are inaccurate (B). Choices D and E are completely off base, misreading the passage. The author decries the "standard responses" (D) and he never questions his own idea of a better term (E).

20. **B.** The author alludes to "nervous breakdown" as a phrase that, like "depression," is ill-chosen, but, unlike it, is passing out of use. His objection to "nervous breakdown" is not because it is "bland," but because it appears to blame the victims for their illness. He never suggests the term is more evocative (A). Choice C is incorrect because the author's purpose in bringing up the term "nervous breakdown" is not merely to add another example of a poor phrase. He does not contrast the two terms (D), and he does not connect "nervous breakdown" to what the uninformed layman feels (E).

21. **C.** Because the author presents depression as "dreadful and raging," as horrible and malevolent, we can assume he would choose "utterly desolated," the most powerful adjective of the five, and reject the four other choices as too weak to describe its "horrible intensity."

22. **E.** The passage uses the phrase "strong protest" in its first sentence, and this position does not change. Choice A is incorrect because the author does not approve of the term depression, although he is unhappily resigned to its use. Both words are inaccurate in choice C. While choices B and D do have one negative word, "disapproval" and "dislike," they are not strong enough for the author's overall attitude, and each is preceded by an inaccurate word, "amused" and "cool."

23. B. Though the passage does incidentally give the history of the word (A) and some of its meanings (C), its central idea is to protest the "bland tonality" of the term "depression." The author reveals his dislike of the phrase "nervous breakdown," and he does mention the archaic word "melancholia" (E), but the passage is focused on the word "depression," not on the shortcomings of medical language (D) in general.

24. A. Though the author would probably agree with choices B, C, and D, the central issue of the passage is the misleading meaning of the word "depression" when it refers to the illness. Choice E is inaccurate because the passage complains about the one word, not about all words.

The passage referred to in questions 25–36 is from John Locke's "An Essay Concerning Human Understanding" (1690).

25. B. Any of these five choices can technically define the word "periods," but in this context, the best choice is "complete sentences." In most multiple-choice exams, a question calling for the definition of a word will ask about a word with several legitimate meanings, and you must look carefully at the context in the passage to determine your answer, and, in particular, the specific sentence in which the word appears. Notice how the entire paragraph supports that words put together with "the right construction of grammatical rules" would become sentences. Choice A may deceive some, but the author's point in the first paragraph eliminates it. Since the paragraph's idea is that one who uses words without having ideas behind them "only make[s] a noise without any sense or signification," and simply produces "bare sounds and nothing else," the phrase "sound conclusions" (A) can be considered a contradiction to the passage's context. Choices C, D, and E do not fit the context of the passage.

26. A. The antecedent of "ones" is "words" in line 22. The "them" that follows ("that compose them") refers to "ideas" (C).

27. D. The first sentence uses a figure of speech, a simile, which pictures an imagined bookseller who has a warehouse of unbound volumes without titles. The second sentence is literal, describing a man who has complex ideas but cannot find the words to express them. The other answer choices do not accurately describe the shift between the two sentences. If you need a definition for any of the terms listed in the answer choices, look in Appendix A.

28. E. The simile compares the man who lacks the words to express his complex ideas to the bookseller whose books are only loose sheets of paper, with no means of binding them together. The other answer choices are images within the sentence, but they do not accurately answer the question.

29. A. The author uses analogies (comparisons) to support his arguments. In the first paragraph, he compares a man who has words but no thoughts to books with titles and no words inside. In the second paragraph, he compares a man who has complex ideas but no words to express them to a bookseller who has volumes of pages that are not bound into any books. The remaining answer choices are not in both paragraphs.

30. A. In this context, the word "fair" means equitable or honest. The other answer choices do not fit the context of the paragraph.

31. D. The "substances" are imagined thoughts that "never have been" and do not have "any correspondence with the real nature of things," and are therefore contrasted with realities, the things that represent "real and true knowledge." Shadows (A), if anything, compares to the use of "substances," since shadows have little substance. Ideas (B) and the author's use of "substances" are similar; he claims substances are imagined ideas. That reasoning also makes choice C inaccurate, as imaginings, in context, are the substances that don't reflect the real truth. In context, names (E) also refers to the imagined substances.

32. E. Paragraphs 1 and 2 are related; the first presents someone who has words but no ideas, and the second, someone who has ideas but no words. Paragraphs 3 and 4 describe two related misuses of words: using one word to mean many things, and using words with meanings different from those that are commonly accepted. The fifth paragraph discusses imaginary notions.

33. D. The last paragraph recapitulates the contents of the first five. It does not develop the arguments (A) or question the validity of the arguments (B). No new issues are raised in the last paragraph (C). Choice E is incorrect for two reasons: The last paragraph does not develop ideas, it summarizes them, and the last paragraph summarizes all previous paragraphs, not just the fourth and fifth.

34. A. In classical myth, a chimera was a monster with the head of a lion, the body of a goat, and the tail of a serpent. The word has come to mean an impossible fantasy, and the adjective "chimerical" means imaginary, unreal, or absurd. Even if you are not familiar with the word, notice how the other answer choices simply do not fit the context accurately, if at all. In choice B, conundrum means an intricate and complicated problem to be solved, which does not relate to the passage's content. The passage does not discuss religious revelations (C) or philosophical distinctions (E). Logical conclusions (D) contradicts the passage, which discusses illogical use of language.

35. D. The fourth paragraph describes the man who uses familiar words to mean something different from what everyone else understands them to mean.

36. C. The third paragraph describes the man who uses a word "sometimes in one, sometimes in another signification."

The passage referred to in questions 37–46 is excerpted from "Laughter," an essay written by Joseph Addison in 1711 for *The Spectator.*

37. B. Lines 8–13 are an example of parallel construction; they employ a series of infinitive phrases, all dependent on the phrase "what an absurd thing it is . . . to pass . . . to observe . . . to make use." The lines are not an example of a periodic sentence (A), in which the central meaning is placed in a main clause at the end. The complex sentence from which these lines are taken is technically three sentences, and they all present the main idea at the beginning: "Everyone has his flaws . . . the greatest blemishes are often found . . . what an absurd thing it is. . . . " The lines in the question are not a conditional sentence (C), which states a condition and its likely consequence, frequently using the "if . . . then . . . " construction. Choice D is completely inaccurate; the lines do not contain a metaphor, let alone an extended one. Choice E is unreasonable; the lines do not contain an indirect question; instead, they present a declarative statement, essentially claiming "what an absurd thing it is. . . . "

38. C. The sentence begins with a simile, introduced by "As." The simile compares "many eminent critics" and "many admirable buffoons." There is only one simile in the paragraph. The incorrect answer choices are not in the paragraph.

39. A. The passage begins with the criticism of the "ungenerous tempers" that are given to ridicule. The second paragraph further develops this idea. It does not suggest any exceptions to the previous ideas (B), shift focus (C), provide any comic relief (D), or transition to the third paragraph's ideas (E).

40. C. The single long sentence in this paragraph contrasts and deplores the infrequent use of ridicule to mock "vice and folly" with the more common practice of jesting at the expense of "virtue and good sense."

41. D. The phrase makes clear what the author sees as the significance of the earlier phrase, "virtue and good sense." Choices A, B, and C contradict the passage. Choice E is irrelevant; it does not answer the question.

42. B. The paragraph argues that ridicule would be useful if it were directed against "vice and folly"—that is, immoral conduct and foolishness. Choice C might look attractive at first, but the author would be shocked to see human weakness ridiculed. Choice D, solemnity, may sound familiar; however, the phrase in the passage claims that ridicule is used to attack "everything that is solemn and serious." The author does not approve of such ridicule. It makes no sense to think that the author would approve of ridiculing the youth (A) or raillery (E), which refers to joking banter.

43. D. The best choice is "instinctive capacity and acquired knowledge." The passage contrasts the arts of the ancients that depend upon "genius" rather than "experience," the source of the inferior productions of the modern world. Choice A is never addressed in the last paragraph. Choices B and E do not reflect the context of the paragraph. In choice C, the second phrase, "active participation," is inaccurate.

44. A. In the fourth paragraph, "doggerel" (B), "humour" (C), "burlesque" (D), and "raillery" (E) are all forms of comic speech or writing, but "embellishments" are not necessarily comic.

45. C. Since modern writers surpass the ancient in the "arts of ridicule," they should be more accomplished in satire, the only one of these forms that depends chiefly upon ridicule.

46. **A.** Given his praise of the "first ages of the world, when the great souls and masterpieces of human nature were produced," the author would probably value the ancient epics more highly than the literary works of later periods. Drama of the Middle Ages (B), religious lyrics of the Renaissance (C), Elizabethan tragedy (D), and contemporary comedy (E) were not written during "the first ages of the world" as were ancient epics.

The passage referred to in questions 47–55 is from W. E. B. Du Bois' commencement address at Harvard University, 1890.

47. **C.** The speaker uses the term "Strong Man" throughout the passage to refer to those who conquer others under the guise of advancing progress and spreading civilization. The second paragraph firmly establishes this idea with phrases such as "now advancing civilization by murdering Indians" and "the peculiar champion of a people fighting to be free in order that another people should not be free." Choices A and E contain positive ideas that are contradictory to Du Bois' criticism. The first phrase of choice B about physical force is accurate, but the next idea, using force to merely command others, is off base because the Strong Man does not simply command others; rather, he conquers them. Choice D does not reflect the evidence in this passage, wherein the Strong Man does not try to convince others of his righteousness before taking action.

48. **E.** The statements in choices A, B, C, and D all present specific criticisms of Jefferson Davis, but only choice E includes a criticism of both Davis and his society. By stating that the standard by which Jefferson Davis is judged is *fundamentally incomplete,* the speaker criticizes both Davis and those in society that admire him.

49. **A.** Choice A, which opens the second paragraph, is an obvious attempt to keep the speech from being perceived as merely a personal attack on Jefferson Davis alone, because the speaker indicates that he wants to consider "the type of civilization which [Davis'] life represented." Choice B is incorrect because it specifically refers to Jefferson Davis and, in turn, personally criticizes him. The phrase in choice C is incorrect because it does not specifically refer to Davis, but rather, it refers to the consequences of embracing the "Strong Man." Choice D does not discuss Jefferson Davis specifically, and choice E does not present a personal attack on Jefferson Davis. Be sure to read each question carefully and, in this case, focus only on the specific words of the phrases in the answer choices.

50. **D.** The first paragraph concludes with the speaker's claim that the standard by which Jefferson Davis is judged is "fundamentally incomplete"; the second paragraph expands upon this idea and further explores the flaws of Teutonic civilization's standards. Choice A is too vague to clarify the rhetorical purpose of the second paragraph. Choice B contradicts the intent of the speech; it does not present examples of Jefferson Davis' successes; rather, the speech criticizes him. Choice C is incorrect because the second paragraph does not offer any illustration of Jefferson Davis' Teutonic connection. Choice E might seem tempting, but the word "modify" is inaccurate; the second paragraph expands upon the ideas in the first paragraph, it does not change or revise them.

51. **C.** The speaker's attitude toward Davis combines recognition of Davis' achievements with criticism of Davis' arrogant actions. Because the speaker's disapproval of Davis runs throughout this passage, one cannot conclude that the speaker is accepting of Davis (A). Choice B is simply too strong a statement; the speaker is not overly preoccupied with slavery. In choice D, the word "incredulous," meaning disbelieving or skeptical, does not accurately describe the speaker's attitude, and the passage offers no evidence that the speaker is surprised that Davis misled many people. Choice E is incorrect because the speaker does not actually find anything admirable in Davis.

52. **B.** The sentence in question is strongly negative; its tone is both "sardonic," which means tauntingly contemptuous, and "sarcastic," which means bitterly scornful. Based on the tone of this passage, you can eliminate any answer choice with positive, or even neutral, connotations. Therefore, choice A can be eliminated because of the word "balanced." The word "revengeful" in choice C is inaccurate; the passage offers no evidence for this idea. The positive word "reverent" in choice D makes it inaccurate. Choice E is incorrect because of the word "reflective," which does not describe the sentence in this question.

53. **D.** Notice the phrasing that follows choice D and you will see that the speaker is being ironic; he states that Jefferson Davis' means of "advancing civilization" were carried out "by murdering Indians." One might argue that the speaker is also being ironic when he claims Davis defied disease (B), but choice D is clearly intended to be more ironic than choice B. All of the other choices appear to be straightforward and sincere.

54. A. The speaker's overall message deals with the way in which Jefferson Davis personifies a government that actually inhibits the true progress of civilization. Notice how the speaker makes this connection as he states "Under whatever guise, however a Jefferson Davis may appear, as man, as race, or as a nation, his life can only logically mean this: the advance of a part of the world at the expense of the whole: the overwhelming sense of the I and the consequent forgetting of the Thou. It has thus happened, that advance in civilization has always been handicapped by shortsighted national selfishness." Choice D may seem appealing, but the idea that if some people are free, others cannot also be free, is merely a minor point the author includes. The other answer choices do not accurately summarize the speaker's overall message about the way civilization advances.

55. A. The speaker implies that America is shaped by men such as Jefferson Davis, men who embody "individualism coupled with the rule of might," choice A. The speaker does not agree that Americans should embrace the concept of the Strong Man (B). Also, the idea in choice C, that some Americans still admire pre–Civil War Southern society, is probably true, but this idea is not implied in the passage. Similarly, choice E is not based on the evidence in this passage. Choice D is simply too strong of a statement; the speaker undoubtedly wishes that America would never again be deceived by the Strong Man, but the passage offers no evidence that he actually believes this is likely.

Section II: Free-Response Questions

Question 1

Scoring Guide

Score	Description	Criteria
9	Successful	Essays that earn a score of 9 meet the criteria for essays that receive a score of 8. In addition, they are especially sophisticated in their explanation and argument. They may also present particularly remarkable control of language.
8	Successful	Essays that receive a score of 8 respond to the prompt successfully, using at least three sources from the prompt. They take a position that defends, challenges, or qualifies the claim that professional athletes are overpaid. They effectively argue their position and support the argument with appropriate and convincing evidence. The prose demonstrates an ability to control an extensive range of the elements of effective writing, but may not be entirely flawless.
7	Satisfactory	Essays that earn a score of 7 fit the description of essays that score a 6, but provide more complexity in both argumentation and explanation and/or demonstrate a more distinguished prose style.
6	Satisfactory	Essays that earn a score of 6 respond to the prompt satisfactorily, incorporating at least three sources from the prompt. They take a position that defends, challenges, or qualifies the claim that professional athletes are overpaid. They adequately argue their position and support it with appropriate evidence, although without the precision and depth of the top-scoring essays. The writing may contain minor errors in diction or syntax, but the prose is generally clear.
5	Plausible	Essays that earn a score of 5 take a plausible position that defends, challenges, or qualifies the claim that professional athletes are overpaid. They support the position with generally appropriate evidence, but they may not adequately use at least three sources from the prompt. These essays may be inconsistent, uneven, or limited in the development of their argument. Although the writing usually conveys the student's ideas, it may demonstrate lapses in diction or syntax or an overly simplistic style.

Score	Description	Criteria
4	Inadequate	Essays that earn a score of 4 respond to the prompt inadequately. They may have difficulty taking a position that defends, challenges, or qualifies the claim that professional athletes are overpaid. The evidence may be particularly insufficient, or may not use at least three sources from the prompt. The prose may basically convey the student's ideas but suggests immature control over the elements of effective writing.
3	Inadequate	Essays that earn a score of 3 meet the criteria for a score of 4 but reveal less ability to take a position. The presentation of evidence and argumentation is likely to be unconvincing. The writing may show less control over the elements of effective writing.
2	Little success	Essays that earn a 2 demonstrate little success at taking a position that defends, challenges, or qualifies the claim that professional athletes are overpaid, and show little ability to present it with appropriate evidence from the sources in the prompt. These essays may misunderstand the prompt, fail to establish a position with supporting evidence, or substitute a simpler task by replying tangentially with unrelated, erroneous, or unsuitable explanation, argument, and/or evidence. The prose frequently demonstrates consistent weaknesses in the conventions of effective writing.
1	Little success	Essays that earn a score of 1 meet the criteria for a score of 2 but are undeveloped; especially simplistic in their explanation, argument, and/or evidence; or weak in their control of writing.

High-Scoring Essay

In recent decades, athletes' salaries have soared, allowing them to collect millions in yearly earnings for merely displaying their physical gifts. Although athletes are arguably the world's most physically gifted individuals, their preposterous salaries are unjustifiable when their jobs are limited to seasonal games intended for purely entertainment purposes. Magnified by the allure of extravagant wealth, athletes become sedated by the extrinsic value of playing their respective sports, which in turn negatively affects society's younger generation. Salaries that run in the ten-millions and even in the hundred-millions are not only excessive, but also unwarranted for individuals who simply play a game for their jobs.

While some sports such as tennis and golf entail all-year-round games, most of the mainstream and high-paying sports, such as basketball, baseball, and football, are limited to seasons that are played over the course of several months. Especially when athletes are paid on the basis of their performance over a fraction of the year, their absurd salaries do not properly reflect their job's length, no matter what author P. K. claims in "Athletes Are Underpaid." And although some may argue that athletes must train in the off-season to maintain their peak-condition, it is no different than the unpaid preparation that teachers must sacrifice before each school year. Furthermore, the games in which athletes participate last for an average of three hours per game. It is illogical that athletes are paid in the millions for their performances for a couple of hours per game, when other professions judge individuals' production over the compilation of full day's work. Once again, the preparation that athletes must endure is not a relevant argument, since it is ultimately during the games that fans are entertained. People do not pay for preparation; people pay for the action and pleasure of games.

While society may value sports, consumer choice, according to Gene Callahan, reflects one of the reasons for the rich salaries that athletes receive. However, this fact does not fully account for all of the reasons that athletes' salaries are as such (Source C). Many goods in society are vastly overpriced, and although individuals continue to succumb to outrageous prices by giving in, it may be that society is simply at the receiving end of corruption and inflation. Humans are naturally drawn to what is portrayed as rich and wealthy. It is evident that exorbitant prices for sports venues do not have a proper effect on individuals' decision making, which leads to the fact that society is ultimately submitting to the immoral standards of sports entertainment. This is not limited to American sports at all. In fact, as Source D points out, cricket players in India average

$3,612,726 annually, and many European soccer players earn between $1,960,080 (Italy) and $3,184,110 (Britain). It appears the world values sports more than many other commodities.

The argument that "players sacrifice a lot to make it to the big show," is faulted in the fact that athletes sacrifice no more than other professionals who aspire to become teachers and researchers (Source A). Many professions require intense "sacrifice" and yet do not offer the outrageous remuneration professional sports offers. Why should the basketball player's "sacrifice" be worth more than any other professional's? Athletes' salaries are climbing at unprecedented rates, as over a ten-year period, some salaries in the NBA skyrocketed by 472%, which resulted in about a $14 million increase (Source A). Meanwhile, the salaries of prominent government leaders throughout the world seem paltry by comparison: Putin's $136,000, Hollande's $194,251 and Xi Jingping's $22,000 seem like the peanuts sold in NFL stadiums when compared to actual NFL players' salaries (Source B). It boggles the mind that world leaders are compensated only a fraction of professional athletes; after all, which profession is more important?

Although athletes may boast amazing and rare skills, million dollar salaries are definitely not reasonable, when their productivity level lies entirely in entertainment purposes. Although athletes encompass elite physical skills, it is nearly impossible to compare their gifts with those of others. Although societal attitudes may be at the root of this imbalance, in which the value of entertainment may supersede the value of life, the disparity in athletes' salaries as compared to most other professional salaries illustrates a self-evident problem. Regardless of deciding where to place the blame for allowing such overpriced salaries, it is clear that athletes receive too much for their supposed sacrifice and production year in and year out.

As athletes continue to receive more than what they are worth, youngsters who delve their interest in modeling their lives after sports superstars are negatively influenced by greed and discontent. The questionable plight of players' unions seeking even greater salaries for athletes combined with the instances in which athletes "opt out of contracts" only to sign bigger and better ones for "stability" purposes, elicits a message of insatiability and pure greed (Source F). Youngsters begin with the innocent passion of playing sports—similar to how professional athletes began—but when they are exposed to the attempts of athletes and agents in receiving more and more millions of dollars, they can become corrupted. Athletes who boast contracts that reach up to $252 million dollars are unconditionally blinded by the allure of money (Source F). While their gross incomes are unfair and unjust, their commitment to negotiating for millions of dollars adds an immoral image that unavoidably plagues the rest of society and the younger generation.

Amidst the façade of athletic talent and physical stature, athletes' ridiculous earnings have reached excessive and unprecedented levels that are not warranted, given their limited entertainment-driven performances. The myopia of athletes in merely attempting to find the longest and richest contract further illustrates the pathos of outrageous and disproportionate salaries in the world of sports. After all, it's only a game.

Analysis of the High-Scoring Essay

This essay earns a high score because it is on topic and thoroughly developed. The student begins with an understanding that athletes are indeed "physically gifted individuals" but acknowledges that this gift, coupled with athletes' limited season, does not warrant their multi-million-dollar salaries. The introduction sets up the content and organization of the essay well, demonstrating that the student has planned his or her ideas successfully in advance.

The second paragraph focuses on the aspect that most highly paid athletes only perform for a limited time in a limited season, and, therefore, should not receive such exorbitant salaries. Comparing the time athletes train to the time teachers prepare brings the argument to the level of everyman and draws an apt analogy. Certainly an AP Reader can relate to working long hours, but so can every other person who works as hard. By extension, wouldn't all professionals prefer to be paid so handsomely for their preparation? Although this logic demonstrates clear thinking on the student's part, the idea that fans only pay for action and not preparation is not as convincing as it could be. The student would be better served to expand this argument by considering counterarguments and then logically dismissing them.

The next paragraph discusses society's value system and acknowledges the truth that many people in society are willing to pay dearly for those things they deem worthy. The student makes the point even more forceful by discussing that "humans are naturally drawn to what is portrayed as rich and wealthy," intimating that humans do not always know the true value of things; rather, we are influenced by the value judgments of others. The paragraph is further enhanced by exploring sports salaries throughout the globe. This level of analysis demonstrates the maturity of the student.

The following paragraph uses multiple sources from the prompt to compare the actual salaries of many professions. It is as thorough an examination of the data as one could expect in a timed essay. The student continues by addressing the value of certain professions, namely world leaders who carry more important influence, and makes the point that the value of athletes' jobs pales in comparison. The student's comparison of world leaders' salaries to peanuts (sold in stadiums) makes a Reader chuckle, even though the wording is cumbersome. Overall, this paragraph is particularly convincing in its logical and fact-based presentation, and helps earn the essay's high score.

The writer then explores the effect that athletes have on the young, pointing out how young people are so easily influenced by the glitz and glamour of professional athletes. Then, by discussing the example of how an athlete can opt out of a contract in order to sign an even more lucrative one, the student makes a logical connection between the corrupting power of money triumphing over the intrinsic fun of playing a game and how easily a youth's belief system can be swayed by this self-centered behavior. This point is important to all of society, as this student clearly proves.

The concluding paragraph shows that this student does not run out of steam, but rather ends the essay forcefully, using striking phrases such as "the myopia of athletes," and "the pathos of outrageous and disproportionate salaries." The last sentence, concise and pithy, reminds us to place sports into the big picture of society; after all, it is only a game. This concludes the essay with finality, with conviction.

Although this essay does have some flaws, both in minor wording issues and minor lapses in logic, they are not serious enough to keep this essay from receiving a high score. Its intelligent presentation and well-developed discussion clearly demonstrate that the student's efforts are worthy of a high score. It should earn a score of 9.

Medium-Low-Scoring Essay

With the general trend of popularity in sports, athletes have signed contracts worth a lot of money, however, many argue how fair this is despite the fact that athletes have irreplaceable talents and are ultimately paid for the amount of attention they receive. America's emphasis on sports makes the million dollar contracts of athletes just and necessary.

Although there is a disparity in the incomes that athletes earn with the incomes of professionals such as teachers, firefighters and truckers, there are only a limited number of athletes represented in the professional ranks compared to the many individuals in relatively common professions. Given the minority of athletes, the amount of money that they are paid is warranted, if there were as many professional athletes as there were teachers, then it would be vastly unjust, but this is not the case. Furthermore, athletes' talents that they display in their respective sports are unique and unmatchable. After honing their skills for countless years, only a few select individuals who display exceptional athletic abilities are rewarded for their training.

The reasoning behind the rich contracts of athletes is ultimately the valuable God-given talents that athletes have over other individuals. Athletes who grace the covers of magazines and serve as role models for many youngsters are arguably the fittest and most disciplined individuals in society, the achievements that they reach in sports are historically unique and therefore are met with fanatical acceptance through enthusiastic fanfare. People may argue that other professions should receive more incentive for their work, but the fact is that those people should stop putting their money into sports and instead devote it to education (Source C). Many individuals display insurmountable passion for sports. And in turn are willing to pay the money to see their favorite athletes.

Additionally, unlike most other professions, athletics is distinctive in the fact that athletes are constantly under the scrutiny of the press and the opinions of fans. Athletes are human, they are plagued with a flow of attention. Although attention may have beneficial outcomes, it can also be excruciating and undesirable. Athletes living under this spotlight, sacrifice their personal lives as they continue to perform at high-caliber levels of competition. In turn, the incomes that athletes earn are not merely represented through their accomplishments on the field, but also serve as compensation for the loss of privacy in becoming an athlete.

Given the excitement and exuberance for sports throughout society, athletes are given salaries based on their popular demand. Ultimately, athletes are paid really well all around the world (Source D). With money coming from television, ticket sales and other outlets, athletes' salaries are not generated from nothingness, but in actuality in terms of what fans pay to see these athletes perform. Rather than continuing to deem sports as overpriced, individuals must realize that athletes are simply earning what they are given. Athletes are in reality like every other individual in society and should be given the same rights. When individuals cry afoul regarding contract disputes, athletes are merely exercising the exact rights that other individuals exercise when they seek signing bonuses and other incentives. While the blame continues to revolve around athletes and their supposed extorted earnings, the reality is that athletes are for the most part earning every dollar that they receive. For many individuals, sports is everything, and amidst that fervor, fans are willing to put in the money to watch athletes in action. If people are willing to support athletes, yet criticize them, then the problem lies within the populous of society. The true difference between sports and many other professions is that sports entails a large fan-base. In turn, the revenues coming from sports are immense. Just as any front-office executive, team owners merely reward their players with what the organization earns from yearly revenues.

Inevitably through the uniqueness of athletes' skills and achievements in their respective sports, their grossing salaries that consistently run in the million dollar ranges are both just and reasonable. Professional athletes are rare and given their incredible talents, their rich contracts are merely substantiated from the amount of work that they put in and the passionate fanfare they encounter.

Analysis of the Medium-Low-Scoring Essay

This essay, while deceptively lengthy, does not construct a convincing argument, nor does it incorporate the minimum of three sources from the prompt, as directed. Ultimately, this essay demonstrates how a student can write a long essay but basically go nowhere. The language is not particularly striking, and it displays a disturbing number of grammatical and mechanical errors.

The essay begins with a simplistic thesis: that professional athletes justly deserve a large salary because America emphasizes sports. The Reader is left wondering where this logic will lead.

The first body paragraph displays organizational problems, beginning with a discussion of the disparity in the ratio of professional athletes to other professions, then moving into the skills an athlete must hone to succeed. The student also displays gaps in logic; for example, claiming that athletes deserve more money simply because they make up a minority of the workforce. This illogical claim is followed by the equally puzzling remark that if there were as many professional athletes as teachers, "then it would be vastly unjust."

Many of the student's phrases seem hollow and do not help to propel the essay forward. For instance, some statements, such as "athletes' talents . . . are unique and unmatchable," are simply untrue and really say nothing. The student does include two sources from the prompt, but merely uses them to make the point that society values sports without a deeper analysis of how this affects athletes' incomes.

The next brief paragraph does not make a strong argument, but merely asserts the claim that, because athletes are "under scrutiny," they deserve more money to compensate for their loss of privacy. However, if the student were to take this argument to its logical conclusion, then many professions would also deserve multi-million-dollar salaries simply because the jobs propel one into the public eye.

The paragraph that follows presents contradictory ideas. The student previously declared that athletes are unique and therefore deserve their high salary, but now claims that athletes are "in reality like every other individual in society." Self-contradictory thinking like this cannot help an essay's score.

The conclusion repeats the essay's main idea, that athletes deserve their salary because they are "rare" and have "incredible talent." But it's a sentiment the Reader has heard before, and so the conclusion offers no food for thought, merely summary.

Finally, take note of how the sentence fragments, run-on sentences, punctuation errors, and frequent verb mistakes distract the Reader from the essay's content. Do not let the essay's length deceive you; its many errors, lack of substance and source examples, and logical fallacies should earn a score of 4, no more than a 5.

Question 2

Scoring Guide

Score	Description	Criteria
9	Successful	Essays that earn a score of 9 meet the criteria for essays that receive a score of 8. In addition, they are especially sophisticated in demonstrating the clear understanding of the connection between President Obama's rhetorical strategies and his message. They may also present a particularly remarkable control of language.
8	Successful	These well-written essays show successful analysis of *how* President Obama's use of rhetorical strategies helps to deliver his message The thesis is thoughtful and articulate. They develop their analysis with evidence and explanations that are appropriate and convincing, referring to the passage explicitly or implicitly. Successfully convincing, these essays demonstrate a command of essay-writing skills. Although not necessarily flawless, these essays are written with a mature style and diction.
7	Satisfactory	These essays meet the requirements for essays that score a 6 and, in addition, demonstrate a thorough understanding of the connection between rhetorical strategies and message, while providing stronger and more relevant insights. The prose style is generally more mature.
6	Satisfactory	These essays demonstrate a satisfactory comprehension of *how* President Obama's rhetorical strategies help to develop his message, but their theses may be less explicit than those of the top-scoring essays. The evidence offered may be less convincing, but the essays still demonstrate clear thinking. The presentation of evidence, either implicit or explicit, may not be as clear as that of the top-scoring essays. Although well written, these essays may contain some errors, while maintaining satisfactory control over diction and the essay's requirements.
5	Plausible	These essays show some understanding of *how* President Obama's rhetorical strategies develop his message but may not clearly demonstrate the relationship between details of the speech and his message. These essays may merely identify the strategies without effectively discussing them. The evidence or explanations used may be uneven, inconsistent, or limited. Acceptable organization and development may be evident, but the style may not be as sophisticated as that of higher-scoring essays, perhaps containing some lapses in diction or syntax.
4	Inadequate	These low-scoring essays fail to convince. The weak and inadequate analysis may not demonstrate a clear understanding of how President Obama's rhetorical strategies create his message. These essays may misunderstand the speech, misrepresent the strategies President Obama uses, or analyze these strategies insufficiently. The evidence or explanations used may be inappropriate, insufficient, or less convincing. The thesis may be unsubstantiated, paragraph development may be weak, and thinking may be superficial. Frequent errors in composition that distract the Reader may be present.
3	Inadequate	Essays earning a score of 3 meet the criteria for a score of 4 but demonstrate less understanding of President Obama's strategies and show a lack of depth in their insights. These essays may show little control over the elements of writing.
2	Little success	These poorly written essays lack coherence and clarity. They may attempt with little success to identify the use of rhetorical strategies in the speech. The thesis may be overly obvious or absent. Little or no evidence may be offered, and any connection between the evidence and the thesis may be shallow or nonexistent. These essays may be unusually short, and persistent grammatical problems may exist.
1	Little success	These poorly written essays meet the criteria for a score of 2 but are undeveloped, especially shallow in insight, and weak in the control of language.

High-Scoring Essay

The whole world was watching and listening as newly elected President Obama stepped up to the microphone on January 21, 2009, representing a campaign that was associated with hope and dignity and change. Traditionally, an inaugural speech is one of inspiration, one of optimism, one of assurance for the future. Indeed, President Obama adheres to this tradition, eloquently and effectively, as he takes the helm as the leader of the United States.

Frequently throughout his remarks, President Obama tactically refers to the past, reminding us of America's strengths during adversity, before looking to the future. He begins by mentioning the forty-four presidents who have come before him, surely establishing his credibility as the new president as he joins those august men. But he does not merely allude to past presidents as a tool to reflect upon himself; he instead immediately segues into the fact that many presidents faced metaphorical "gathering clouds and raging storms," through which the country carried on, thanks to Americans' remaining "faithful to the ideals of our forebears and true to our founding documents." His introduction, therefore, connects to the audience by reminding them of America's past greatness and suggesting more greatness to come. His repetition in the parallel phrasing, "so it has been; so it must be . . . " musically reinforces this goal.

President Obama then explores how this greatness has been achieved, again reaching into American history for examples. He acknowledges that America's greatness has been a hard path, a journey taken by frequently obscure "risk-takers . . . doers . . . makers of things." His repetition of "For us, they packed up . . . and traveled. . . . For us, they toiled . . . and settled . . . endured . . . and plowed. . . . For us, they fought and died. . . ." hammers in the collective idea that Americans overcome hardship, that Americans endure harsh conditions, that Americans sacrifice for their country. Indeed, his powerful diction, parallel construction, and harsh imagery compound his message, ultimately reminding us that we are "bigger than the sum of our individual ambitions, greater than all the differences of birth or wealth or faction." These are the oratorical tools that great speech writers use.

It is interesting to note that his inaugural address continues not by bringing up what problems America faces today, but by probing what questions we ask today. This changes the thrust from negative to potentially positive and influences the way an audience emotionally responds; we do not want to hear about problems in an inaugural address, but we do want to know about what questions we can answer. President Obama acknowledges that our challenges may be new and the way we meet them will also have to be new, but in doing so he again uses the approach of reminding us of our past, how "honesty and hard work, courage and fair play, tolerance and curiosity, loyalty and patriotism," are "old" and "true" forces of progress. Through collectively embracing these values, we want to enthusiastically cheer on America as we jointly work, "giving our all to a difficult task."

The President concludes his oration appropriately with another reference to our history, but this time a very specific one, one often taught in American schools: that of the horrible winter endured by soldiers during the American Revolution in Valley Forge. Reminding us of America's past struggle for "that great gift of freedom," knowing that the struggle was successful in creating a nation that has endured ever since, this allusion to hardship propels the audience to rise to greatness and, "with eyes fixed on the horizon" continue to overcome any new challenges. Emotionally, President Obama has his audience in the palm of his hand as he connects America's past to its present and future, for who can deny that the suffering of those soldiers in the winter of 1777–1778 led to a great and prosperous nation? Who can deny that America as a great and prosperous nation still maintains its place in the world today? Who can deny that we will work hard so that it can continue?

Analysis of the High-Scoring Essay

AP Readers always appreciate and reward well-written, thoughtful essays; this high-scoring essay indeed deserves to be amply rewarded. It begins by arousing a Reader's anticipation, reminding one of the intense public interest that surrounded President Obama's inaugural speech in 2009 and how his campaign was associated with positive ideals: hope, dignity, and change. The student then connects President Obama's optimistic message with previous presidents' addresses, subtly establishing President Obama's credentials. The student completes the introductory paragraph explicitly claiming that President Obama's speech was both eloquent and effective.

The second paragraph explores the rhetorical strategy of using historical examples to make a point. While introducing this idea, the student creates a positive connection to the Reader with the phrase "reminding us of America's strengths during adversity." The student understands how Obama's rhetorical strategy of mentioning past presidents establishes "his credibility" without having to use the term "ethos," a word that is so often drilled into AP students. The essay continues by noticing one of the metaphors Obama uses, that of "gathering clouds and raging storms," and connects it to America's ability to overcome hardship. The student then directly states that President Obama's introduction "connects to the audience," because we understand and appreciate his historical allusions. The student also notices President Obama's rhetorical strategy of parallel construction, mentioning that his use "musically reinforces" the speech's goal. Although one might want the student to further develop how this stylistic device enhances the speech, one can reward the student for noticing it and having something accurate to say about its effect.

The essay continues examining President Obama's historical examples, ones that do not refer to specific individuals or singular events, but to the many "obscure" Americans who helped build the country. The student again notices Obama's parallel construction, and in doing so, the student, in turn, eloquently employs his or her own parallel construction, repeating the phrase "that Americans . . . " three times. The student's phrasing is particularly effective for several reasons: It mirrors the effectiveness of the original speech, and, in the process, it helps prove the student's idea that Obama's speech "hammers in the collective idea" of Americans' success. The student mentions that "powerful diction, parallel construction, and harsh imagery" are tools of great speech writers. This perceptive analysis of how rhetorical strategies help deliver a message is thoughtful and, because of the student's sophisticated style, particularly articulate.

The fourth paragraph discusses a point that not many students notice: how President Obama's choice of exploring questions that America faces, instead of identifying them as problems to be solved, turns something potentially negative into something positive. The student does not merely make this point, but continues to explore the effect, pointing out how it influences the way the audience responds. The student again brings up how President Obama uses historical allusions to Americans' fortitude and connects that to audience reaction, claiming that "we want to enthusiastically cheer" as America faces the future.

The student's final paragraph examines how President Obama concludes his speech, again understanding how his historical allusion to the Revolutionary War not only reminds us of our past but also compels us to future greatness. Without having to use the word "pathos," the student claims that "President Obama has his audience in the palm of his hand." The student effectively ends the essay with a series of questions, all using parallel construction with the phrase "who can deny that . . . " Ending any essay with a series of questions can be risky, because one general bit of advice is that essays should answer questions, not ask them. However, this student's questions are thought-provoking and do not remotely imply that the student does not know the answers. Instead, they are rhetorical questions; we know what the student intends the answers to be.

Overall, this essay is clearly on topic and well developed. Its organization explores the speech chronologically, walking through it from its introduction to its conclusion. A Reader will be glad that the student did not choose to organize around rhetorical strategies, such as devoting one paragraph to historical allusion, one to parallel construction, and so forth. Although organizing in that fashion may give many students comfort, it is ultimately not as sophisticated as the organization exhibited in this essay. Finally, the student's style is very pleasing, using sophisticated diction and syntax. Any AP Reader will reward this student for what he or she does so well, and a Reader will award this essay a high score of 9.

Low-Scoring Essay

All presidents give an inaugural speech. Some are great speeches, some are forgettable. President Obama's 2009 inaugural speech was good, making a positive impact on all who heard it or read it today.

Obama talks of unity, something he thinks the nation needs. He thinks the country had strong leaders in the past who helped America. He wants to do the same. In his speech his message is that we have to work hard because "hard work" has "been the quiet force of progress throughout our history."

He uses historical examples to prove his point that "throughout our history" we have worked hard. He talked about Concord, Gettysburg, Normandy, and Khe Sahn, which was during the Vietnam War. These historical examples help prove his point. He also talked about the American Revolutionary War.

He also tries to be uplifting by using phrases like "reaffirming the greatness of our nation" and "vital trust between a people and their government" and "return to these truths" and "with hope and virtue."

President Obama's speech tries to unify the country by using historical examples and uplifting diction.

Analysis of the Low-Scoring Essay

The student who wrote this low-scoring essay appears to appreciate President Obama's inaugural speech, but little more can be said for its presentation. Instead of analyzing *how* the speech's rhetorical strategies develop its message, the student merely paraphrases or directly quotes the speech.

It begins with a short, off-topic introduction that does not address the prompt; instead it claims the speech was "good" and had a "positive impact." The Reader of the essay has no idea what criteria the student uses to judge quality or impact. Unfortunately, just as the student claims that "some [speeches] are forgettable," this introduction is also forgettable.

The second paragraph simply tells the Reader what President Obama said, that he spoke of unity and the need for strong leaders. The student does not attempt to identify any rhetorical strategies, let alone analyze how they add effect. Notice the weak wording as the student summarizes the speech's message, claiming that "we have to work hard," misquoting the speech phrase of "hard work." This is both unnecessary and redundant.

In the third paragraph, the student finally identifies a rhetorical strategy, that of using "historical examples," but has no more to say than that they "prove his point." Perhaps one might want to reward the student for knowing that the battle of Khe Sahn occurred during the Vietnam War, but that hardly qualifies as analysis. The comment is as bland as noticing that President Obama "also talked about the American Revolutionary War."

The entire fourth paragraph, consisting of only one sentence, copies four phrases from the speech and claims the President uses them to be "uplifting." Again, sadly, we have no analysis.

The one-sentence conclusion merely repeats the three concepts of the three body paragraphs: unity, historical examples, and uplifting diction, and then abruptly ends. Although a Reader wants to reward the student for trying, the essay earns a low score because it is not on topic and its paragraph development borders on being anorexic. The essay's organization is not bad, and its language, albeit simplistic, is not riddled with errors. To improve, the student needs to practice connecting what he or she sees in the speech to how its strategies make it more effective. It should earn a score of 4, maybe as low as a 3.

Question 3

Scoring Guide

Score	Description	Criteria
9	Successful	Essays earning a score of 9 meet the criteria for essays that are scored an 8 and, in addition, are especially full or apt in their analysis or reveal particularly remarkable control of language.
8	Successful	These well-written essays demonstrate clear ideas about Franklin's assertion that people can use reasoning to justify anything they want to do, and they support their ideas with thoughtful, relevant evidence. They illustrate a sound awareness of the logical requirements of an argumentative essay. Stylistically, these essays are mature, using sophisticated sentence structure and diction. The writing need not be error-free, but it clearly shows the ability to construct an effective essay through a combined command of language and logic.
7	Satisfactory	Essays earning a score of 7 fit the description of essays that are scored a 6, but provide more complete analysis and a more mature prose style.
6	Satisfactory	These essays advance a thesis about Franklin's idea that people can use reasoning to justify anything they want to do, and any assertions may be satisfactory and well presented. However, they may provide weaker evidence or explanatory logic to support any assertions. The style of these essays is appropriate to the task, but perhaps with less maturity than that of the top-scoring essays. Some errors in diction or syntax may be present, but the writing demonstrates satisfactory control over the conventions of writing and presents ideas clearly.

Score	Description	Criteria
5	Plausible	These average essays develop a plausible position on Franklin's idea that people can use reason to justify anything they want to do. The evidence and explanations used to support that position may be uneven, inconsistent, or limited. The writing may contain lapses in syntax or diction, but it adequately conveys the student's ideas.
4	Inadequate	These essays inadequately develop a position on Franklin's assertion that people can use reason to justify anything they want to do. The evidence and explanations may be inappropriate to the topic, insufficient, or unconvincing. The argument may have lapses in coherence or development. The prose generally conveys the student's ideas but may be inconsistent in controlling the elements of effective writing.
3	Inadequate	Essays earning a score of 3 meet the criteria for a score of 4 but demonstrate less success in developing a position about Franklin's idea. These essays may show less control over the elements of writing.
2	Little success	These essays demonstrate little success in developing a position on Franklin's idea that people can use reason to justify anything they want to do. The student may misunderstand the prompt or substitute a simpler task by responding to the prompt tangentially with irrelevant or inaccurate explanation. The writing often demonstrates consistent weaknesses, such as grammatical problems, a lack of development or organization, or a lack of coherence or control.
1	Little success	These poorly written essays meet the criteria for a score of 2 but are undeveloped, especially simplistic in their analysis, and weak in their control of language.

High-Scoring Essay

It is his reason that separates man from the creatures of the wild. Reason also fathers conscience, to act as a counterweight to the volatile animal passions of which his sentience has suddenly made him aware. If this were the only function of reason, to launch conscience, the world could theoretically be a better place. Imagine a society where a criminal, about to rob a hapless victim, stops as his mind reasons out the consequences. Reaching the reasonable conclusion that any punishment would be longer lasting and worse than the immediate benefits of his crime, the robber stops. Unfortunately, in reality, the human mind just does not work this way. Reason is not entirely an agent of good, of conscience. Reason can enter Promethean combat with the conscience it creates and shrewdly invent a means for its owner to justify some of his baser impulses.

Ben Franklin addresses man's propensity to justify and explain away his actions through reasoning, to allow caprices and animal impulses to persist. His Autobiography makes the valid point that once someone has his mind set on doing something, reason frequently acts as a tool to circumvent conscience rather than as an agent of that conscience.

Indeed, virtually any action can be justified through some semblance of reason, no matter how faulty the logic, how heinous the crime. For every violent act, for every deceit, a dozen specious premises rise to the task of denying any wrongdoing by the criminal. For example, study the logic which convinced looters during any recent riots in American inner cities that they were justified in robbing innocent storekeepers. This kind of reasoning, sadly, occurs daily in the minds of humanity.

Empirical approaches to life, from the Socratic Method to Hegelian philosophy, have relied on reason to explain both the natural world and the human response to that world. Moral relativism and "situational ethics" depend on reason of a sort. Proponents of such philosophies insist that man must abandon preconceptions, that he must judge each situation as it happens, and use reason to determine what is morally correct under each set of specific circumstances which arise. But it is not only relativists who look to reason as a means of understanding and reacting to the world. Strict Draconian moral codes find their justification in reason as well. Man's actions, whether representing the "rule of law," or the most liberal definitions of right and wrong, are always defended with arguments paying homage to reason. This holds as true for the Supreme Court justice as for the urban pickpocket . . . whether the subject feels he is doing the will of God and country, or knows he is shrewdly evading responsibility. Reason is the tool of man's shell game with his conscience.

Franklin, then, is essentially correct. After a moment of balancing "between principle and inclination," man seizes upon the "convenience" of being a "reasonable creature, since it enables one to find or make a reason for everything one has a mind to do." What one has a mind to do may be quixotic or craven, vainglorious or altruistic, but whatever the case, man can use reason to nullify the conscience that is its offspring.

Analysis of the High-Scoring Essay

This high-scoring essay begins with a relevant discussion of reason and its function. Introducing the idea that "reason . . . fathers conscience," the student provides a hypothetical example of a robber who stops mid-crime because his reason has convinced him the punishment would exceed the gain. The thesis follows, with the interesting concept that reason can engage in "Promethean combat" with the conscience to justify any human action. The student is obviously linguistically talented; the sophisticated diction and syntax are impressive and set the Reader's expectations high for the remainder of the essay.

The next paragraph acknowledges Ben Franklin as the inspiration for this topic and capsulizes Franklin's remarks about reason. This paragraph serves as a direct tie to the essay question, but it does not move the essay forward. Fortunately, the next paragraphs are much more impressive.

The third paragraph suggests that humans use reason to justify any kind of action, even immoral actions, and provides another relevant example: looters during recent riots who feel justified in their unlawful actions. The parallel structure in the phrase "no matter how faulty the logic, how heinous the crime" is pleasing to the ear and is another sign of the student's sophisticated writing style.

The fourth paragraph includes a pertinent review of several philosophies and "empirical approaches" that use reason as a way of determining one's actions. This paragraph notes that all those taking positions, from Supreme Court justices to common thieves, use reason to justify actions. The paragraph ends with a somewhat mixed but still effective metaphor: "Reason is the tool of man's shell game with his conscience." This student continues to impress with stylistic sophistication and intellectual panache. High-scoring essays demonstrate the ability to think analytically and deeply, avoiding a surface-level presentation, and communicate ideas with mature techniques, just as this essay does.

The concluding paragraph returns to Franklin's insight, that humans will always find a reasonable way to explain any action. The student once more uses sophisticated style and diction with phrasing like "quixotic or craven, vainglorious or altruistic." This student possesses the command of language evidenced only in top-scoring essays. This essay might be improved if it recognized Franklin's obviously playful tone and responded in kind, at least to some extent. But, overall, the essay is on topic, philosophically insightful, and intelligently presented, and provides sufficient convincing examples from real-life situations. It definitely deserves a high score of 8.

Low-Scoring Essay

Ben Franklin is one of our most important Founding Fourfathers. Like Alexander Hamilton and others who never achieved the presidency, he still had a profound impact on the U.S. His importance is shown in his autobiography, where he discusses vegetarianism and the morality of eating fish among other topics.

Ben Franklin contemplates how people can change their mind about things, such as whether it's O.K. to eat animals that have been alive (like fish). He acknowledges that sometimes people are tempted to do something they might think wrong, just as he was tempted by the delightful smell of fish cooking when he was on a boat trip. Franklin also explains that people use reason to approve their actions. His ideas about reason are right. Man frequently employs reason to back up his deeds, whether they are right or wrong. It seems that everyone can find a way to defend their actions. I have personally seen this trait at work, both in myself and my friends.

By using reason, Franklin proved that eating the fish, even though he believed in vegetarianism before, wasn't wrong after all. In the end, Ben Franklin says that it is a good thing that he is a reasonable creature. He means that he was reasonable enough to be open-minded about eating fish; he changed his mind accordingly after listening to his reason. I think Franklin was correct in this point too. It's important to be open-minded about things and not to eliminate what you're willing to try. Like Franklin, we shouldn't be scared to try something new if our reason can explain it to us.

Thus, Ben Franklin shows that reason is a valid tool in helping man to defend his actions, because without reason his actions might be stuck in the same old ways. He would never try some thing new. And Benjamin Franklin, as he was a great man of our country, is someone to whom that was important.

Analysis of the Low-Scoring Essay

This poorly written essay would score in the low range. The first paragraph is ineffective. It fails to address the question of the validity of Franklin's assertions on justifying one's actions through reasoning. The paragraph lacks a thesis and includes such irrelevant information as the reference to Alexander Hamilton. The student also demonstrates a weak command of language, misspelling words such as "Founding Fourfathers."

The second paragraph improves a bit and approaches the topic. Beginning with a paraphrase of Franklin's fish-eating experience, the student gives an opinion on the validity of using reason. But this thesis is especially weak, merely claiming that Franklin was "right." The student offers no evidence to convince the Reader, but rather claims only to have personally seen some examples.

The next paragraph discusses the need for one to be reasonable in order to try new things. The student is on shaky ground once again, exhibiting simplistic ideas with no support.

The conclusion merely summarizes the essay and still avoids the topic. This essay deserves a low score because it offers no proof for its assertions, its treatment of the topic is superficial, and its presentation is riddled with errors and unsophisticated diction. It is a clear example of a score of 4.

Scoring

Use the following worksheet to arrive at a probable final AP grade on Practice Exam 4. Because being objective enough to estimate your own essay score is sometimes difficult, you might give your essays (along with the sample essays) to a teacher, friend, or relative to score, if you feel confident that the individual has the knowledge necessary to make such a judgment and that he or she will feel comfortable doing so.

Section I: Multiple-Choice Questions

$$\underline{\hspace{3cm}} - (\underline{\hspace{3cm}}) = \underline{\hspace{3cm}}$$

    right answers   wrong answers   multiple-choice
                                  raw score

$$\underline{\hspace{3cm}} \times 1.2272 = \underline{\hspace{3cm}} \text{ (of possible 67.5)}$$

    multiple-choice   multiple-choice
      raw score   converted score

Section II: Free-Response Questions

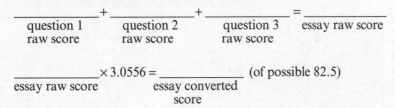

$$\underline{\hspace{2cm}} + \underline{\hspace{2cm}} + \underline{\hspace{2cm}} = \underline{\hspace{2cm}}$$

    question 1   question 2   question 3   essay raw score
    raw score   raw score   raw score

$$\underline{\hspace{3cm}} \times 3.0556 = \underline{\hspace{3cm}} \text{ (of possible 82.5)}$$

    essay raw score   essay converted
                          score

Final Score

$$\underline{\hspace{3cm}} + \underline{\hspace{3cm}} = \underline{\hspace{3cm}} \text{ (of possible 150)}$$

multiple-choice   essay   final
converted score   converted score   converted score

Probable Final AP Score	
Final Converted Score	**Probable AP Score**
150–114	5
113–98	4
97–81	3
80–53	2
52–0	1

Appendix A

Glossary

Terms for the Multiple-Choice and Free-Response Sections

Some of the following terms may be used in the multiple-choice questions and/or answer choices, or in the free-response section instructions. You might choose to incorporate others into your essay writing; for example, to help identify and explain the effect of a literary device used by an author or to help build your argument.

ad hominem argument: From the Latin meaning "to or against the person," this is an argument that appeals to emotion rather than reason, to feeling rather than intellect.

allegory: The device of using character and/or story elements symbolically to represent an abstraction in addition to the literal meaning. In some allegories, for example, an author may intend the characters to personify an abstraction such as hope or freedom. The allegorical meaning usually deals with a moral truth or a generalization about human existence. Allegory is more commonly used in fiction than in nonfiction.

alliteration: The repetition of sounds, especially initial consonant sounds, in two or more neighboring words (as in "she sells seashells"). Although the term is not usually used in the multiple-choice section, you may want to analyze any alliteration you find in any essay passage. The repetition can reinforce meaning, unify ideas, and/or supply a musical sound.

allusion: A direct or indirect reference to something that is presumably commonly known, such as an event, book, myth, place, or work of art. Allusions can be historical (such as referring to Hitler), literary (such as referring to Kurtz in *Heart of Darkness*), religious (such as referring to Noah and the flood), or mythical (such as referring to Atlas). There are, of course, many more possibilities, and a single work may use multiple layers of allusion.

ambiguity: The multiple meanings, either intentional or unintentional, of a word, phrase, sentence, or passage. Ambiguity can also include a sense of uncertainty or inexactness that a work presents.

analogy: A similarity or comparison between two different things or the relationship between them. An analogy can explain something unfamiliar by associating it with, or pointing out its similarity to, something more familiar. Analogies can also make writing more vivid, imaginative, and intellectually engaging.

anaphora: Deliberately repeating beginning clauses or phrases in sentences to create effect. For example, Winston Churchill famously claimed, "We shall not flag or fail. We shall go on to the end. We shall fight in France. We shall fight on the seas and oceans. We shall fight with growing confidence and growing strength in the air. We shall defend our island, whatever the cost shall be." His repetition of "We shall . . ." creates a rhetorical effect of solidarity and determination. See also *epistrophe,* which is the opposite of anaphora.

anecdote: A short, narrative account of an amusing, unusual, revealing, or interesting event. A good anecdote has a single, definite point and is used to clarify abstract points, to humanize individuals so that readers can relate to them, or to create a memorable image in the reader's mind.

antecedent: The word, phrase, or clause referred to by a pronoun. The antecedent of a pronoun will be a noun. The multiple-choice section of the AP exam occasionally asks for the antecedent of a given pronoun in a long, complex sentence or in a group of sentences.

antithesis: A figure of speech involving a seeming contradiction of ideas, words, clauses, or sentences within a balanced grammatical structure. The resulting parallelism serves to emphasize opposition of ideas. The familiar phrase "Man proposes, God disposes" is an example of antithesis, as is John Dryden's description in *The Hind and the Panther:* "Too black for heaven, and yet too white for hell."

aphorism: A terse statement of known authorship that expresses a general truth or moral principle. (If the authorship is unknown, the statement is generally considered to be a folk proverb.) An aphorism can be a memorable summation of the author's point.

apostrophe: A figure of speech that directly addresses an absent or imaginary person or personified abstraction, such as liberty or love, or an inanimate object. The effect may add familiarity or emotional intensity. William Wordsworth addresses John Milton as he writes "Milton, thou shouldst be living at this hour: England hath need of thee," and John Donne speaks directly to death when he writes "Death, be not proud."

asyndeton: A deliberate choice to eliminate conjunctions that would normally join phrases or clauses. It creates speed and urgency. For example, "I came. I saw. I conquered" has much more force than "I came, and then I saw, and then I conquered."

atmosphere: The emotional mood created by the entirety of a literary work, established partly by the setting and partly by the author's choice of objects that are described. Even such elements as a description of the weather can contribute to the atmosphere. Frequently, atmosphere foreshadows events. See also *mood.*

caricature: A representation, especially pictorial or literary, in which the subject's distinctive features or peculiarities are deliberately exaggerated to produce a comic or grotesque effect. Sometimes caricature can be so exaggerated that it becomes a grotesque imitation or misrepresentation. Synonymous words include *burlesque, parody, travesty, satire,* and *lampoon.*

chiasmus: A figure of speech based on inverted parallelism. It is a rhetorical figure in which two clauses are related to each another through a reversal of terms. The purpose is usually to make a larger point or to provide balance or order. In classical rhetoric, the parallel structures did not repeat words, such as is found in Alexander Pope's *Essay on Man:* "His time a moment, and a point his space." However, contemporary standards allow for repeated words; a commonly cited example comes from John F. Kennedy's inaugural address: ". . . ask not what your country can do for you—ask what you can do for your country."

clause: A grammatical unit that contains both a subject and a verb. An independent, or main, clause expresses a complete thought and can stand alone as a sentence. A dependent, or subordinate, clause cannot stand alone as a sentence and must be accompanied by an independent clause. Examine this sample sentence: "Because I practiced hard, my AP scores were high." In this sentence, the independent clause is "my AP scores were high," and the dependent (or subordinate) clause is "Because I practiced hard." See also *subordinate clause.*

colloquialism: Slang or informality in speech or writing. Not generally acceptable for formal writing, colloquialisms give language a conversational, familiar tone. Colloquial expressions in writing include local or regional dialects.

conceit: A fanciful expression, usually in the form of an extended metaphor or a surprising analogy between seemingly dissimilar objects. A conceit displays intellectual cleverness due to the unusual comparison being made.

connotation: The nonliteral, associative meaning of a word; the implied, suggested meaning. Connotations may involve ideas, emotions, or attitudes. See also *denotation.*

deductive reasoning: The process of logic in which one takes a rule for a large, general category and assumes that specific individual examples within that general category obey the same rule. For example, a general rule might be that "Objects made of iron will rust." The logician who then encounters a shovel made of iron can assume deductively that the iron shovel will rust just as other iron objects do. Deduction determines the truth about specific examples using a large general rule. See its opposite, *inductive reasoning.*

denotation: The strict, literal, dictionary definition of a word, devoid of any emotion, attitude, or color. See also *connotation.*

diction: Related to style, diction refers to the writer's particular word choices, especially with regard to their correctness, clearness, or effectiveness. For the AP Language and Composition Exam, you should be able to describe an author's diction (for example, formal or informal, ornate or plain) and understand the ways in which diction can complement the writer's purpose. Diction, combined with syntax, figurative language, literary devices, and so on, creates a writer's style. See also *syntax.*

didactic: From the Greek, "didactic" literally means "instructive." Didactic works have the primary aim of teaching or instructing, especially teaching moral or ethical principles.

epistrophe: Deliberately repeating ending clauses or phrases in sentences to create effect. For example, President Lyndon B. Johnson used epistrophe that urged people to come together for a common cause when he addressed the U.S. Congress in 1965: "There is no Negro problem. There is no Southern problem. There is no Northern problem. There is only an American problem. And we are met here tonight as Americans—not as Democrats or Republicans—we are met here as Americans to solve that problem." See also its opposite, *anaphora.*

ethos: From the Greek word for "character," ethos is one of the three rhetorical appeals, coined by Aristotle, that refer to the ways a writer or speaker persuades a reader or an audience. Ethos establishes credibility and believability and sets up trust. The word "ethic" comes from "ethos." See also *logos* and *pathos.*

euphemism: From the Greek for "good speech," euphemisms are a more agreeable or less offensive substitute for generally unpleasant words or concepts. A euphemism may be used to adhere to standards of social or political correctness, or to add humor or ironic understatement. Saying "earthly remains" rather than "corpse" is an example of a euphemism.

extended metaphor: A metaphor developed at great length, occurring frequently in or throughout a work. See also *metaphor.*

figurative language: Writing or speech that is not intended to carry a literal meaning and is usually meant to be imaginative and vivid. See also *figure of speech.*

figure of speech: A device used to produce figurative language. Many figures of speech compare dissimilar things. Figures of speech include the following: *apostrophe, hyperbole, irony, metaphor, metonymy, oxymoron, paradox, personification, simile, synecdoche,* and *understatement.*

generic conventions: This term describes traditions for each genre. These conventions help to define each genre; for example, they differentiate between an essay and journalistic writing or an autobiography and political writing. On the AP Language and Composition Exam, try to distinguish the unique features of a writer's work from those dictated by convention.

genre: The major category into which a literary work fits. The basic divisions of literature are prose, poetry, and drama. However, "genre" is a flexible term; within these broad boundaries are many subdivisions that are often called genres themselves. For example, prose can be divided into fiction (novels and short stories) or nonfiction (essays, biographies, autobiographies, and so on). Poetry can be divided into such subcategories as lyric, dramatic, narrative, epic, and so on. Drama can be divided into tragedy, comedy, melodrama, farce, and so on. On the AP Language and Composition Exam, expect the majority of the passages to be from the following genres: autobiography, biography, diaries, criticism, and essays, as well as journalistic, political, scientific, and nature writing.

homily: This term literally means "sermon," but more informally, it can include any serious talk, speech, or lecture involving moral or spiritual advice.

hyperbole: A figure of speech using deliberate exaggeration or overstatement. Hyperbole often has a comic effect; however, a serious effect is also possible. Often, hyperbole produces irony at the same time.

imagery: The sensory details or figurative language used to describe, arouse emotion, or represent abstractions. On a physical level, imagery uses terms related to the five senses: visual, auditory, tactile, gustatory, or olfactory imagery. On a broader and deeper level, however, one image can represent more than one thing. For example, a rose may present visual imagery while also representing the color in a woman's cheeks. An author, therefore, may use complex imagery while simultaneously employing other figures of speech, especially metaphor and simile. In addition, this term can apply to the total of all the images in a work. On the AP Language and Composition Exam, pay attention to *how* an author creates imagery and the effect of that imagery.

inductive reasoning: The process of logic that begins reasoning from a specific case or cases and then derives a general rule or prediction that may or may not necessarily be true. It draws inferences from observations in order to make generalizations. Induction uses evidence more than logic when it says "A, B, and C are true, so D should also be true." This can result in a more uncertain conclusion than the more certain *deductive reasoning*. Inductive arguments are, hence, always open to question since the conclusion is a larger idea than the evidence on which it is based. This breadth allows it to be used where deductive methods may not work; for example, in prediction or invention. One advantage of inductive reasoning is that starting from specifics and building up to a larger generality can be less threatening than starting with the big ideas, which can make inductive arguments more persuasive, as people may understand the process better than a more clinical deduction.

infer: To draw a reasonable conclusion from the information presented. When a multiple-choice question asks for an inference to be drawn from the passage, the most direct, most reasonable inference is the safest answer choice. If an inference is implausible, it's unlikely to be the correct answer. Note that if the answer choice is something that is directly stated in the passage, it is *not* inferred and is, therefore, not the correct answer.

invective: An emotionally violent, verbal denunciation or attack using strong, abusive language.

irony: The contrast between what is stated explicitly and what is really meant; the difference between what appears to be and what is actually true. Irony is used for many reasons, but frequently, it's used to create poignancy or humor. In general, three major types of irony are used in language:

1. In *verbal* irony, the words literally state the opposite of the writer's (or speaker's) true meaning.

2. In *situational* irony, events turn out the opposite of what was expected. What the characters and readers think ought to happen does not actually happen.

3. In *dramatic* irony, facts or events are unknown to a character in a play or piece of fiction but known to the reader, audience, or other characters in the work.

jargon: The specific words or phrases used in a trade, occupation, or field of study, such as sports jargon, medical jargon, police jargon, or military jargon. To the uninitiated, these phrases can sometimes be confusing.

juxtaposition: Placing dissimilar items, descriptions, or ideas close together or side by side, especially for comparison or contrast.

logical fallacy: A mistake in verbal reasoning. Technically, to be a fallacy, the reasoning must be potentially deceptive; it must be likely to fool at least some of the people some of the time. Many types of logical fallacies (which you can easily look up) have been identified, such as *ad hominem argument,* appeals to emotion, bandwagon, begging the question, circular reasoning, hasty generalization, non sequitur argument, post hoc argument, slippery slope, or straw man argument.

logos: One of Aristotle's three rhetorical appeals that refer to the ways a writer or speaker persuades a reader or an audience. Logos, the appeal to logic, means to convince an audience by use of logic or reason, such as citing facts and statistics, historical and literal analogies, or certain authorities on a subject. "Logos" is the Greek word for "word." The word "logic" is derived from "logos." See also *ethos* and *pathos.*

loose sentence: A type of sentence in which the main idea (independent clause) comes first, followed by dependent grammatical units such as phrases and clauses. If a period were placed at the end of the independent clause, the clause would be a complete sentence. A work containing many loose sentences often seems informal, relaxed, and conversational. See also *periodic sentence.*

metaphor: A figure of speech using implied comparison of seemingly unlike things or the substitution of one for the other, suggesting some similarity. For example, consider the title of Carson McCullers' novel *The Heart Is a Lonely Hunter*. Metaphorical language makes writing more vivid, imaginative, thought-provoking, and meaningful. See also *simile.*

metonymy: A term from the Greek meaning "changed label" or "substitute name," metonymy is a figure of speech in which the name of one object is substituted for that of another closely associated with it. A news release that claims "the White House declared" rather than "the President declared" is using metonymy. This term is unlikely to be used in the multiple-choice section, but you might see examples of metonymy in an essay passage. See also *synecdoche.*

modes of discourse: This term encompasses the four traditional categories of written texts. See also *rhetorical modes.*

1. Exposition, which refers to writing that intends to inform and demonstrate a point
2. Narration, which refers to writing that tells a story or relates a series of events
3. Description, which refers to writing that creates sensory images, often evoking a mood or atmosphere
4. Argumentation, which refers to writing that takes a stand on an issue and supports it with evidence and logical reasoning

mood: This term has two distinct technical meanings in English writing. The first meaning is grammatical and deals with verbal units and a speaker's attitude. The *indicative* mood is used only for factual sentences. For example, "Joe eats too quickly." The *subjunctive* mood is used for a doubtful or conditional attitude. For example, "If I were you, I'd get another job." The *imperative* mood is used for commands. For example, "Shut the door!" The second meaning of mood is literary, meaning the prevailing atmosphere or emotional aura of a work. Setting, tone, and events can affect the mood. In this usage, mood is similar to tone and atmosphere.

narrative: The telling of a story or an account of an event or series of events.

onomatopoeia: A figure of speech in which natural sounds are imitated in the sounds of words. Simple examples include such words as "buzz," "hiss," "hum," "crack," "whinny," and "murmur." This term usually is not used in the multiple-choice section. If you identify examples of onomatopoeia in an essay passage, note the effect.

oxymoron: From the Greek for "pointedly foolish," an oxymoron is a figure of speech in which the writer groups apparently contradictory terms to suggest a paradox. Simple examples include "jumbo shrimp" and "cruel kindness." This term usually does not appear in the multiple-choice questions, but there is a chance you will see it used by an author in an essay passage or find it useful in your own essay writing.

paradox: A statement that appears to be self-contradictory or opposed to common sense, but upon closer inspection contains some degree of truth or validity. The first scene of *Macbeth,* for example, closes with the witches' cryptic remark, "Fair is foul, and foul is fair. . . ."

parallelism: Also referred to as parallel construction or parallel structure, this term comes from Greek roots meaning "beside one another." It refers to the grammatical or rhetorical framing of words, phrases, sentences, or paragraphs to give structural similarity. This can involve, but is not limited to, repetition of a grammatical element such as a preposition or a verbal phrase. A famous example of parallelism begins Charles Dickens' novel *A Tale of Two Cities:* "It was the best of times, it was the worst of times, it was the age of wisdom, it was the age of foolishness, it was the epoch of belief, it was the epoch of incredulity. . . ." The effects of parallelism are numerous, but, frequently, parallelism acts as an organizing force to attract the reader's attention, add emphasis and organization, or simply provide a pleasing musical rhythm. Another famous example comes from the concluding line of Tennyson's poem "Ulysses," as the speaker claims, "To strive, to seek, to find, and not to yield." Many specific terms identify different forms of parallelism, such as *anaphora, asyndeton, epistrophe,* and *symploce.* See also *antithesis* and *chiasmus.*

parody: A work that closely imitates the style or content of another work with the specific aim of comic effect and/or ridicule. As comedy, parody distorts or exaggerates distinctive features of the original. As ridicule, it mimics the work by repeating and borrowing words, phrases, or characteristics in order to illuminate weaknesses in the original. Well-written parody offers insight into the original, but poorly written parody offers only ineffectual imitation. Usually an audience must grasp literary allusion and understand the work being parodied to fully appreciate the nuances of the newer work. Occasionally, however, parodies take on a life of their own and don't require knowledge of the original.

pathos: One of Aristotle's three rhetorical appeals, pathos is a writer's or speaker's attempt to inspire an emotional reaction in an audience—often a deep feeling of suffering, but sometimes joy, pride, anger, humor, patriotism, or any other strong emotion. In its critical sense, pathos signifies a scene or passage designed to evoke the feeling of pity or sympathetic sorrow in a reader or viewer. "Pathos" is the Greek word for both "suffering" and "experience." The words "empathy" and "pathetic" are derived from "pathos." See also *ethos* and *logos.*

pedantic: An adjective that describes words, phrases, or a general tone that is overly scholarly, academic, or bookish.

periodic sentence: A sentence that presents its central meaning in a main clause at the end. An independent clause, it is preceded by a phrase or clause that cannot stand alone. For example, "Ecstatic with my AP scores, I let out a loud shout of joy!" The effect of a periodic sentence is to add emphasis and structural variety. See also *loose sentence.*

personification: A figure of speech in which the writer presents or describes concepts, animals, or inanimate objects by endowing them with human attributes or emotions. Personification is used to make these abstractions, animals, or objects appear more vivid to the reader.

point of view: In fictional literature, this is the perspective from which a story is told. There are two general divisions of point of view, first-person narrator and third-person narrator, and many subdivisions within those. However, on the AP English Language and Composition Exam, the term *point of view* is synonymous with the author's *attitude.*

polysyndeton: Deliberately using many conjunctions to join items in a sentence to create an overwhelming effect. For example, Cormac McCarthy used polysyndeton in this passage from his novel *The Crossing:* "He got the fire going and lifted the wolf from the sheet and took the sheet to the creek and crouched in the dark and washed the blood out of it and brought it back and he cut forked sticks from a mountain hackberry and drove them into the ground with a rock and hung the sheet on a trestlepole . . ." Notice how joining every action with the conjunction "and" separates and intensifies the actions.

predicate adjective: One type of subject complement—an adjective, group of adjectives, or adjective clause that follows a linking verb. It is in the predicate of the sentence, and modifies or describes the subject. For example, in the sentence "My boyfriend is tall, dark, and handsome," the group of predicate adjectives ("tall, dark, and handsome") describes "boyfriend."

predicate nominative: A second type of subject complement—a noun, group of nouns, or noun clause that renames the subject. It, like the predicate adjective, follows a linking verb and is located in the predicate of the sentence. For example, in the sentence "Abe Lincoln was a man of integrity," the predicate nominative is "man of integrity," as it renames Abe Lincoln. Occasionally, this term or the term *predicate adjective* appears in a multiple-choice question.

prose: One of the major divisions of genre, prose refers to fiction and nonfiction, including all its forms, because they are written in ordinary language and most closely resemble everyday speech. Technically, anything that isn't poetry or drama is prose. Therefore, all passages in the AP Language and Composition Exam are prose. Of course, prose writers often borrow poetic and dramatic elements.

repetition: The duplication, either exact or approximate, of any element of language, such as a sound, word, phrase, clause, sentence, or grammatical pattern. When repetition is poorly done, it bores, but when it's well done, it links and emphasizes ideas while giving the reader the comfort of recognizing something familiar. See also *parallelism.*

rhetoric: From the Greek for "orator," this term describes the principles governing the art of writing effectively, eloquently, and persuasively.

rhetorical modes: This flexible term describes the variety, conventions, and purposes of the major kinds of writing. Sometimes referred to as *modes of discourse,* the four most common rhetorical modes and their purposes are as follows:

1. The purpose of *exposition* (or expository writing) is to explain and analyze information by presenting an idea, relevant evidence, and appropriate discussion. The AP Language and Composition Exam essay questions are frequently set up as expository topics.
2. The purpose of *argumentation* is to prove the validity of an idea or point of view by presenting sound reasoning, thoughtful discussion, and insightful argument that thoroughly convince the reader. Persuasive writing is a type of argumentation that has the additional aim of urging some form of action. Many AP Language and Composition Exam free-response questions ask you to form an argument.

3. The purpose of *description* is to recreate, invent, or visually present a person, place, event, or action so that the reader can picture what is being described. Sometimes a writer engages all five senses in description; good descriptive writing can be sensuous and picturesque. Descriptive writing may be straightforward and objective or highly emotional and subjective.

4. The purpose of *narration* is to tell a story or narrate an event or series of events. This writing mode frequently uses the tools of descriptive writing.

rhetorical question: A question that is asked merely for effect and does not expect a reply. The answer is assumed. For example, in Shakespeare's *Julius Caesar,* the character Brutus asks, "Who is here so vile that will not love his country?"

sarcasm: From the Greek meaning "to tear flesh," sarcasm often involves bitter, caustic language that is meant to hurt or ridicule someone or something. It may use irony as a device, but not all ironic statements are sarcastic (that is, intending to ridicule). When well done, sarcasm can be witty and insightful; when poorly done, it's simply cruel.

satire: A work that targets human vices and follies, or social institutions and conventions, for reform or ridicule. Regardless of whether or not the work aims to reform humans or their society, satire is best seen as a style of writing rather than a purpose for writing. It can be recognized by the many devices used effectively by the satirist, such as irony, wit, parody, caricature, hyperbole, understatement, and sarcasm. The effects of satire are varied, depending on the writer's goal, but good satire—often humorous—is thought-provoking and insightful about the human condition.

simile: An explicit comparison, normally using "like," "as," or "if." For example, remember Robert Burns' famous lines, "O, my love is like a red, red rose / That's newly sprung in June. / O, my love is like a melody, / That's sweetly played in tune." See also *metaphor.*

subject complement: The word (with any accompanying phrases) or clause that follows a linking verb and complements, or completes, the subject of the sentence by either (1) renaming it or (2) describing it. The former is technically called a predicate nominative, the latter a predicate adjective. See also *predicate nominative* and *predicate adjective* for examples of sentences. This term is occasionally used in a multiple-choice question.

subordinate clause: Like all clauses, this word group contains both a subject and a verb (plus any accompanying phrases or modifiers). But unlike the independent clause, the subordinate clause cannot stand alone; it does not express a complete thought. Also called a dependent clause, the subordinate clause depends on a main clause, sometimes called an independent clause, to complete its meaning. Easily recognized key words and phrases usually begin these clauses—for example: "although," "because," "unless," "if," "even though," "since," "as soon as," "while," "who," "when," "where," "how," and "that." See also *clause.*

syllogism: From the Greek for "reckoning together," a syllogism (or syllogistic reasoning) is a deductive system of formal logic that presents two premises—the first one called major and the second minor—that inevitably lead to a sound conclusion. A frequently cited example proceeds as follows:

- Major premise: All men are mortal.
- Minor premise: Socrates is a man.
- Conclusion: Therefore, Socrates is mortal.

A syllogism's conclusion is valid only if each of the two premises is valid. Syllogisms may also present the specific idea first ("Socrates") and the general idea second ("All men").

symbol: Generally, a symbol is anything that represents or stands for something else. Usually, it is something concrete—such as an object, action, character, or scene—that represents something more abstract. However, symbols and symbolism can be much more complex. One system classifies symbols into three categories:

1. *Natural* symbols use objects and occurrences from nature to represent ideas commonly associated with them (such as dawn symbolizing hope or a new beginning, a rose symbolizing love, a tree symbolizing knowledge).

2. *Conventional* symbols are those that have been invested with meaning by a group (religious symbols, such as a cross or Star of David; national symbols, such as a flag or an eagle; or group symbols, such as skull and crossbones for pirates or the scales of justice for lawyers).

3. *Literary* symbols are sometimes also conventional in the sense that they are found in a variety of works and are generally recognized. However, an individual work's symbols may be more complicated, such as the whale in *Moby Dick* and the jungle in *Heart of Darkness*. On the AP Language and Composition Exam, try to determine what abstraction an object symbolizes and to what extent it is successful in representing that abstraction.

symploce: A type of *parallelism* that combines *anaphora* and *epistrophe,* symploce occurs when words or phrases are repeated at both the beginning and at the ending of clauses or verses. President Bill Clinton used symploce in a prayer service at Oklahoma City in 1995 when he said, "When there is talk of hatred, let us stand up and talk against it. When there is violence, let us stand up and talk against it."

synecdoche: A rhetorical figure of speech in which a part of an object represents the whole, or the whole of an object may be used to represent a part. For example, a cowboy who boasts of owning "sixty head of cattle" is not referring to their heads alone, but sixty living, whole cows. See also *metonymy*.

syntax: The way a writer chooses to join words into phrases, clauses, and sentences. In other words, syntax refers to the arrangement or order of grammatical elements in a sentence. Syntax is similar to *diction,* but you can differentiate the two by thinking of syntax as referring to groups of words, while diction refers to individual words. In the multiple-choice section of the AP Language and Composition Exam, expect to be asked some questions about how an author manipulates syntax. In the free-response section, you will need to analyze how syntax produces effects. When you are analyzing syntax, consider such elements as the length or brevity of sentences, unusual sentence constructions, the sentence patterns used, and the kinds of sentences the author uses. The author may use questions, declarations, exclamations, or rhetorical questions; sentences are also classified as periodic or loose, simple, compound, or complex. Syntax can be tricky for students to analyze. First try to classify what kind of sentences the author uses, and then try to determine how the author's choices amplify meaning—in other words, why they work well for the author's purpose.

theme: The central idea or message of a work, the insight it offers into life. Usually, the theme is unstated in fictional works, but in nonfiction, the theme may be directly stated, especially in expository or argumentative writing. Frequently, a theme can be stated as a universal truth; that is, a general statement about the human condition, society, or humanity's relationship to the natural world.

thesis: In expository writing, the thesis statement is the sentence or group of sentences that directly express the writer's opinion, purpose, meaning, or proposition. Expository writing is usually judged by analyzing how accurately, effectively, and thoroughly a writer has proven the thesis.

tone: Similar to mood, tone describes the writer's attitude toward his or her material, the audience, or both. Tone is easier to determine in spoken language than in written language. Considering how a work would sound if it were read aloud can help identify a writer's tone. Some words describing tone are "playful," "serious," "businesslike," "sarcastic," "humorous," "formal," "ornate," and "somber." As with attitude, a writer's tone in the exam's passages can rarely be described by one word. Expect that an explanation will be more complex. See *attitude* in "Terms for the Free-Response Section," on the next page.

transition: A word or phrase that links different ideas, a transition is used especially, although not exclusively, in expository and argumentative writing. Transitions effectively signal a shift from one idea to another. A few commonly used transitional words or phrases include the following: "furthermore," "consequently," "nevertheless," "for example," "in addition," "likewise," "similarly," and "on the contrary."

understatement: The ironic minimizing of fact, understatement presents something as less significant than it actually is. The effect can frequently be humorous and emphatic. Understatement is the opposite of *hyperbole.* Two specific types of understatement exist:

1. *Litotes* is a figure of speech by which an affirmation is made indirectly by denying its opposite. It uses understatement for emphasis, frequently with a negative assertion. For example, "It was no mean feat" means it was quite hard. "He was not averse to drink" means he drank a lot.

2. *Meiosis,* the Greek term for "understatement" or "belittling," is a rhetorical figure by which something is referred to in terms less important than it really deserves. It describes something that is very impressive with its simplicity. An example is when Mercutio calls his mortal wound a "scratch" in *Romeo and Juliet.*

wit: In modern usage, wit is intellectually amusing language that surprises and delights. A witty statement is humorous, while suggesting the speaker's verbal power in creating ingenious and perceptive remarks. Wit usually uses terse language that makes a pointed statement. Historically, wit meant basic understanding. Its meaning evolved to include speed of understanding, and finally (in the early 17th century), it grew to mean quick perception, including creative fancy.

Terms for the Free-Response Section

The following words and phrases have appeared in recent AP Language and Composition Exam essay prompts. Although what follows is not a comprehensive list of every word or phrase you might encounter, it will help you understand what you're being asked to do for a topic.

argument: In the AP free-response section, this is a global term for one of your essays (also called an argumentation or argumentative essay) in which you will establish an assertion (or group of assertions) and support that idea with evidence and logical explanation. The phrasing in the prompt you will often see on the exam asks you to "defend, challenge, or qualify" an idea (or ideas). See Chapter 2 for a complete discussion of the argument essay.

attitude: A writer's intellectual position or emotion regarding the subject of the writing. In the free-response section, expect to be asked what the writer's attitude is and how his or her language conveys that attitude. Also be aware that, although the singular term "attitude" is used in this definition and on the exam, the passage will rarely have only one attitude. More often than not, the writer's attitude will be more complex, and the student who presents this complexity—no matter how subtle the differences—will appear to be more astute than the student who only uses one adjective to describe attitude. Of course, don't force an attitude for which there is no evidence in the passage; instead, understand that an accurate statement of a writer's attitude is not likely to be a blatantly obvious idea. If it were that simple, the exam committee wouldn't ask you to discuss it.

audience: The person(s) who is reading a text, listening to a speaker, or observing a performance. On the AP English Language and Composition Exam, be aware of who would most likely be eager to read or hear the passage.

concrete detail: Strictly defined, concrete refers to nouns that name physical objects—a bridge, a book, or a coat. Concrete nouns are the opposite of abstract nouns (which refer to concepts like freedom and love). However, as used in the free-response section of the AP Language and Composition Exam, this term has a slightly different connotation. The directions may read something like this: "Provide concrete details that will convince the reader." This means that your essay should include details from the passage; at times, you'll be allowed to provide details from your own awareness of the world—from your readings, observations, experiences, and so forth.

descriptive detail: When an essay prompt uses this phrase, look for the writer's sensory description. Descriptive details appealing to the visual sense are usually the most predominant, but don't overlook other sensory details. As usual, after you identify a passage's descriptive details, analyze their effect.

device: Devices are the figures of speech, syntax, diction, and other stylistic elements that collectively produce a particular artistic effect.

language: When you're asked to "analyze the language," concentrate on how the elements of language combine to form a whole—how diction, syntax, figurative language, and sentence structure create a cumulative effect.

narrative device: The tools of the storyteller (also used in nonfiction), such as ordering events so that they build to a climactic moment or withholding information until a crucial or appropriate moment when revealing it creates a desired effect. On the essay portion of the exam, this term may also apply to biographical and autobiographical writing.

narrative technique: The style of telling the story, even if the passage is nonfiction. Concentrate on the order of events and on their detail in evaluating a writer's technique.

persuasive device: When asked to analyze an author's persuasive devices, look for the words in the passage that have strong connotations—words that intensify the emotional effect. For example, consider the different connotations in the terms "civil war," "rebellion," and "revolution." In addition, analyze how these words complement the writer's argument as it builds logically. Speeches are often used in this context because they are generally designed to persuade.

persuasive essay: When asked to write a persuasive essay, you should present a coherent argument in which the evidence builds to a logical and relevant conclusion. Strong persuasive essays often appeal to the audience's emotions or ethical standards.

resources of language: This phrase refers to all the devices of composition available to a writer, such as diction, syntax, sentence structure, and figures of speech. The cumulative effect of a work is produced by the resources of language a writer chooses.

rhetorical features: This phrase refers to how a passage is constructed. If you are asked to consider rhetorical features or structure, look at the passage's organization and how the writer combines images, details, or arguments to serve his or her purpose.

rhetorical strategies: This phrase, used to identify one of the three essays you will write in the free-response section of the exam (and sometimes used in the multiple-choice section), is a global term that refers to all the strategies a writer can use. See Chapter 2 for a complete discussion of the rhetorical strategies essay. The term basically encompasses three elements:

1. *Structure,* which refers to the writer's organization
2. *Purpose,* which refers to why the writer wrote the piece and his or her goal
3. *Style,* which is made up of many elements such as diction, syntax, figurative language, attitude, tone, pacing, selection of detail, and modes of discourse

sentence structure: If appropriate in your essay analysis, look at the type of sentences the author uses. Remember that the basic sentence structures are simple, compound, and complex, and variations are created by combining sentences. Also consider variation (or lack of it) in sentence length; any unusual devices in sentence construction, such as repetition or inverted word order; and any unusual word or phrase placement. As with all devices, be prepared to discuss the effect of the sentence structure. For example, a series of short, simple sentences or phrases can produce a feeling of speed and choppiness, which may suit the author's purpose. This type of analysis is most appropriate for the rhetorical strategies essay prompt.

stylistic devices: An essay prompt that mentions stylistic devices is asking you to note and analyze all of the elements in language that contribute to style—such as diction, syntax, tone, attitude, figures of speech, connotations, and repetition.

synthesis: One of the three essay types you will be asked to write on the essay portion of the AP exam. After reading the given sources that relate to the same issue(s), you will combine, synthesize, and analyze the information from at least three of the sources as you develop your position and your unique perspective on the issue(s). See Chapter 2 for a complete discussion of the synthesis essay.

Past AP Essay Topics

In the following chart, presented in reverse chronological order, you will find a paraphrasing of every AP English Language and Composition essay topic since 2008. Although an exact topic is never reused, when you read this information you should look for trends and patterns in the essay topics. Examine the different modes the essay category requires. For example, understand the difference between writing a synthesis essay, a rhetorical strategies essay, and an argument essay. Be aware that the real exam will not be printed like this; it will not label the topic as a "synthesis" topic, a "rhetorical strategies" topic, or an "argument" topic. However, you should be able to understand what category the topic fits into from your practice.

The topics are printed in the same order as they appeared on the actual exam for each year.

Year	Question Category	Passage (Title of Passage and Author)/Topic
2017	Synthesis	Consider to what extent the Internet age has changed the role of public libraries, examining their relevance in today's society and any ways in which they might change to meet the needs of a transforming world. Develop a position that discusses the function, if any, that public libraries should serve in the future.
	Rhetorical Strategies	In 1960, Clare Boothe Luce, an American journalist and politician, delivered a speech to the Women's National Press Club in which she decried the penchant of the American press to sacrifice journalistic integrity in favor of what is perceived as the public's demand for sensational stories. The introduction to her speech is presented. Analyze how Luce uses her opening to prepare the audience for her message.
	Argument	In an excerpt from *Empire of Illusion,* author Chris Hedges presents the idea that artifice is the most important skill for politicians to use when trying to persuade the public. He points out that successful politicians need to have a narrative, whether it is accurate or not, and that mastering the art of entertainment is essential to being perceived as real and honest; actual sincerity and competency are not necessary, but the appearance of these qualities is. Using appropriate and specific evidence, develop your position on the truthfulness of Hedges' ideas.
2016	Synthesis	English has become the dominant global language in such fields as international finance, science, and politics over the last several decades. Concurrently, learning a foreign language in English-speaking countries has declined. Develop your position on whether monolingual English speakers are at a disadvantage in today's world.
	Rhetorical Strategies	The eulogy written by Margaret Thatcher, the former prime minister of Great Britain, and delivered to the American people in honor of former U.S. President Ronald Reagan is presented. Analyze the rhetorical strategies Thatcher uses as she memorializes the leader with whom she had worked closely.
	Argument	In 1891, Irish author Oscar Wilde claimed that disobedience is a virtue that eventually promotes social progress. Using appropriate examples, present your stand on the extent to which you feel Wilde's assertion is valid.

continued

Year	Question Category	Passage (Title of Passage and Author)/Topic
2015	Synthesis	Consider that the intended purpose of honor codes or honor systems in schools, colleges, and universities is to cultivate integrity. Develop a position on whether or not your school should institute, uphold, amend, or abolish an honor code or honor system.
	Rhetorical Strategies	An article written by the labor union organizer and civil rights leader Cesar Chavez on the tenth anniversary of Martin Luther King Jr.'s assassination is excerpted. Analyze the rhetorical strategies Chavez uses to present his stand on nonviolent resistance.
	Argument	An anthropologist who studied first-year university students observed that their friendly greetings, such as "How are you?" and "Let's get in touch," were not intended to be literal, but merely polite. Develop your position on the role and value of polite speech within a culture or community with which you are familiar. Use appropriate examples for support.
2014	Synthesis	In light of the fact that many recent college graduates face a dim prospect for employment, develop a position on the value of a college education, given its cost. Consider to what degree college helps students prepare for more than just a job.
	Rhetorical Strategies	A letter of advice from Abigail Adams to her son, John Quincy Adams, is reproduced. Her son was traveling with his father, John Adams, who was, at the time, a U.S. diplomat and later the second U.S. president. She urges her son to use adversity to grow, mature, and develop virtue. Analyze the rhetorical strategies Adams uses to offer advice.
	Argument	In 2010, authors Po Bronson and Ashley Merryman published a *Newsweek* article that laments the decline in the public's "creativity quotient" since 1990. The article explores the far-ranging need for creativity in solving many of the world's problems. While explaining your definition of creativity, write a letter to your school board taking a stand on whether or not the creation of a class in creative thinking is advisable.
2013	Synthesis	Examine what factors any group or agency should contemplate when choosing to create a monument to honor great achievements or deep sacrifice, and also discuss what considerations need to be addressed in the creation of any monument of an event or person.
	Rhetorical Strategies	In a passage from Richard Louv's 2008 book, *Last Child in the Woods,* he laments the separation between people and nature. Analyze the rhetorical strategies Louv uses to advance his point.
	Argument	Three positions on the relationship between ownership and one's sense of self are presented. Plato argues that owning material objects damages a person's character. Aristotle counters that owning tangible objects helps to develop moral character. Jean-Paul Sartre suggests that ownership extends beyond the tangible, and that to master some skill equates to "owning" it. Develop a position on the relationship between ownership and personality, using examples from your reading, experiences, or observations to support your opinion.

Year	Question Category	Passage (Title of Passage and Author)/Topic
2012	Synthesis	Develop a position on whether or not the delivery days and services of the United States Postal Service should be restructured because of the decreased volume that the post office has faced over the last decade.
	Rhetorical Strategies	Opening remarks from President John F. Kennedy's news conference in 1962 are presented. The president criticized the nation's largest steel companies for raising steel prices, and he urged stable prices and wages during a period of economic instability. Analyze the rhetorical strategies President Kennedy used to convey his thoughts.
	Argument	Two different perspectives are presented. William Lyon Phelps, an American educator and writer, states that one can accomplish anything if one has an absolute sense of certainty and powerful beliefs. Bertrand Russell, a British author, mathematician, and philosopher, counters that people need to contemplate their opinions with a degree of doubt. Develop a position on the relationship between certainty and doubt. Use appropriate evidence to support your stand.
2011	Synthesis	Locavores are people who, considering nutrition as well as sustainability, have decided to eat locally grown or produced products as often as possible. Identify the key issues associated with the locavore movement and examine their implications for the community.
	Rhetorical Strategies	A speech to the convention of the National American Woman Suffrage Association in Philadelphia on July 22, 1905, is presented by Florence Kelley, a U.S. social worker and reformer who fought successfully for child labor laws and improved conditions for working women. Analyze the rhetorical strategies Kelley uses to convey her message about child labor to her audience.
	Argument	A passage from *Rights of Man,* a book written by the pamphleteer Thomas Paine in 1791 after the American Revolution, is presented. In it he claims one would think that America is least likely to have unity, given that its people are from different backgrounds, speak different languages, and worship different religions; however, he asserts America does have unity, which comes from a government that is based on the needs of society and basic rights of man. Paine asserts that in America the poor are not oppressed, the rich not privileged, and that taxes are few, resulting in no need for riots. Examine the extent to which Paine's characterization of America holds true today. Use appropriate evidence to support your argument.
2010	Synthesis	Given the pros and cons of modern, fast-paced information technology, evaluate the most important factors that a school should consider before using particular technologies in curriculum and instruction.
	Rhetorical Strategies	A 1791 letter is presented from Benjamin Banneker, the son of former slaves who became a farmer, astronomer, mathematician, surveyor, and author, to Thomas Jefferson. Analyze the ways in which Banneker uses rhetorical strategies to argue against slavery.
	Argument	A quotation from Alain de Botton's 2004 book, *Status Anxiety,* posits that, since humorists can say things others cannot or will not, the primary goal of humorists is not simply to entertain but to present "with impunity" ideas that might be "dangerous or impossible to state directly." Defend, challenge, or qualify de Botton's claim about the vital role of humorists in society. Use specific, appropriate evidence to develop your position.

continued

Year	Question Category	Passage (Title of Passage and Author)/Topic
2009	Synthesis	Develop a position about what issues, such as ethical and financial considerations, should be considered most important in making decisions about space exploration.
	Rhetorical Strategies	Two passages that satirize the language of two groups that hold opposing attitudes about environmentalism are presented from Edward O. Wilson's 2002 book, *The Future of Life*. Analyze how Wilson's satire illustrates the unproductive nature of such discussions.
	Argument	A quotation from the Roman poet Horace claims people's talents rise to the occasion when faced with adversity. Defend, challenge, or qualify Horace's assertion about the role that adversity plays in developing a person's character. Perhaps consider problems such as financial difficulty, political hardship, danger, or misfortune. Use appropriate evidence from your reading, observation, and/or experience.
2008	Synthesis	Develop a position on whether or not the penny coin should be eliminated.
	Rhetorical Strategies	A passage is presented from *The Great Influenza,* in which author John M. Barry writes about scientists and their research in the 1918 flu epidemic. Analyze the ways in which Barry uses rhetorical strategies to describe scientific research.
	Argument	Evaluate the advantages and disadvantages of corporate sponsorship for schools and point out why you find one position more credible than the other.

Suggested Reading List

Following is a list of important authors and some of their works that are similar to those used on the AP English Language and Composition Exam. The list is not meant to be all-inclusive or required reading for every student, but reading extensively from works on this list and analyzing the authors' use of language will be excellent preparation for the exam. These works are largely available from reputable libraries and online sources such as Project Gutenberg (www.gutenberg.org).

Autobiography, Biography, Journal, and History

Maya Angelou

Gather Together in My Name

The Heart of a Woman

I Know Why the Caged Bird Sings

Singin' and Swingin' and Gettin' Merry Like Christmas

Any of her speeches

Walter Jackson Bate

John Keats

Samuel Johnson

Charles A. Beard

An Economic Interpretation of the Constitution of the United States

The Rise of American Civilization (with Mary R. Beard)

James Boswell

The Life of Samuel Johnson

Van Wyck Brooks

An Autobiography

Days of the Phoenix: The 1920s I Remember

From a Writer's Notebook

Thomas Carlyle

The French Revolution

Past and Present

Bruce Catton

Mr. Lincoln's Army

A Stillness at Appomattox

Winston Churchill

Blood, Toil, Tears and Sweat: The Speeches of Winston Churchill

Europe Unite: Speeches 1947 and 1948

History of the English-Speaking Peoples

In the Balance: Speeches 1949 and 1950

Marlborough: His Life and Times

My Early Life

Their Finest Hour

Any of his speeches

Charles Dana

Any of his nonfiction

Thomas De Quincey

Confessions of an English Opium-Eater

Frederick Douglass

The Life and Times of Frederick Douglass

My Bondage and My Freedom

Narrative of the Life of Frederick Douglass

Leon Edel

Bloomsbury: A House of Lions
Henry James: A Life
Stuff of Sleep and Dreams
Telling Lives

Dave Eggers

A Heartbreaking Work of Staggering Genius
Zeitoun

Richard Ellmann

Eminent Domain: Yeats among Wilde, Joyce, Pound, Eliot, and Auden
James Joyce
Oscar Wilde

Antonia Fraser

Cromwell
King James I of England
Mary Queen of Scots
The Warrior Queens
The Weaker Vessel

Edward Gibbon

The History of the Decline and Fall of the Roman Empire

Alex Haley

The Autobiography of Malcolm X: As Told to Alex Haley

Lillian Hellman

Scoundrel Time
An Unfinished Woman: A Memoir

William Dean Howells

Years of My Youth

Alfred Kazin

New York Jew
Starting Out in the Thirties
A Walker in the City

Helen Keller

The Story of My Life

Ross King

Brunelleschi's Dome: How a Renaissance Genius Reinvented Architecture
The Judgment of Paris: The Revolutionary Decade That Gave the World Impressionism
Michelangelo and the Pope's Ceiling

Maxine Hong Kingston

China Men
The Woman Warrior

T. E. Lawrence

The Revolt in the Desert
Seven Pillars of Wisdom

Gerda Lerner

The Creation of Patriarchy
The Female Experience: An American Documentary
The Majority Finds Its Past: Placing Women in History

Thomas Macaulay

Critical and Historical Essays
History of England from the Accession of James II

Samuel Eliot Morison

Admiral of the Ocean Sea: A Life of Christopher Columbus
The Growth of the American Republic
The Life and Letters of Harrison Gray Otis, Federalist

John Henry Newman

Any of his nonfiction

Francis Parkman

The Oregon Trail
Pioneers of France in the New World

Samuel Pepys

The Diary of Samuel Pepys

Richard Rodriguez

Days of Obligation: An Argument with My Mexican Father
Hunger of Memory: The Education of Richard Rodriguez
Any of his essays

Mari Sandoz

The Battle of the Little Big Horn
Old Jules

Arthur M. Schlesinger Jr.

The Age of Jackson
The Age of Roosevelt
The Bitter Heritage
Robert Kennedy and His Times
A Thousand Days: John F. Kennedy in the White House

George Trevelyan

English Social History

Barbara Tuchman

Bible and Sword: England and Palestine from the Bronze Age to Balfour
A Distant Mirror: The Calamitous 14th Century
The Guns of August
The March of Folly: From Troy to Vietnam
The Proud Tower: A Portrait of the World Before the War, 1890–1914

Richard Wright

Black Boy (American Hunger)

Anzia Yezierska

The Open Cage
Red Ribbon on a White Horse: My Story

Essays, Fiction, and Criticism

Joseph Addison

Selections From The Spectator, Tatler, Guardian, and Freeholder V1 (edited with Richard Steele)

James Agee

The Collected Short Prose of James Agee
A Death in a Family

Michael Arlen

An American Verdict
The Camera Age: Essays on Television
Exiles

Matthew Arnold

Any of his criticism

Margaret Atwood

Cat's Eye
The Handmaid's Tale
Negotiating with the Dead: A Writer on Writing
Payback: Debt and the Shadow Side of Wealth

Francis Bacon

The Advancement of Learning
The New Atlantis

James Baldwin

Another Country
The Devil Finds Work
The Evidence of Things Not Seen
The Fire Next Time
Go Tell It on a Mountain
If Beale Street Could Talk
Notes of a Native Son

G. K. Chesterton

Heretics
St. Francis of Assisi
St. Thomas Aquinas
The Victorian Age in Literature

Kenneth Clark

Another Part of the Wood
Civilisation
The Other Half
The Story Behind the Mortgage and Housing Meltdown: The Legacy of Greed

Samuel Taylor Coleridge

Any of his criticism

Arlene Croce

Any of her criticism

Joan Didion

A Book of Common Prayer
Salvador
Slouching Towards Bethlehem
The Year of Magical Thinking
Any of her essays

Ralph Waldo Emerson

Journals and Miscellaneous Notebooks
Any of his essays

Northrop Frye

Anatomy of Criticism
Fearful Symmetry: A Study of William Blake
Fools of Time: Studies in Shakespearean Tragedy

Paul Fussell

Bad: Or, the Dumbing of America
The Great War and Modern Memory
"Thank God for the Atom Bomb" and Other Essays

Nadine Gordimer

Face to Face
My Son's Story
Not for Publication
Telling Times: Writing and Living (1954–2008)
Any of her essays

William Hazlitt

Any of his criticism

Zora Neale Hurston

Dust Tracks on a Road: An Autobiography
Jonah's Gourd Vine
Their Eyes Were Watching God

Ruth Prawer Jhabvala

Heat and Dust
In Search of Love and Beauty

Samuel Johnson

The Lives of the Poets
The Selected Essays from the Rambler, Adventurer, and Idler

Pauline Kael

5001 Nights at the Movies
I Lost It at the Movies
State of the Art

Hugh Kenner

A Colder Eye

Charles Lamb

Tales from Shakespeare
Any of his essays

Stephen Leacock

Frenzied Fiction
Last Leaves
Winnowed Wisdom

Norman Mailer

Ancient Evenings
The Armies of the Night
The Naked and the Dead
Pieces and Pontifications

Mary McCarthy

Cannibals and Missionaries
Memories of a Catholic Girlhood
"The Writing on the Wall" and Other Literary Essays

N. Scott Momaday

The Names: A Memoir
The Way to Rainy Mountain

Michel de Montaigne

Any of his essays

Vladimir Nabokov

Lectures on Literature
Pnin
Speak, Memory

V. S. Naipaul

Among the Believers: An Islamic Journey
The Return of Eva Peron

Joyce Carol Oates

Contraries: Essays

The Edge of Impossibility

First Person Singular: Writers On Their Craft

New Heaven, New Earth: The Visionary Experience in Literature

On Boxing

Woman Writer

Tillie Olsen

Mother to Daughter, Daughter to Mother

Silences

Tell Me a Riddle

Yonnondio: From the Thirties

George Orwell

Animal Farm

Down and Out in Paris and London

Shooting an Elephant

Cynthia Ozick

Art and Ardor: Essays

The Cannibal Galaxy

The Din in the Head

Walter Pater

Any of his criticism

Adrienne Rich

Of Woman Born: Motherhood as Experience and Institution

On Lies, Secrets, and Silence

John Ruskin

Modern Painters

Praterita: Outlines of Scenes and Thoughts, Perhaps Worthy of Memory in My Past Life

Any of his criticism

George Santayana

The Life of Reason: Or, the Phases of Human Progress

The Sense of Beauty

George Bernard Shaw

The Intelligent Woman's Guide to Socialism and Capitalism

Any of his criticism

Peter Singer

Animal Liberation: A New Ethics for Our Treatment of Animals

Ethics in the Real World: 82 Brief Essays on Things That Matter

How Are We to Live?

The Life You Can Save: Acting Now to End World Poverty

The Most Good You Can Do: How Effective Altruism Is Changing Ideas About Living Ethically

Susan Sontag

"Against Interpretation"

"AIDS and Its Metaphors"

"Illness as Metaphor"

Styles of Radical Will

Regarding the Pain of Others

Richard Steele

Selections From The Spectator, Tatler, Guardian, and Freeholder V1 (edited with Joseph Addison)

John Updike

Assorted Prose

Hugging the Shore: Essays and Criticism

Self-Consciousness

Gore Vidal

Matters of Fact and Fiction

Perpetual War for Perpetual Peace: How We Got to Be So Hated

Reflections upon a Sinking Ship

Views from a Window: Conversations with Gore Vidal

Alice Walker

In Love and Trouble

You Can't Keep a Good Woman Down

Eudora Welty

The Eye of the Story: Selected Essays and Reviews

The Golden Apples

Losing Battles

One Writer's Beginnings

E. B. White

Essays of E. B. White

One Man's Meat

Oscar Wilde

Any of his criticism

Edmund Wilson

Axle's Castle: A Study in the Imaginative Literature of 1870–1930

The Devils and Canon Barham: Ten Essays on Poets, Novelists, and Monsters

Letters on Literature and Politics

Patriotic Gore: Studies in the Literature of the American Civil War

The Shores of Light

Virginia Woolf

The Common Reader

"The Death of the Moth"

The Moment and Other Essays

Roger Fry: A Biography

A Room of One's Own

Three Guineas

A Writer's Diary

Political Writing and Journalism

Roger Angell

Five Seasons: A Baseball Companion

Late Innings

Once More Around the Park

Hannah Arendt

Between Past and Future

The Human Condition

On Revolution

The Origins of Totalitarianism

Simone de Beauvoir

The Coming of Age

The Prime of Life

The Second Sex

William F. Buckley

God and Man at Yale

The Governor Listeth

On the Firing Line

J. Hector St. John de Crèvecoeur

Letters from an American Farmer

Elizabeth Drew

American Journal: The Events of 1976

The Corruption of American Politics: What Went Wrong and Why

Washington Journal: The Events of 1973–1974

W. E. B. Du Bois

The Autobiography of W. E. B. Du Bois

The Negro

The Souls of Black Folk

Worlds of Color

Nora Ephron

Crazy Salad: Some Things About Women

Wallflower at the Orgy

Frances Fitzgerald

America Revisited

Cities on a Hill

Fire in the Lake

Janet Flanner

Janet Flanner's World: Uncollected Writings, 1932–1975

Men and Monuments

Paris Was Yesterday: 1925–1939

John Kenneth Galbraith

The Affluent Society
Ambassador's Journal
The Anatomy of Power
The Nature of Mass Poverty

Charlotte Perkins Gilman

The Charlotte Perkins Gilman Reader
"Herland"

Ellen Goodman

At Large
Close to Home
Keeping in Touch
Making Sense
Paper Trail: Common Sense in Uncommon Times

Thomas Hobbes

The Citizen: Philosophical Rudiments Concerning Government and Society
Leviathan

Thomas Jefferson

Any of his writings

George Kennan

American Diplomacy, 1900–1950
Democracy and the Student Left
Sketches from a Life

John F. Kennedy

A Nation of Immigrants
Profiles in Courage
Why England Slept
Any of his speeches

Martin Luther King Jr.

Stride Toward Freedom
A Testament of Hope
The Trumpet of Conscience
Any of his speeches

John Locke

An Essay Concerning Human Understanding
Two Treatises of Government

Andy Logan

The Man Who Robbed the Robber Barons

Niccolo Machiavelli

The Prince

John McPhee

The Headmaster
A Sense of Where You Are

H. L. Mencken

The Bathtub Hoax and Other Blasts and Bravos from the Chicago Tribune
A Book of Prefaces
A Choice of Days
H. L. Mencken's Smart Set Criticism
In Defense of Women
Prejudices

John Stuart Mill

On Liberty
The Subjection of Women
Utilitarianism

Thomas More

Utopia

Jan Morris

Destinations: Essays from Rolling Stone

Barack Obama

The Audacity of Hope: Thoughts on Reclaiming the American Dream
Dreams from My Father: A Story of Race and Inheritance
Any of his speeches

Olive Schreiner

The Story of an African Farm

William L. Shirer

Berlin Diary
Nightmare Years
Twentieth Century Journey

Red Smith

The Red Smith Reader
To Absent Friends

Lincoln Steffens

The Autobiography of Lincoln Steffens
The Shame of the Cities
Upbuilders

Alexis de Tocqueville

Democracy in America
The Old Regime and the French Revolution

Calvin Trillin

American Fried
An Education in Georgia
Third Helpings
Uncivil Liberties

Theodore H. White

Breach of Faith: The Fall of Richard Nixon
Fire in the Ashes
In Search of History
The Making of the President: 1960

Tom Wolfe

Any of his essays

Mary Wollstonecraft

Letters Written during a Short Residence in Sweden, Norway, and Denmark
A Vindication of the Rights of Men, in a Letter to the Right Honorable Edmund Burke
A Vindication of the Rights of Woman, with Strictures on Political and Moral Subjects

Science and Nature Writing

Isaac Asimov

The Exploding Suns
In Joy Still Felt (autobiography)
In Memory Yet Green (autobiography)
Until the Sun Dies

Jacob Bronowski

The Origins of Knowledge and Imagination
A Sense of the Future

Rachel Carson

The Sea Around Us
Silent Spring
Under the Sea Wind

Annie Dillard

An American Childhood
Holy the Firm
Living by Fiction
Pilgrim at Tinker Creek
Teaching a Stone to Talk: Expeditions and Encounters
The Writing Life

Gretel Ehrlich

The Future of Ice: A Journey into Cold
The Solace of Open Spaces

Jane Goodall

Africa in My Blood
The Chimpanzees of Gombe
Hope for Animals and Their World: How Endangered Species Are Being Rescued
Innocent Killers
Reason for Hope: A Spiritual Journey
Visions of Caliban

Stephen Jay Gould

Ever Since Darwin
Hen's Teeth and Horse's Toes
The Mismeasure of Man
Time's Arrow, Time's Cycle
An Urchin in the Storm

Richard P. Hallion

On the Frontier: Experimental Flight at NASA Dryden (with Michael Gorn)

Storm Over Iraq: Air Power and the Gulf War

Taking Flight: Inventing the Aerial Age from Antiquity Through the First World War

The Wright Brothers: Heirs of Prometheus

Barbara Kingsolver

Animal, Vegetable, Miracle: A Year of Food Life

Holding the Line: Women in the Great Arizona Mine Strike of 1983

Last Stand: America's Virgin Lands

Any of her essays

Peter Matthiessen

At Play in the Fields of the Lord

Far Tortuga

In the Spirit of Crazy Horse

The Snow Leopard

The Tree Where Man Was Born

Margaret Mead

And Keep Your Powder Dry: An Anthropologist Looks at America

Blackberry Winter

Coming of Age in Samoa

Carl Sagan

The Dragons of Eden

A Path Where No Man Thought

Lewis Thomas

The Fragile Species

Late-Night Thoughts on Listening to Mahler's 9th Symphony

The Lives of a Cell: Notes of a Biology Watcher

The Medusa and the Snail

E. O. Wilson

The Ants

Half Earth

Letters to a Young Scientist

On Human Nature

The Social Conquest of Earth